The Cowgirl

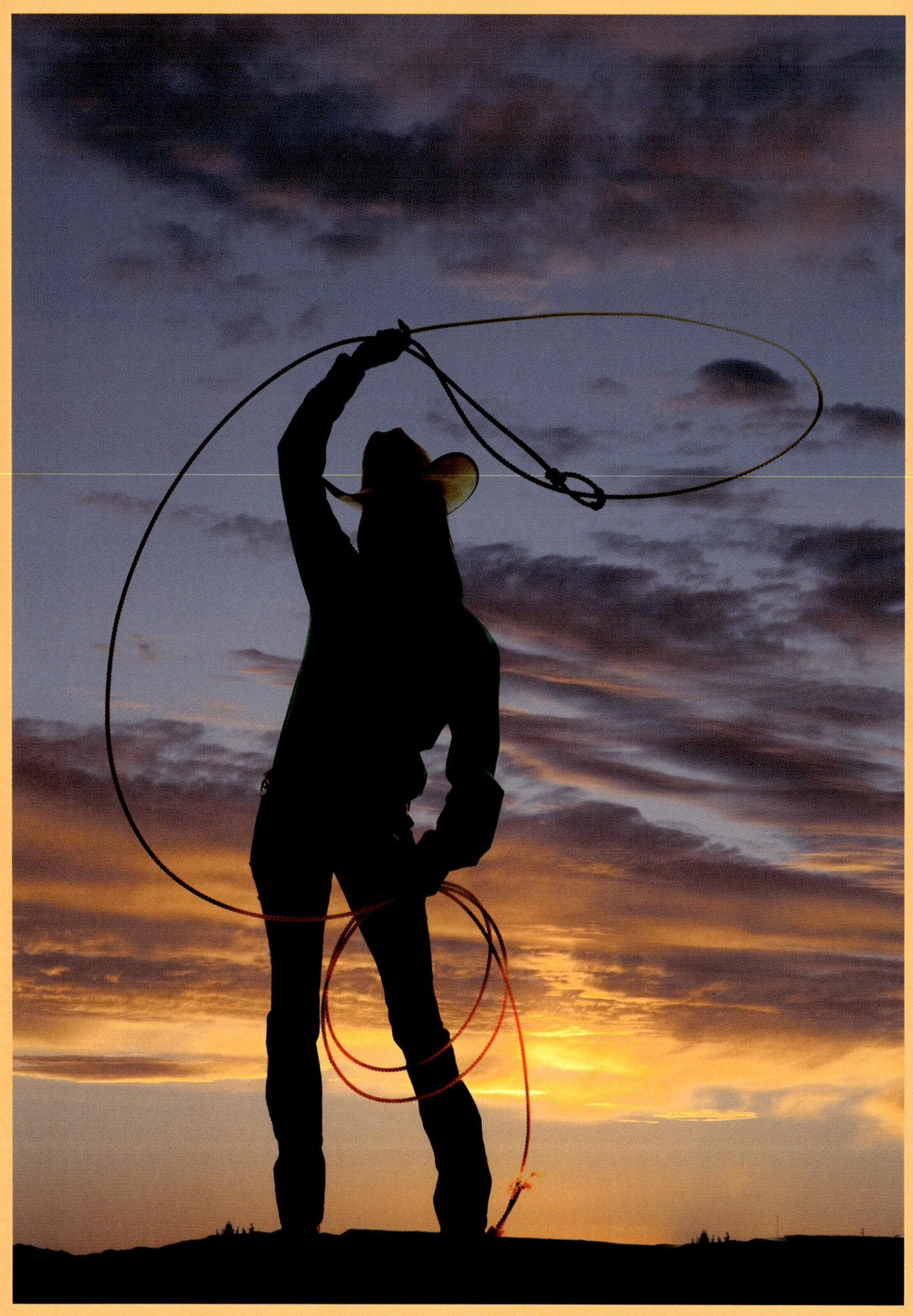

The Cowgirl

A Cultural Phenomenon from Ranches to Runways

Amanda Devan

EPIC INK

Contents

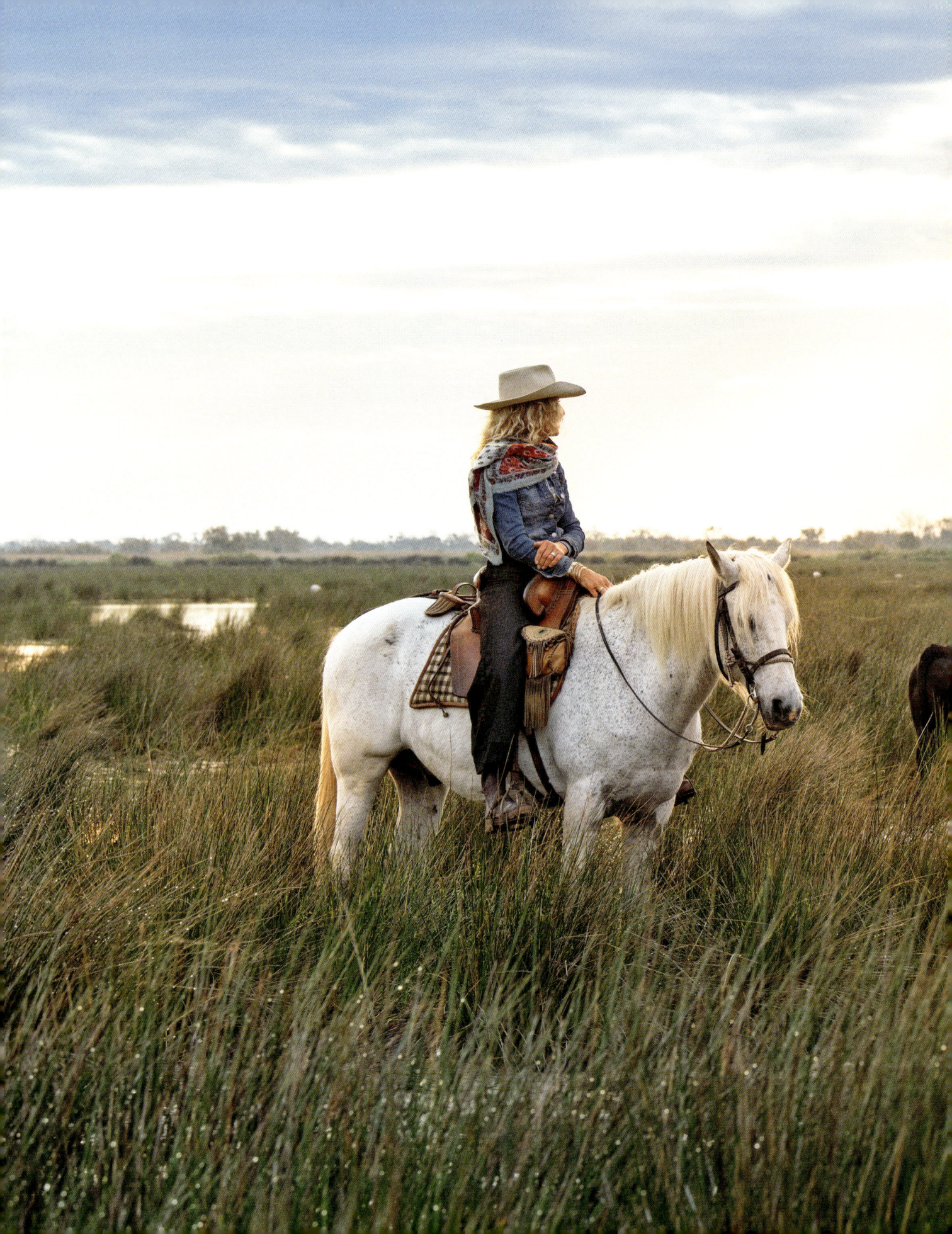

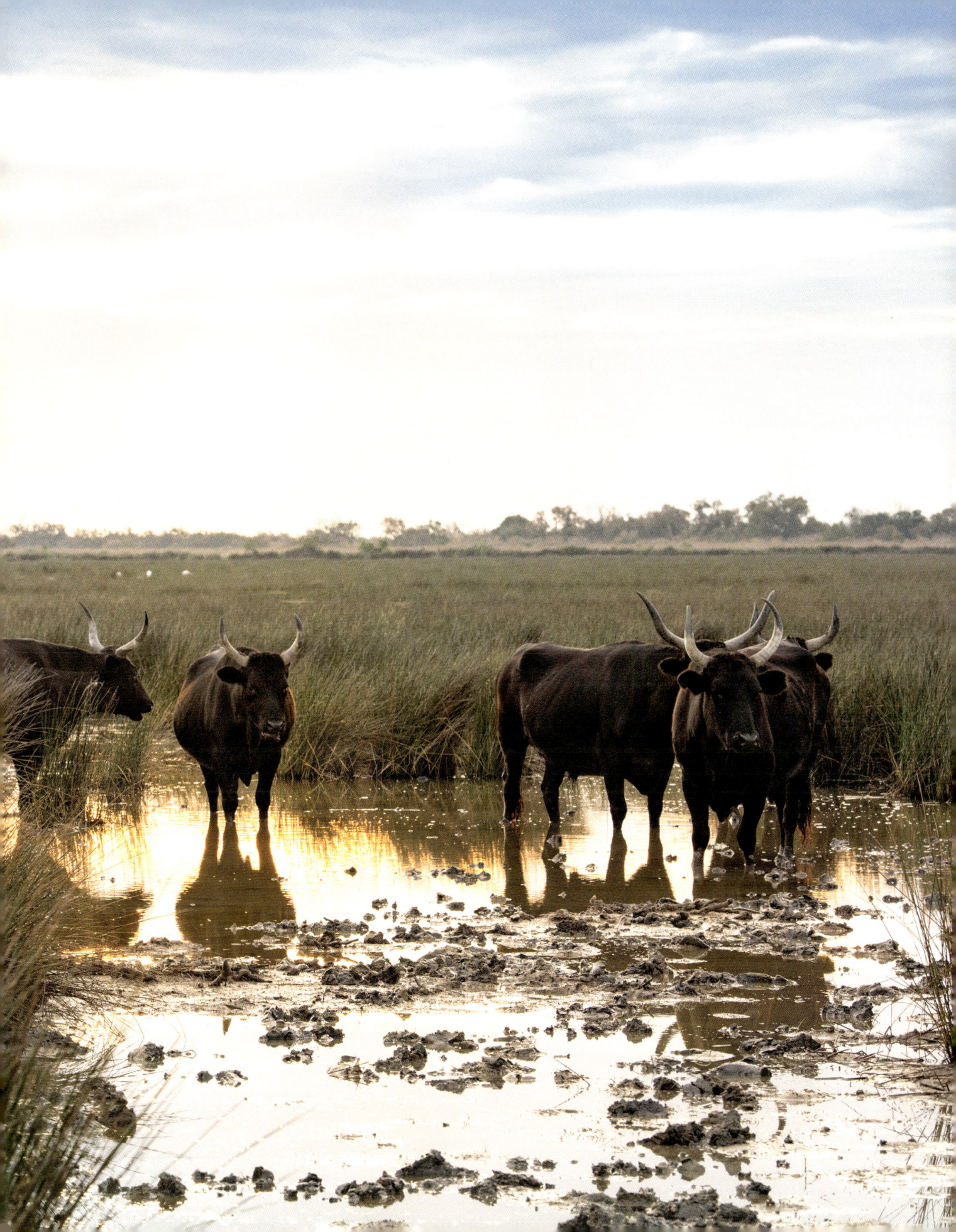

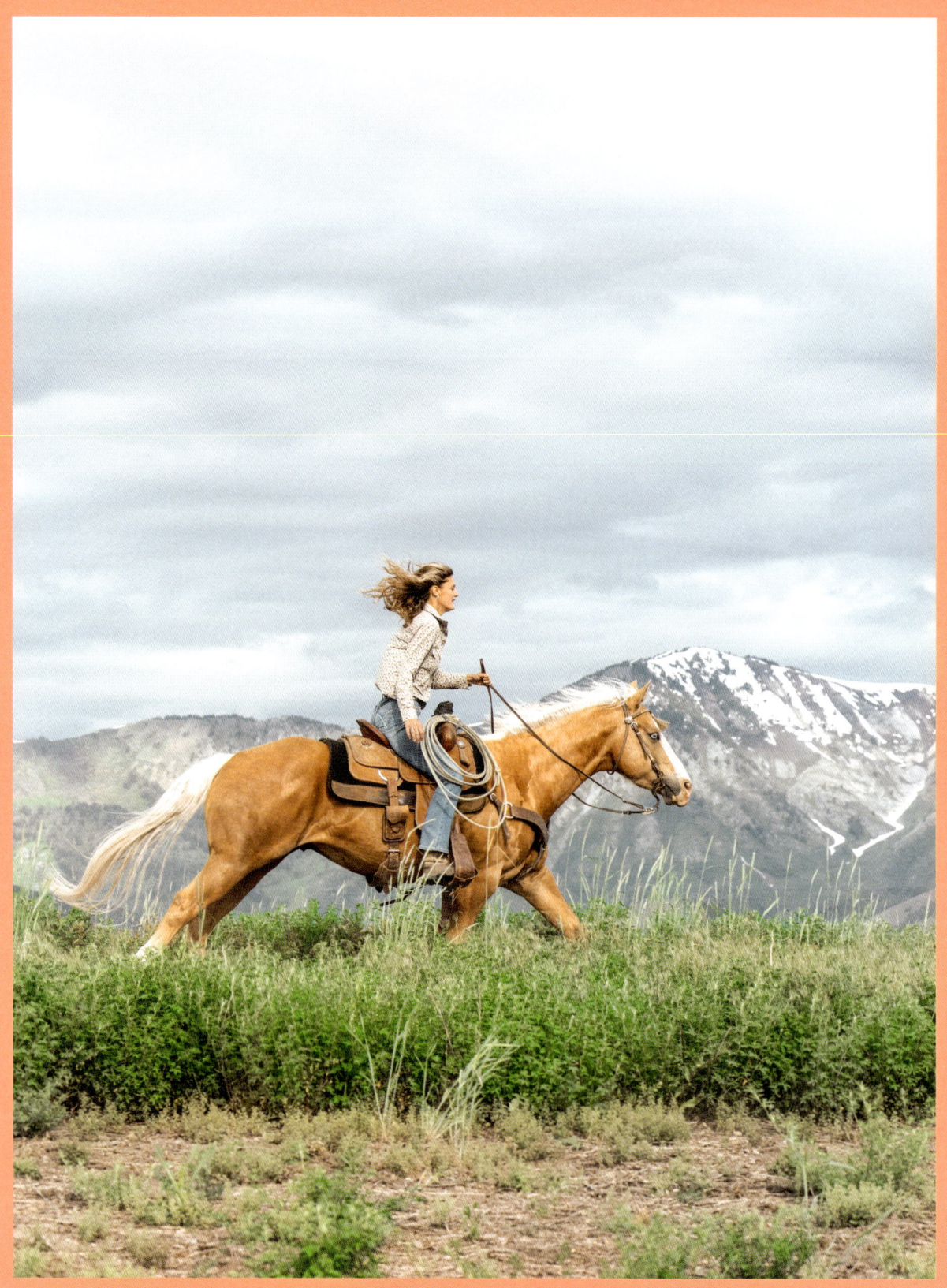

Introduction: Cowgirl Culture

← Have horse, will travel.

↑ PREVIOUS PAGE
A cowgirl is always at home in the saddle.

The idea of the cowgirl means different things to different people. For some people, it's largely appearance-based. They see a woman at a country music concert in cutoff jeans, cowboy boots, and a flannel shirt, and call her a cowgirl. Others see the cover art on Beyoncé's *Cowboy Carter* album and think, because she is on horseback and is from Texas, she is the epitome of a cowgirl. For me, the idea of the cowgirl is based in a woman's mindset, nature, and work-ethic. I was lucky enough to grow up around women who broke horses and handled cattle on a ranch every day. When I think of "cowgirls," I think of those women.

The term itself is controversial in the Western community. For women who saddle up every day and work ranches alongside cowboys, "cowgirl," is widely considered a condescension, downplaying their skills and abilities. On the other hand, there are also plenty of women who embrace the term as celebration of strong women in the vastly male-dominated Western industry. For them, "cowgirl," is an umbrella term that provides a space to recognize the hardworking females who might otherwise be overshadowed by their male counterparts. Sort of like the Supporting and Lead Actress awards at the Oscars, which put the focus on women explicitly rather than bundling men and women into the same category.

Personally, I think there is space to recognize and celebrate the unique characteristics and accomplishments of women in the Western world without detracting from their incredible horsemanship, ranching, and farming skills.

While we all have a different picture in our minds of what it means to be a cowgirl, what we will explore throughout this book is the common thread that ties those ideas together. The truth of the matter is, thankfully, the Western, farming, and agriculture industries have all grown their female workforces, and the once-tight parameters around the idea of the "cowgirl," just aren't there anymore. The word "cowgirl," while still relevant to those who are working and living within the parameters of Western culture, has evolved to be less about the job title and more about the spirit in her heart.

I was raised on a ranch. My dad is a horseman and a cowboy, and he met my mother at a horse show in Jackson, Mississippi. My brother and I were horseback riding before we could walk (literally). We learned to love and appreciate the land and animals around us from an early age.

At home, I was always on horseback and helping around the barn. To this day, I know which pens the cattle go in, and symptoms to look for when one of the cattle might be sick. I know how to move cattle quietly and efficiently. I know how to wrap a horse's legs to give them tendon support when they're sore.

But I was also a cheerleader and a dancer. I was girly. Anxiety surged through my bones and everything scared me. Most of all, I hated to be in trouble. I was not a rebel—not defiant in any sense of the word. I pushed my teenage limits minimally for fear of consequences.

I envied my friends who would fearlessly swing a leg over a cold-backed horse just to see how fast it would run. I romanticized their relationships when they would sneak away to see their high school sweethearts because their love felt more important than any consequence they could foresee. They were brave and passionate. They always did what they wanted to do. It may read like selfishness, but up close it was something entirely different— they respected their parents, and they were responsible, but they were also free. That made them cowgirls in my eyes.

My friend Jaylee is years younger than me but so much braver in every sense of the word. She would jump on her pony bareback and ride him full-speed into the brush, laughing the whole way and coming back scraped and cut. She would get bucked off in the arena and laugh it off, jumping right back on to keep riding.

Lindy Burch was the first woman to really significantly establish herself in the National Cutting Horse Association as a professional female rider. She had her bachelor's in Zoology and master's in Endocrinology from UCLA and was in the process of obtaining her doctorate. She overcame scrutiny from her male peers, built her business from scratch, and chose this life over a career as a veterinarian.

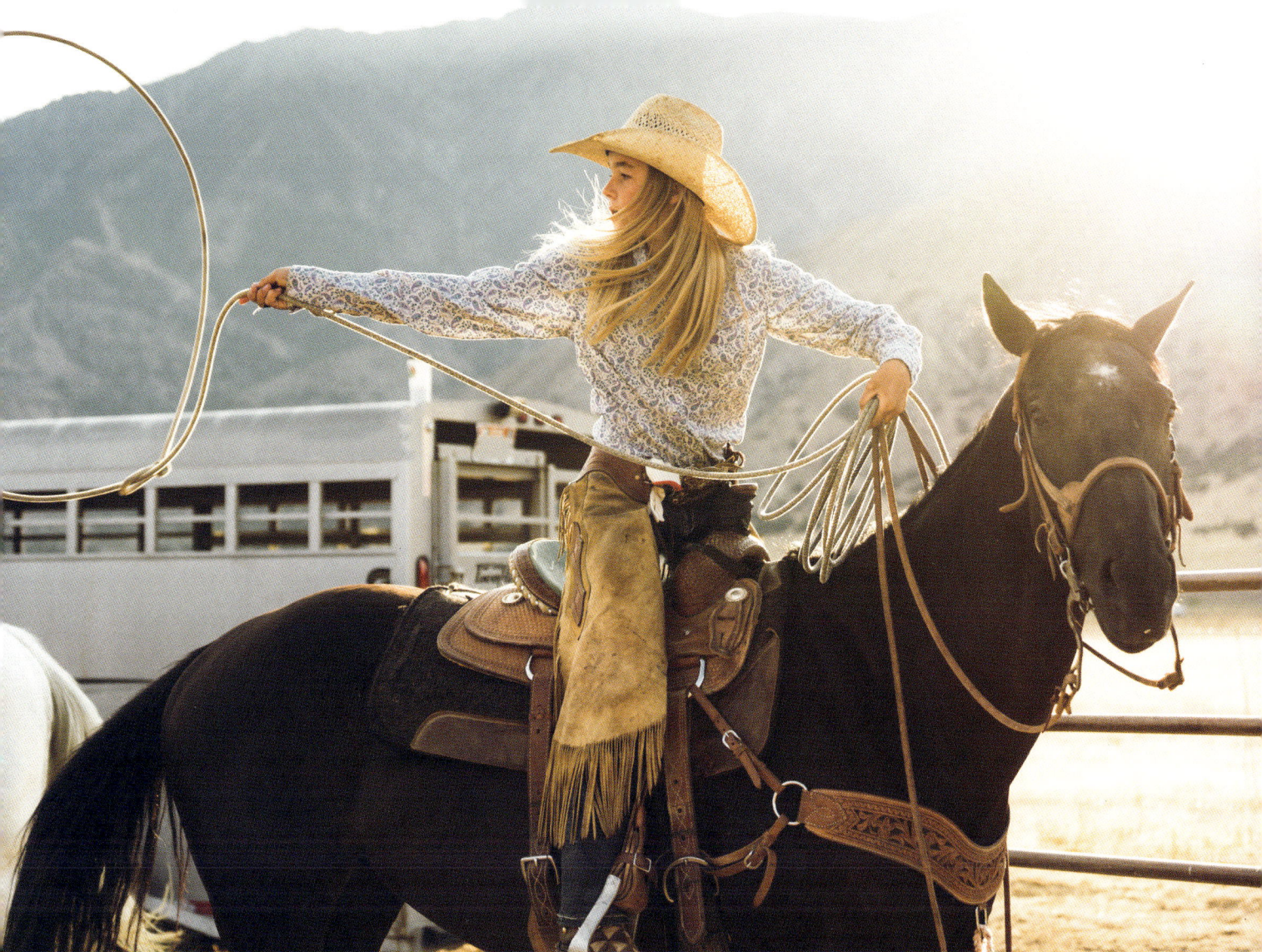

↑ A rodeo cowgirl-
in-training
practices roping in
a Utah arena.

Anne Marion was the Four Sixes Ranch heiress. She was a silver-spoon child who attended boarding school in Switzerland, and had every opportunity to live whatever kind of life she wanted. The life she wanted was on the Sixes, and she helped make groundbreaking decisions for that ranch's horse program that would set them apart for decades to come.

When I thought about these women who were cowgirls through-and-through, I didn't see myself in them. I never felt brave, independent, or free. I never felt like I knew enough to stand on my own two feet or would be strong enough to handle what might come my way if I tried. I felt like I was half-cowgirl. I don't know how I would describe the other half—weak, maybe? I've come a long way since then, but this kind of mindset and identity crisis is still relevant in Western culture today—the idea that a cowgirl is just one thing. The reality is that she is so much more complex than we give her credit for.

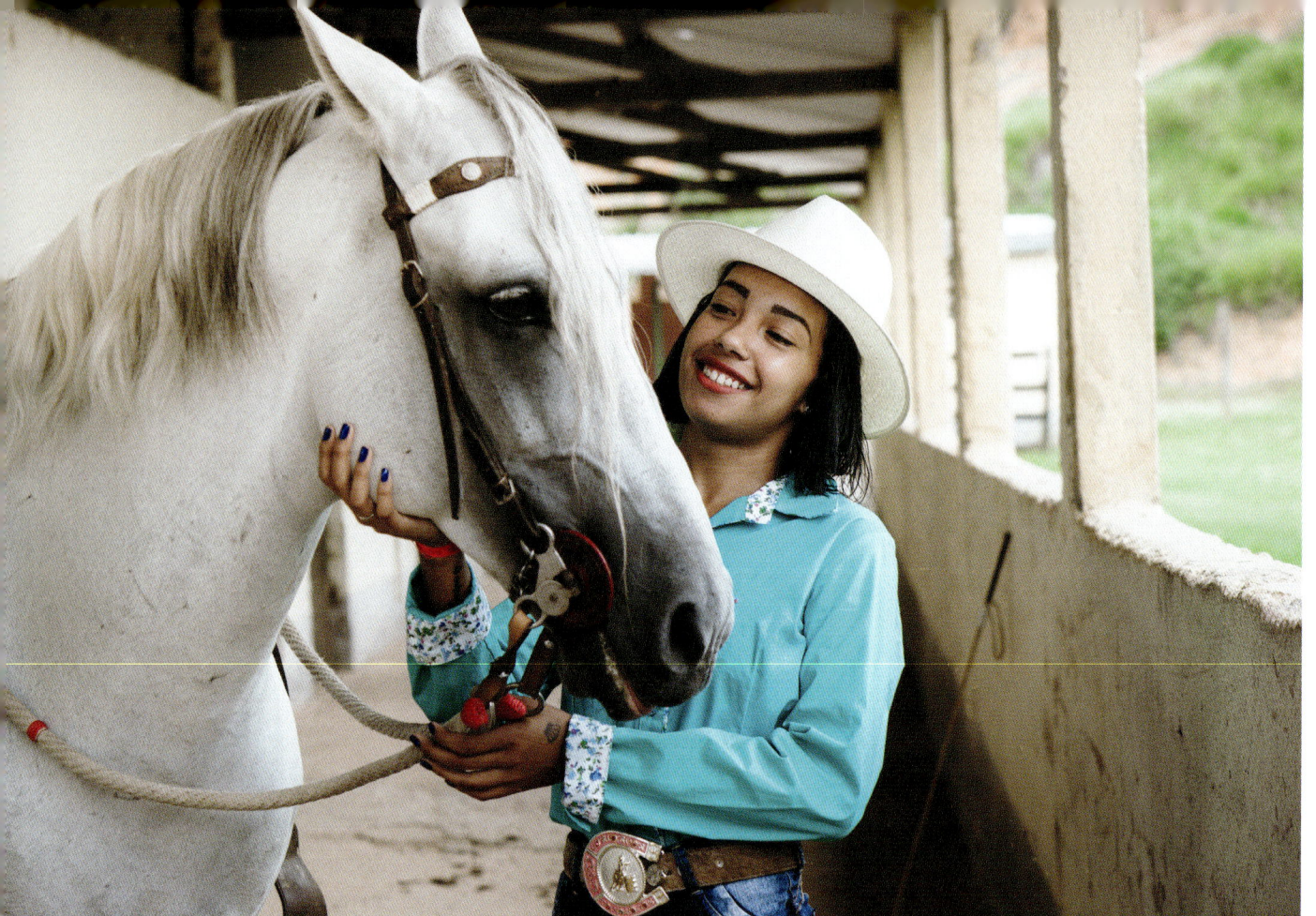

Have you ever heard the phrase, "All hat, no cattle?" It wasn't until later in my life that I realized that neither the hat nor the cattle really made the cowgirl. What makes the cowgirl is the heart and the mind. What does she love? What does she fear? What drives her? When I examined these things about myself as I grew older and more confident, I found that I had much more in common with the strong women around me than I thought; I also realized that they had more in common with women in corporate America, in non-profits, and in social work—more than they would likely ever know.

I started to draw parallels between the strong women around me. Our job titles, stories, and socioeconomic backgrounds are different, but I realized the cowgirl spirit is the common thread that ties us all together. Those defining characteristics of the women I befriended and admired could be tracked across cultures—maybe not every woman was riding a fast horse for the plot, but they showed strength, bravery, and a lust for life in so many other ways.

Being a cowgirl is a way of life—one that is deeply rooted in strength, independence, and connection. Born from the rugged landscapes of the

Cowgirl culture transcends borders. Here, a young woman bonds with her horse in a stable in Brazil.

American West, cowgirl culture is defined by a collective of women who embody authenticity, resilience, tenacity, empathy, and an unapologetic sense of freedom. They break barriers, defy expectations, and carve their own space in a world that is desperately trying to put them in a box. And they do all that while advocating for and progressing the Western industry, be it through ranching, marketing a Western brand, developing new livestock pharmaceuticals, and in many other ways.

Men have always been expected to get results by whatever means necessary. If a man is pushy, he's ambitious; if he's unrealistic, he's got big ideas; if he's harsh, he has high expectations. If a woman is pushy, she's rude; if she's unrealistic, she's unreasonable; if she's harsh, she's emotional. The rules have always been different for women. The expectations and standards are so much higher, and the recognition so much lower—and if you happen to be successful, you're seen as an exception. It's a tale as old as time.

The spirit of the cowgirl lives inside the women who won't be told who they are or where they belong. The cowgirl movement is a testament to these ideals. From the nineteenth century Wild West show performers to early women drovers and rodeo queens who fought for their place on horseback, to the modern women who dare to walk unapologetically into uncharted territory and do what they love despite societal norms—these women are all mavericks in their own right.

The cowgirl movement is a call to all women to stand tall in their proverbial boots and spurs and ride daringly into their next big thing—and to do it all with both grit and grace. And the cowgirl spirit is accessible to all. It's a rebellion against conformity, and it's happening all around us every day, on horseback or not. Cowgirl culture is a celebration of individuality and of success. It's a rallying cry that transcends geography and generations.

The cowgirl archetype reminds us of the power of being our authentic selves. It's not just about what you wear—though few things bring me as much joy as a great pair of boots—but about the spirit and tenacity you carry in your heart. Throughout this book, we'll explore the vibrant history of Western women who paved the way for the mold-breakers who followed them. We'll see their iconic style and their unstoppable mentality, and understand why the cowgirl legacy endures to this day.

The culture of the cowgirl continues to inspire generations of women to a relentless pursuit of freedom from societal norms and expectations. The cowgirl remains a symbol of empowerment and individuality for women everywhere.

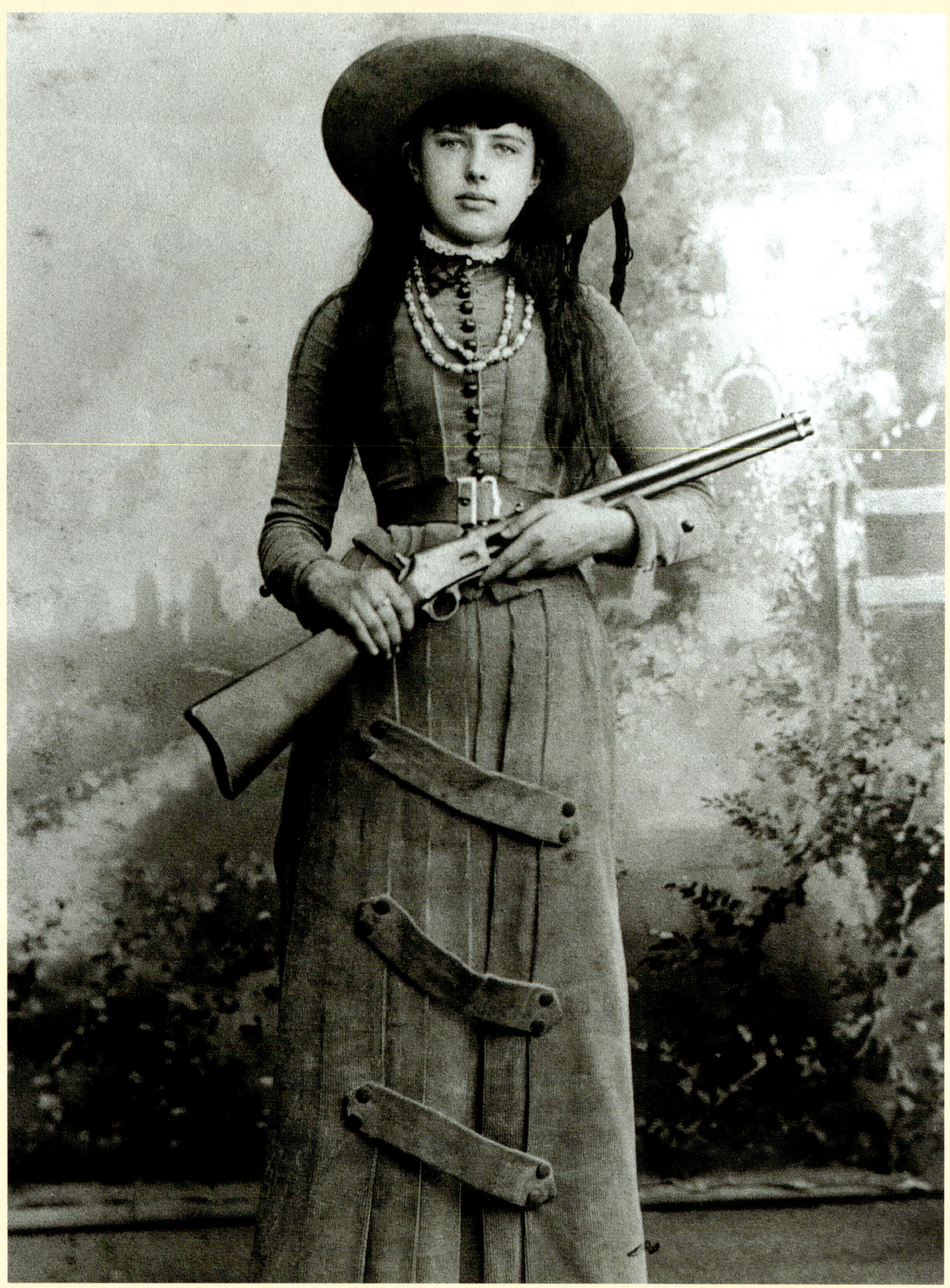

The West Goes Cowgirl

In nineteenth-century America, women's roles were largely dictated by the Cult of Domesticity, or the Cult of True Womanhood—a belief that a woman's primary role was taking care of the home, and that they were expected to have four virtues: piety, purity, submissiveness, and domesticity. While there were women who embraced their role at home, others began to advocate for equal rights and a woman's right to participate in and shape public culture.

Although these advocates laid the foundation for early activism—suffrage, property rights, educational opportunities, and so on—not all women were included in this movement. While white women sought liberation from domestic constraints, Black, Indigenous, and other Women of Color were often denied even the most basic recognition of their womanhood. Despite this, these women were still actively resisting these ideals through abolitionist movements, labor activism, and other forms of advocacy.

Women—across race and class—have always pushed boundaries. In this chapter, we will explore the Cult of Domesticity's lasting impact, the women who defied it, and how the cowgirl's spirit of independence became a powerful symbol for women reclaiming their place in the world.

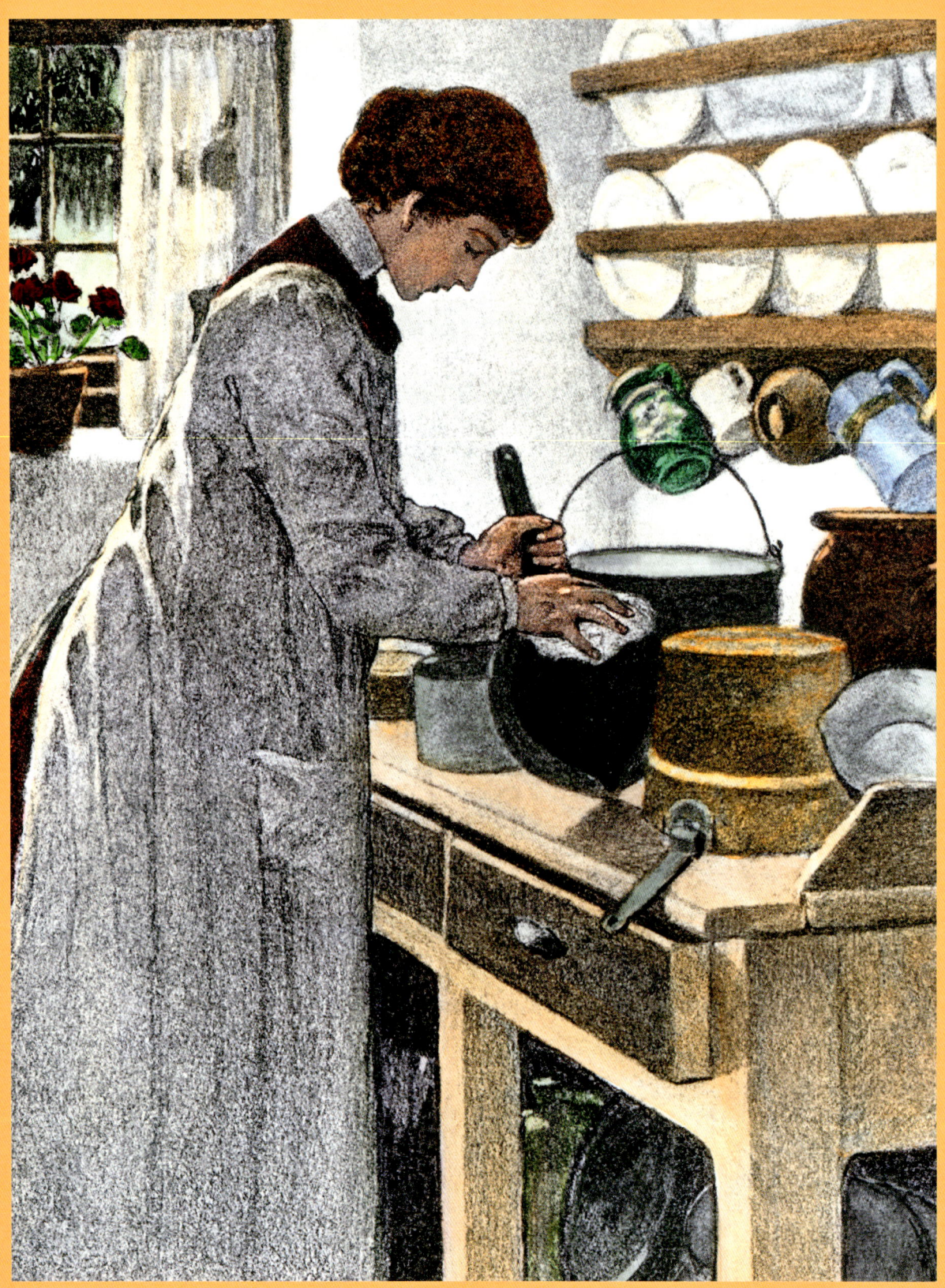

Down with Domesticity

Many magazines and works of literature in the nineteenth century instilled the idea that women were too weak and sensitive to take on economic responsibilities. It was believed that since men were participating members of the workforce, they should therefore manage the family's finances.

On the other hand, women were expected to take their place inside the home, creating a safe, nurturing, well-kept environment for their family. These qualities promised to make the women who adopted them more "Christlike," and therefore, morally superior (and thus, more desirable), to their male counterparts who were apparently held to much lower standards, even back then. For these reasons, many women in America embraced these ideals; however, a significant number of women felt stifled by their narrowly defined role in society.

Historian Barbara Welter explored the ideals of the time in her 1966 article, "The Cult of True Womanhood: 1820–1860," and examined how these ideas were incorporated into literature and magazines, including the highly influential 1800s women's fashion magazine, *Godey's Lady's Book*, which played a key role in shaping social norms at the time.

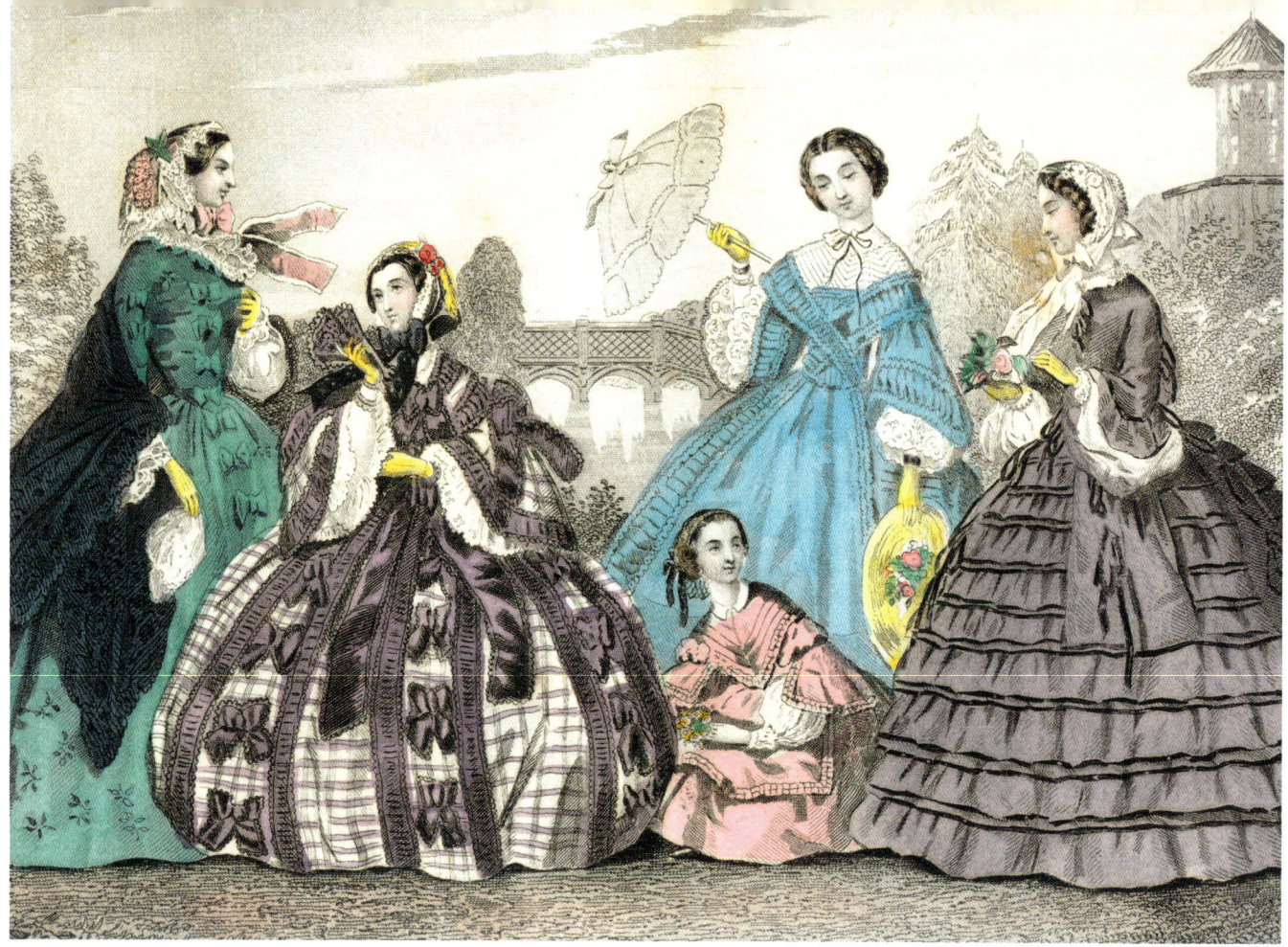

Godey's Lady's Book, was the most widely circulated magazine prior to the Civil War and primarily targeted white, upper-middle-class women. Published in Philadelphia, Pennsylvania, from 1830 to 1898, the magazine boasted 150,000 readers in 1860, making it the most successful women's fashion magazine at that time. The issues contained poetry, articles, engravings from prominent writers, and more—all of which heavily influenced the way people thought women should behave. As the magazine's portrayal of women's roles gained popularity, many began scrutinizing these ideals.

As society progressed, questions began to arise about the roles of women beyond the domestic sphere. An awakening was on the horizon—if women were morally superior to men, why weren't they considered competent enough to participate in the economy and politics? This was the founding principle of women's reform activism and the Suffrage movement. So, while some American women were finding their footing managing their homes, others were painting picket signs for protests.

↑ Fashion plate from *Godey's Lady's Book.*

→ This illustration was printed on a postcard issued in 1900 by the National American Woman Suffrage Association.

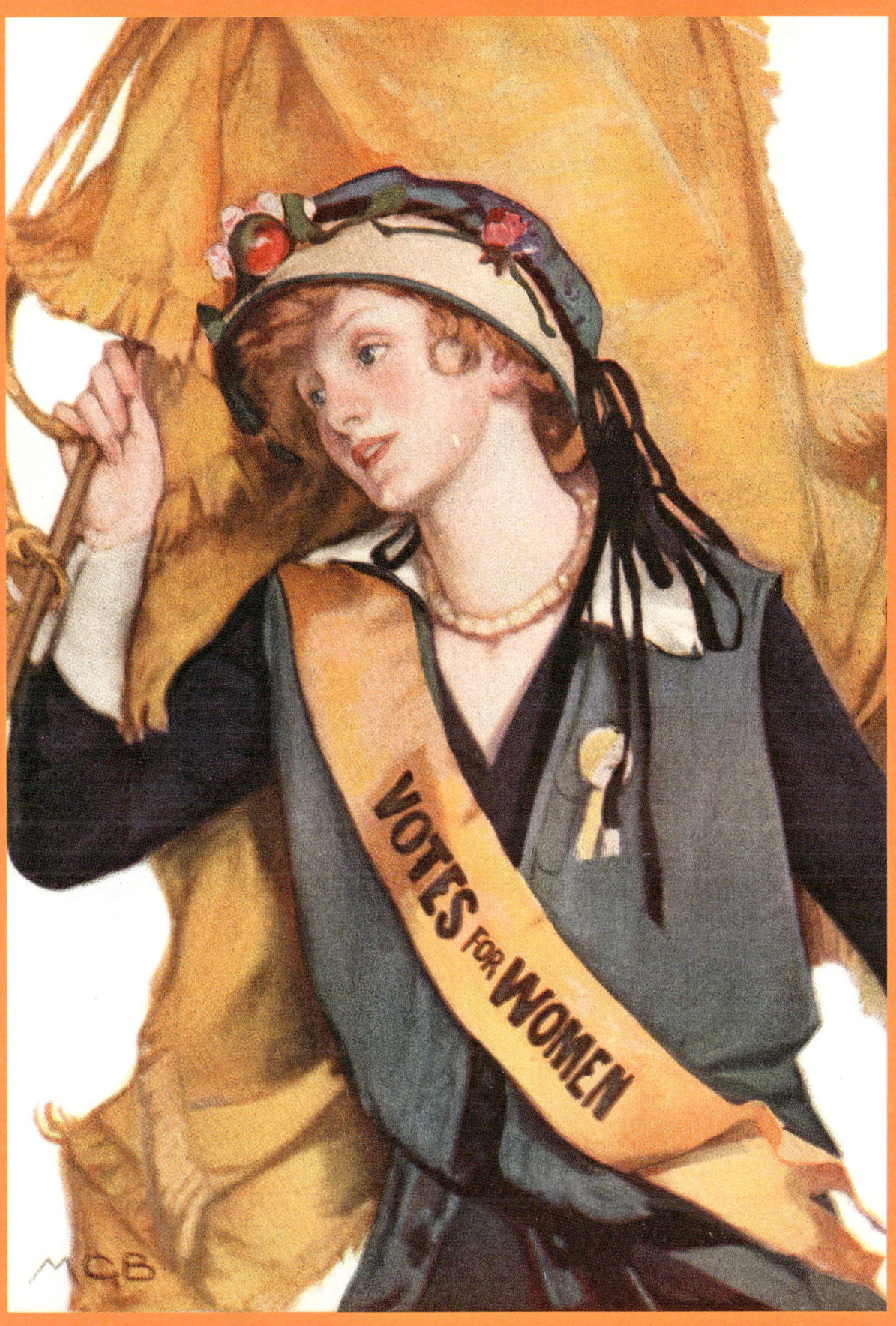

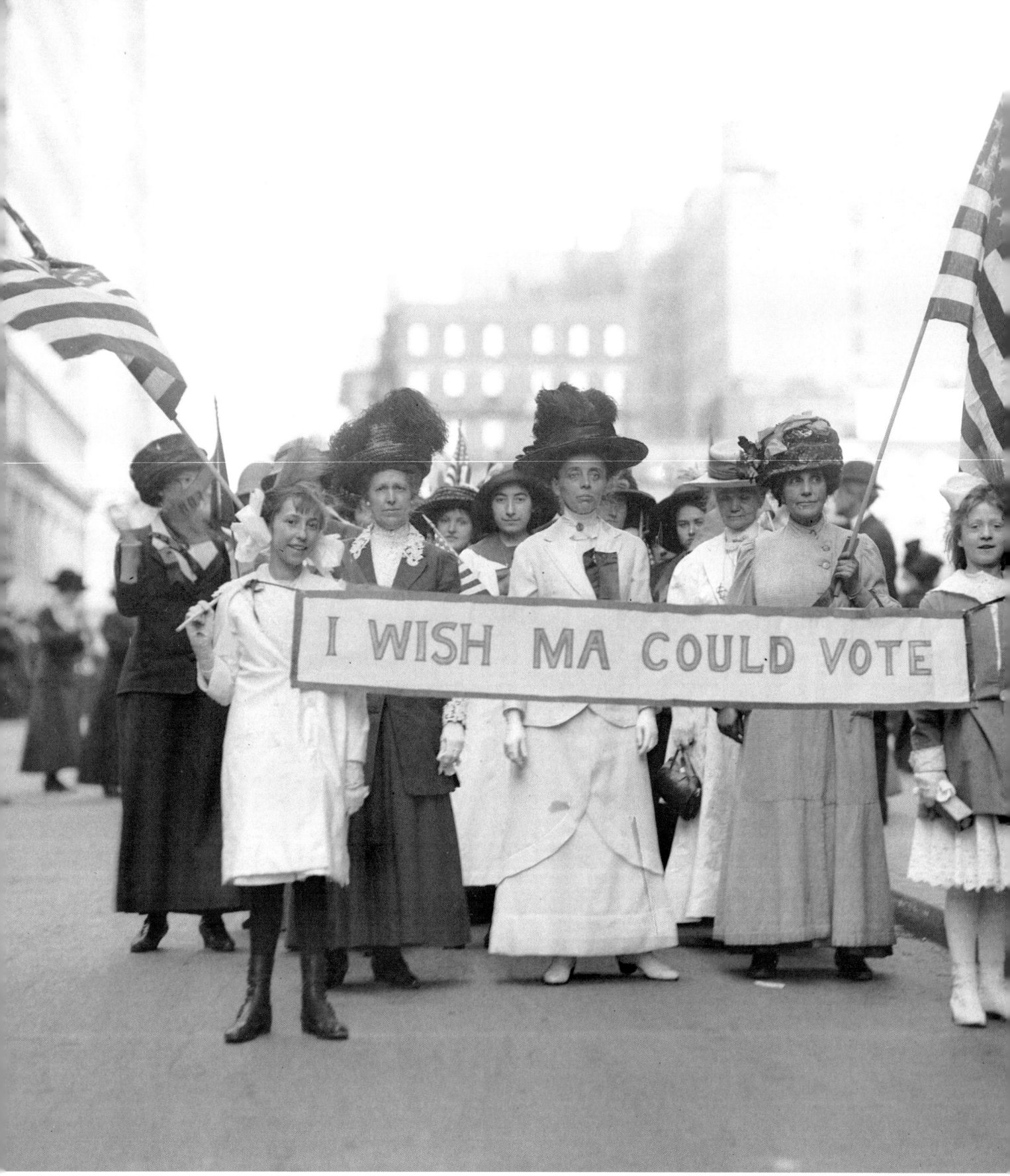

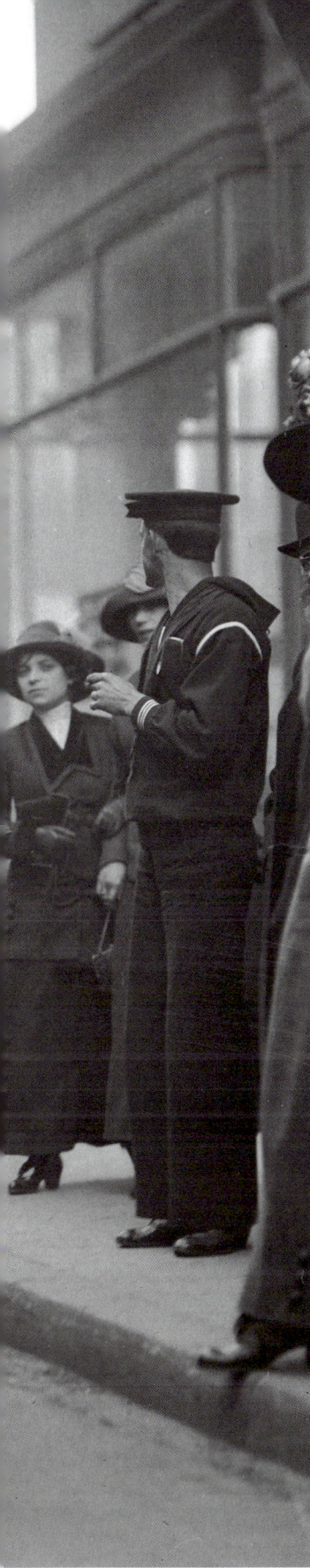

← A group of American women's suffrage activists march in a parade, circa 1913.

Yet, these ideals of domesticity did not apply equally to *all* women. The Cult of Domesticity was largely inaccessible to Black, Indigenous, and other Women of Color in the nineteenth century as Black and Indigenous women were enslaved and the validity of their personhood and humanity systematically denied. Even after slavery was abolished in 1865, Black women continued to work as domestic servants, sharecroppers, and factory workers, making the domestic role of "true womanhood" unattainable.

Indigenous women were also facing displacement and violence through the Indian Removal Act of 1830, which incited what is known as the "Trail of Tears," the forced removal and migration of over sixty thousand Indigenous Americans from their homes. Many thousands died of starvation, disease, and exposure as they were marched on foot away from their ancestral lands, classifying this as one of the worst massacres in US history.

While white women sought freedom from their domestic roles, many Women of Color were fighting simply to be recognized as women in a society that often dehumanized them. The Suffrage movement, though rooted in gender equality, frequently excluded Women of Color, prioritizing white women's rights over racial solidarity. This exclusion persisted well into the twentieth century.

Despite this, Black and Indigenous women still fought against exclusionary ideals like the Cult of Domesticity through abolitionist movements and community organizing, resisting displacement by fighting to retain aspects of their culture.

As American society evolved, so did the role of women, and since then, women—from different cultures and classes—have continuously fought for autonomy in their own ways.

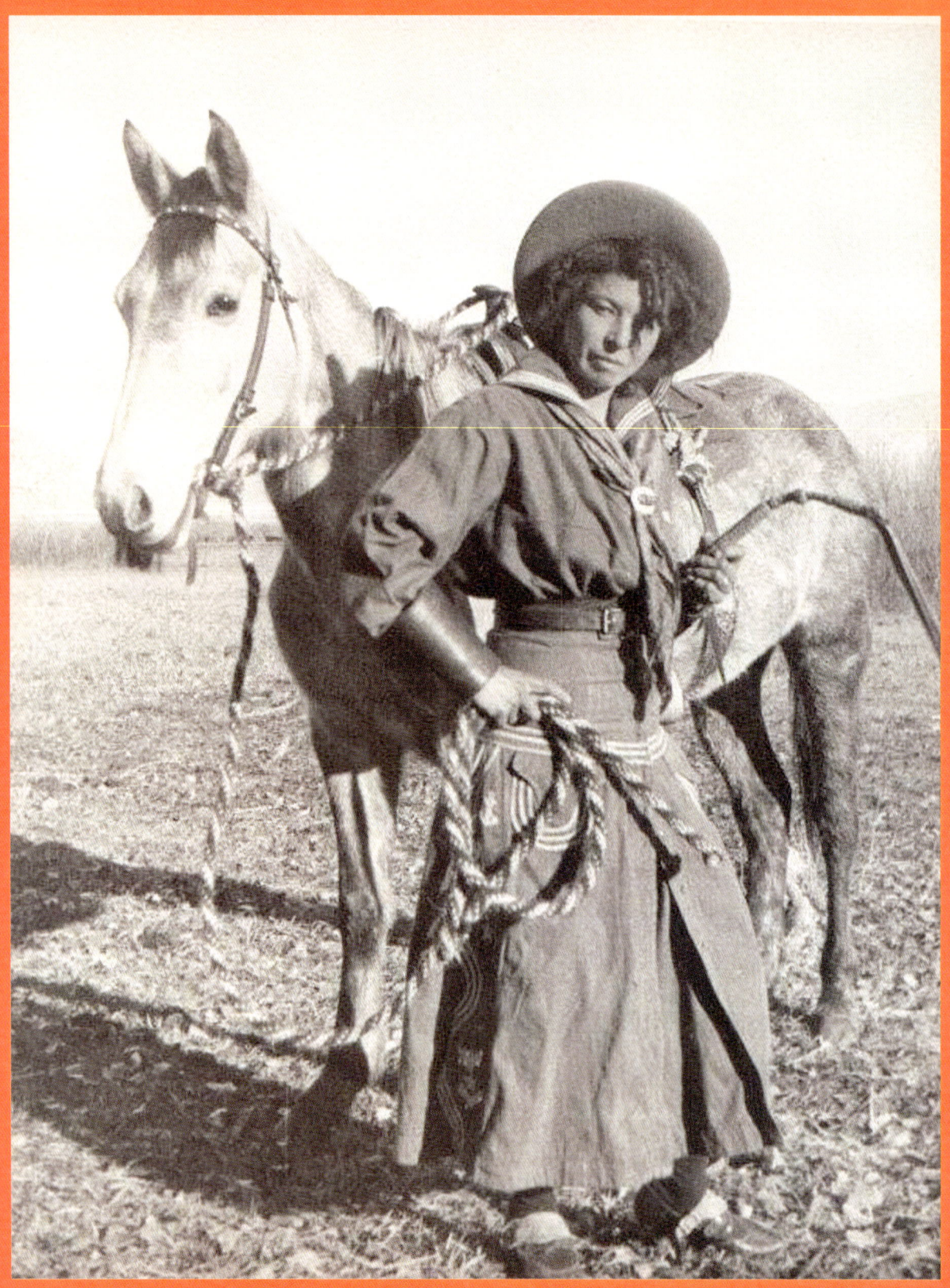

Heading West

The woman in this photograph is often identified as Nellie Brown, a Black cowgirl making her way in the American west in the 1800s.

A new chapter in American history was underway as the women's rights movement began. In 1848, the first women's rights convention was held in Seneca Falls, New York. While women gathered in the east for the Suffrage movement, American men were drawn to the West for the California Gold Rush, igniting economic and cultural changes.

The West also reflected racial divides. While white women had the opportunity to craft an image of independence and adventure as cowgirls, Black, Latina, and Indigenous women were often overlooked in these narratives. However, they played crucial roles in ranching, cattle driving, and rodeo culture. Figures like Mary Fields, also known as "Stagecoach Mary"—a formerly enslaved woman who became a legendary mail carrier—and Indigenous horsewomen who worked alongside men, challenged gender and racial barriers, yet their contributions remain underrepresented in mainstream history.

The news of the gold rush spread throughout the country, and Americans collectively loaded their wagons and headed west. By the end of the Civil War, more than four hundred thousand people moved west, and with them went American goods, products, and services. Commerce was going to take off in a new territory, and for many women, that meant a huge opportunity was on the horizon.

With business opportunities booming, ranchers moved west with the rest of the country. Drovers took herds to Texas, Kansas, Wyoming, Montana, Arizona, and eventually, California. And as demand to move cattle and manage ranches grew, so did the demand for cowboys. And with cowboys

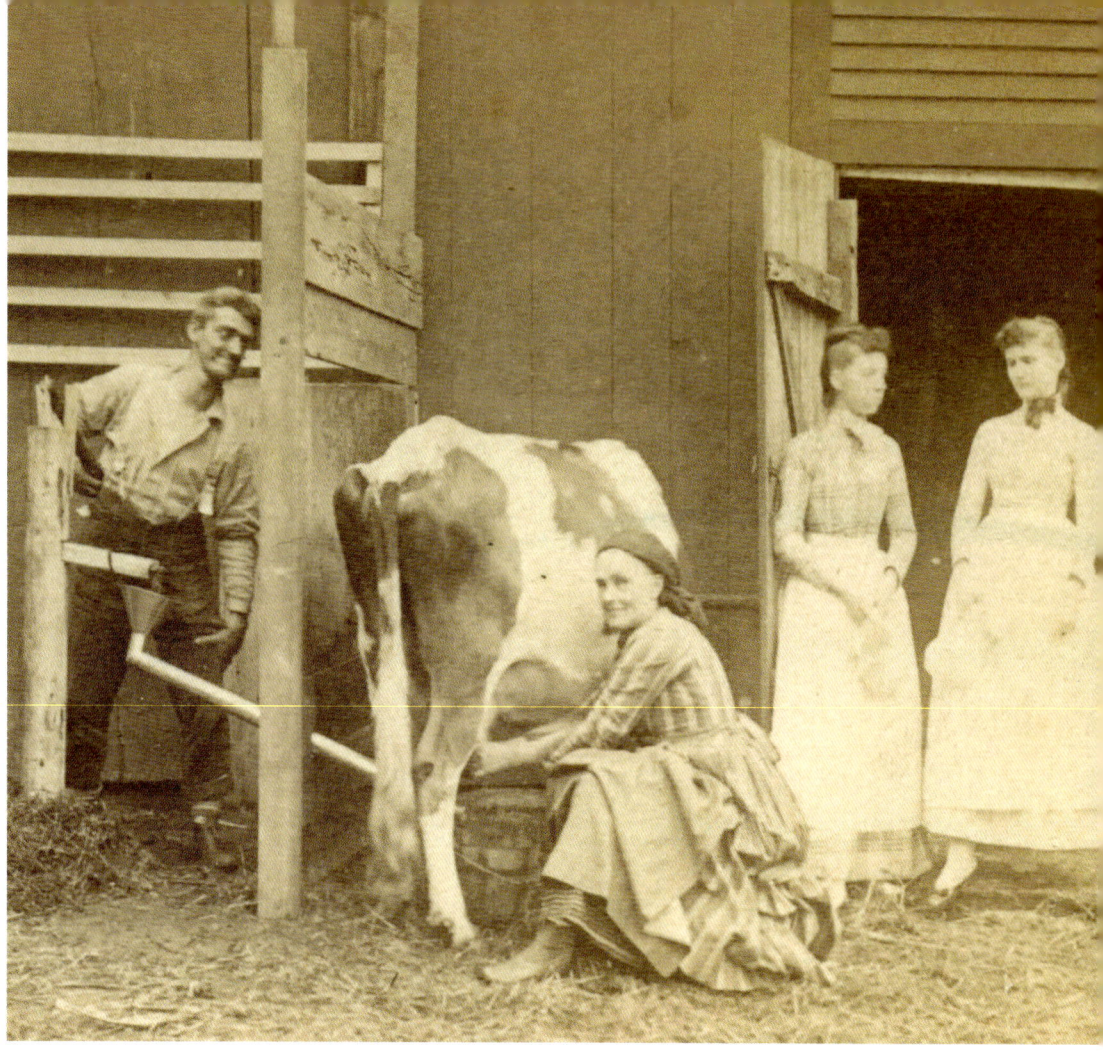

Farm work has always been women's work too. Here, a woman milks a cow while her family looks on.

came their wives, daughters, and sisters. The first skilled cowgirls can likely be traced back to some of the women in these early ranching families, including Mexican ranching families. In these families, the girls learned all of the same skills as the boys so everyone could lend a hand on the ranch. Women of Color, including Latina vaqueras, Indigenous, and Black women also played a pivotal role in the development of ranching and cowboy culture, participating in cattle drives, herding cattle, pushing the boundaries of horsemanship, and challenging gender roles.

Women were often tasked with running the ranch while the men were away on cattle drives for days, weeks, or even months. Despite systematic displacement, this was also true for Indigenous women who also adapted to the demands of ranching life. They worked alongside men as skilled horsewomen and managed livestock while also resisting ongoing colonization.

Another thing that hasn't changed since the nineteenth century: the sheer grit it takes to be a rancher. These women had to survive in harsh climates as well as keep the animals alive and the land tended to. They were isolated and

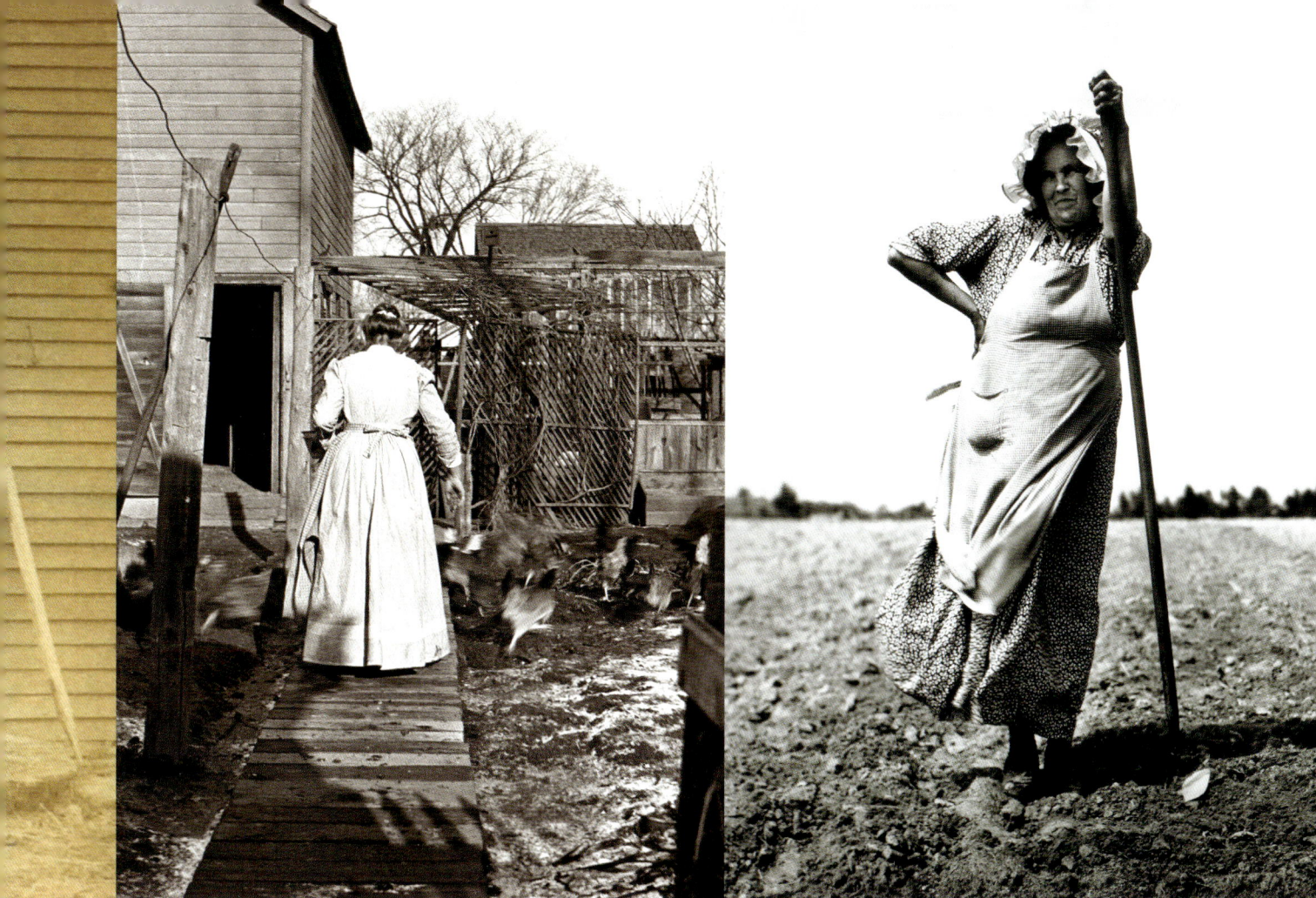

↑ Feeding the chickens, circa 1910.

→ Planting tobacco in Durham, North Carolina, circa 1940.

alone, often for long periods of time. It wasn't uncommon for the matriarch of the household to take over ranching operations completely if her husband passed away, often claiming her own land to start a new operation. This proved important when Congress passed the Homestead Act of 1862, which stated that unmarried women over the age of twenty-one, whether single, divorced, or widowed, could claim 160 acres (65 hectares) of land in the Western regions of the country.

Because women could only claim the land if they were considered the head of their household, establishing land ownership for married women was a much more difficult feat. In addition, although this act was passed in 1862, it wasn't until the 1866 Civil Rights Act and ratification of the Fourteenth Amendment that Black women were able to participate—although they still faced many barriers—and Black families were eventually able to own land. Bertie Brown, a Black homesteader in Montana, was one of the first Black women to successfully claim an independent homestead in 1891.

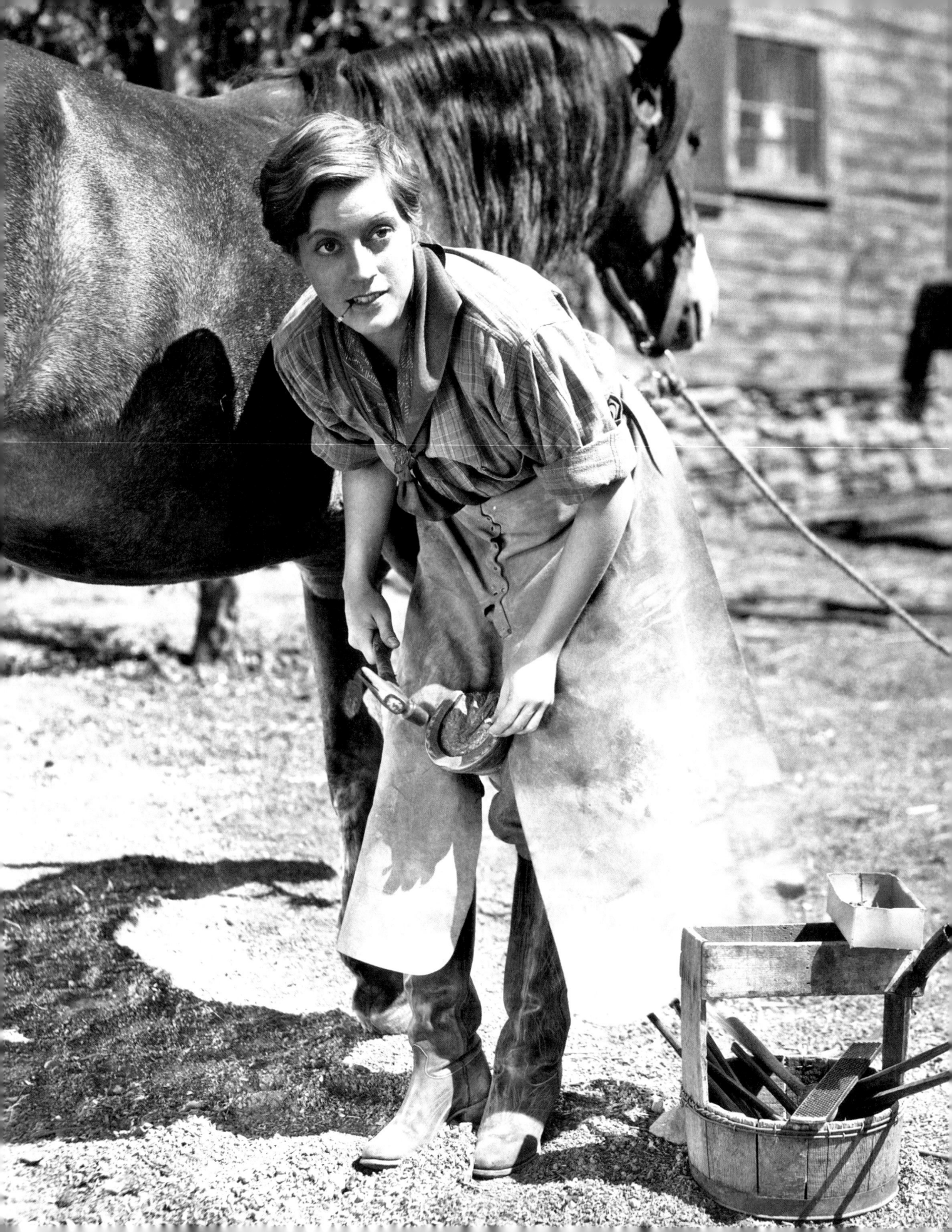

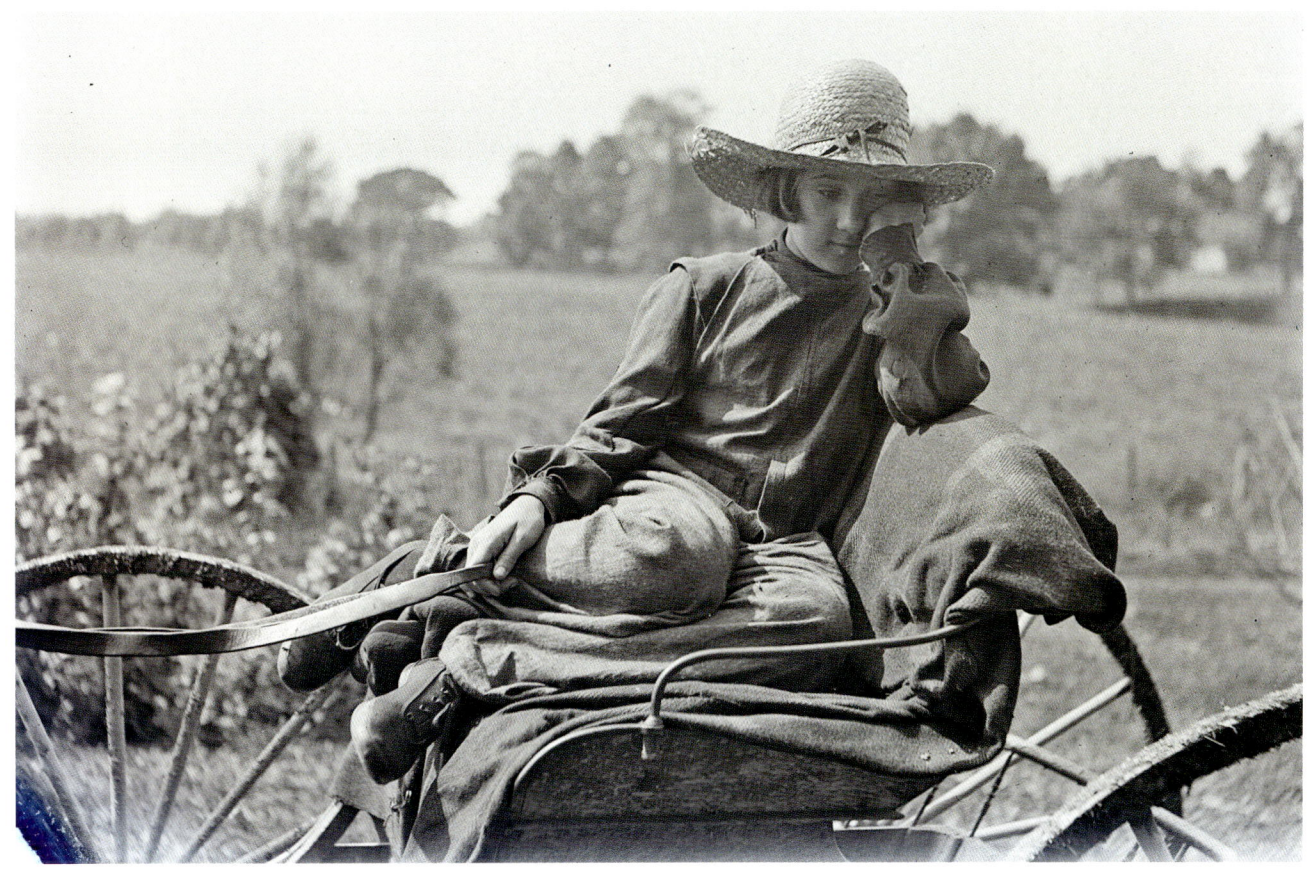

↑ A young woman holds the reins to a wagon, circa 1900.

← A woman shoes a horse.

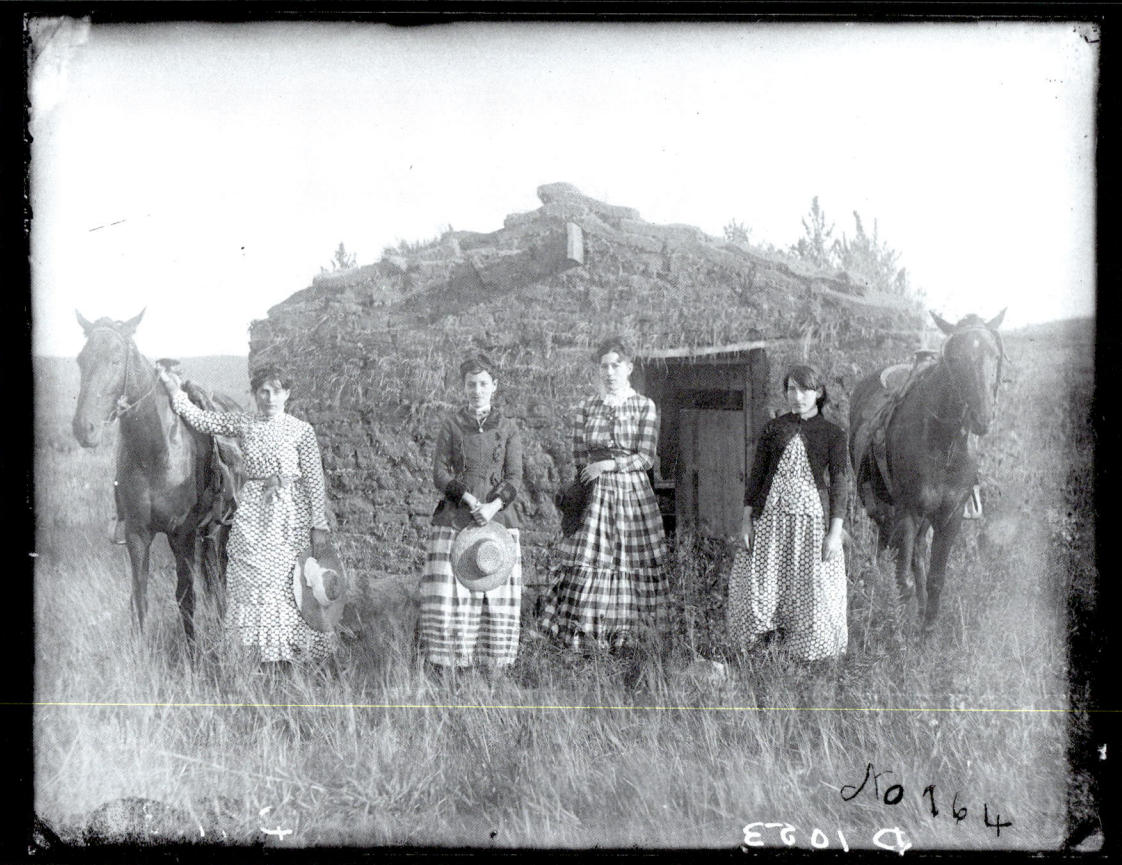

While women in the West were seeing a glimmer of hope for a new role in society, women in other parts of the country were frustrated with the lack of actual advancement in the Suffrage movement. Women of Color also continued to face challenges, from access to land ownership to broader inclusion in activism.

In 1886, the Statue of Liberty was erected in New York City, New York, as a gift from France. It was a symbol of freedom and democracy, but at a time when women could not yet vote and Women of Color were disenfranchised, making it an ironic symbol of inequality. Thus, a boat packed with more than two hundred women's rights activists sailed by Lady Liberty with a message of their own, holding signs that read, "American women have no liberty."

Many nineteenth-century American women were finding their footing in activism and in their evolving societal roles. The term "cowgirl" first appeared in literature in 1885, in reference to the evolving popularity of Wild West shows where women were featured in various riding exhibitions and competitions. Many women also participated in cattle drives, often masquerading as men because it wasn't considered a safe endeavor for women to drive cattle through the back country alone. Some things never change—right?

↑ A photograph of the Chrisman sisters in front of their sod house in Custer County, Nebraska, taken by Solomon D. Butcher in 1886. From left to right: Harriet (Hattie), Elizabeth (Lizzie), Lucy (Lutie), and Jennie Ruth (Ruth). The horses are Bet (on the left) and Jessie.

→ An older woman leads her horse.

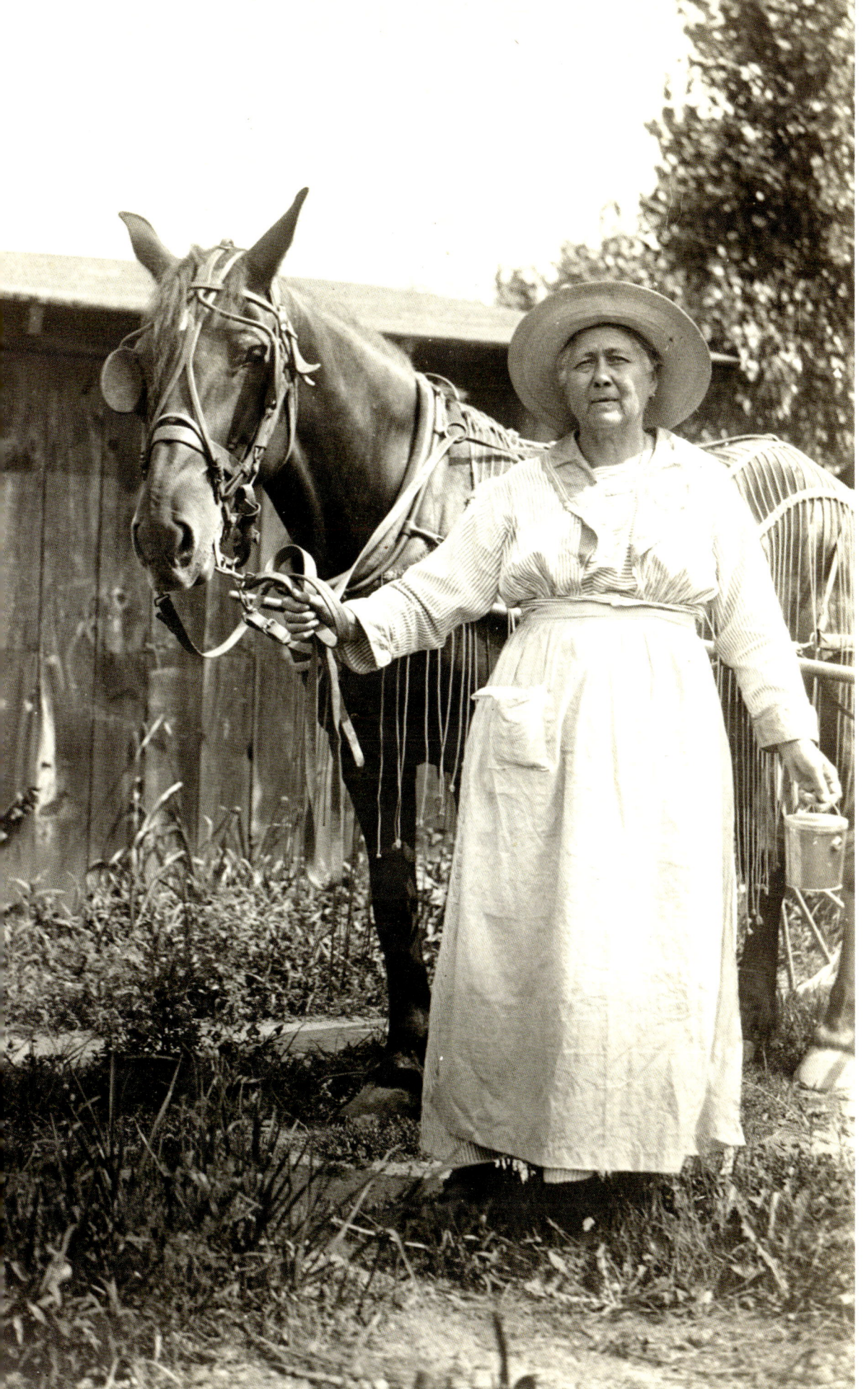

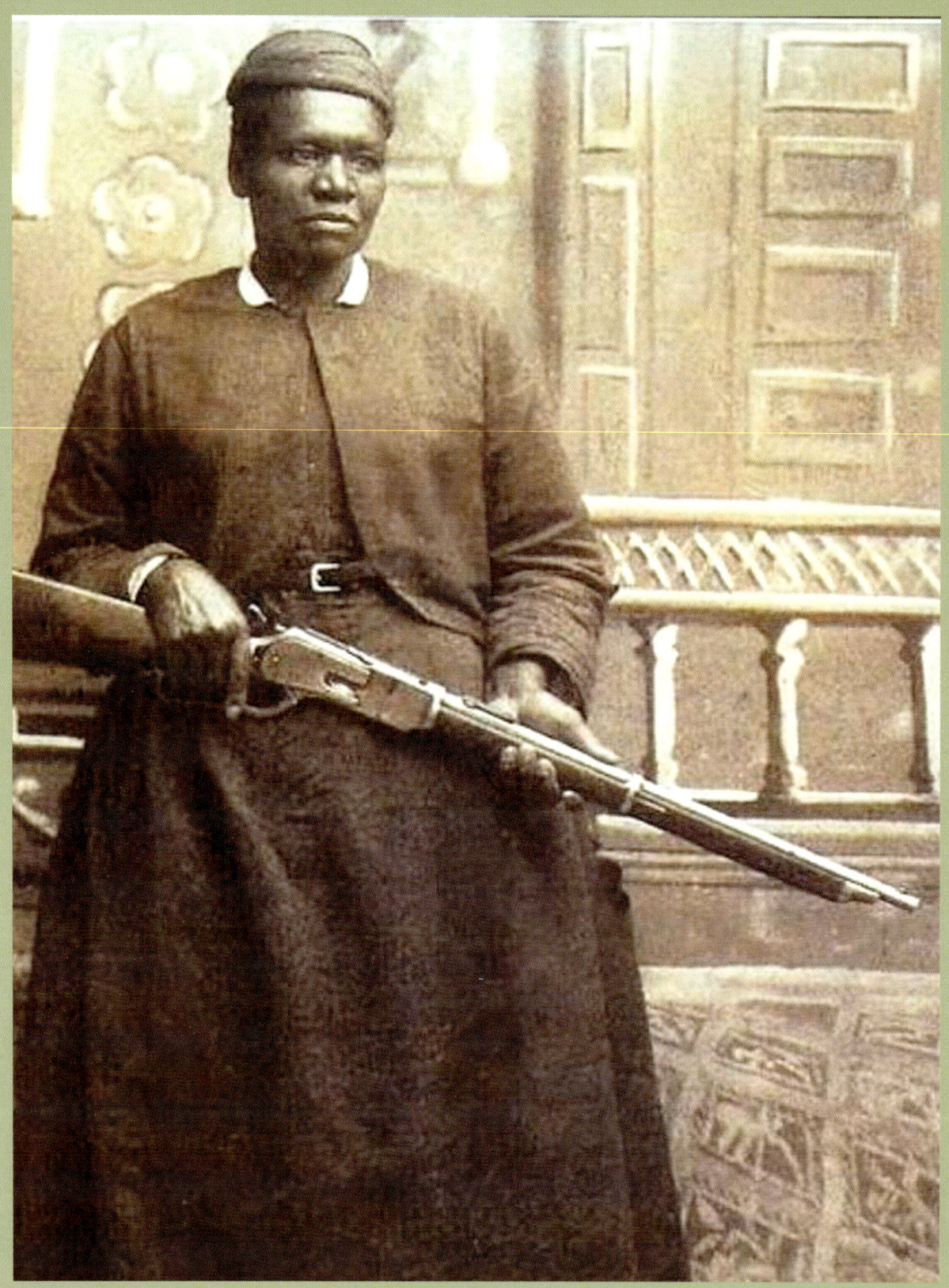

Cowgirl Pioneers

← Mary Fields (circa 1832-1914), the first Black woman mail carrier in the United States.

Among the first cowgirl pioneers was Mary Fields. Fields, mentioned earlier in this chapter, was born enslaved in Tennessee and was emancipated at the end of the Civil War. She held various jobs but ultimately became the second female to carry mail on a Star Route for the US Postal Service and the first Black woman to do so, earning her the nickname "Stagecoach Mary." The job was dangerous for women, especially a recently emancipated Black woman, due to the lawless nature of the frontier. Women were often seen as easy targets for criminals, especially if they traveled alone. But Fields was six feet (1.8 meters) tall and was known to carry two guns on her while she worked. She became a beloved member of her community in Cascade, Montana, known for her fearlessness and generosity, especially her kindness to children.

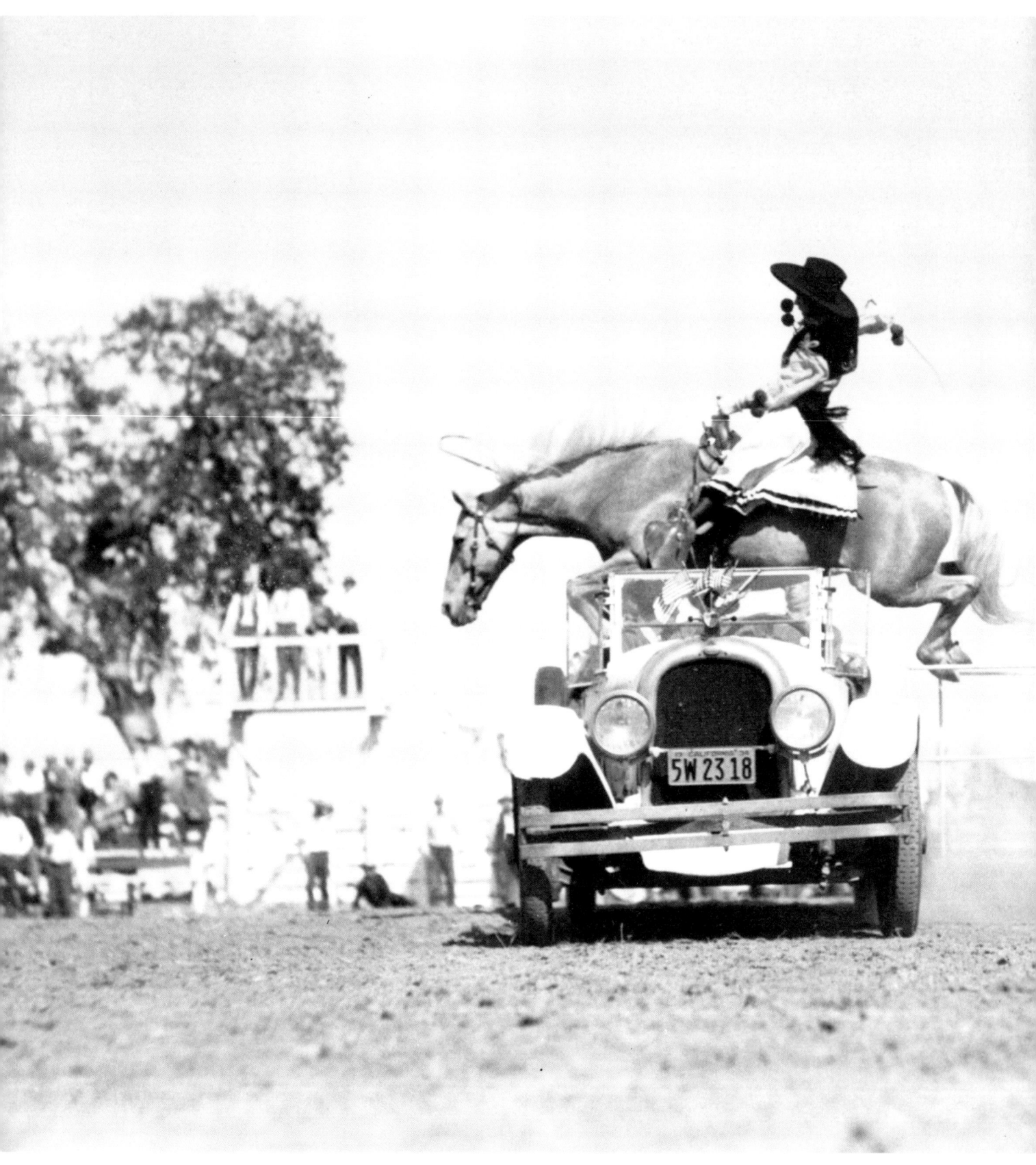

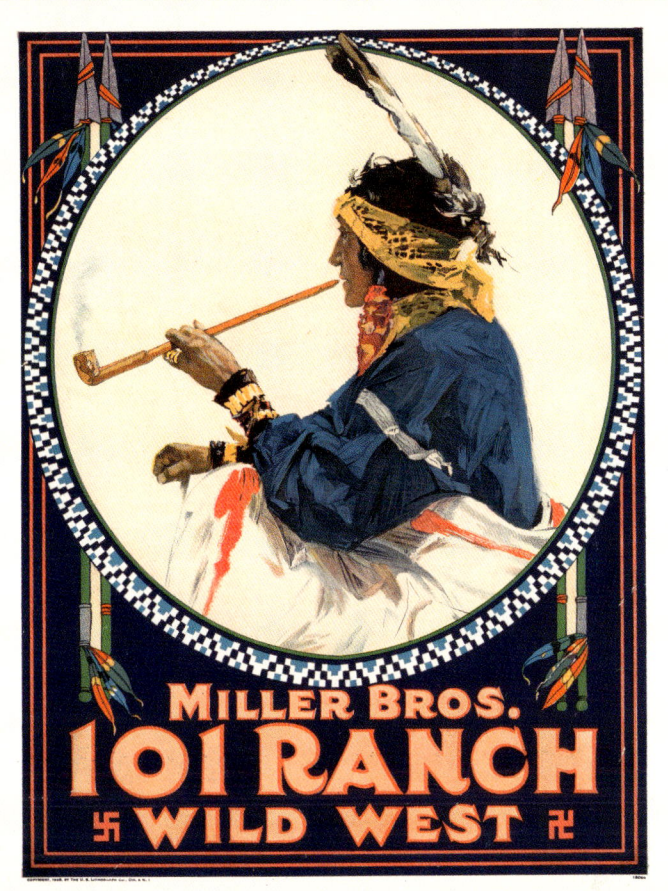

↑ Vintage advertising poster for the Miller Brothers 101 Ranch Wild West Show, circa 1909.

← In the 1920s and '30s, trick rider Bonnie Gray (1891–1988) was known for jumping her horse King Tut over automobiles and their passengers.

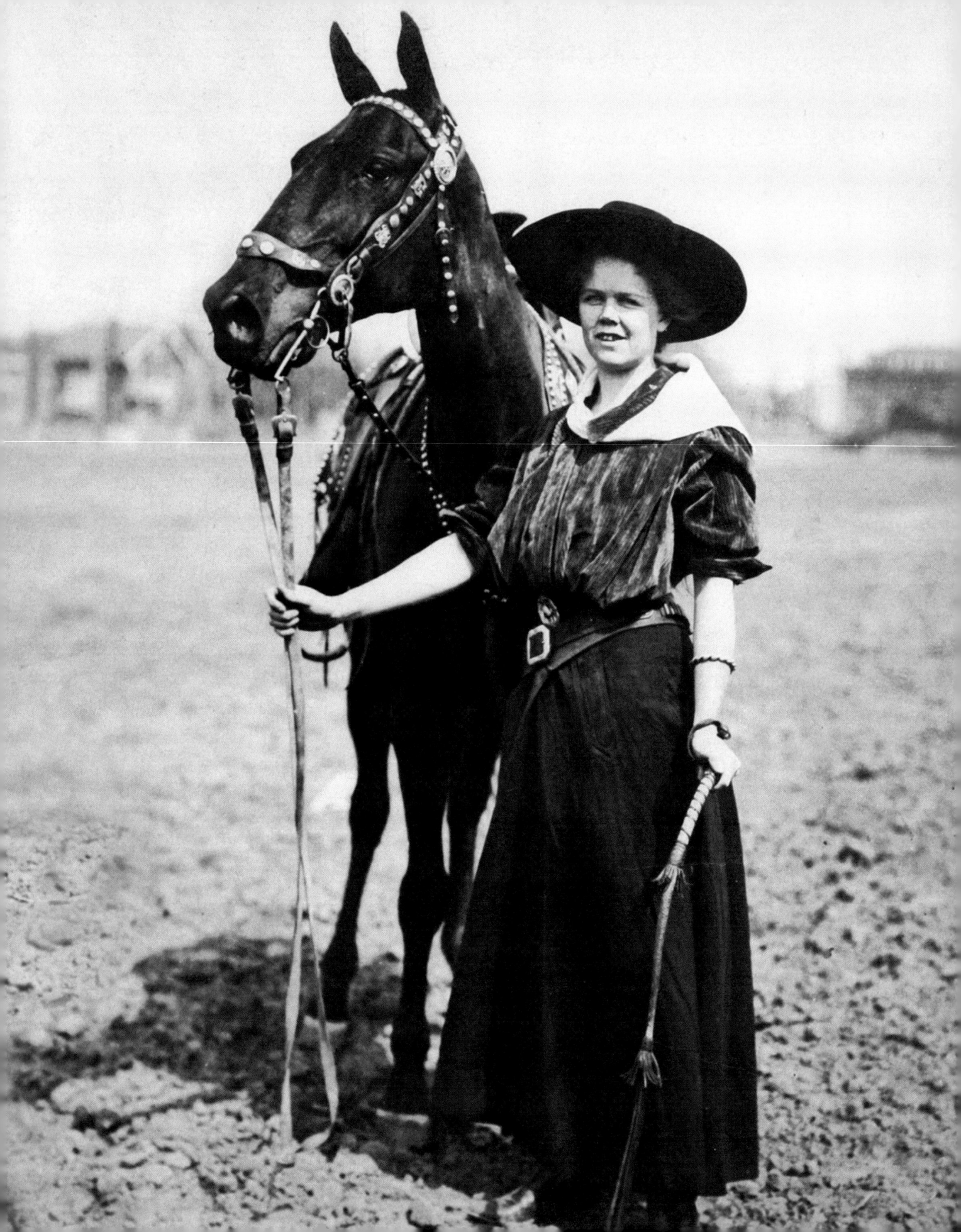

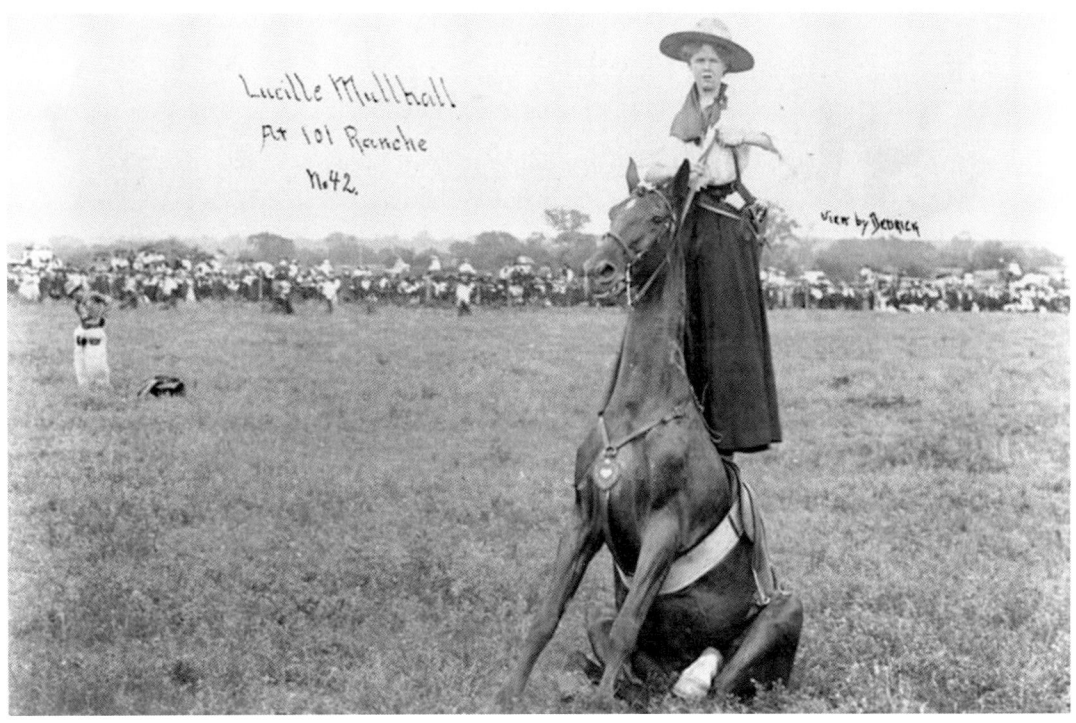

Lucille Mulhall at the Miller Brothers 101 Ranch.

Lucille Mulhall, circa 1899. Mulhall performed in rodeos and Wild West shows for over thirty years.

Lucille Mulhall is often said to have been the "first" cowgirl, at least in name, as she was referred to by the title after Teddy Roosevelt saw her perform at a Wild West show at the Mulhall Ranch. While the term had been used before, this was the first time it was bestowed upon a specific person. The lore suggests that Roosevelt told her he would invite her to the inaugural parade if she could rope a wolf, and she returned three hours later dragging a dead wolf behind her.

Mulhall starred in Mulhall's Wild West Show and the Miller Brothers 101 Ranch Wild West Show. She produced her own rodeo and was among the first women to compete in roping and riding events against men. She was married to Tom Burnett, whose father, Burk Burnett, established the Four Sixes Ranch in Guthrie, Texas.

Another one to pioneer women's participation in the rodeo competition arena was Bertha Blancett. She gained notoriety when she became the first woman to ride a bronc at the Cheyenne Frontier Days in 1904. Her horseback skills earned her a spot in the Miller Brothers 101 Ranch Wild West Show as well.

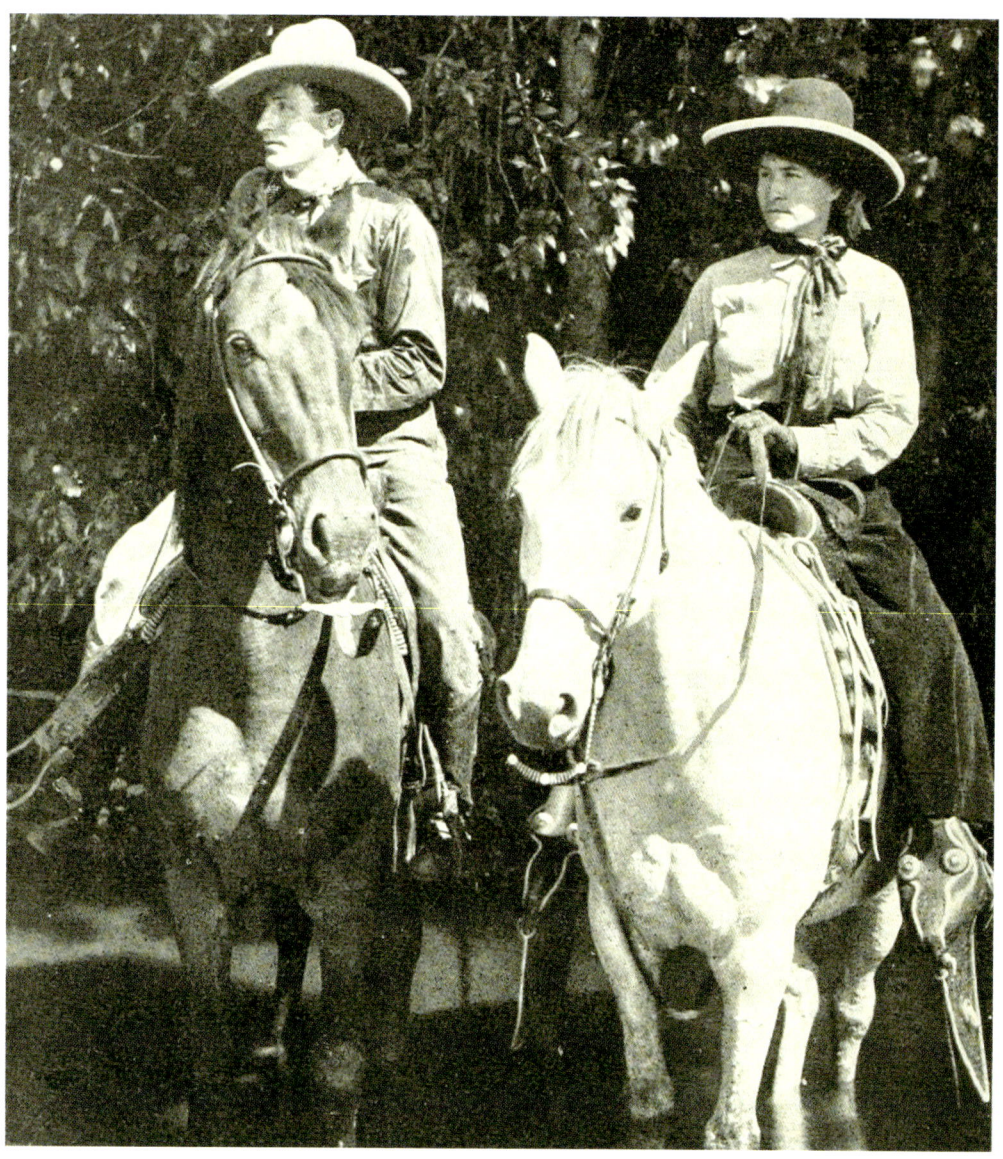

Behind Blancett came Florence Randolph, who rose to stardom when she bested thirteen male competitors in the Roman racing event at the Calgary Stampede. She also won the first trophy awarded to the champion All-Around Cowgirl at the Madison Square Garden Rodeo in 1927, only to be outshined by cowgirl Tad Lucas, who would win three consecutive All-Around Cowgirl titles at the same rodeo in subsequent years.

One thing many cowgirl pioneers had in common was finding their roots in a Wild West show, which were the bread-and-butter of early cowgirls, two of whom would go on to become household names—Annie Oakley and Calamity Jane.

Bertha Blancett (right) and her husband Dell Blancett.

Calamity Jane (1852-1903), born Martha Jane Canary, was a colorful character who claimed to have served as a scout under General George Crook during several prolonged territorial conflicts with Native American tribes. This claim was never verified by official sources. In fact, it was reportedly flat-out denied.

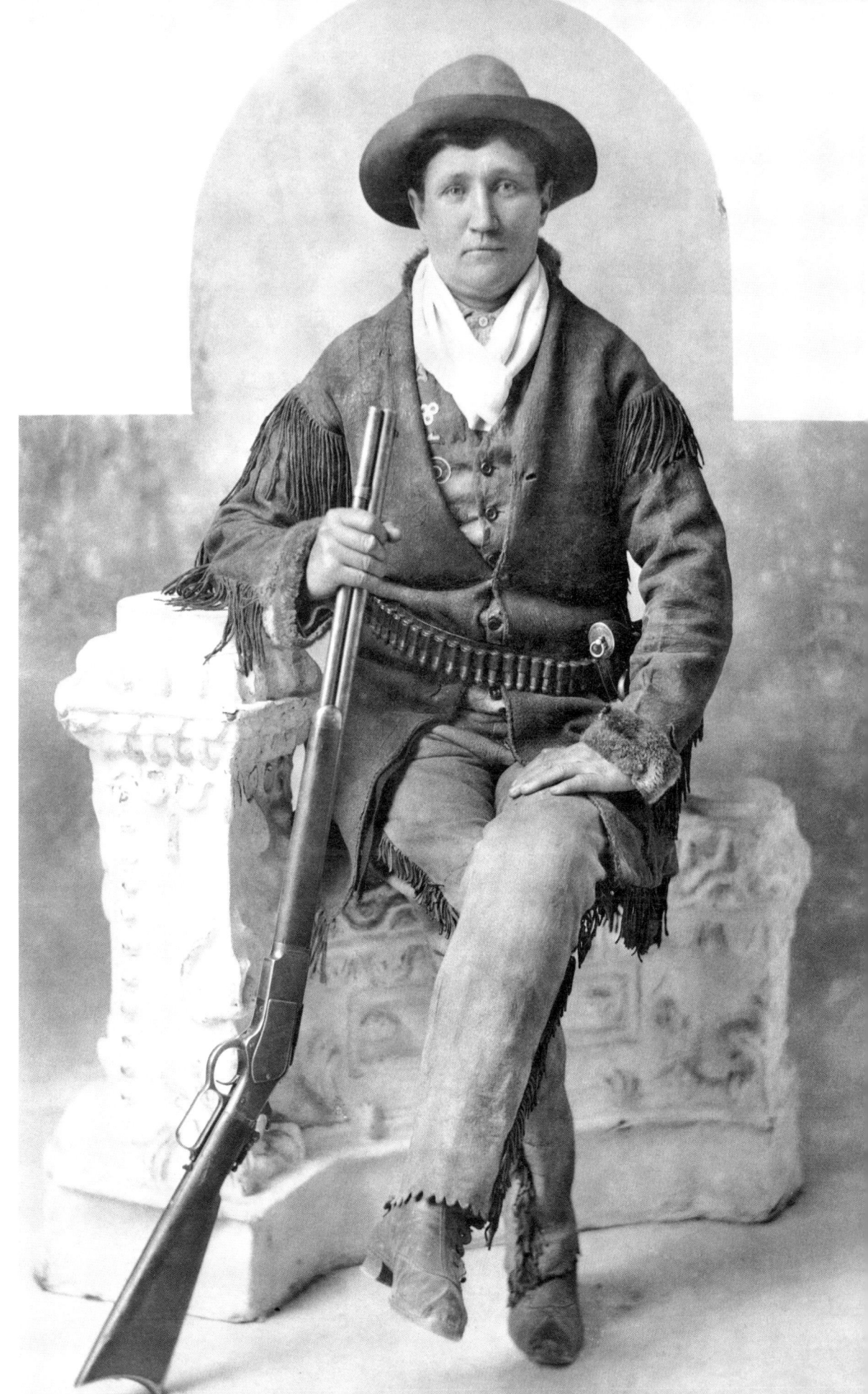

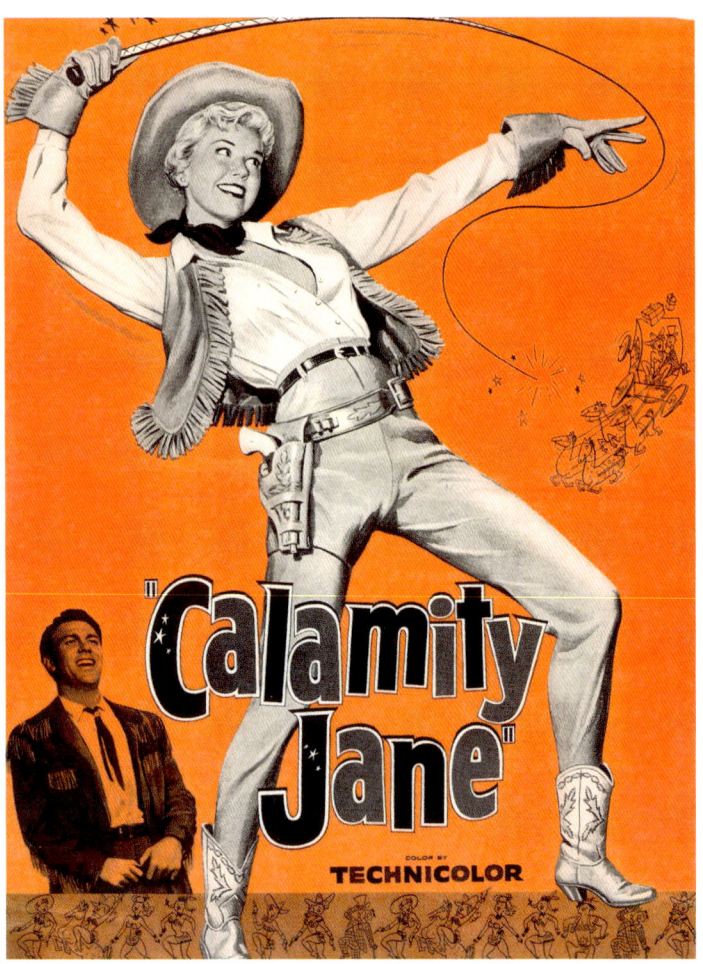

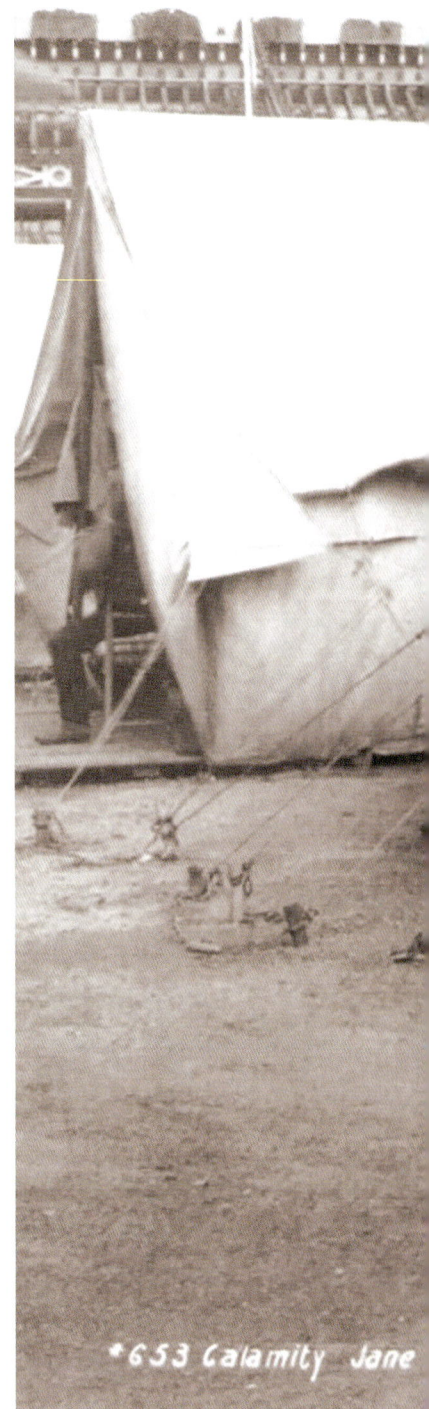

Promotional poster for the 1953 film *Calamity Jane*, starring Doris Day and Howard Keel.

Calamity Jane on horseback, circa 1885.

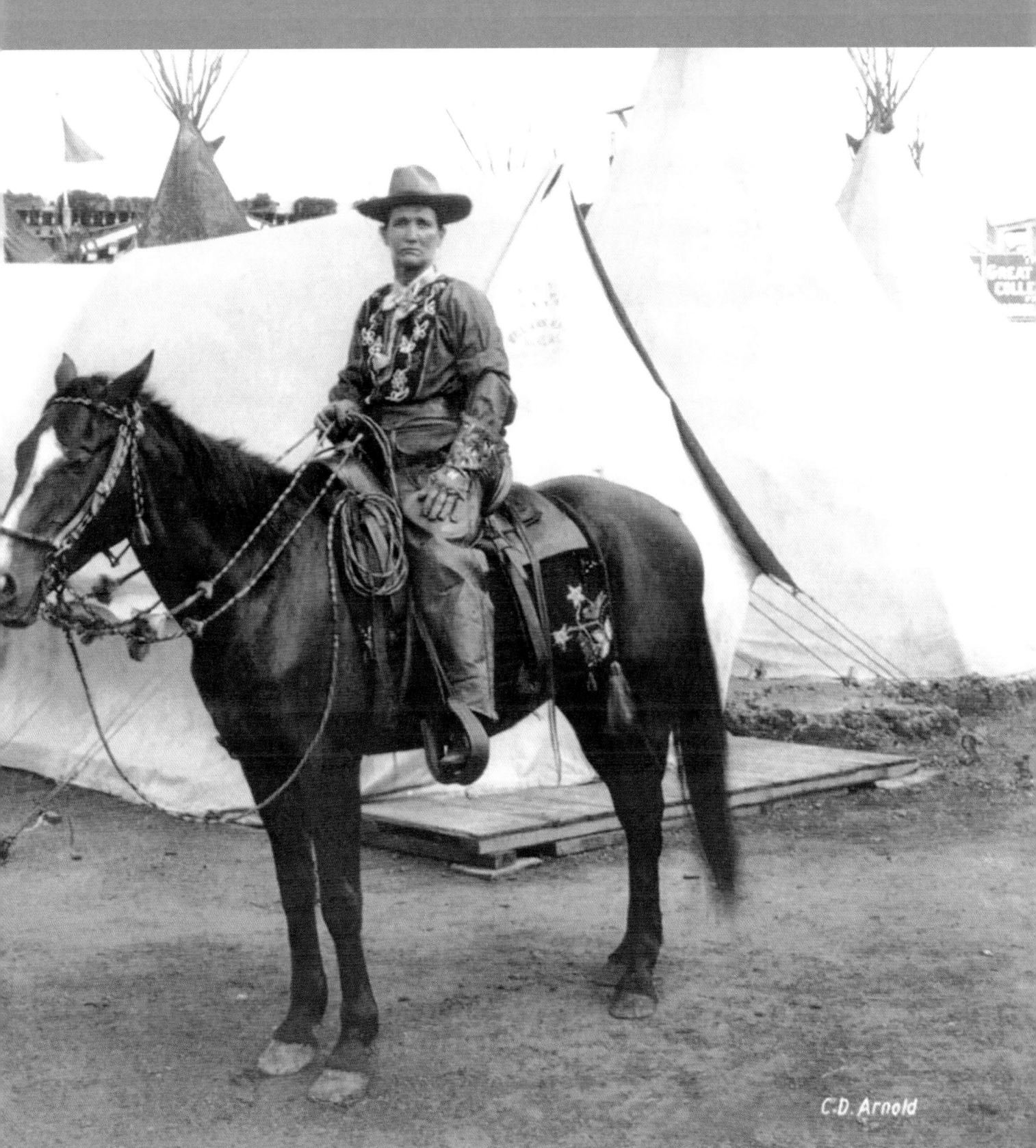

C.D. Arnold

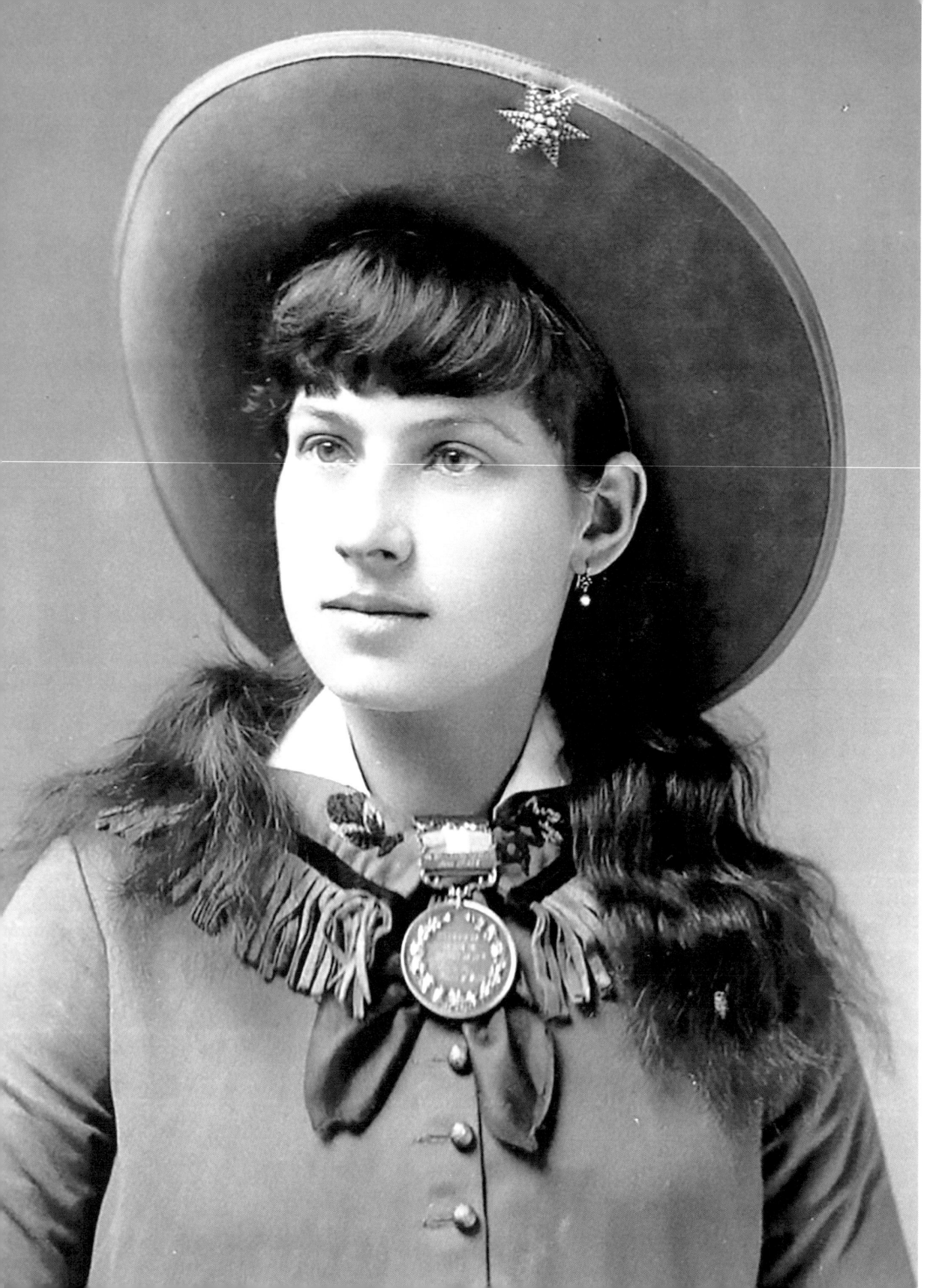

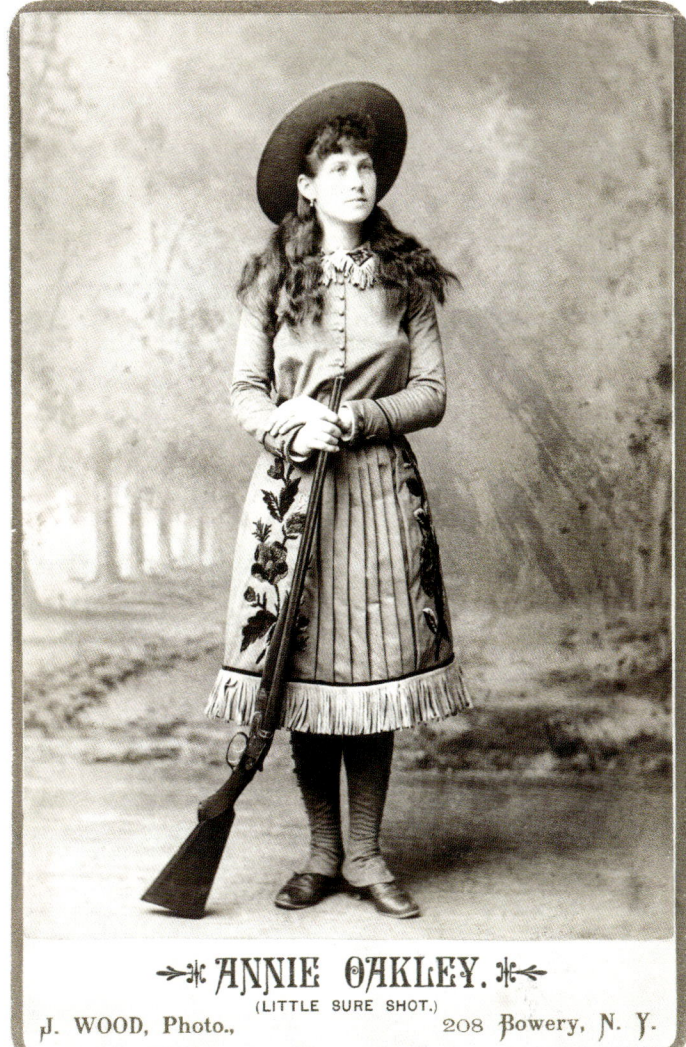

Annie Oakley was given the nickname "Little Sure Shot" by Lakota leader Sitting Bull, who met the sharpshooter in 1884. Oakley, who was only five feet tall, had larger-than-life charisma as a performer.

Portrait of Annie Oakley. At the height of her career, Oakley traveled Europe performing in Buffalo Bill's Wild West Show. She was a true star, earning more than anyone in the touring group (except Buffalo Bill himself).

Phoebe Ann Moses, also known as "Annie Oakley," starred in what was perhaps the most popular Wild West show, Buffalo Bill's Wild West. Oakley hunted to provide for her impoverished family in Ohio as a child, which is how she honed her marksmanship.

Martha Jane Canary, "Calamity Jane," was also a star in Buffalo Bill's Wild West Show. She was widely known as a sharpshooter, a daredevil, and a woman of the frontier. Calamity Jane was an acquaintance of Wild Bill Hickok, infamous for his vigilante ways as a cattle rustler, gambler, and gunslinger.

Familiar with the vigilante life was Pearl Hart, a Canadian cowgirl who, while disguised as a man, committed one of the last recorded stagecoach robberies in the United States. The crime gained notoriety for the simple

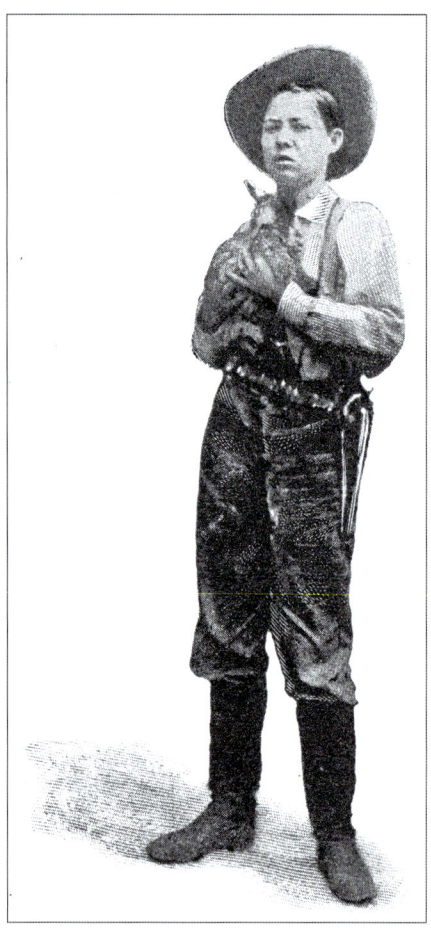

← Pearl Hart, outlaw.

→ Two women wearing chaps.

fact that a woman was the offender. The story became so popular that Hart willingly recounted her story for *Cosmopolitan* magazine when they interviewed her from her jail cell in 1899.

The original cowgirls of the nineteenth century were icons. They were beautiful and brave and tough and vulnerable. They commanded the rooms they entered—even Hart deserves credit for the confidence behind her crime. Most of all, they were larger than life. They were each pioneers in their own right. They had families, or responsibilities, or obstacles to overcome, yet the fire inside them urging them toward their dreams couldn't be extinguished. They found a way to do it all despite the dangers and the scrutiny they faced, a legacy they would unknowingly pass on to modern women in America. From Annie Oakley in 1885 to Tad Lucas in 1927, their names will live on for eternity in cowgirl legacy and lore, though these women were largely a part of the background of America—a side show. But cowgirls were on the cusp of finding their footing and taking over the arena.

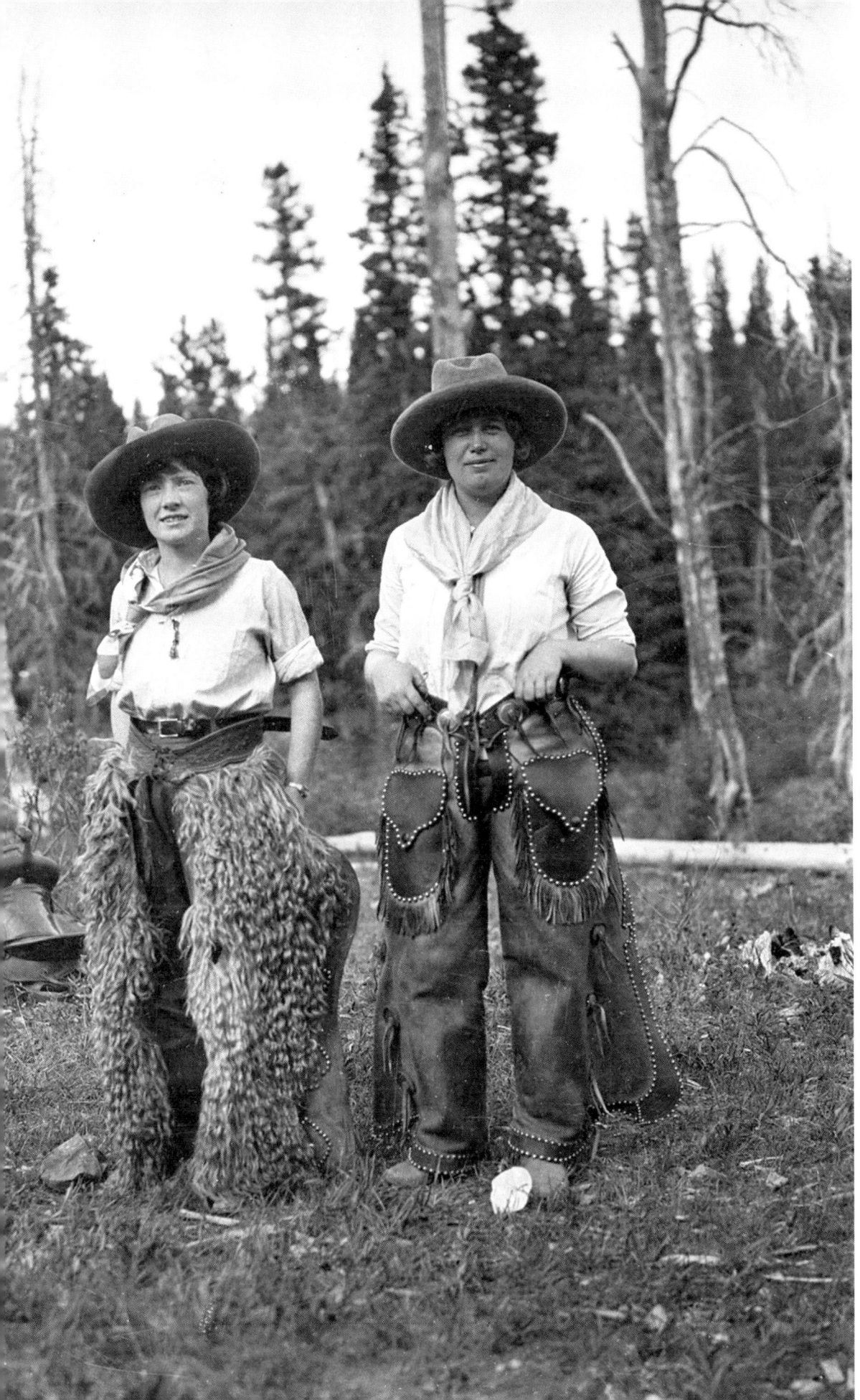

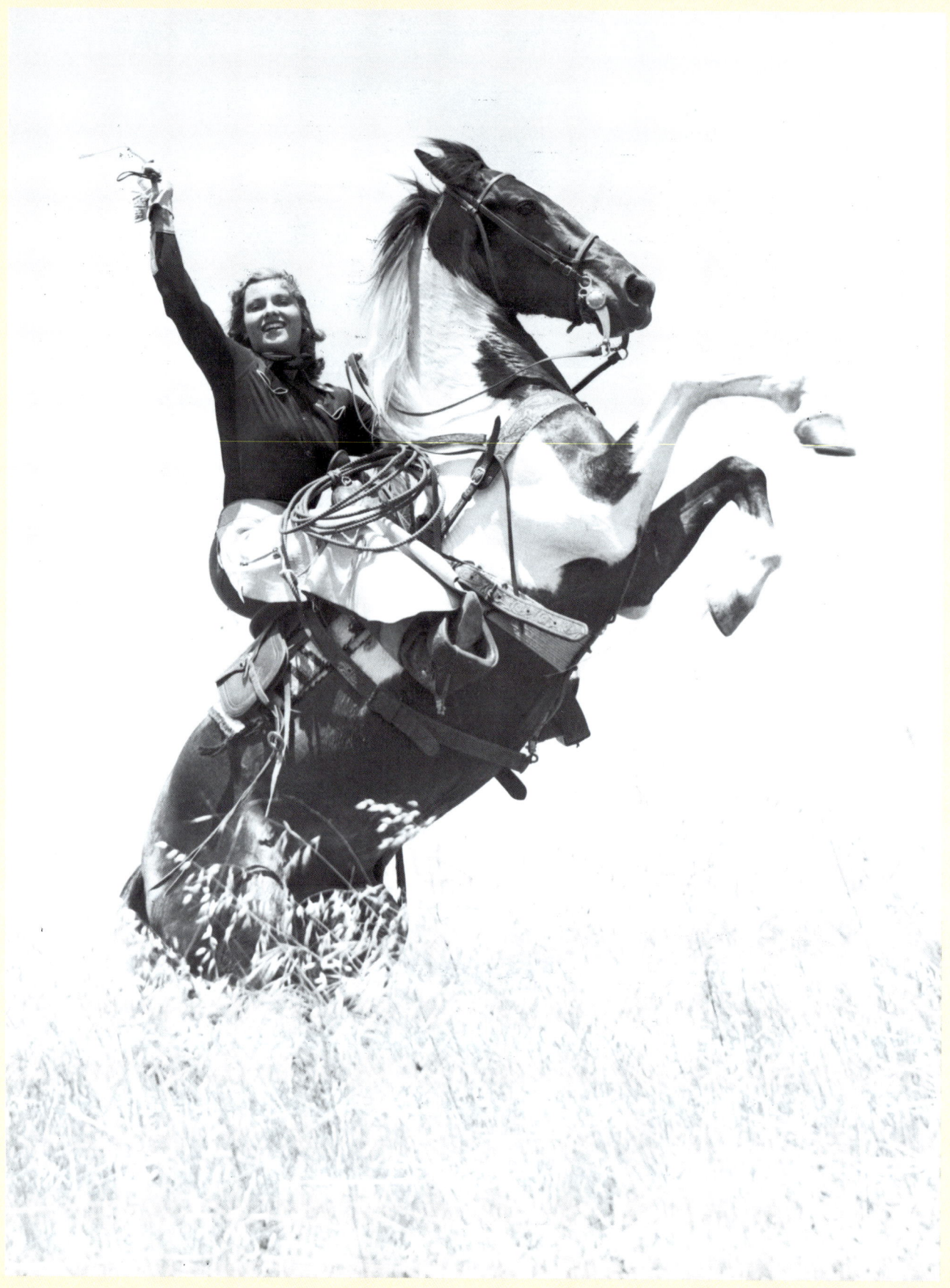

Not Her First Rodeo

Wild West shows were the launch pad of the modern-day rodeo and some of the first public platforms for cowgirls to carve out visible space on horseback. Many of today's American rodeo events—bronc riding, roping, and trick riding—are largely derived from the original Wild West show formats. While these rodeos were important to shaping cowboy culture, rodeo spectacles often distorted frontier life.

Original shows typically included dramatized reenactments of frontier events including stagecoach robberies, battles with Indigenous peoples, and bison hunts. These shows also served as one of the rare public stages where some People of Color—Black cowboys, Mexican vaqueros, and Indigenous riders—could display their horsemanship, roping skills, and more. However, these reenactments often perpetuated harmful stereotypes that glorified colonial violence, particularly with the depictions of the battles with Indigenous people, who were often misrepresented and even, at times, coerced into performing traditional dances and ceremonies in demeaning contexts.

Opportunities for Women of Color in these spaces were even more restricted due to racial segregation, which left them excluded from the spotlight or confined to supporting or stereotypical roles. While People of Color were often essential to the success of the shows, they were rarely given equal recognition.

Despite the deeply problematic elements of Wild West shows, they showcased unique cowboy skills. Eventually, some women began to be included as characters and trick riders, and even joined trick shooting and rough stock riding events, which led to more women participating in rodeo.

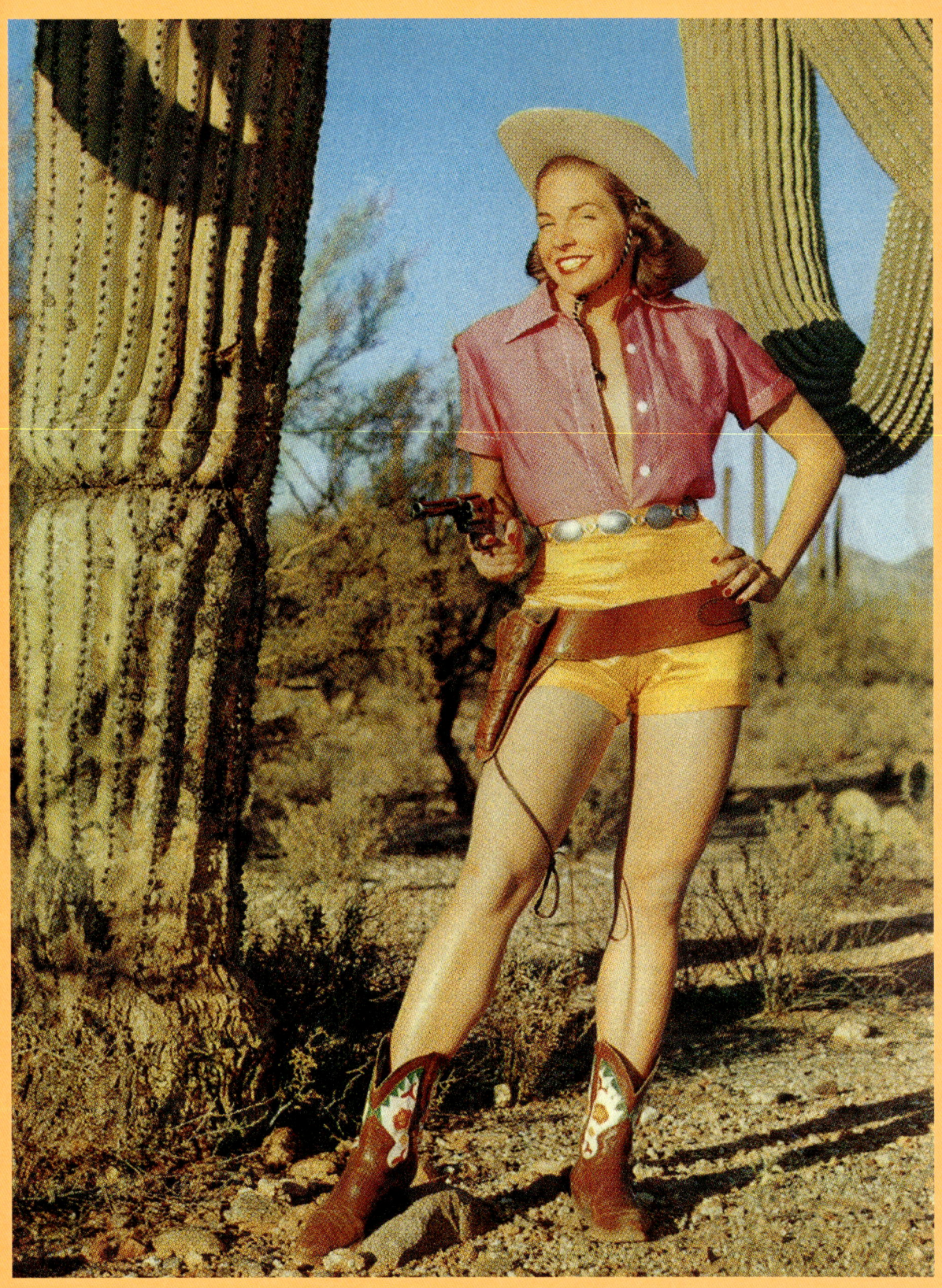

The Wild, Wild West

A vintage illustration of 1950s cowgirl-inspired fashion.

One show that quickly rose to fame was Buffalo Bill's Wild West Show, which opened in Omaha, Nebraska, in 1883. In 1869, novelist Ned Buntline, wrote about a US Army scout and avid buffalo hunter he had met on a train named William F. Cody. The novel, *Buffalo Bill, the King of the Border Men,* wove Cody's story into the growing legend of Buffalo Bill. The novel became a theatrical production, and later, Cody founded Buffalo Bill's Wild West, an outdoor attraction that toured annually and included wild animals, trick riders, theatrical reenactments, shooting exhibits, rodeo events, and more. Many of the riding and roping techniques featured in the show were heavily influenced by Mexican vaqueros, whose deep-rooted charrería traditions—a Mexican equestrian sport showcasing roping, ranching skills, and horsemanship—helped shape the style, skills, and culture of early rodeo.

The shows began as a true stage production depicting Western life but evolved to become open-air productions that romanticized the Western lifestyle and featured action-oriented cowboys and cowgirls. Some storylines were fictionalized but many were dramatizations loosely based on historical events, like military battles, breaking wild horses, and more. Some dramatizations often showcased harmful stereotypes, particularly regarding Indigenous peoples with fictionalized "battles" that reinforced colonial narratives.

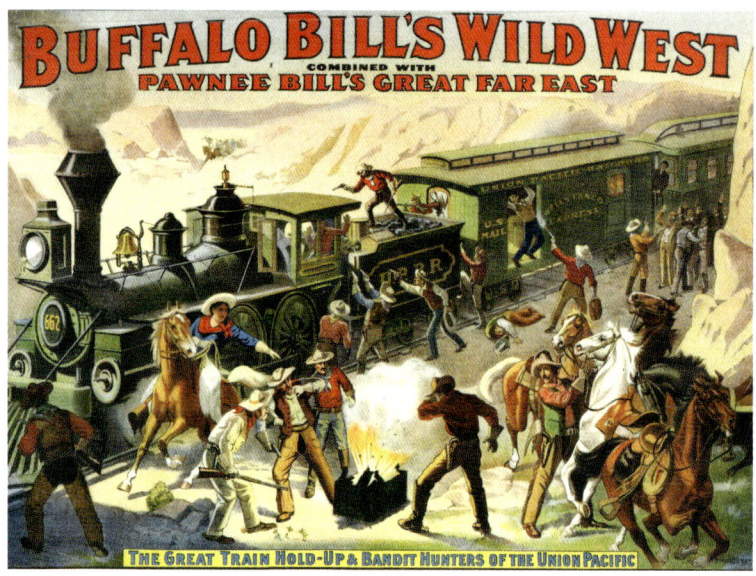

Advertising poster for Buffalo Bill's Wild West Show from the 1910s.

Stunt double Donna Hall (1928-2002) spent her career riding, falling from, and jumping onto horses in Western films. A fearless horsewoman, born and raised in the Los Angeles suburbs, she made her movie debut at age ten.

Despite this, Buffalo Bill's Wild West Show became the prototype for the other shows that would follow, and it lasted until 1915, leaving a lasting impact on popular culture and the development of modern rodeo.

The popularity of Wild West shows attracted enough media and participants that the show organizers were able to coordinate a sort of competition between the shows. Over time, the competitions became more sophisticated and organized, and we got our first taste of modern rodeo in the United States. Though, at the time, the word "rodeo" wasn't even used—these competitions were referred to as frontier days, stampedes, or cowboy contests.

From the inception of the first Wild West show in 1883 women played an important yet often overlooked role in shaping rodeo culture and the spectacles of frontier entertainment. Some women initially made their mark as trick riders and exhibition performers, but over time, they trickled into shooting events and even rough stock riding. These women defied the odds with bravery and confidence as they went toe to toe with some of the most famous cowboys in the world on the public stage. However, society labeled them as inappropriate, unladylike, and rebellious. High society shamed and judged the women who dared participate in these events, yet they persisted, knowing they were doing what they loved. Despite their relentless spirit and effort, women were still not given the same opportunities as men to exhibit their horsemanship skills.

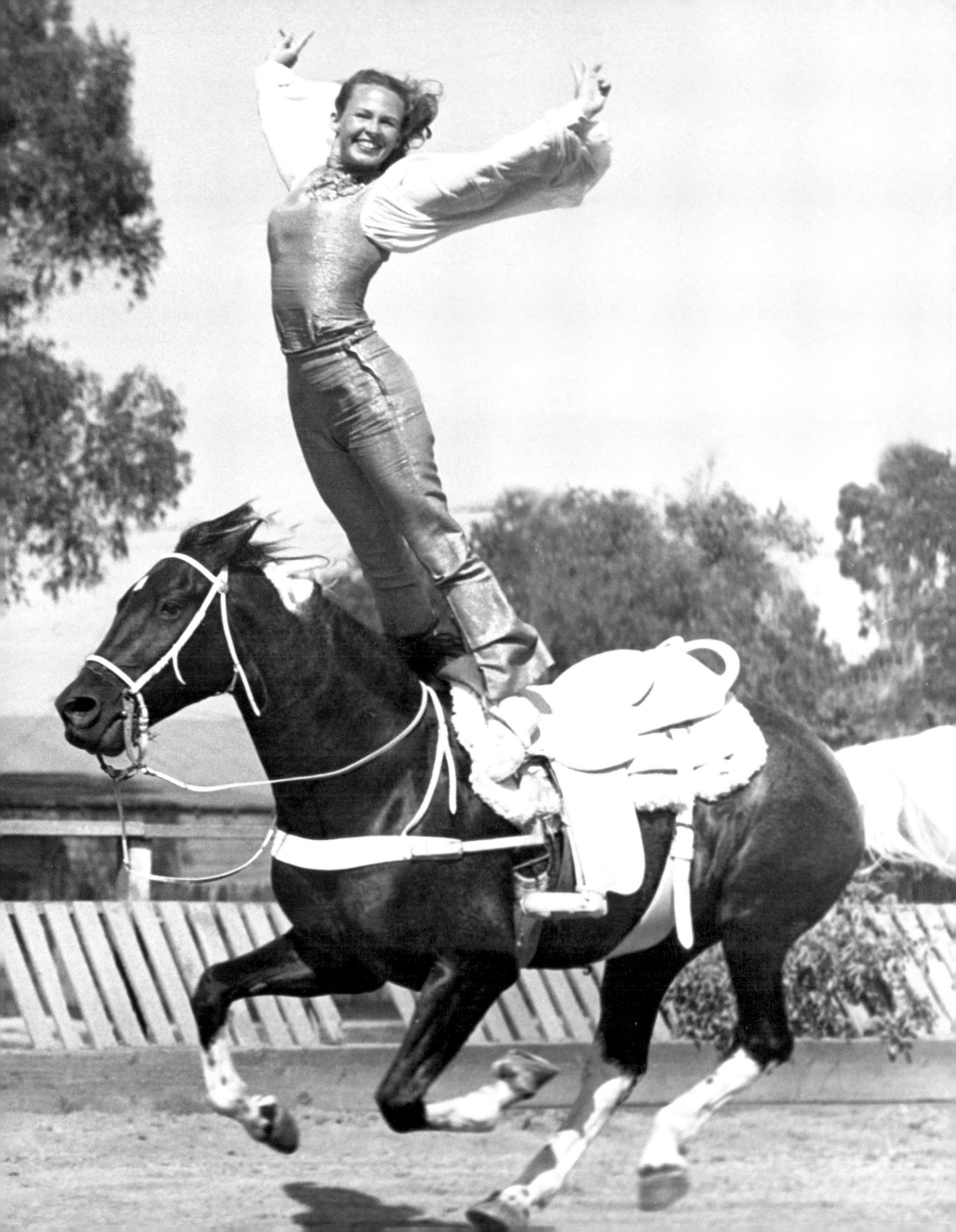

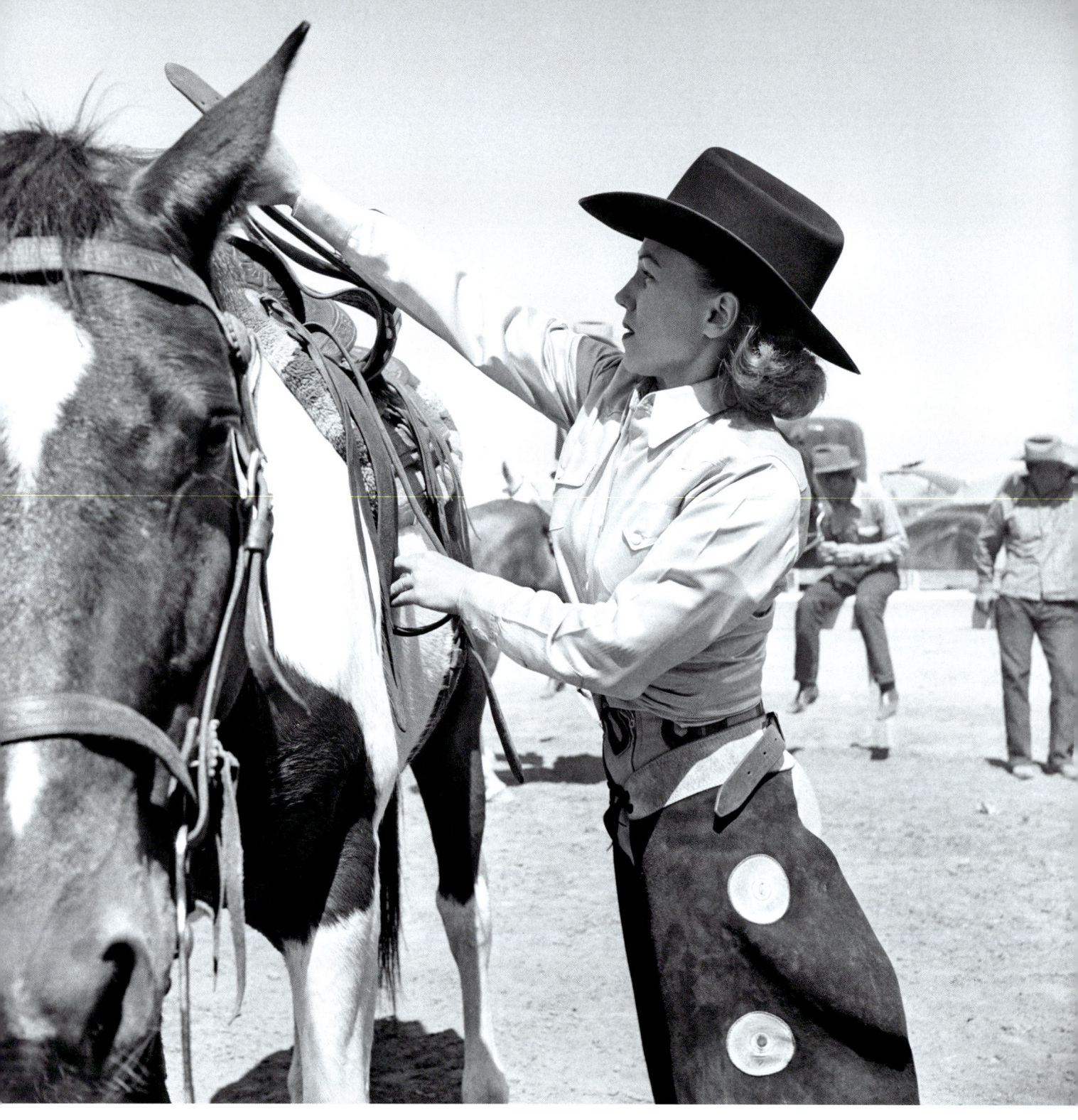

↑ Trick rider Jean Allen at the rodeo in 1946.

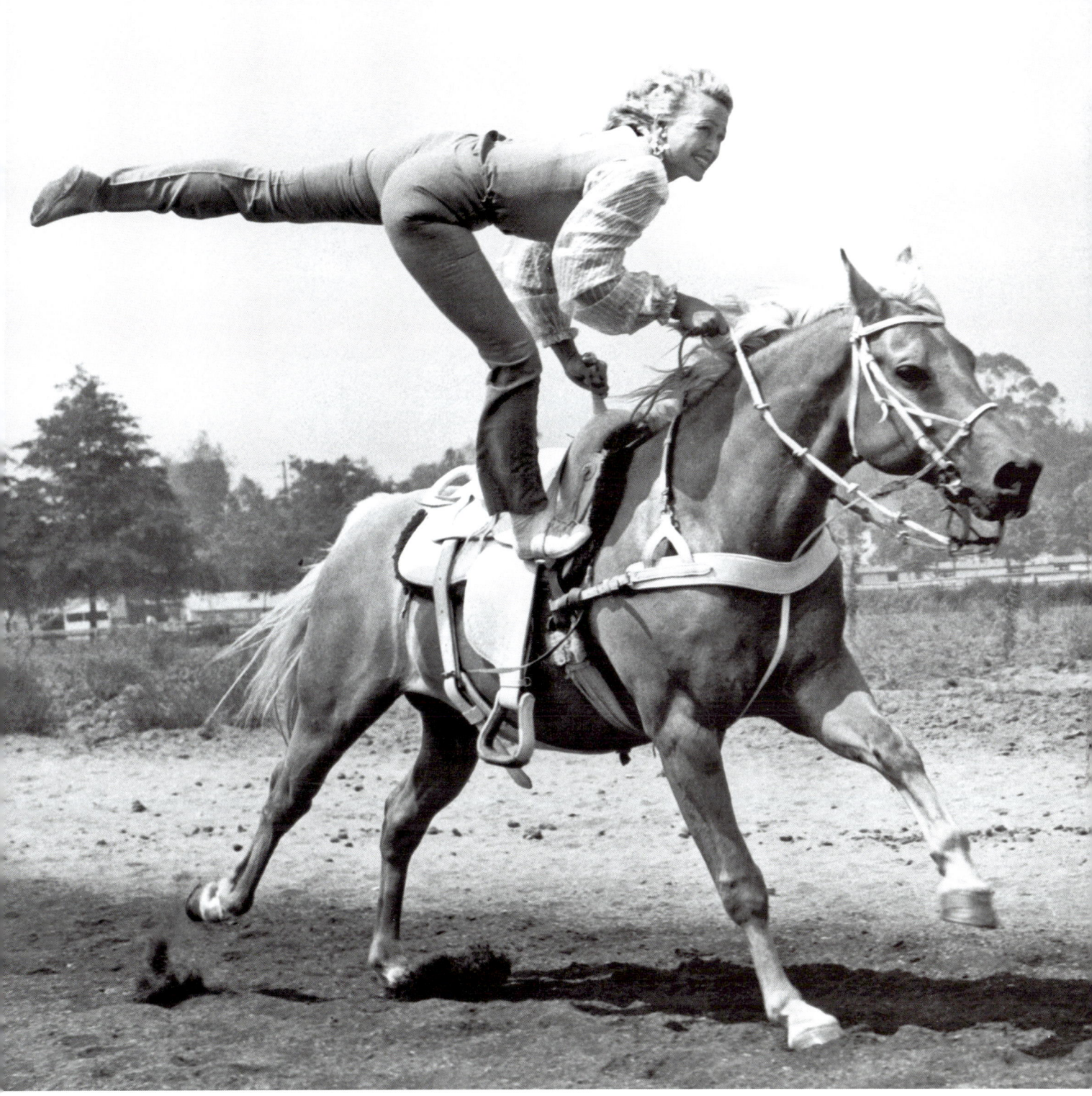

↑ Faye Blessing (1920-1999), a National Cowgirl Hall of Fame inductee, performs on her palomino horse, Flash, in the 1950s.

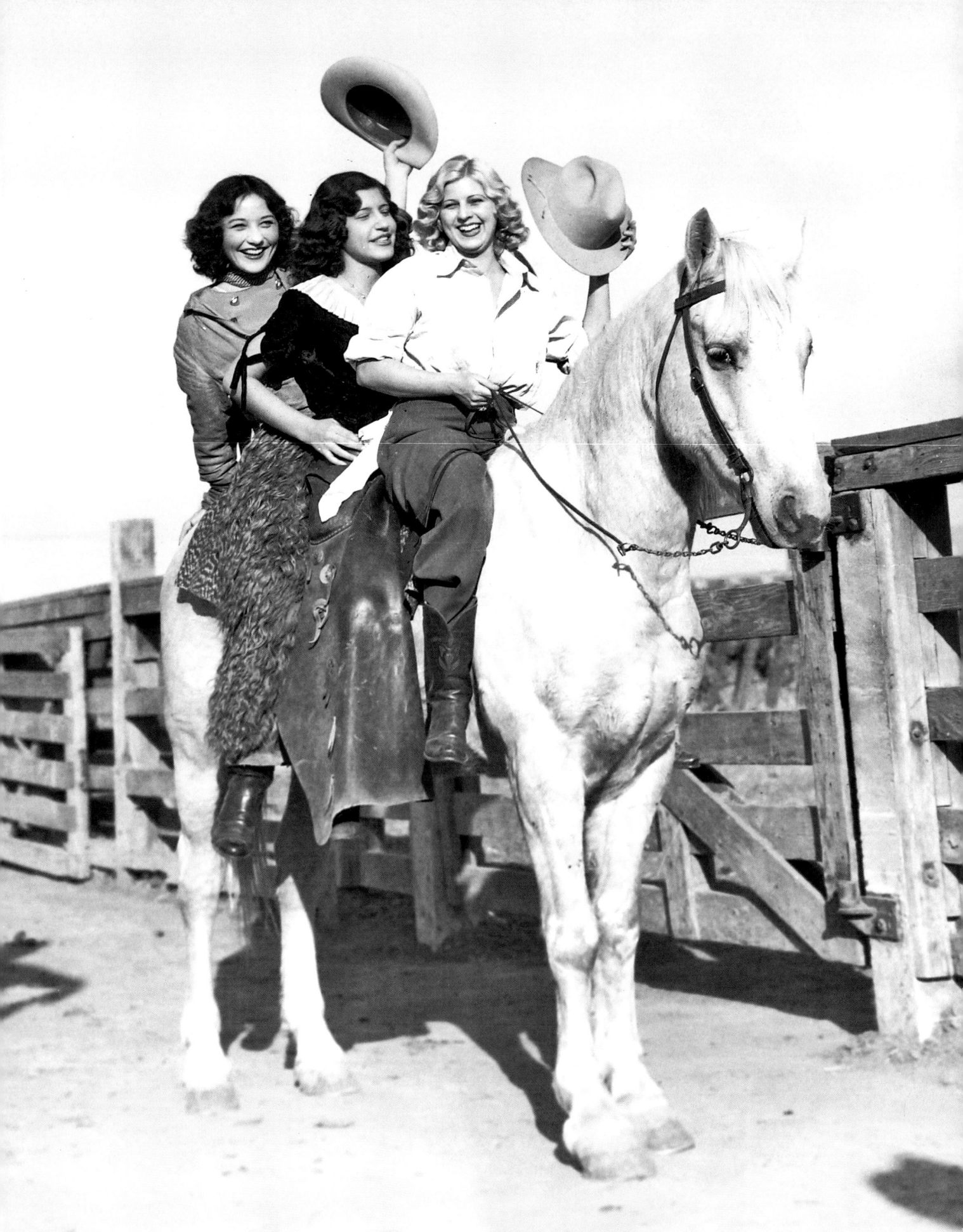

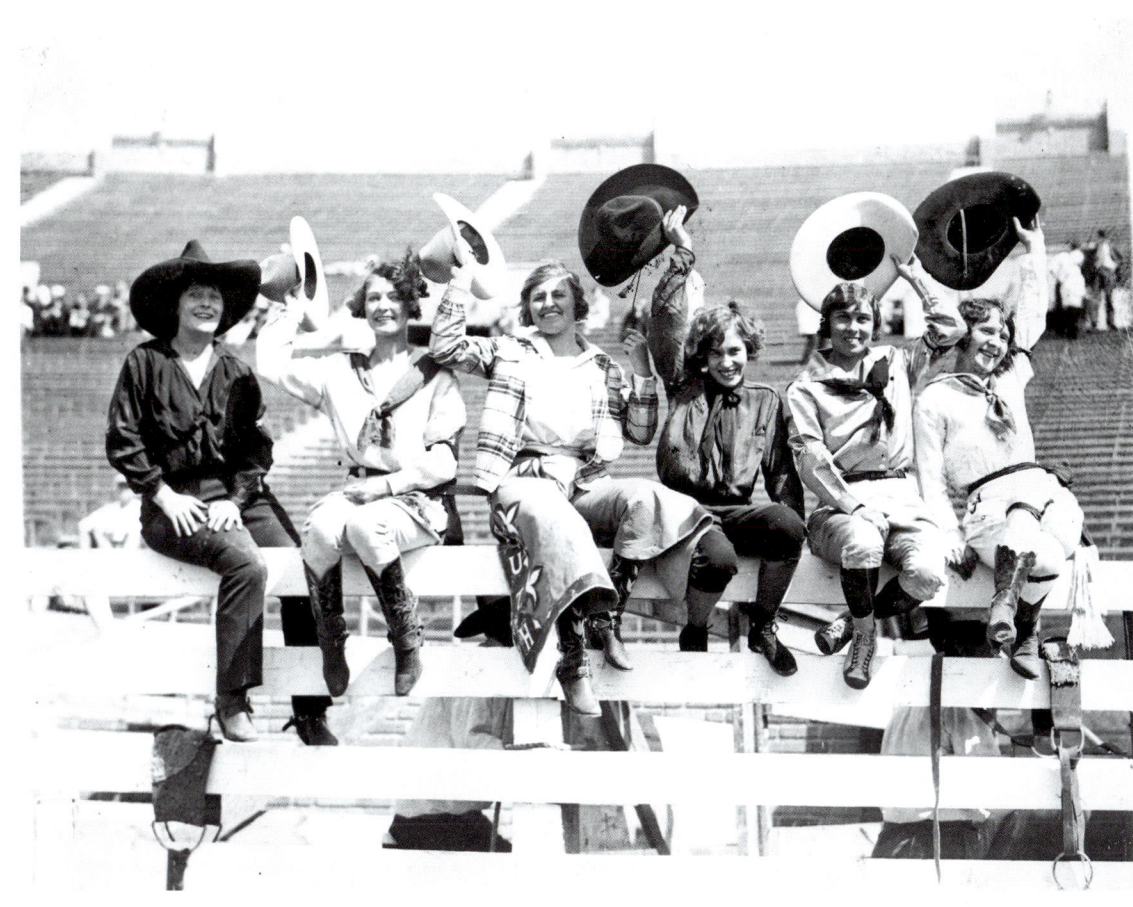

↑ Cowgirls at the World's Championship Rodeo in Philadelphia, Pennsylvania, in 1926. They include Tad Lucas (third from the left) and Bonnie McCarroll (far right). McCarroll was a champion bronc rider in the 1920s. At the Pendleton Roundup in 1929, McCarroll was thrown from her horse during a bronc riding event. She died from her injuries eleven days later.

← Promotional photo for the 1932 World's Congress Rough Rider Rodeo in Los Angeles.

Then, in 1929, a female roughie (rough stock rider), Bonnie McCarroll, died as a result of an injury in bronc riding at the Pendleton Roundup in Pendleton, Oregon. The accident shook the industry—causing more to question whether women should be allowed to participate in such dangerous events. Many women began to pull out of rodeo events nationwide. Event producers and organizers felt the sport of rodeo needed a governing body to help discern what was right for the sport, and to make key decisions, which led to the formation of the Rodeo Association of America (RAA).

The association created a standardized set of rules and established a points system for its competitors. It aimed to regulate rodeo competitions across the country, and it banned women from participating. Wild West shows had waned at this point, due to the rise of rodeo, and even the most tenacious, headstrong women in the country who had already broken the mold once, found themselves on the sidelines with no point of entry.

In 1936, even the cowboy contestants were fed up with the RAA. The association was run solely by organizers and producers, not by cowboys themselves, and didn't take the contestants' needs and welfare into consideration. The breaking point came at the Boston Garden Rodeo, where cowboys went on strike to protest the unfair conditions. This led to the formation of the Cowboy Turtles Association (CTA)—"turtles," because the cowboys had been slow to act against the restrictions of the RAA and "stuck their neck out" in support of what was right. The association became the first contestant-run rodeo organization in the United States, advocating for fair prize money, better judging, and a more honest image for the sport of rodeo. However, even though this was a big win for contestant rights, it primarily benefitted white cowboys, as women and People of Color were still largely excluded from rodeo competitions.

This new association eventually evolved into the Rodeo Cowboys Association (RCA), later renamed Professional Rodeo Cowboys Association (PRCA), in 1945. With the establishment of the RCA, rodeo events became more standardized and quickly became popular attractions.

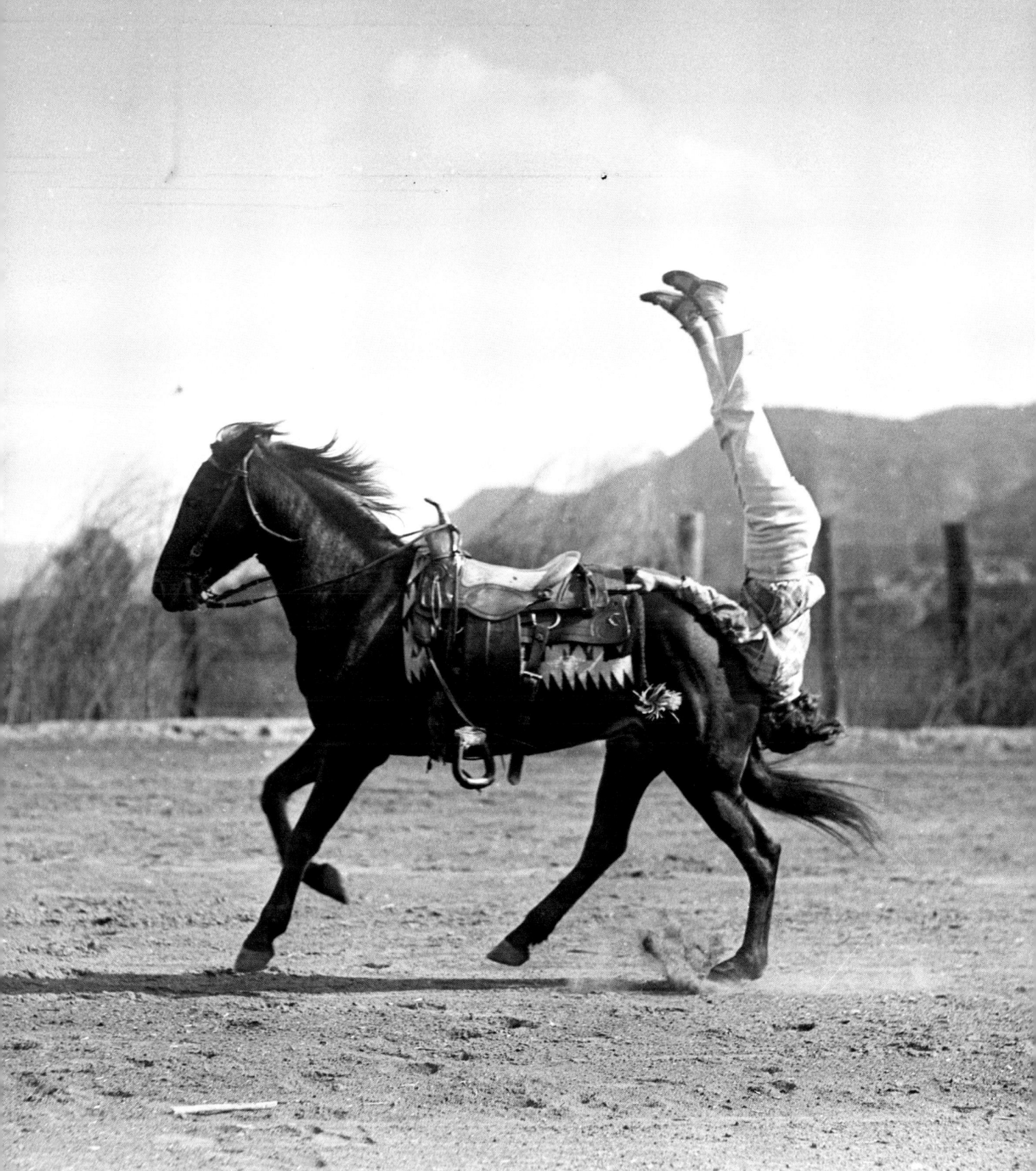

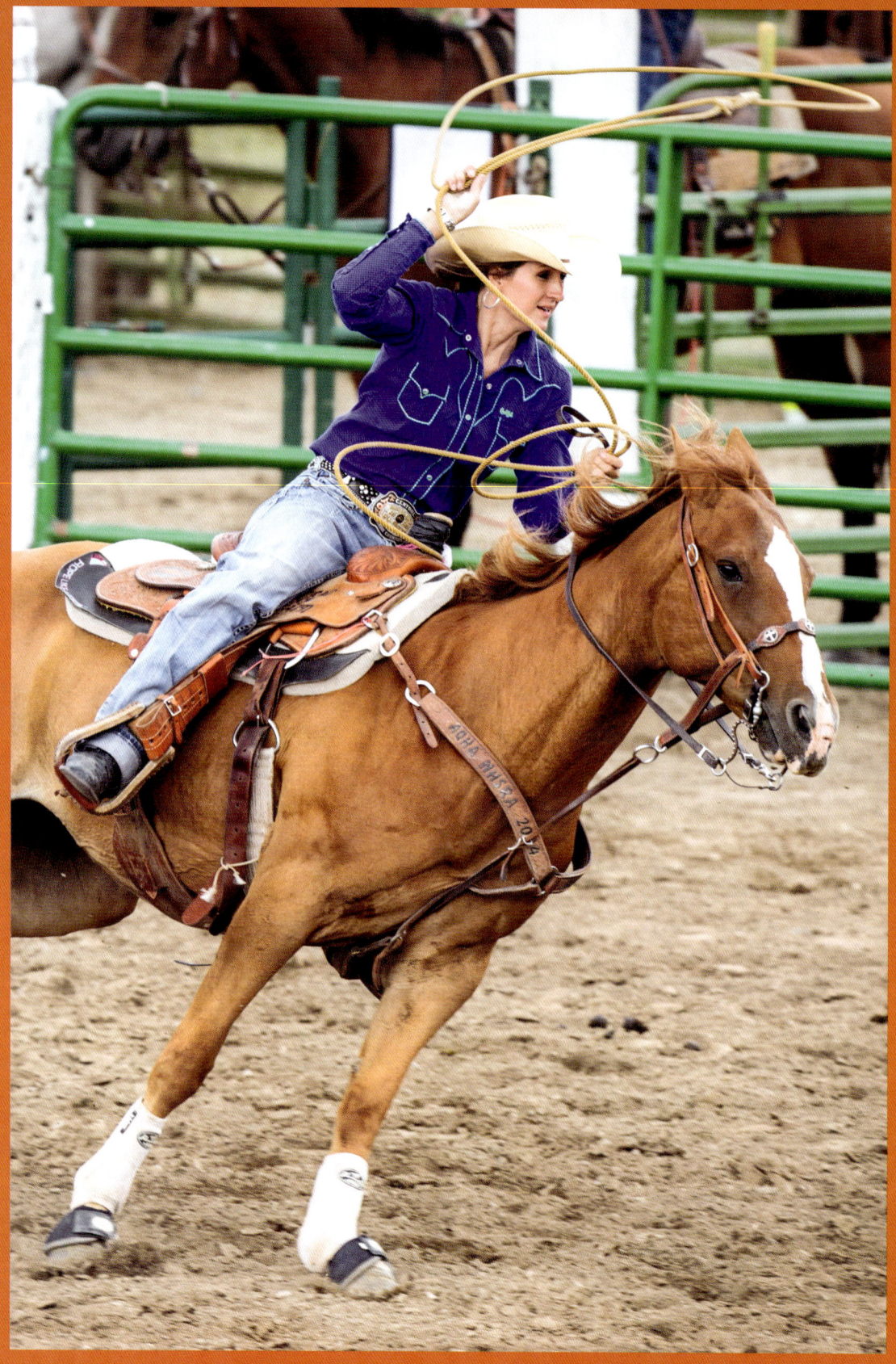

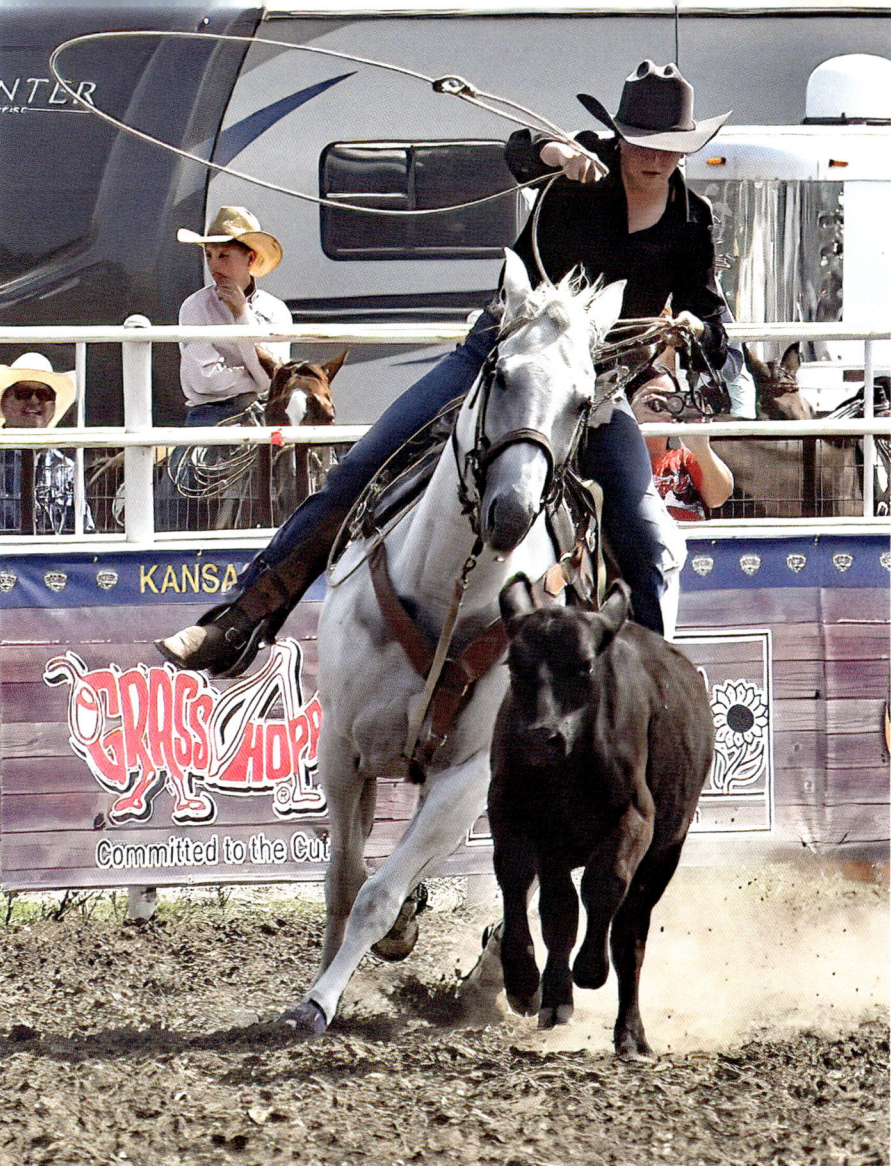

→ Maggie Hart competes in a Breakaway Roping event in Emporia, Kansas, in 2023.

← A cowgirl competes in a Tie-Down Roping event at the Chaffee County Fair and Rodeo in Salida, Colorado.

Mainstream Events

The original events included in the RCA were Bronc Riding, Bull Riding, Calf Roping (now more commonly known as Tie-Down Roping), Steer Roping, Bulldogging (now more commonly known as Steer Wrestling), Team Roping, and Wild Cow Milking. These events, rooted in the daily work of ranching and livestock handling, became the backbone of mainstream rodeo. Each showcases a different skill set—from the raw power and balance needed to ride bucking animals, to the speed, precision, and teamwork required to rope and control cattle. Among the most iconic events are Bronc Riding and Bull Riding, which test a rider's strength, timing, and nerve against powerful, unpredictable animals.

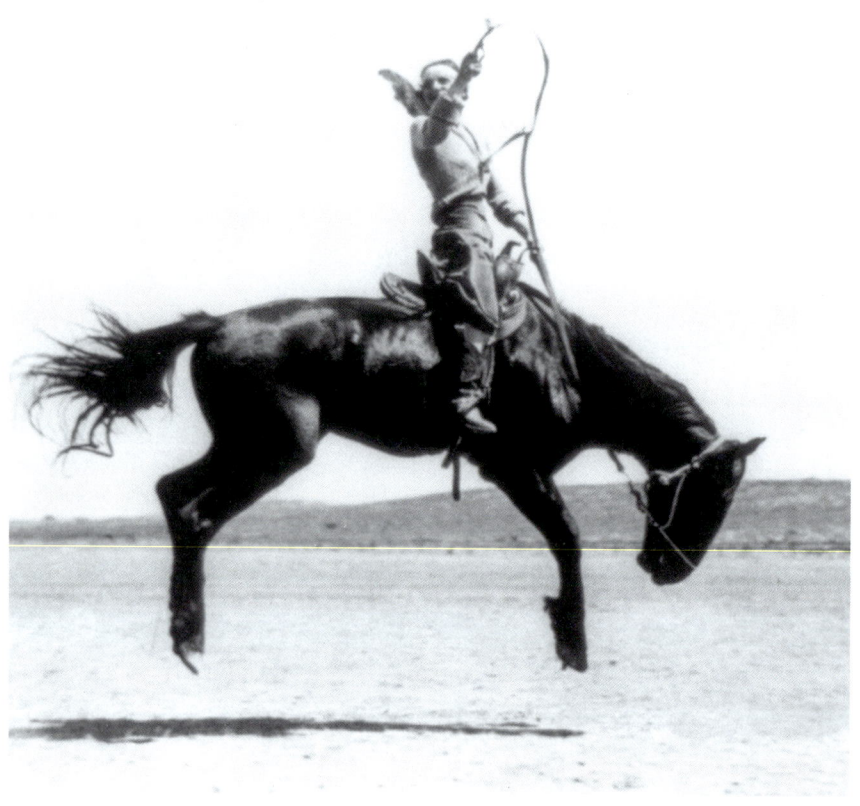

← Cowgirl Kitty Canutt, stage name Kitty Wilks, rides a bronco in 1919.

→ Ruth Reach at the American Rodeo Championship in the 1930s.

BRONC RIDING AND BULL RIDING

In Bronc Riding, which is generally the opening event for a rodeo, the rider attempts to ride a bucking horse for eight seconds. Now, this event has two iterations—Saddle Bronc and Bareback.

In Saddle Bronc, riders sit in a specialized saddle and attempt to ride for eight seconds. They have to keep their feet in the stirrups, and not touch the horse or themselves with their "free hand," which remains in the air, while they hang on with their "riding hand."

In Bareback Riding, there is no saddle. The rider sits on the back of the horse and attaches his riding hand to an apparatus called a "rigging," a leather and rawhide composite piece often compared to a suitcase handle. The rigging attaches to a cinch, which wraps the circumference of the horse's midsection just behind the horse's withers.

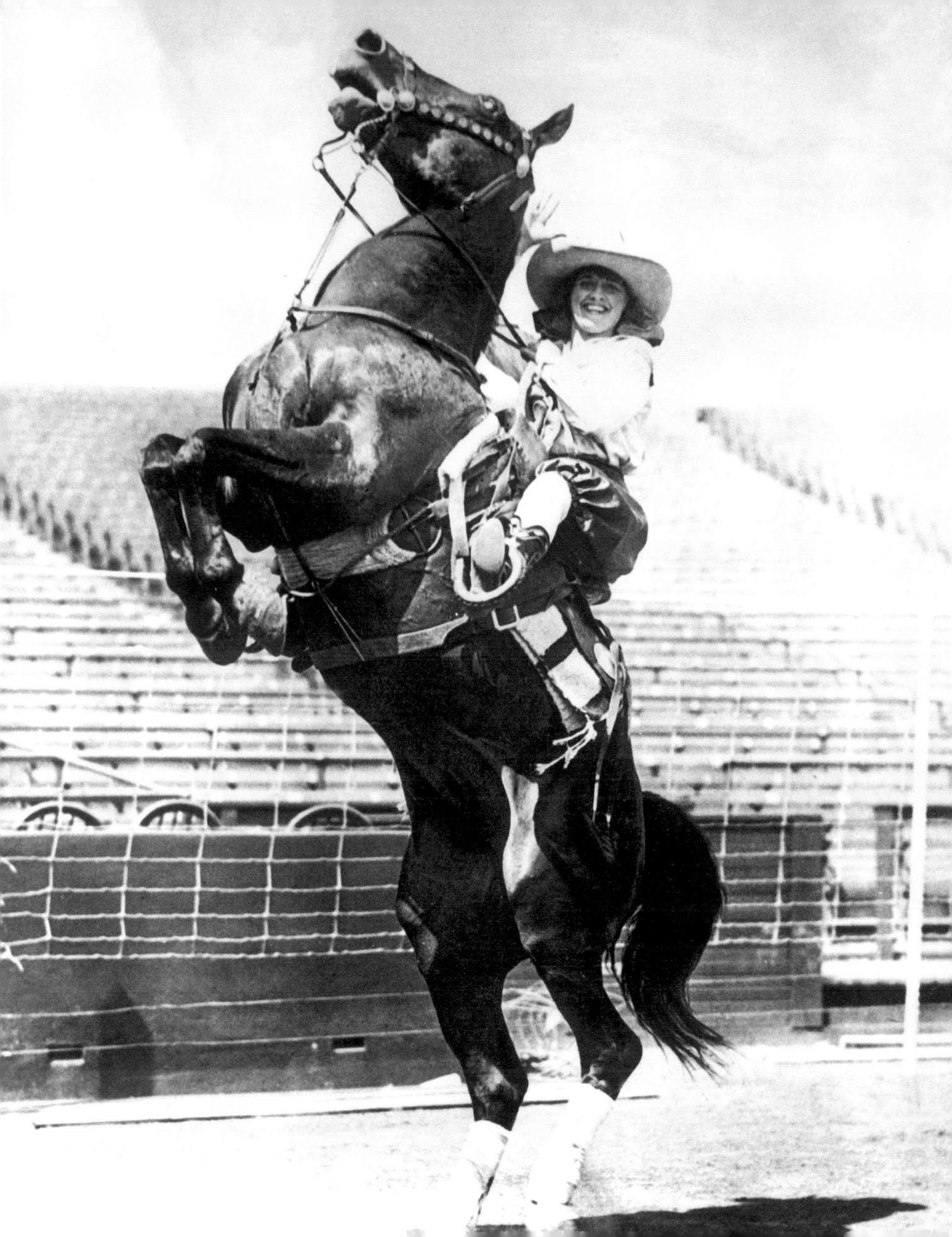

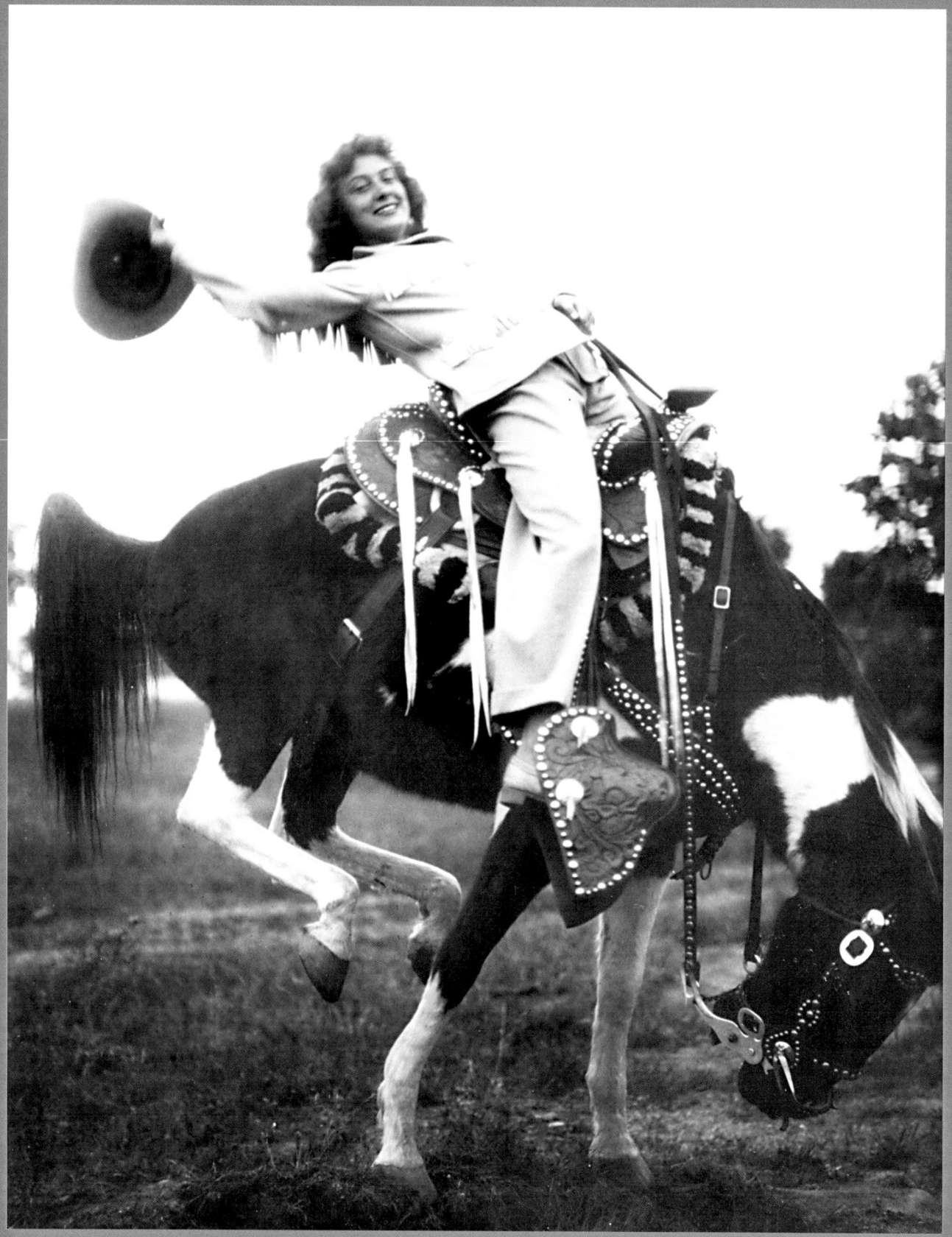

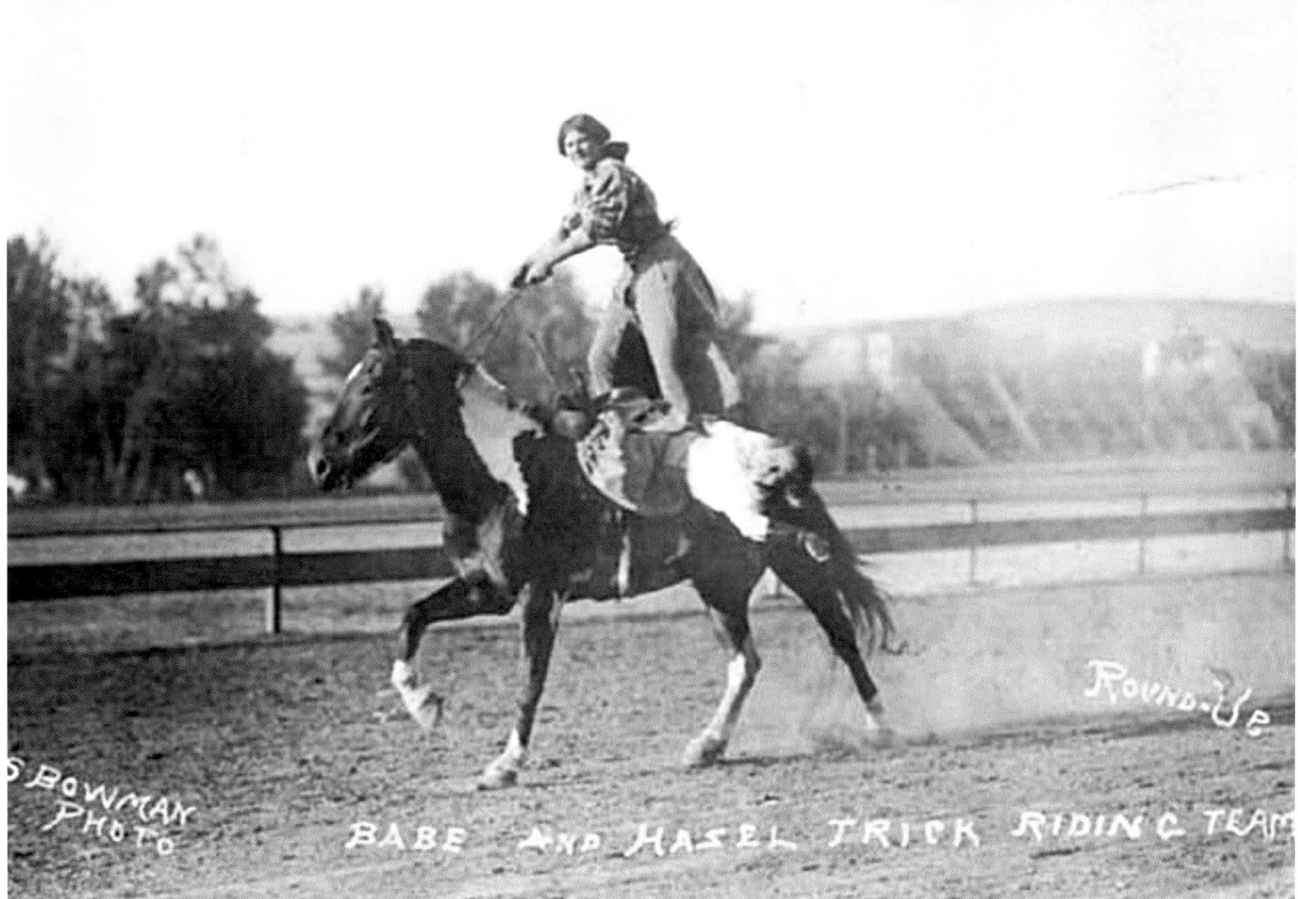

Hazel Walker and Babe Lee perform a trick riding stunt at the Pendleton Roundup.

A woman practices her rodeo skills.

In both events, the objective is to ride through eight seconds of powerful bucking with finesse and control. The strategy is different for every rider, but the trick here is to get in sync with the horse and try to match your movement to theirs to create balance and rhythm. This sport is directly derived from the ranching practice of breaking wild or untamed horses to ride, which has roots in the Mexican vaquero tradition of charreada, a traditional Mexican rodeo-style event that showcases the skills of charros or participants in charrería.

Similarly, Bull Riding, which generally closes a rodeo as the pinnacle event of the night, takes the same core principles of riding through powerful, unpredictable movements but on a different animal—a bull. The rider's hand, as with Bronc Riding, is strapped in using a flat, braided rope. Their "free hand" has to stay in the air without touching any part of the bull or themselves. They are scored on degree of difficulty and control, and that's if they make it to eight seconds.

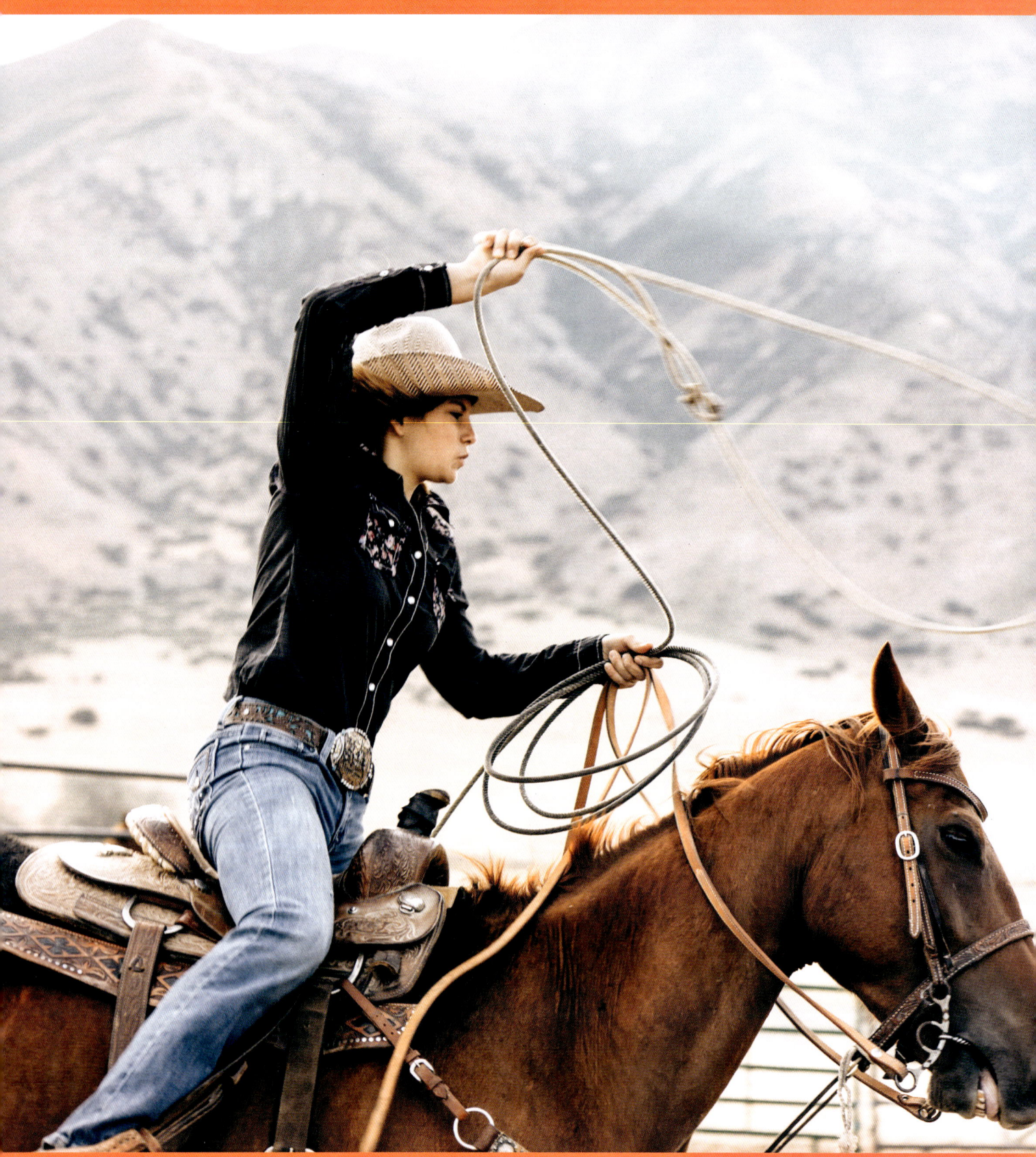

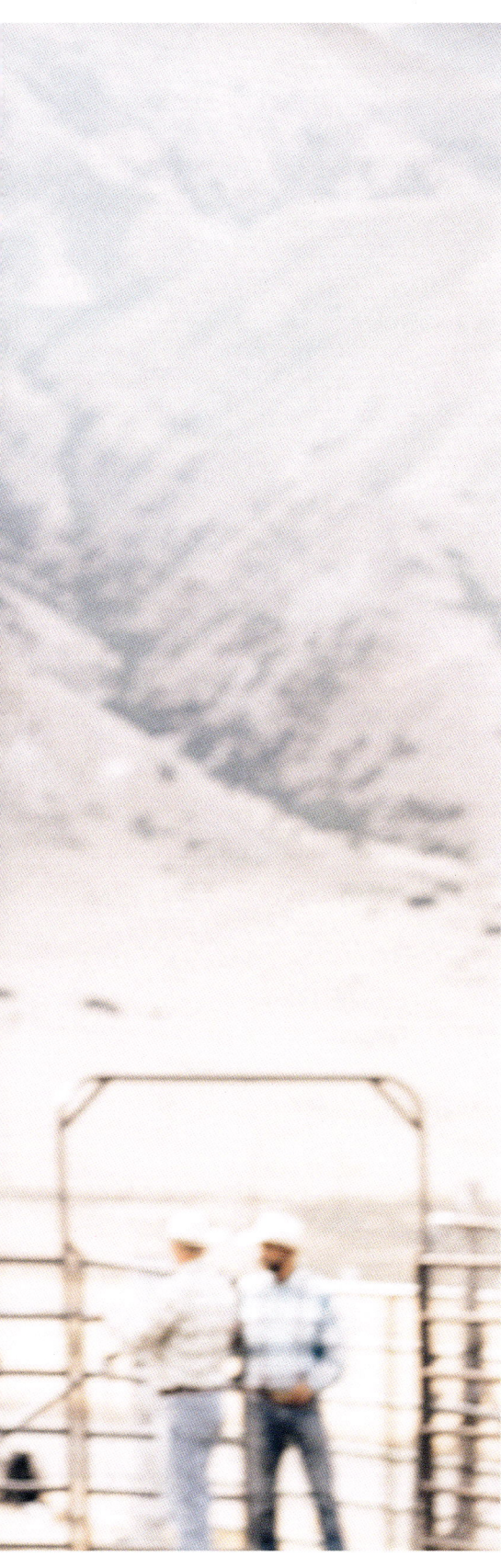

← A young woman ropes a calf.

CALF ROPING

In contrast, Calf Roping, now more commonly referred to as Tie-Down Roping, is a timed event where a rider on horseback ropes a calf or young bovine. Once the rider has the calf roped, they dally the rope to their saddle, quickly dismount, and make their way to the roped calf, where they secure the calf's legs. This skill was necessary for working cow ranches when calves needed to be branded, medicated, or tagged, in an open pasture. To be great at this event, the rider needs to rope quickly, establish control, and get a solid tie on the calf's legs. The rider who can complete the leg-tying in the shortest amount of time, wins.

STEER ROPING AND BULLDOGGING

Steer Roping is another timed event similar to Calf Roping. In this event, the steers, or castrated male cattle, are roped and brought to the ground. It's a more difficult event due to the steer's size compared to the calves. There are a few different iterations of this sport, including Steer Roping, Steer Tripping, and Steer Jerking. The sport is controversial due to concerns for the animals' well-being and the safety of the riders—even though the animals' horns are reinforced for protection—and it's not included in most current sanctioned rodeo events. Bulldogging or Steer Wrestling is another timed event where a horseback rider chases down a steer, dismounts their horse, grabs hold of the steer, and wrestles it to the ground. This is one of the quickest-moving events in rodeo and can be one of the most exciting to watch of the timed events. The rider who wrestles the steer completely to the ground the fastest is the winner.

TEAM ROPING

The Team Roping event is unique as it is the only rodeo event that judges two competitors at once—the Header and the Heeler. The Header is the horseback competitor responsible for roping the steer's head, ideally catching both horns of the steer and pulling them to the left, so the Heeler can then come behind the steer and rope its hind legs. The objective is to gain complete control over the steer, with one competitor controlling its head and the other competitor controlling its hind legs.

This sport derived out of necessity as roping cattle in this manner is often the only way to get them medicated, branded, or treated for any other reason, when working on a ranch. While calves are small enough to hog-tie to complete these tasks, steers are often too large and strong to rely on that method. When that's the case, cowboys rely on the Team Roping technique to get the job done on the ranch. Again, this is a timed event, so the fastest time wins, but both riders have to complete their own portion in order to receive a score.

WILD COW MILKING

Finally, the Wild Cow Milking is an event that is no longer included in mainstream professional rodeos due to safety concerns for the animal and the competitors. But it is still a crowd favorite at ranch rodeos, which are rodeos with a slight variation of events more targeted toward day-to-day ranch work. At ranch rodeos, competitors enter as part of a working ranch team.

The Wild Cow Milking is a team-based competition where the team has to catch a "wild" full-grown cow, which is a female bovine who has given birth and produces milk. In this event, two riders team-rope the cow, two more team members run to them—one to milk the cow and the other to hold the receptacle to milk into. Then, when there is enough milk in the container, the member holding the milk receptacle runs to the finish line. The fastest time wins.

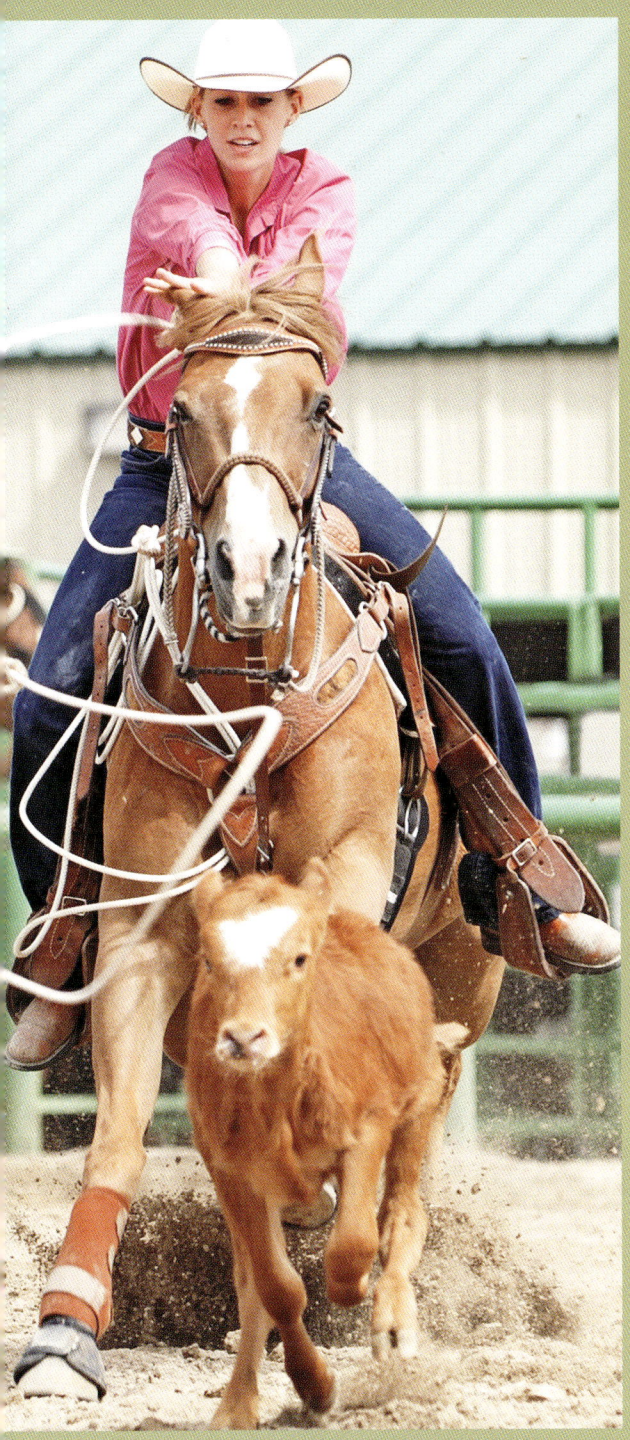

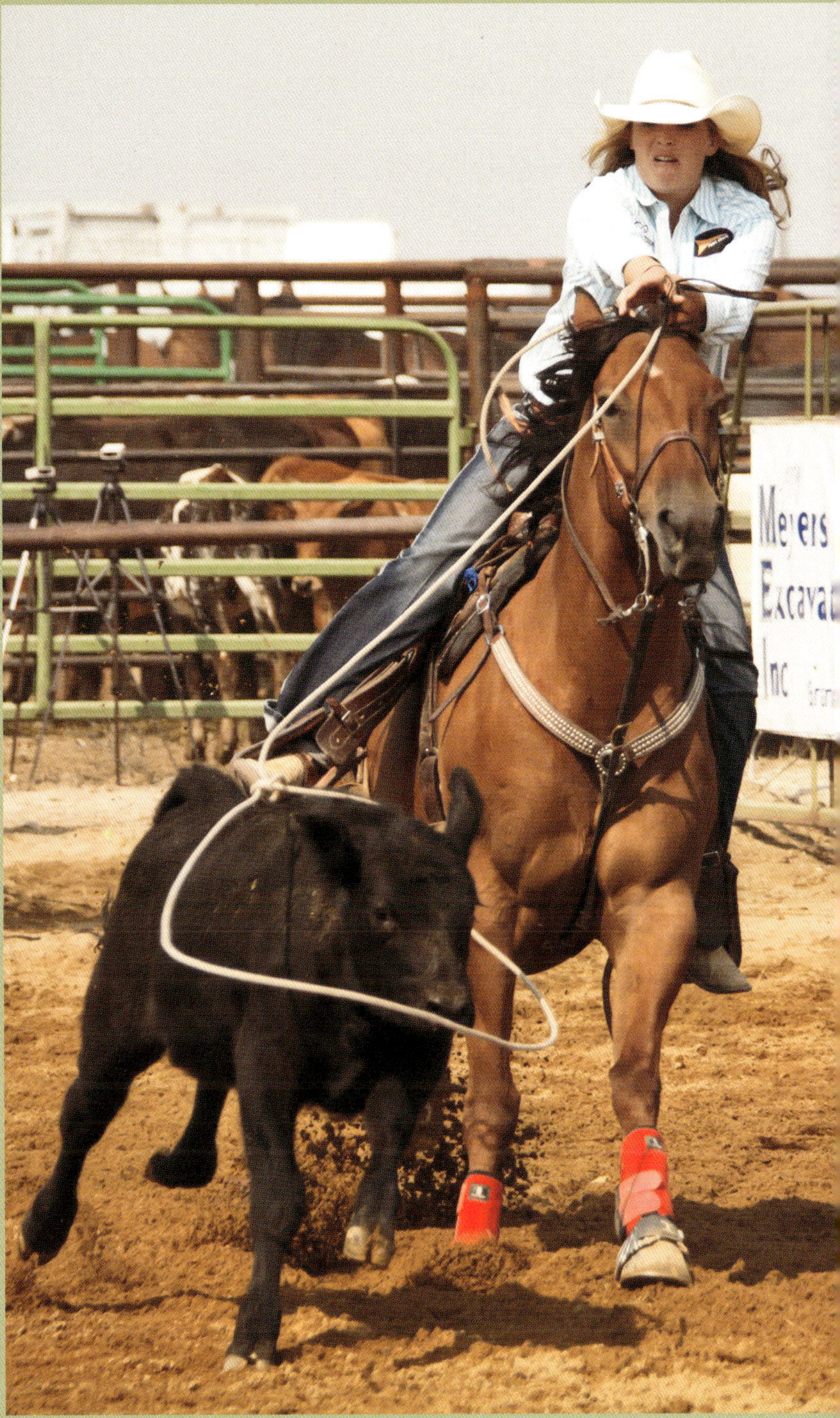

↑ A cowgirl roping a calf.

⇢ A competitor on her saddle horse calf roping at a rodeo in Bruneau, Idaho.

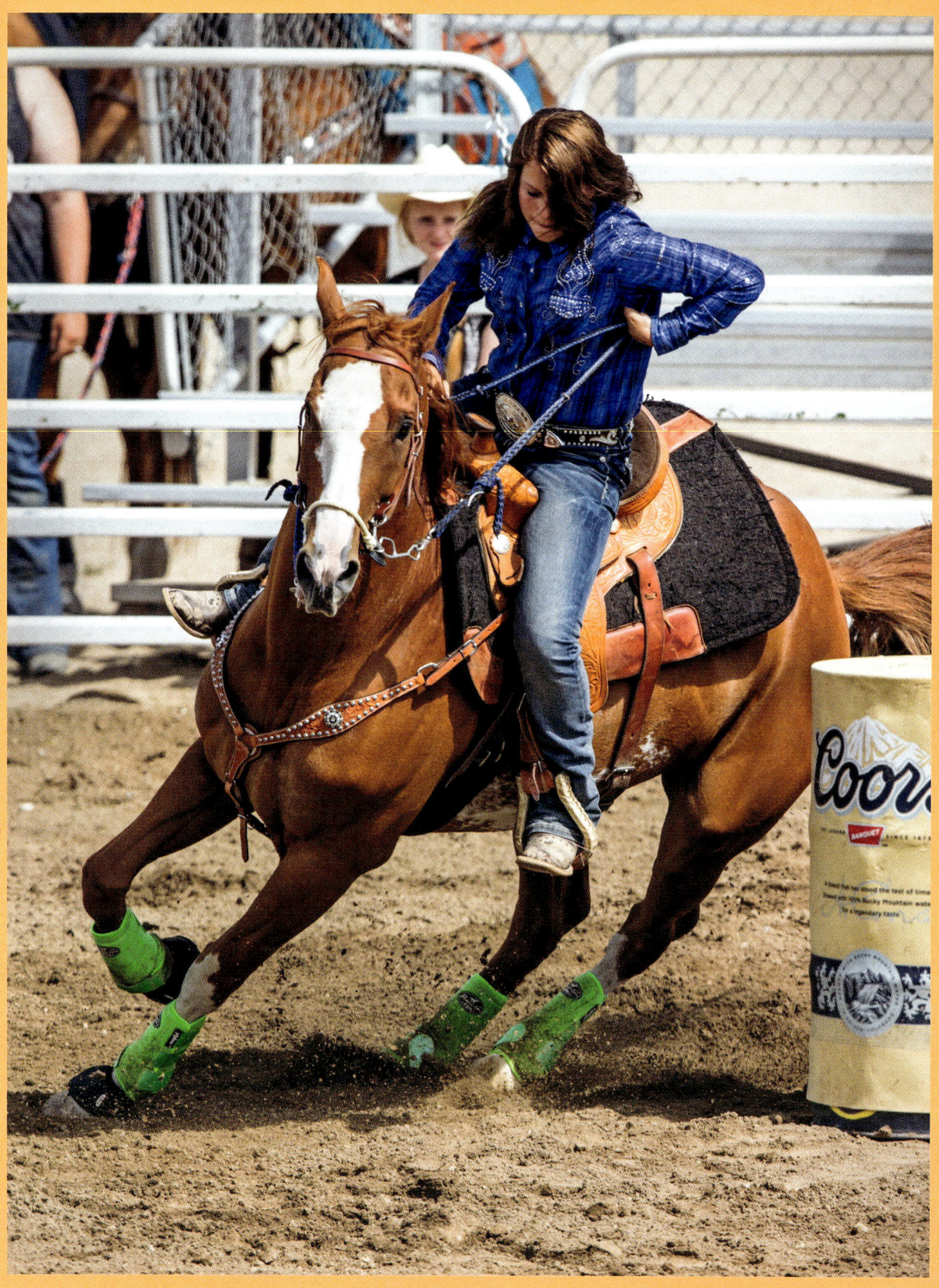

Women Ride Again

← A rodeo cowgirl competes in a barrel racing event at the Chaffee County Fair & Rodeo in Salida, Colorado.

As we know by now, women were still not allowed to join the Rodeo Cowboys Association. But in 1948, more than thirty women gathered in San Angelo, Texas, to take matters into their own hands, and founded the Girls Rodeo Association (GRA)—the first organized rodeo association for women. Their goals were to create competitive opportunities for women while improving their treatment within the sport.

Founding members included Betty Dusek, Nancy Binford, and Thena Mae Farr, all influential women in early rodeo. Dusek would go on to become a Team Roping world champion while Binford and Farr produced the Tri-State All Girl Rodeo, an all-women's rodeo that broke barriers by proving that they could draw crowds and deliver serious competition. The GRA eventually led to the development of the Women's Professional Rodeo Association (WPRA). While this was an amazing step toward gender equality, Women of Color did not begin appearing more visibly in mainstream rodeo events until the 1970s.

The founding event of the Girls Rodeo Association was Barrel Racing. This is when a horseback rider runs their horse into the arena to complete a cloverleaf pattern around three barrels. They cannot knock those barrels down, and they have to make a complete circle around all three. The fastest time wins the event, and it's one of the most exciting sports in rodeo, usually occurring near the end of the event before the Bull Riding.

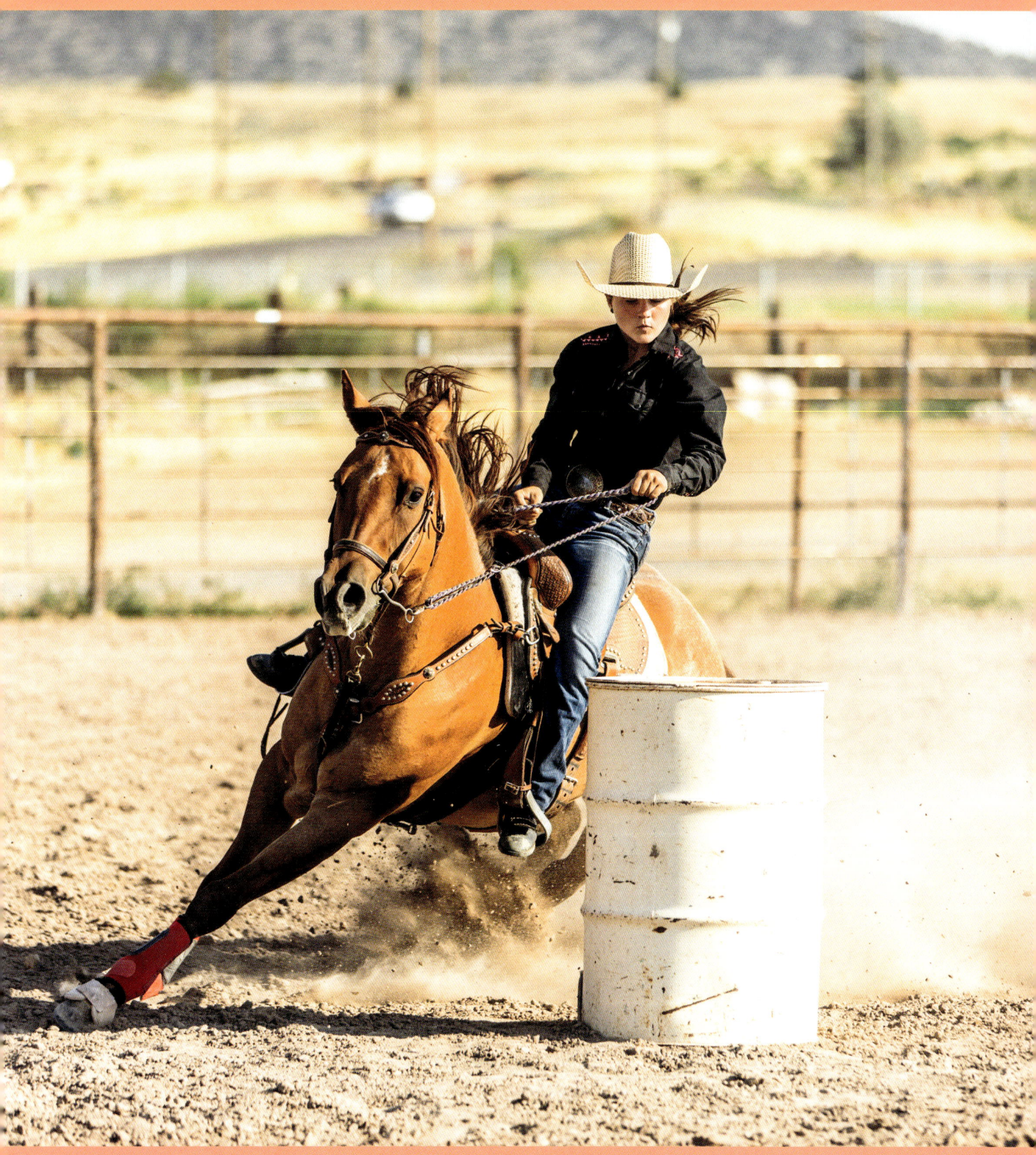

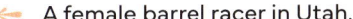
← A female barrel racer in Utah.

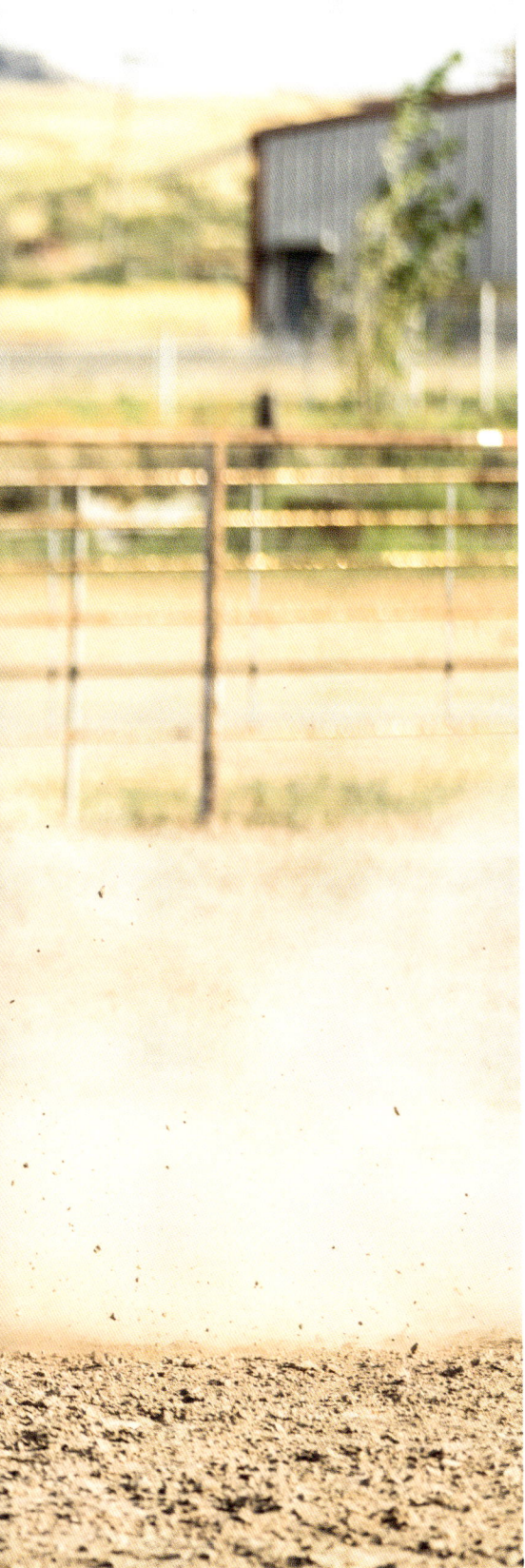

The GRA was the first professional sports organization in the United States created solely by women, for women. However, the decades during which women were sidelined resulted in a significant loss of momentum in rodeo. Their roles had been largely reduced to Miss Rodeo pageants or exhibition-only performances, excluding them from any money-earning competitions or opportunities. Determined to reclaim their place in rodeo, the founders of the GRA launched the organization with sixty approved events and approximately $30,000 in prize earnings to distribute. They knew the road ahead would be steep—a challenge to prove to the men that they were worthy of competing alongside them once again.

In 1955, the Rodeo Cowboys Association, formerly the RAA, signed an agreement with the GRA, stating it would strongly urge rodeo committees to include a GRA-approved barrel race at their events. It also stated that the RCA would not work with any other barrel racing association and would solely collaborate at events with the GRA. This was huge for the sport of barrel racing and women's inclusion in general. Another decade later, in 1967, the Professional Rodeo Cowboy Association (the newest iteration of the RCA) brought barrel racing into the National Finals Rodeo (NFR), where the best of the best rodeo athletes competed every year for a world championship title in their respective events. The payout for the women competing in the WPRA barrel racing at the National Finals was far less than their male counterparts. However, these inequalities were not limited to gender. Racial discrimination also shaped the history of rodeo, affecting talented cowboys and performers alike.

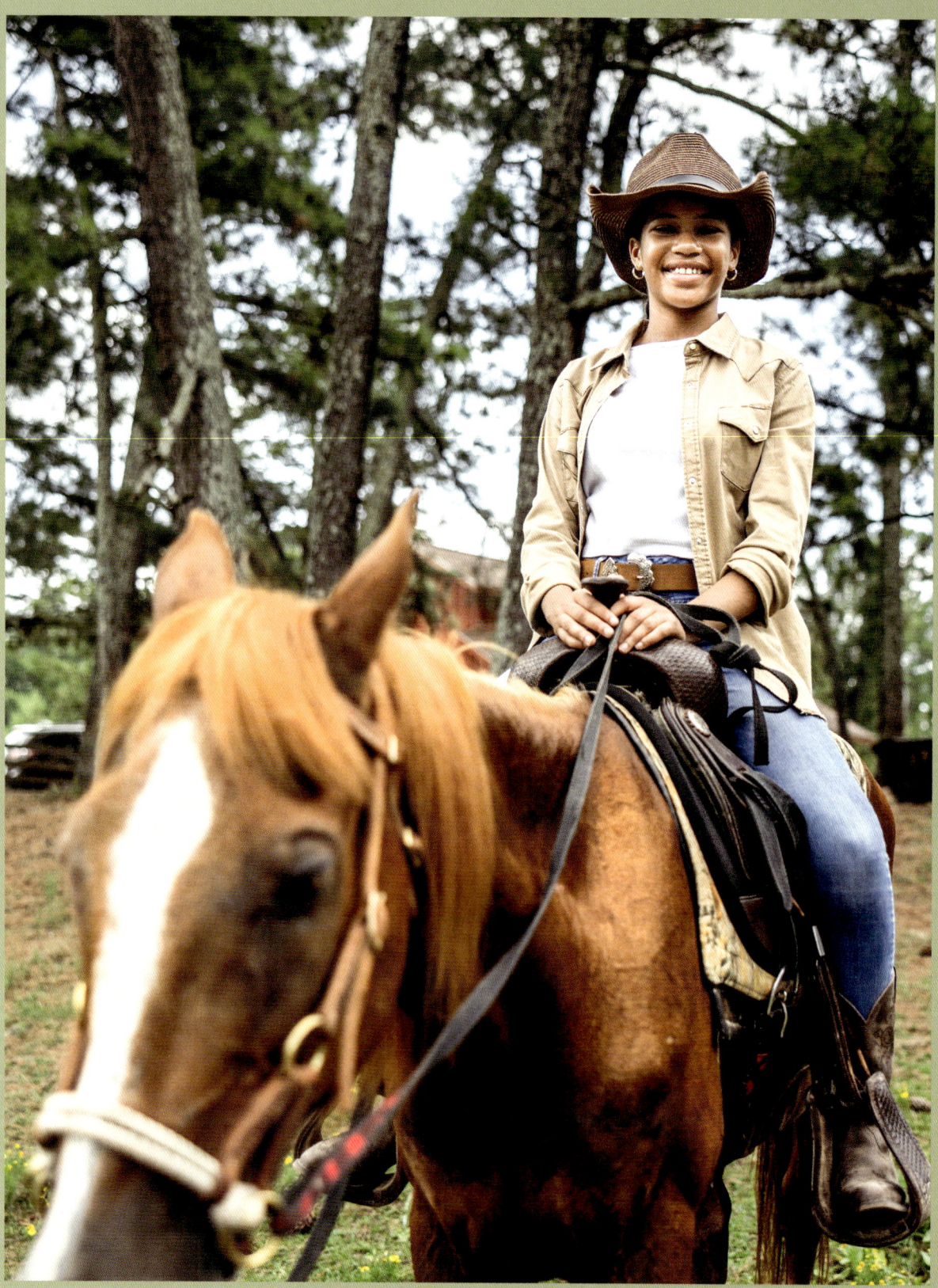

Cowboys of Color

← A portrait of a young woman on horseback in a pasture.

Cowboys of Color played a pivotal yet frequently unrecognized role in the history of rodeo and the American West. Despite facing significant societal barriers, pioneers like Bill Pickett, Nat Love, and Isom Dart made lasting contributions to the culture, craftsmanship, and traditions of the frontier.

Bill Pickett was a Black cowboy, rodeo performer, and actor who became a trailblazer in the world of rodeo in the nineteenth century. He joined the 101 Ranch Wild West Show, produced by the iconic Miller Brothers 101 Ranch in Oklahoma. Although many tour stops barred Pickett from performing due to racial segregation, when he was allowed to take the stage, his performances were unforgettable. Pickett invented a unique style of steer wrestling where he grabbed cattle by the horns, bit them on the lip, and wrestled them to the ground. This method was inspired by the practice of cattlemen using trained bulldogs to catch stray steers, and Pickett believed that if a bulldog could do it, so could he. This innovative technique became known as "bulldogging" and eventually evolved into the modern rodeo event of Steer Wrestling.

Pickett's legacy as the "father of steer wrestling" cemented his place in rodeo history, but his influence extended far beyond the arena. He paved the way for future Black cowboys. He died in 1932 when a bronc kicked him in the head, but his legacy remained alive through the sport of rodeo. Pickett was buried on the 101 Ranch.

Nat Love was another trailblazing Black cowboy of the American West. He was born into slavery in Tennessee in 1854 and gained his freedom after the Civil War as a teenager. As a cowboy, he was highly skilled, worked long

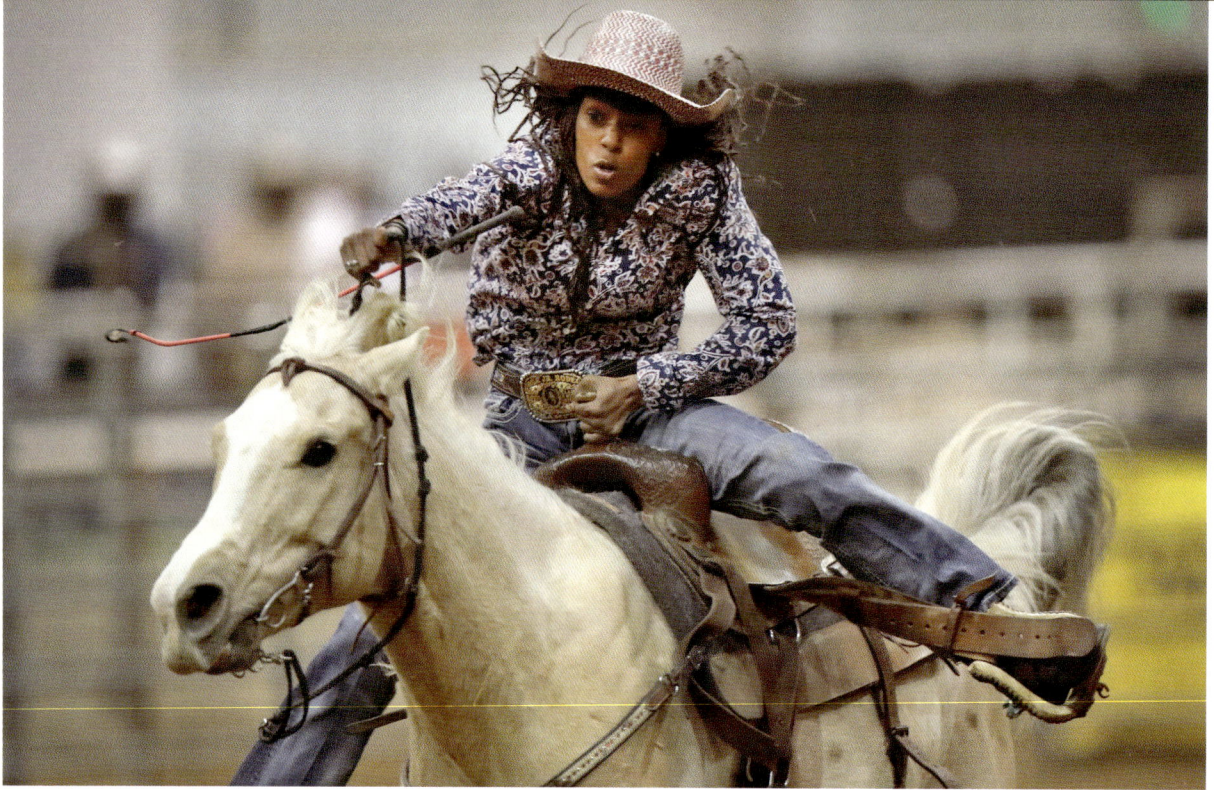

A cowgirl competes in the barrel race at the Bill Pickett Invitational Rodeo (BPIR) in Memphis, Tennessee, in 2017. The BPIR is a Black touring rodeo.

Two generations of Black horsewomen.

cattle drives, tamed wild horses, and even won a rodeo competition in Deadwood, Dakota Territory, which earned him the nickname "Deadwood Dick." His autobiography, *The Life and Adventures of Nat Love*, is one of the few firsthand accounts of a Black man's experience in the cattle-driving era, preserving his powerful legacy of resilience and excellence.

Another Black rancher and cowboy who made his mark on rodeo was Isom Dart. Born in 1858, Dart began his cowboy career wrangling cattle as a teenager. He eventually became known for his incredible horsemanship skills.

In the late nineteenth century, Black cowboys made up 25 percent of working ranch cowboys, but their participation in rodeos began to dwindle. Event and media producer Lu Vason noticed the lack of Black contestants in the 1977 Cheyenne Frontier Days and was inspired to create a space in rodeo dedicated to the Black cowboy. Vason launched an all-Black rodeo in 1984 and named it after Pickett. The Bill Pickett Invitational Rodeo still tours today, with events all over the United States, showcasing the impact of People of Color on cowboy culture.

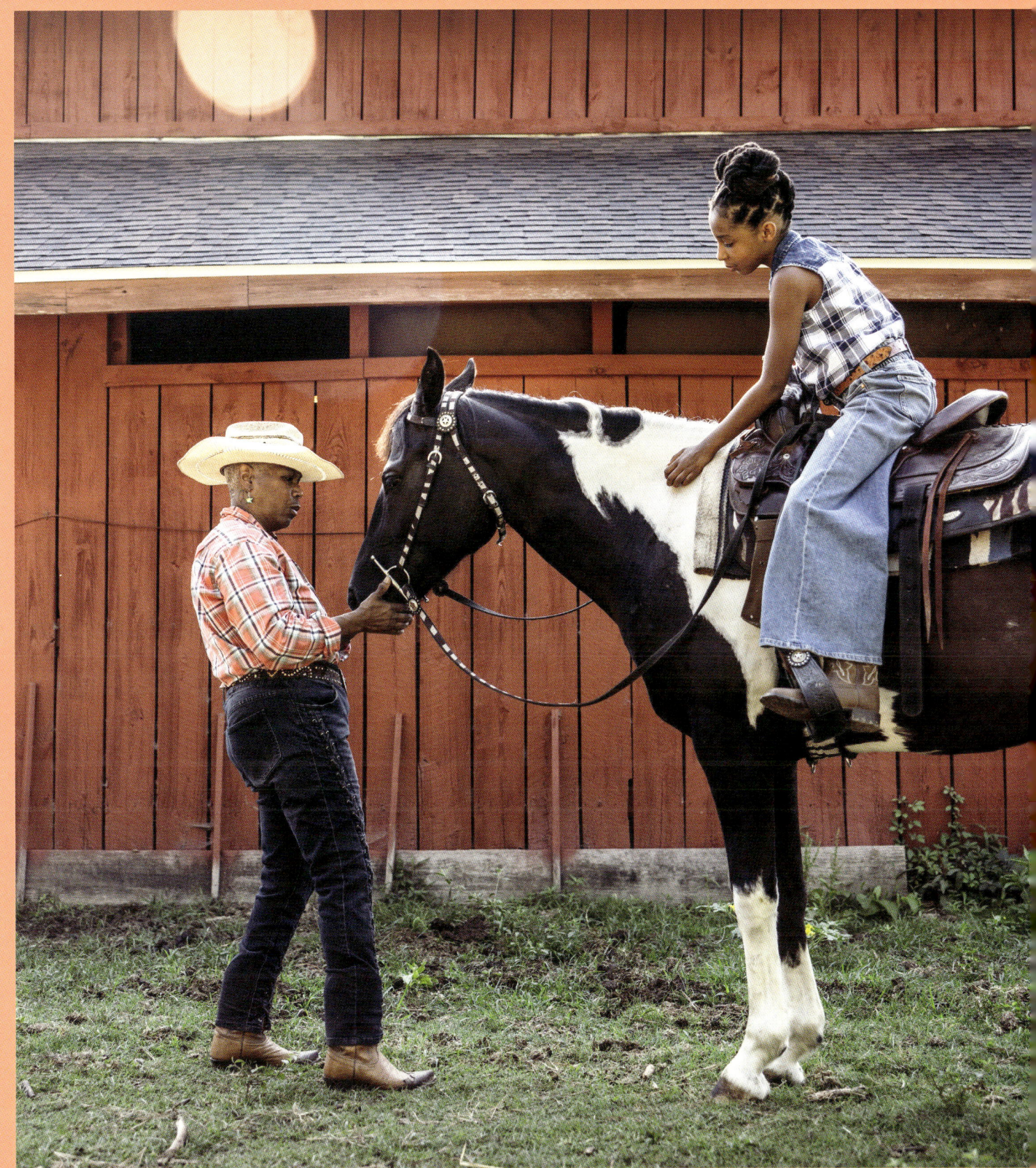

Junior barrel racers Paris Wilburd, Maliyah Pete, and Kortnee Solomon arriving to compete at the Roy Leblanc Invitational rodeo in Oklmulgee, Oklahoma in 2023.

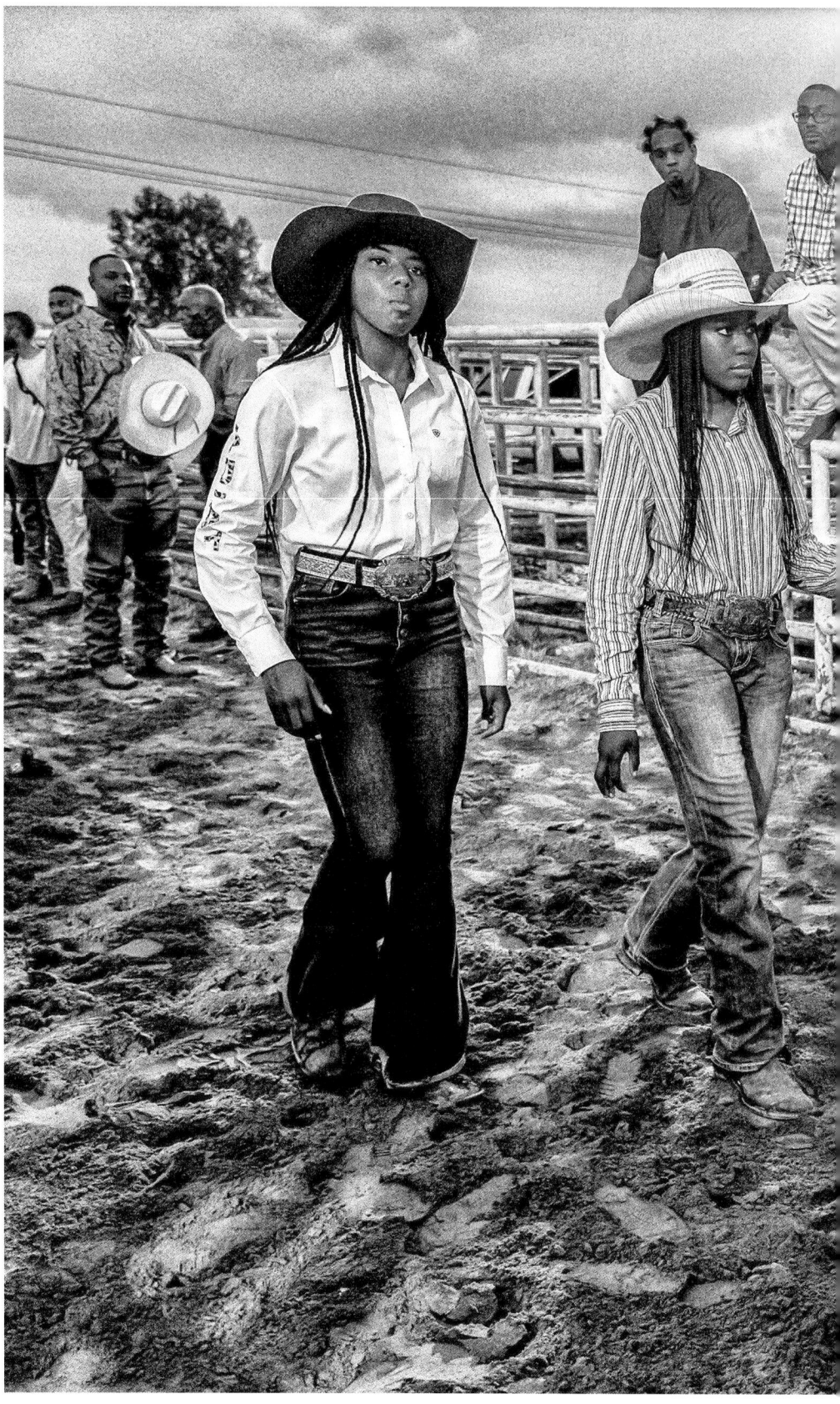

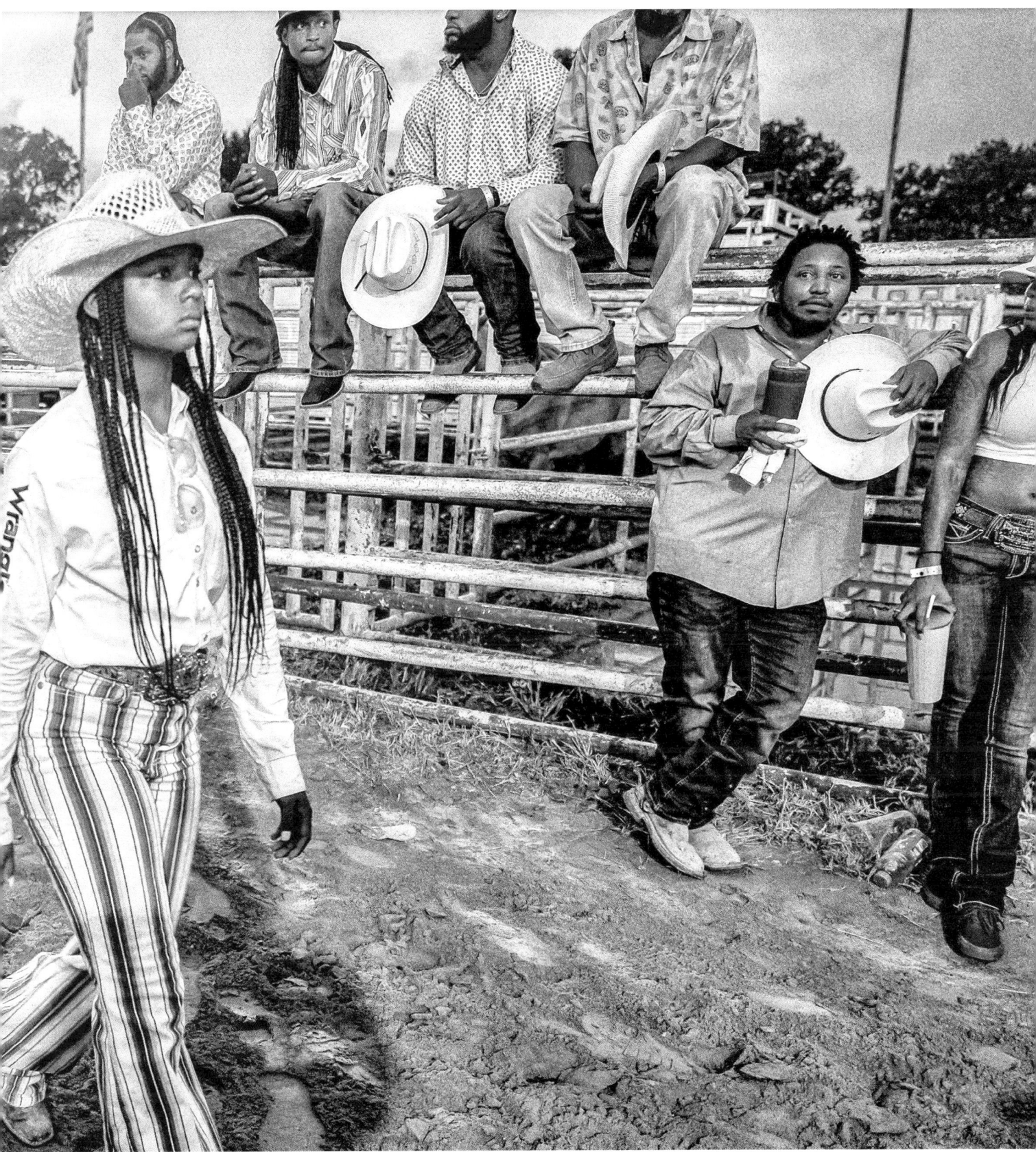

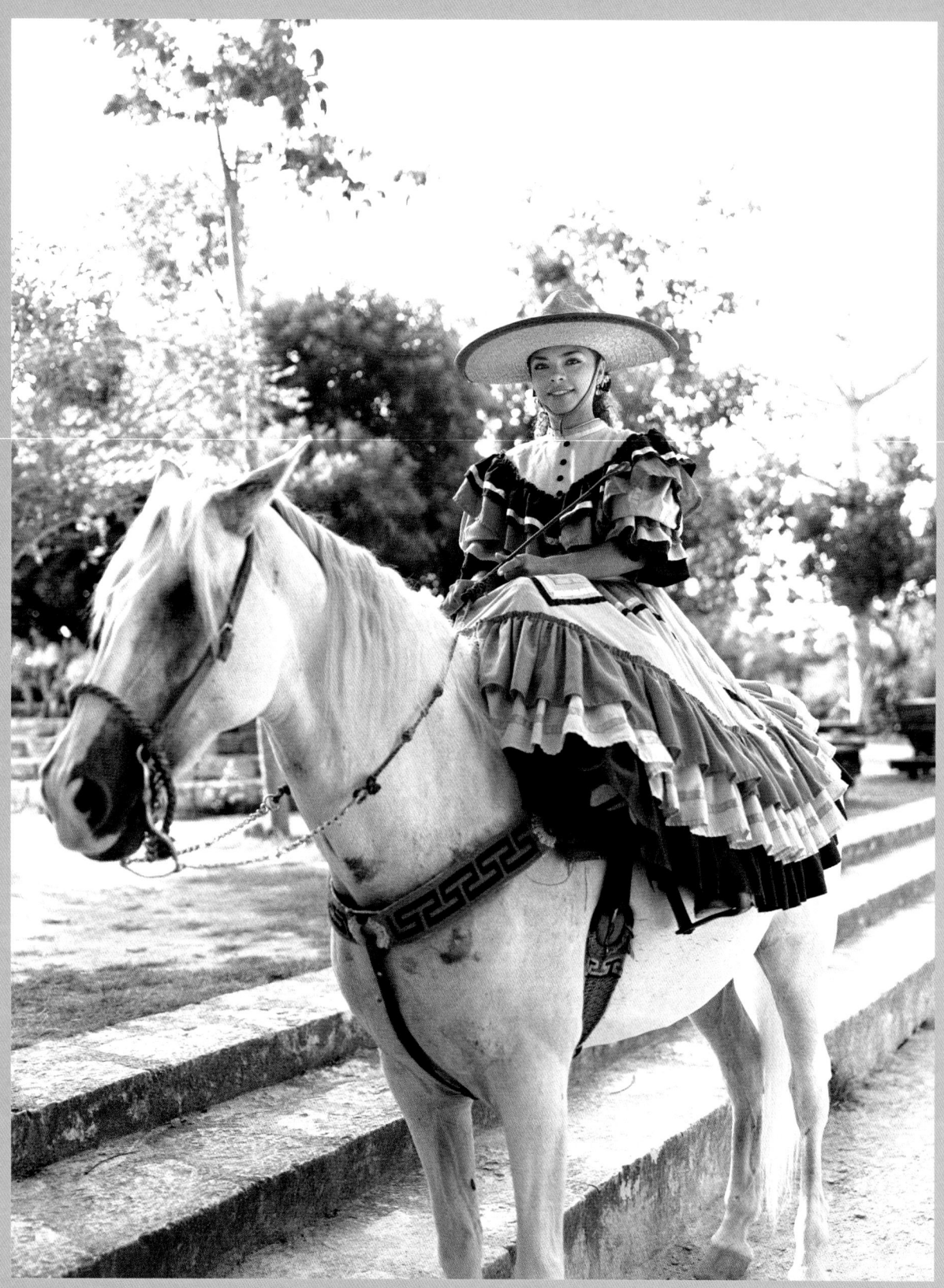

The Original Horsemen

A Mexican cowgirl, or charra, in traditional escaramuza performance dress seated on horseback.

Indigenous peoples were also very much a part of the early days of rodeo, but their participation was stifled over time. In the early days, Wild West shows often portrayed tribe members in a stereotypical and negative light. In fact, most of the American West's celebrated Wild West performers participated in hugely problematic and offensive reenactments of battles and tribal rituals. While they are celebrated for spotlighting the Western way of life, much of the show material that catapulted them to the top was extremely degrading to the Indigenous participants, and to the communities they were meant to represent.

Indigenous people were and are a big part of rodeo culture. They were truly the original trick riders and horsemen. They understood riding and hunting practices that white American settlers were just beginning to grasp.

Many organized rodeos didn't allow for any non-white contestants to qualify for prize money, including Indigenous competitors. As a result, Indigenous people began forging their own path in rodeo and founded their own event coalitions, including the Central Navajo Rodeo Association (CNRA) and the All Indian Rodeo Cowboys Association (AIRCA). Indian rodeo remains a hugely important part of rodeo culture, and an important cultural institution for Indigenous groups, culminating annually at the Indian National Finals Rodeo.

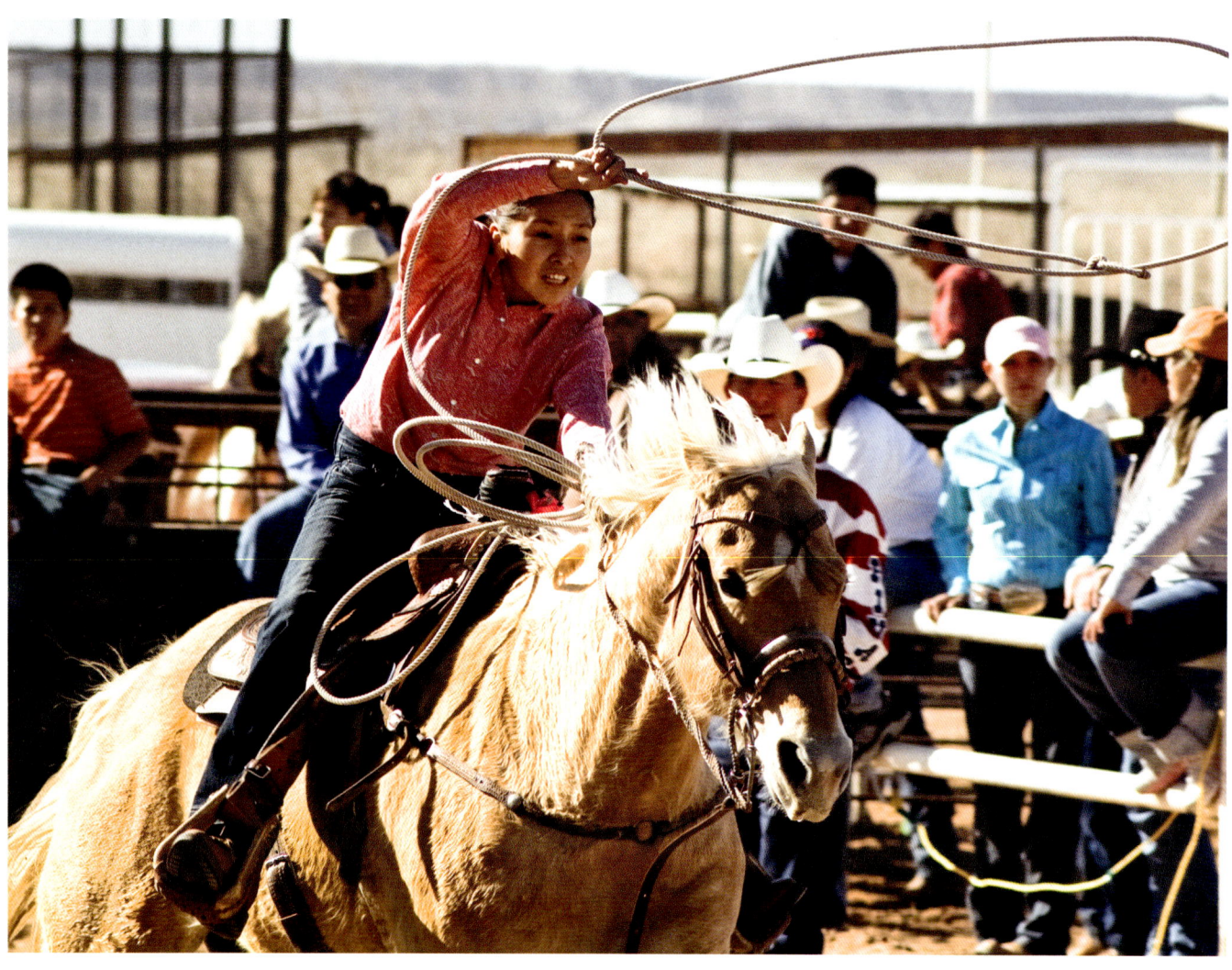

The Professional Rodeo Cowboys Association (PRCA) has made significant strides since the 1900s, and Native American participants are now an integral part of American rodeo culture. With more than one hundred events held nationwide, ProRodeo (professional rodeo events endorsed by the PRCA) contestants include members from 574 Indigenous tribes across the United States, and some rodeo events attract over 20,000 Indigenous participants and spectators. At one such event, the National Anthem was even performed in Apache, celebrating the country's Indigenous heritage. Although Indigenous peoples make up only 3 percent of the US population, the PRCA reports that half of its members are Indigenous cowboys and cowgirls, including renowned athletes such as Derrick Begay, Erich Rogers, and Aaron Tsinigine.

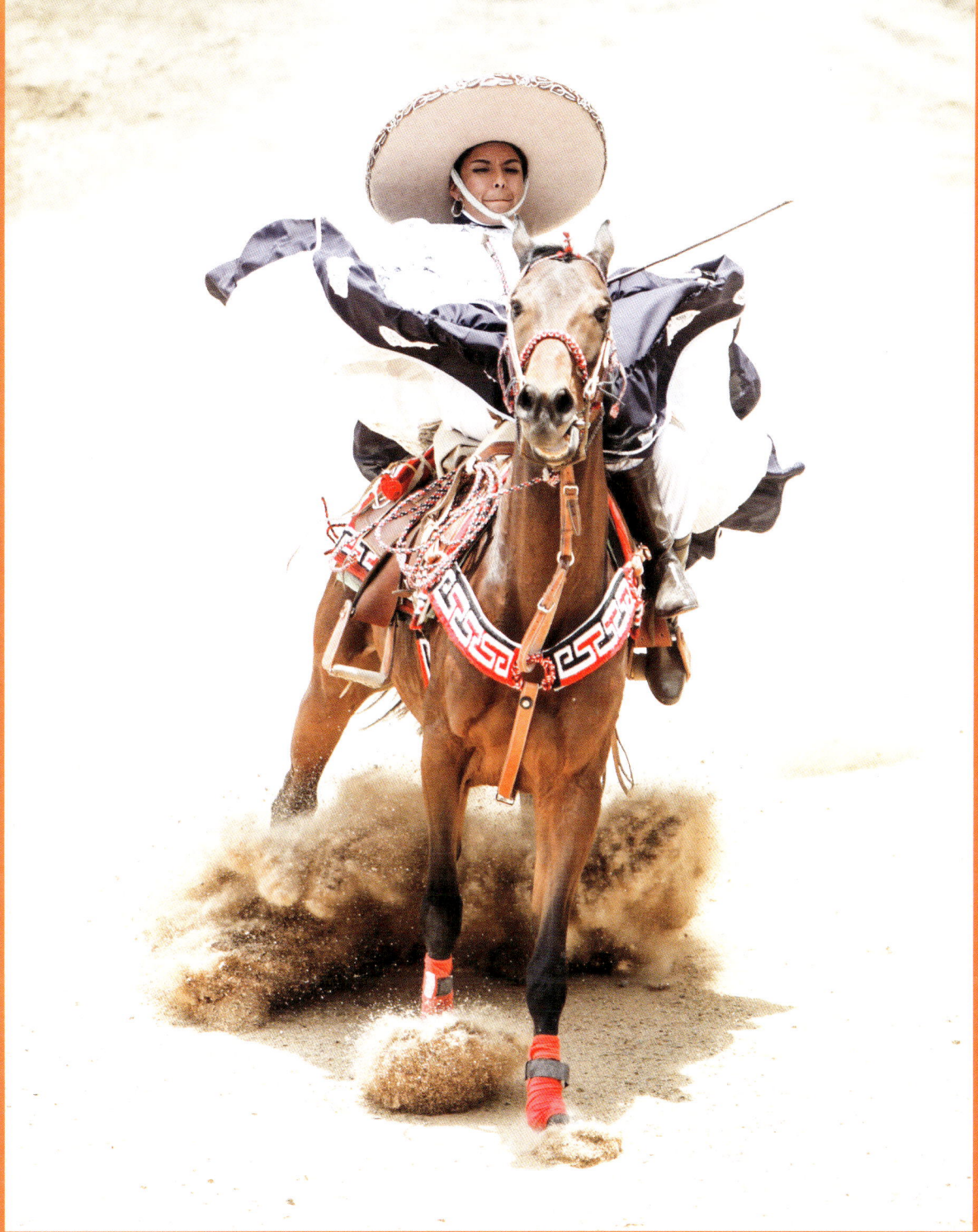

↑ An escaramuza performer in the arena.

← A cowgirl competes in the Breakaway Roping event at the O'odham Tash All-Indian Rodeo.

→ NEXT PAGE A group of women pose in colorful escaramuza attire.

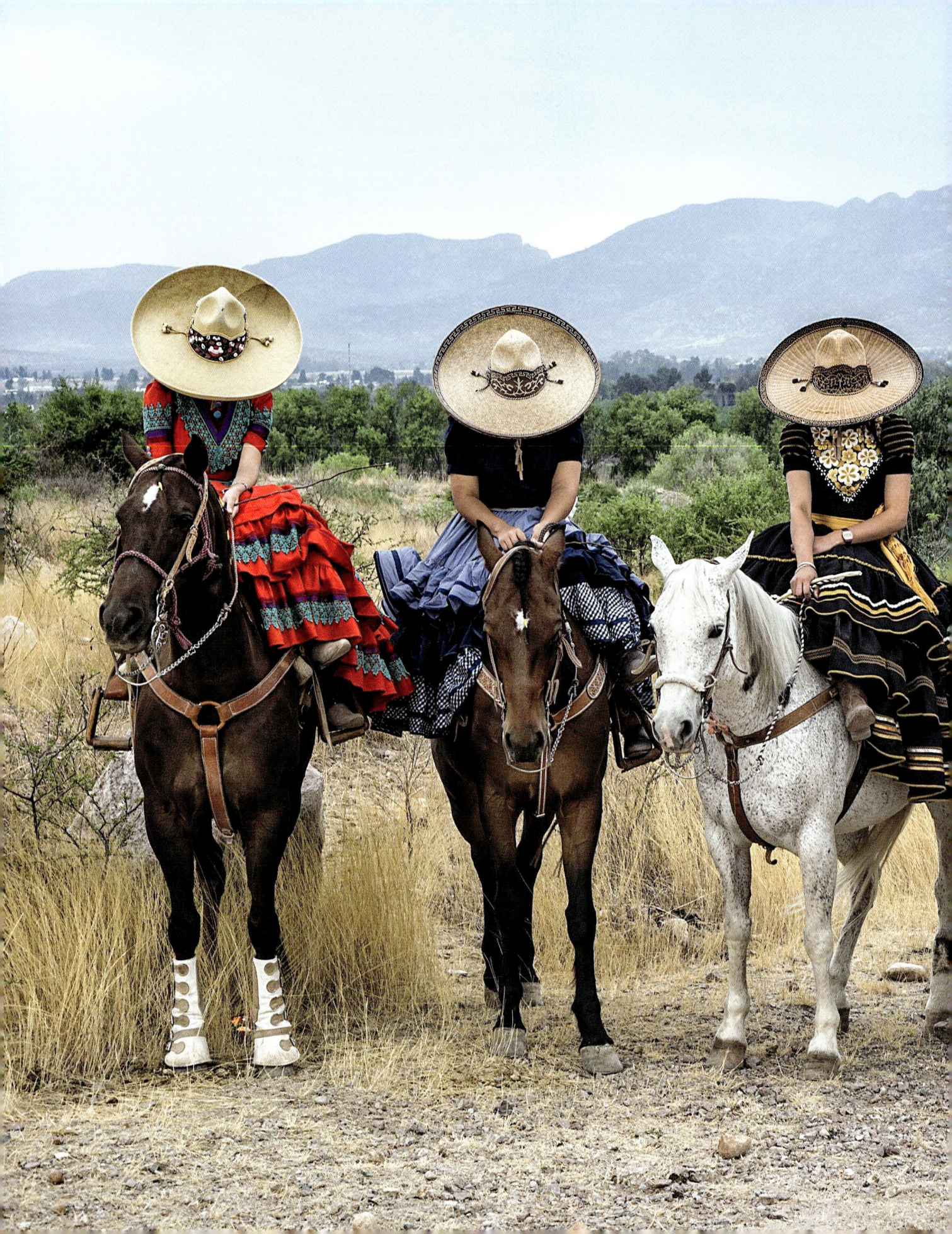

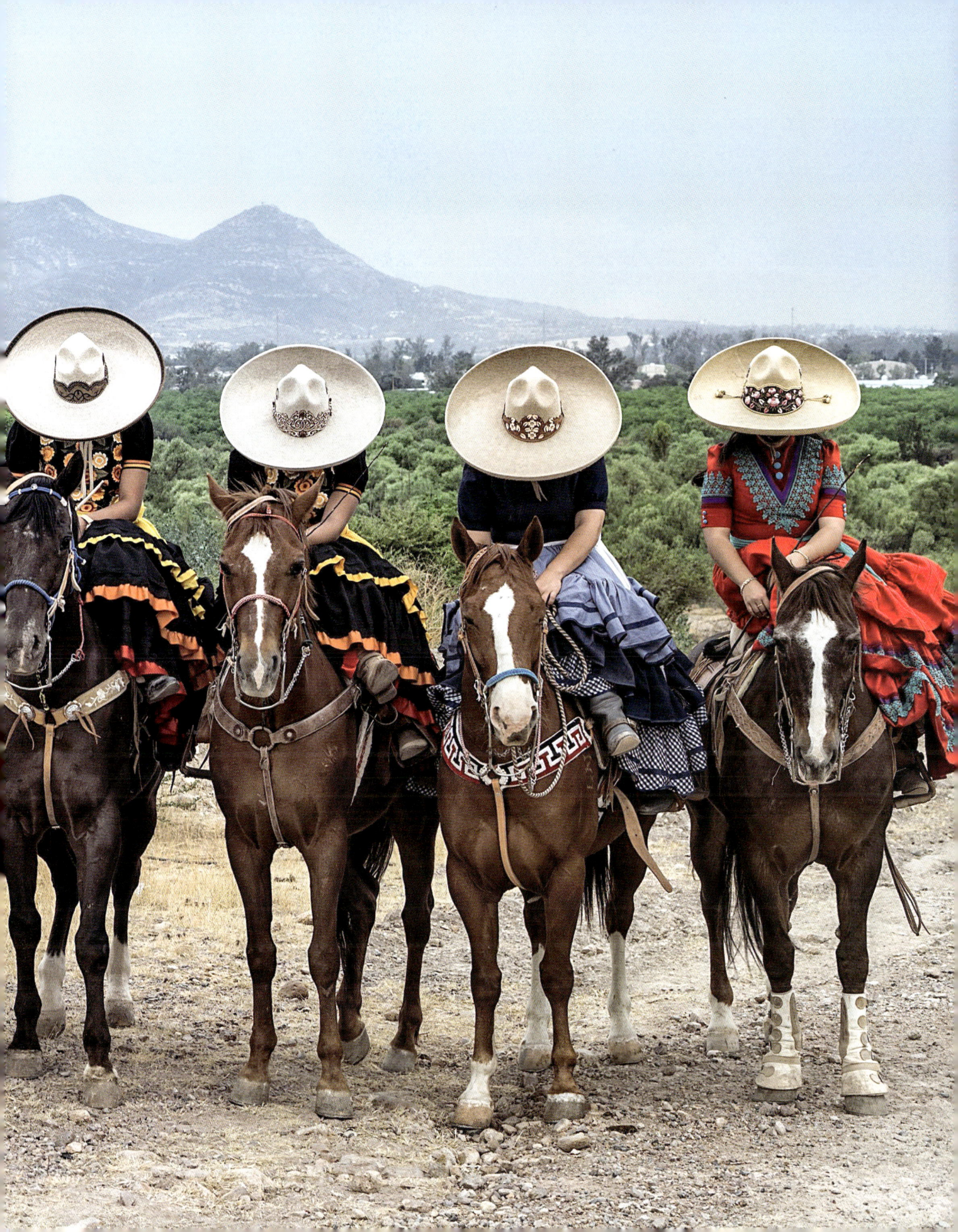

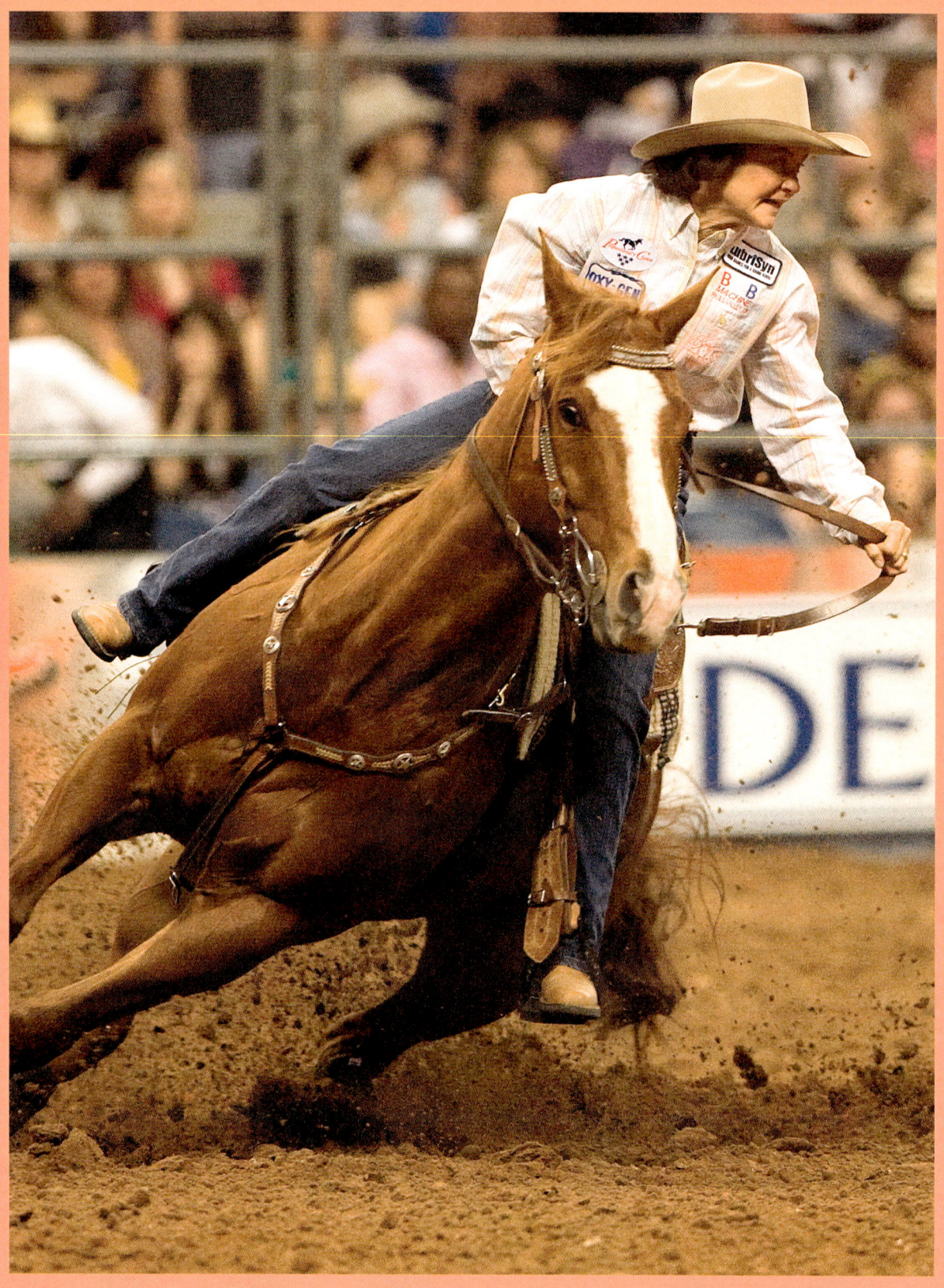

A Line in the Dirt

Representation in cowboy culture was growing, and cowgirls were putting their proverbial boots down to stand firmly for what they believed in. The landscape of rodeo had long been dominated by male competitors, with women facing systemic barriers and limited opportunities. Yet, by the 1980s, women in rodeo were not only gaining visibility but also demanding equality. In 1980, the GRA drew a line in the sand, approving a motion to refuse participation in any PRCA rodeo that did not offer a payout for women equal to or greater than the lowest-paying men's event. This decision marked a pivotal moment in the fight for gender equity in rodeo. The PRCA received the message from the WPRA loud and clear, resulting in more than 98 percent of their rodeos meeting the requirement.

The following year, the GRA officially changed its name to the Women's Professional Rodeo Association. Today, it stands as one of the largest rodeo associations in the world, exclusively open to women eighteen years of age or older. This shift in pay standards gave women in rodeo the incentive they needed to prove that they could compete alongside the men, even on rodeo's grandest stage—the National Finals Rodeo.

The National Finals Rodeo works according to a system of qualification. Throughout the year, riders earn money at rodeos all over the continent. The earnings are tracked year-round and the top fifteen highest-earning riders in each individual rodeo event qualify for the National Finals Rodeo. The numbers contestants wear on their backs to identify themselves go in order of overall earnings for the year. The rodeo contestant who earned the most PRCA money for the entire year, regardless of which event they compete in, wears the number 1, and so on.

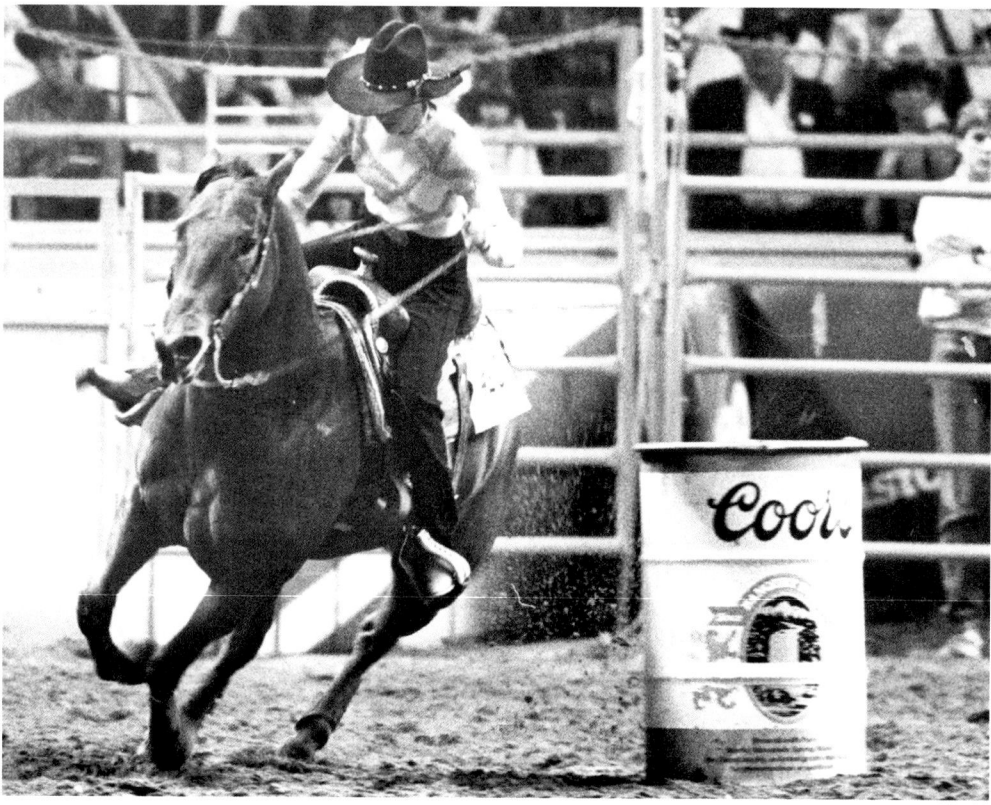

In the history of the NFR, only three women have ever worn the number 1. The first was Charmayne James in 1987, just five years after the motion for equal pay passed. Following in James's bootsteps were two women who would also become iconic barrel racers. Sherry Cervi wore the number 1 in 1995, and Mary Burger in 2016. In 1998, the PRCA began paying the National Finals barrel racers the same amount as their male counterparts. These three women, among many others, were pioneers for the sport of barrel racing and for all women in rodeo.

Barrel racing has become the dominant rodeo sport for women, offering the largest payouts and opportunities.

Women also have begun competing more frequently in other WPRA rodeo sports like Goat Roping, Team Roping, and Breakaway Roping, which is where a horseback rider tries to rope a calf as quickly as possible, and the rope breaks away from the saddle as soon as the calf is caught. While the WPRA crowned its first world champion breakaway roper in 1974, the event wasn't introduced at sanctioned PRCA rodeos until 2017. To this day, the event isn't given the same opportunities or exposure as barrel racing, though the PRCA does have the option to add Breakaway Roping to any event they see fit. Breakaway Ropers are going to be the next group of

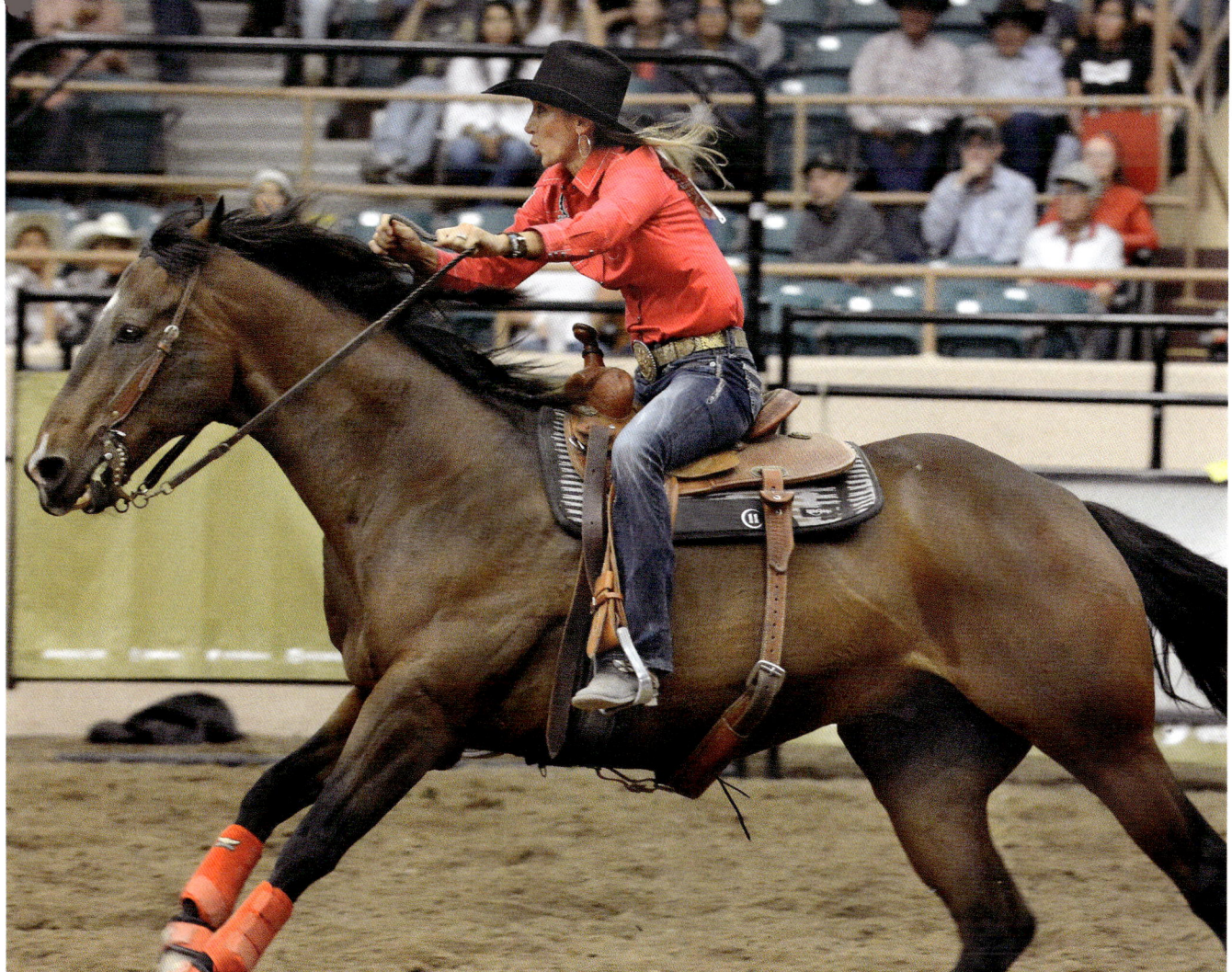

↑ Eleven-time world champion barrel racer Charmayne James at the ERA Premier Tour in 2016.

← Charmayne James competes at the National Western Stock Show in 1986.

Western women to break barriers, that's for certain, but it's unknown how long it will take for Breakaway to become a part of mainstream rodeo.

The event does have a championship in Las Vegas, Nevada, which is held at the same time of year as the National Finals Rodeo, but it is not included in the event itself. In fact, it's in a separate arena, at a separate location, at a different time of day, and is given about a minimal fraction of the promotion the National Finals themselves get.

There is a call each year from National Finals contestants and spectators alike who want to see Breakaway Roping added to the event. Of course, just like with all the hurdles that have been overcome in years past, there are a litany of reasons why it just "won't work": timing, logistics, cost, and so on. But these aren't unfamiliar excuses for the cowgirls of the WPRA. It may take time but if I trust anyone to get the job done, it's rodeo cowgirls.

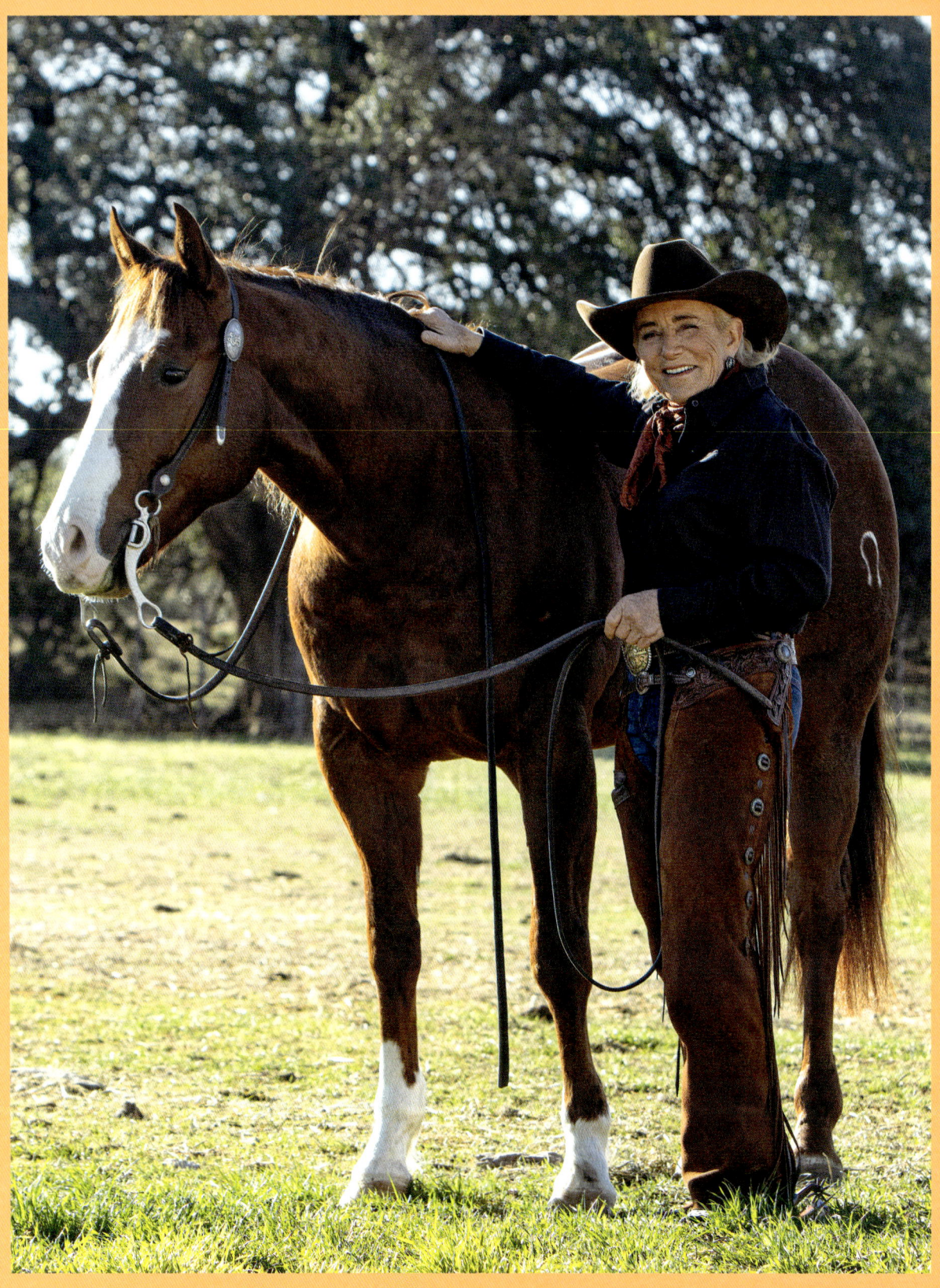

More Than Rodeo

Record-setting cutting horse trainer and horsewoman Lindy Burch was the first woman to win the National Cutting Horse Association World Championship Futurity and the first woman to win the National Cutting Horse Association Open World Championship. She continues to serve as a pioneer for women in the performance horse industry.

In addition to rodeo, women are at the forefront of ranching and performance horse competitions. From the queens of the cutting horse pen—Lindy Burch, Kathy Daughn, Cara Brewer, Morgan Cromer, and Mary Jo Milner—to renowned reiners and cow horse riders like Sarah Dawson, Erin Taormino, and Whitney Hall, and Hall's championship women's ranch rodeo teammates Kelsey Thomas, Kylie Carter, and Stormy Sill—women are getting more competitive and more impressive each year.

These women are some of the best cowgirls I know, and they don't even scratch the surface of the abundance of incredible horsewomen out there. Most of the Western community prefer to humbly move about life unrecognized for doing what they love, especially women who, until recently, didn't have the opportunity to be celebrated in the first place. But they are out there, empowering each other through shared knowledge and skill sets at rodeos, events, ranches, and beyond. It's this kind of shared spirit and determination that make the cowgirl relatable and inspiring—her spirit is one that can be translated across any industry where women work twice as hard for half the recognition. And let's be honest, that's most of them.

One event in particular where Western women come together for empowerment and growth is Art of the Cowgirl in Wickenburg, Arizona, which brings women together in a showcase of not only horsemanship, but also craftsmanship and artistry. Women share their skill sets, learn, create, compete, and come away inspired to lead the next generation of women into the arena, both stateside and beyond.

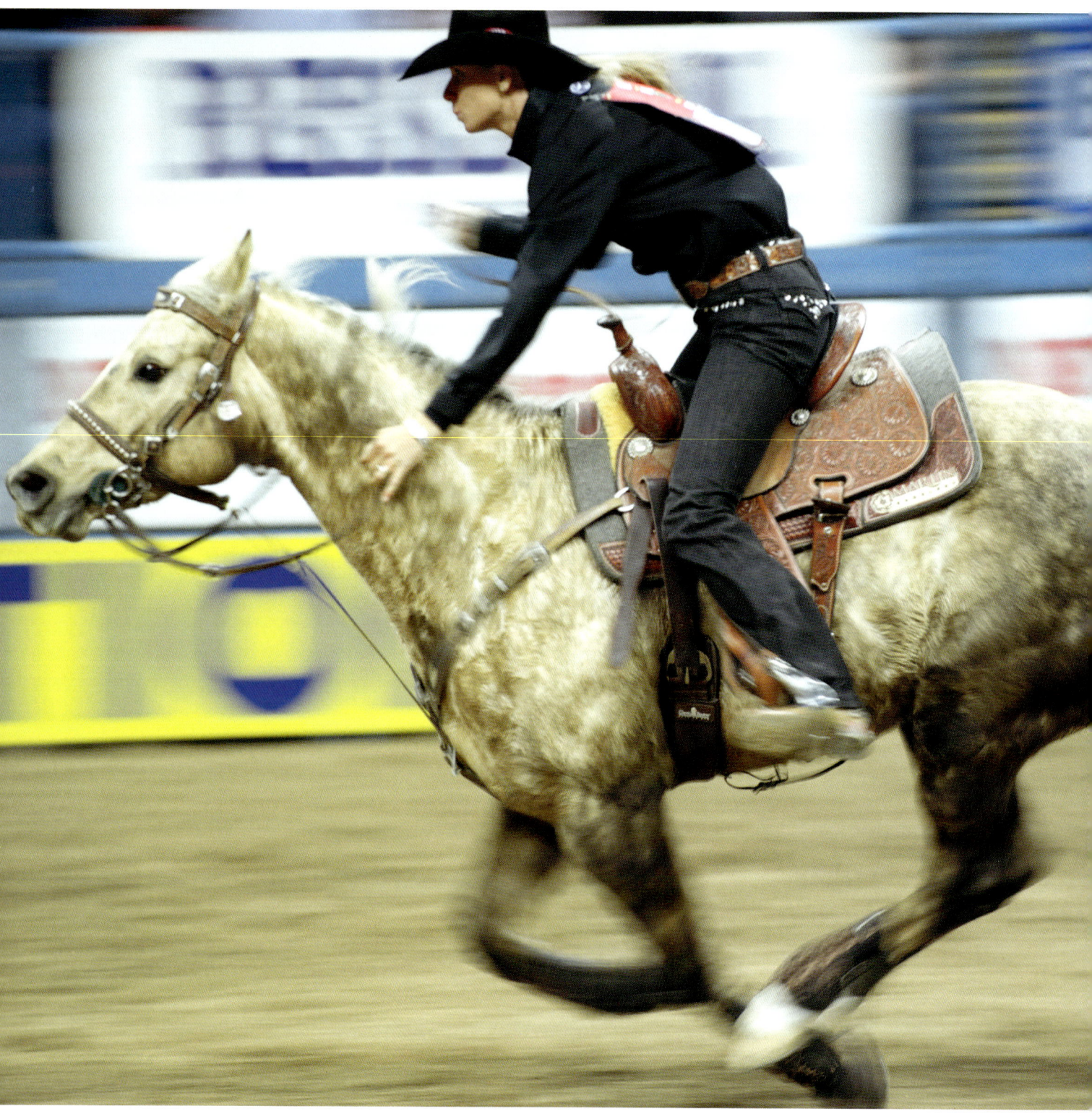

↑ Sherry Cervi competes in the Barrel Racing event at the Wrangler National Finals Rodeo in 2010.

→ Sherry Cervi barrel races in 2011 at the Red Bluff Round-Up in Red Bluff, California.

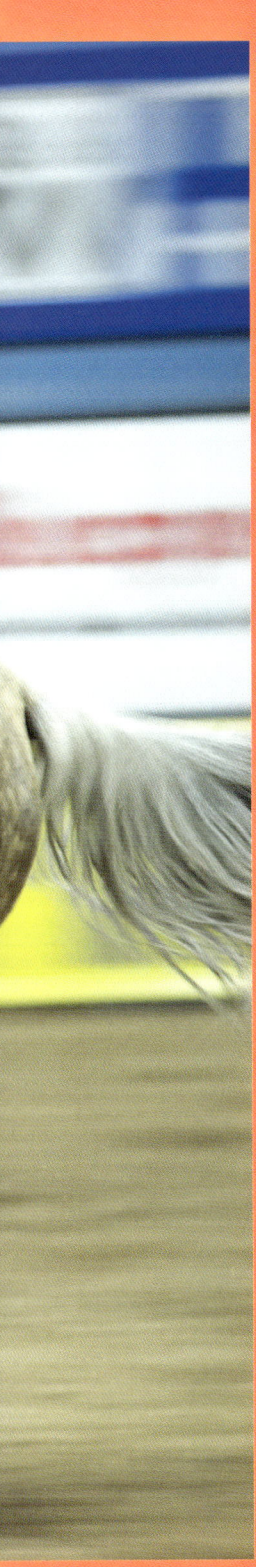

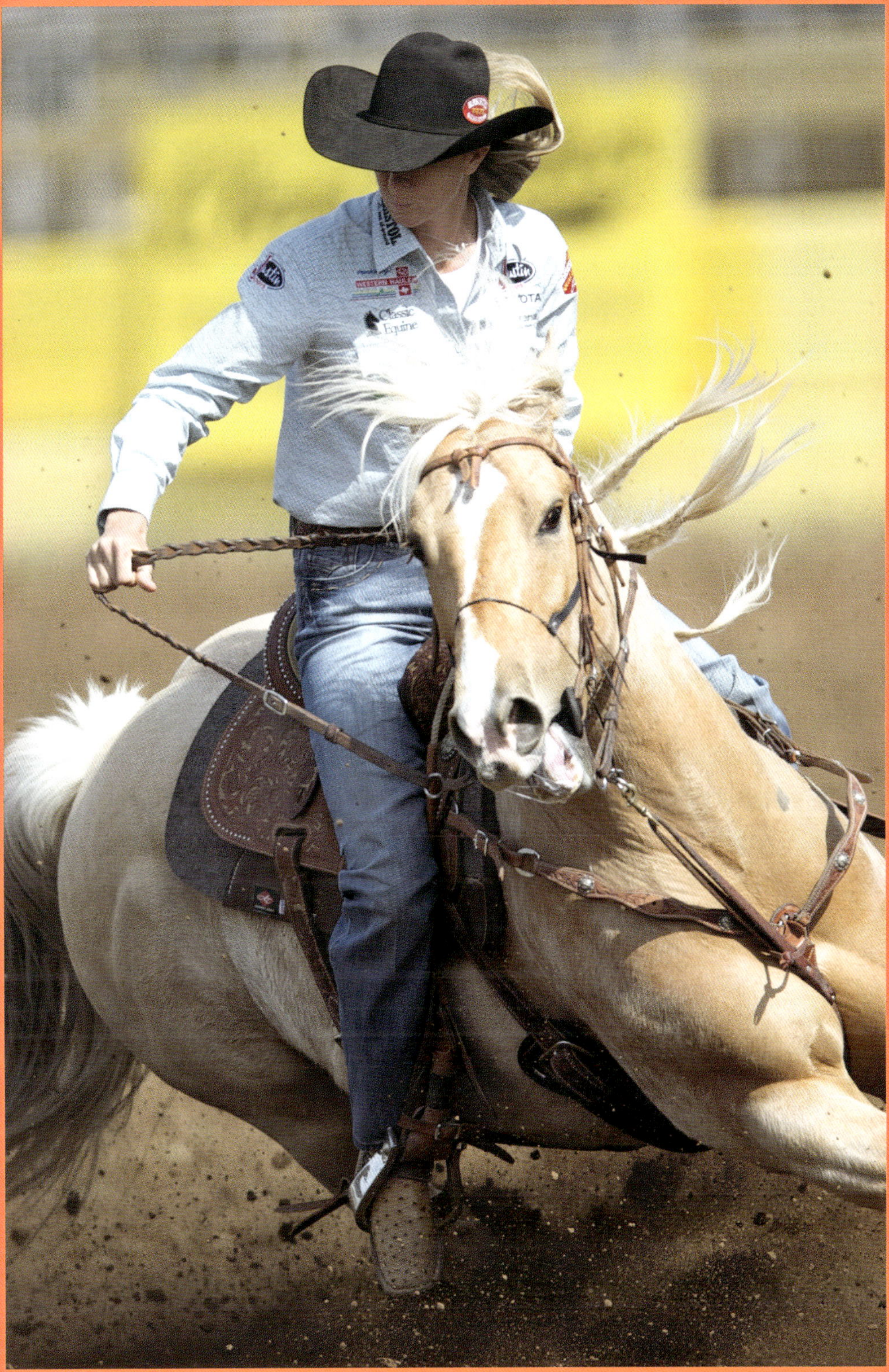

→ **NEXT PAGE** A woman competes in a timed barrel race in an arena in Utah.

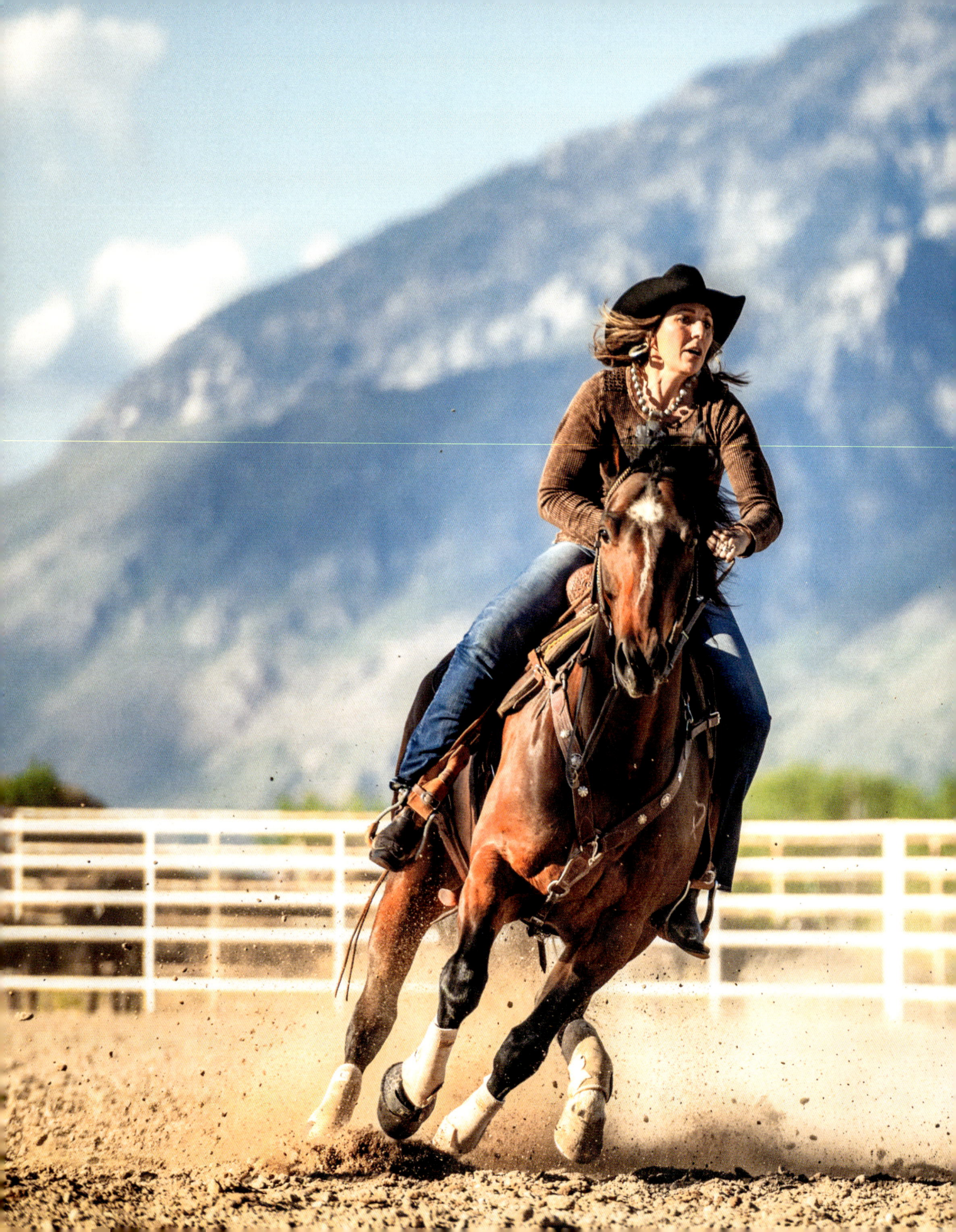

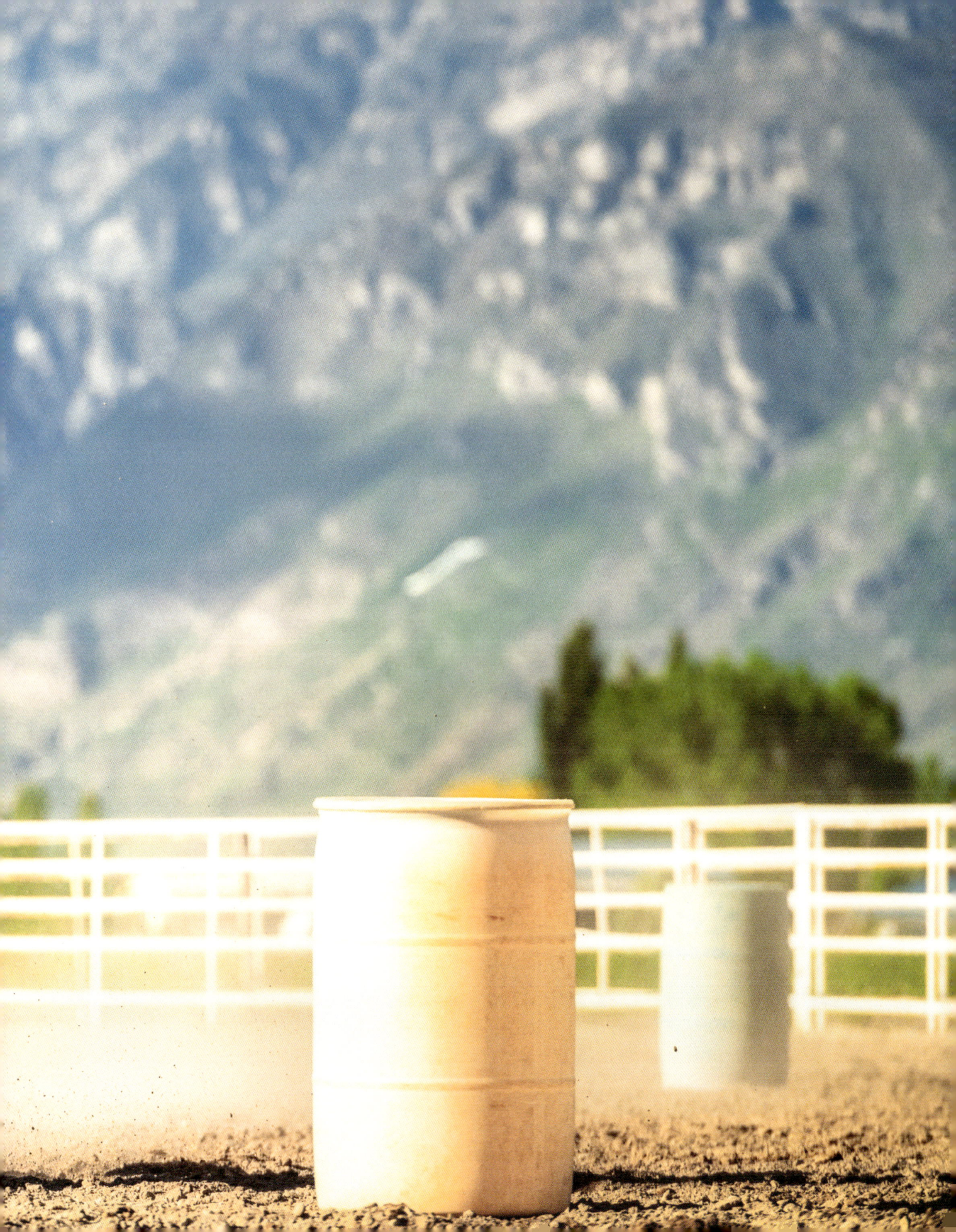

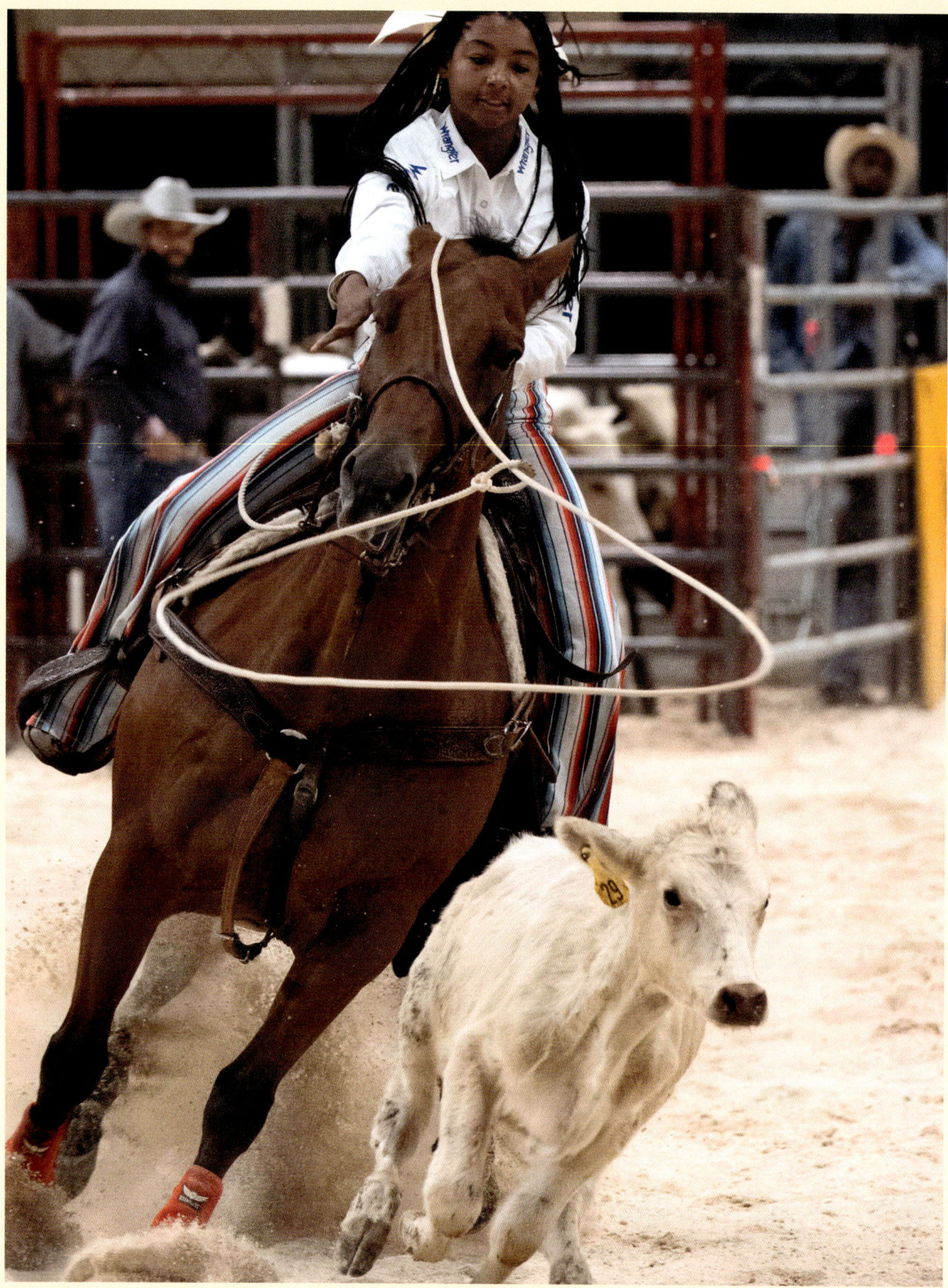

Western Life Around the World

← Kortnee Solomon competes in a Breakaway Roping event at the 2022 Bill Pickett Invitational Rodeo in Upper Marlboro, Maryland.

While the cowboy and cowgirl alike evolved from the American West, cowgirl culture—and Western culture in general—spans far beyond the borders of the United States. Just as the spirit of the cowgirl has an influence and application in many different industries and cultures, Western culture, in turn, was shaped by a blend of global traditions.

The cowboy lifestyle drew significant inspiration from the vaquero traditions of Mexico. Vaquero expertise in cattle herding, roping, and horsemanship heavily influenced American cowboy practices. Indigenous peoples of North America also contributed knowledge of the land, livestock management, and survival skills, which became integral to cowboy culture.

Western culture has been shaped by influences from diverse cultures worldwide and has, in turn, become deeply embedded in societies across the globe. Rodeo and Western traditions thrive worldwide. From North America to South America, Europe, and Australia, few corners of the planet remain untouched by Western culture's reach and influence.

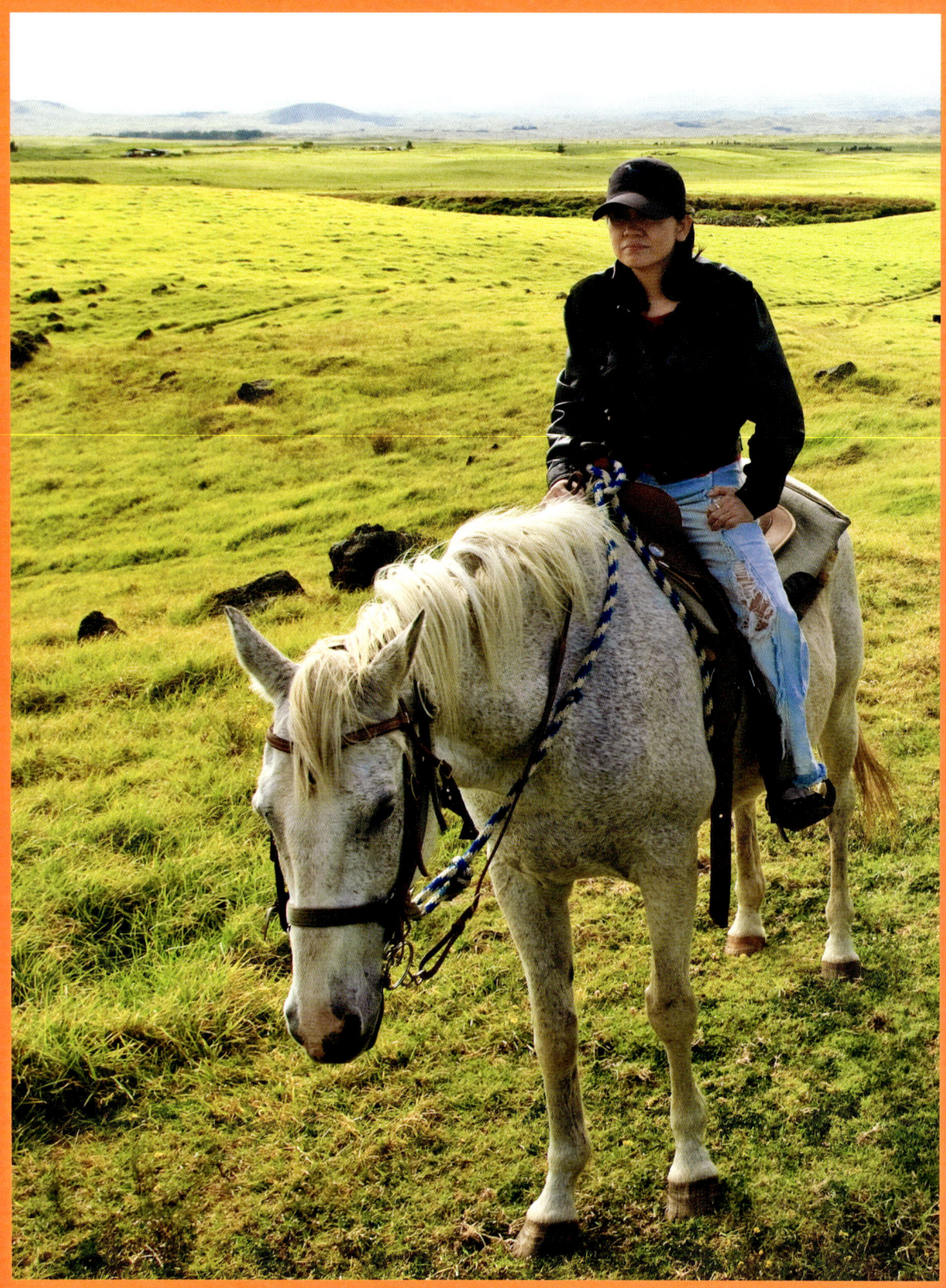

Island Life

← Horseback riding at Parker Ranch on the Big Island of Hawai'i.

Hawaii has a unique and thriving cowboy culture. Mammals were not indigenous to Hawaii with the exception of a couple of species of bats, but Polynesian explorers brought back chickens and pigs, and the islanders learned to raise livestock for consumption. Eventually, cattle were introduced to the island, planting the seeds of Hawaiian ranching culture. Around 1812, Mexican vaqueros were invited to the island to teach the locals about ranching and cattle-handling practices, including how to ride and utilize horses to work cattle. Hawaiians learned to rope and ride and became skilled in ranch life—they created a distinctive Hawaiian cowboy culture.

The Hawaiian cowboys were called paniolo, and when they came to the mainland to compete against American cowboys in various rodeos, they would often outperform them. One highly respected paniolo was James "Kimo" William Ho'opai, Sr., who was a member of the Hawaii Cattlemen's Association Paniolo Hall of Fame.

Women also made key contributions to cowgirl culture in Hawaii and are known as paniolo wahine. The Hawaii Women's Rodeo Association (HWRA) was founded in 1991 and is dedicated to supporting women in rodeo sports. Its most notable event is the annual All-Girl Rodeo, which celebrates the talent and skills of cowgirls.

Today, the Big Island is home to the Parker Ranch, one of the biggest cattle ranches in the United States, with more than 135,000 acres (54,633 hectares) of land. Between the Parker and other ranches on the Hawaiian Islands, cattle production is a large part of Hawaiian agriculture.

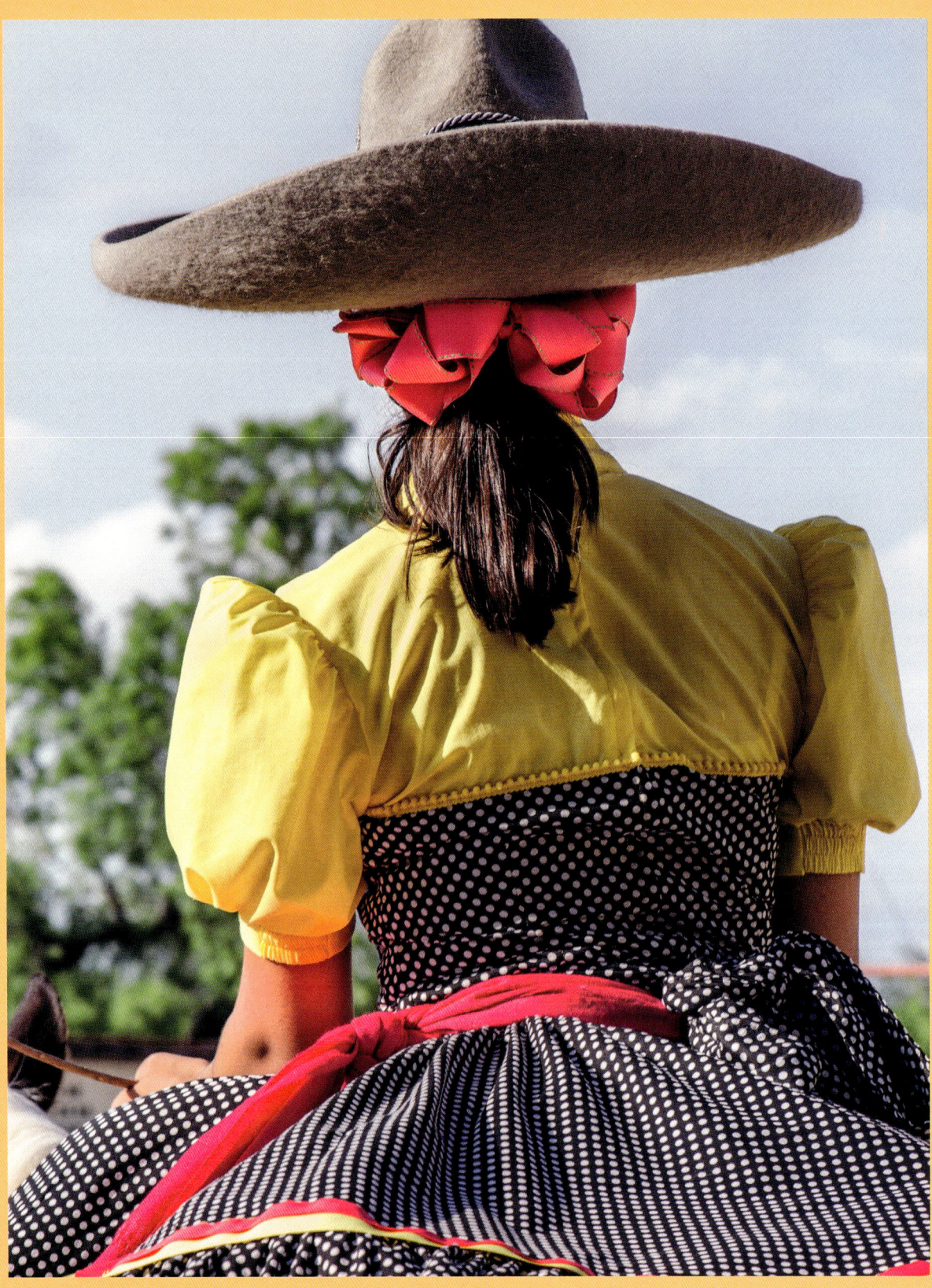

North and South

← A portrait of
an escaramuza
competitor at
Fiesta Week in San
Antonio, Texas.

Canada is home to a massive agricultural economy, especially in Alberta. Likewise, Alberta is home to some of the largest and most historic rodeos and horse shows in the world, like the Calgary Stampede. The Stampede is the world's largest outdoor rodeo and attracts more than one million spectators each year. Canada is also home to major performance horse exhibitors and events, and is a popular competition stop among most major Western event associations.

Moving south to Mexico brings us to the rich history and culture of charrería, a sport derived from early cattle-herding traditions. Charrería is the national sport of Mexico. It began as ranch work competitions between haciendas, not unlike the original ranch rodeo format. Charros, or horsemen, compete in various events to prove their horses' discipline, agility, and cow sense.

Charrería really took off after the Mexican revolution, when charros began organizing individual sporting events rather than focusing on the hacienda teams. Some notable charros include Antonio Arámbula, celebrated for his roping skills and horsemanship; José Andrés Aceves, a prominent figure in bull riding and roping; and Miguel Ángel Vega, a multi-time national champion.

In 1953, women gained the right to vote in Mexico, and that same year, they were also officially allowed to compete in charrería—but women have their own dedicated space in Mexican cowgirl culture as well. Escaramuza is the female-only equestrian event within charrería. It is a synchronized, choreographed routine, usually set to music, performed by women on

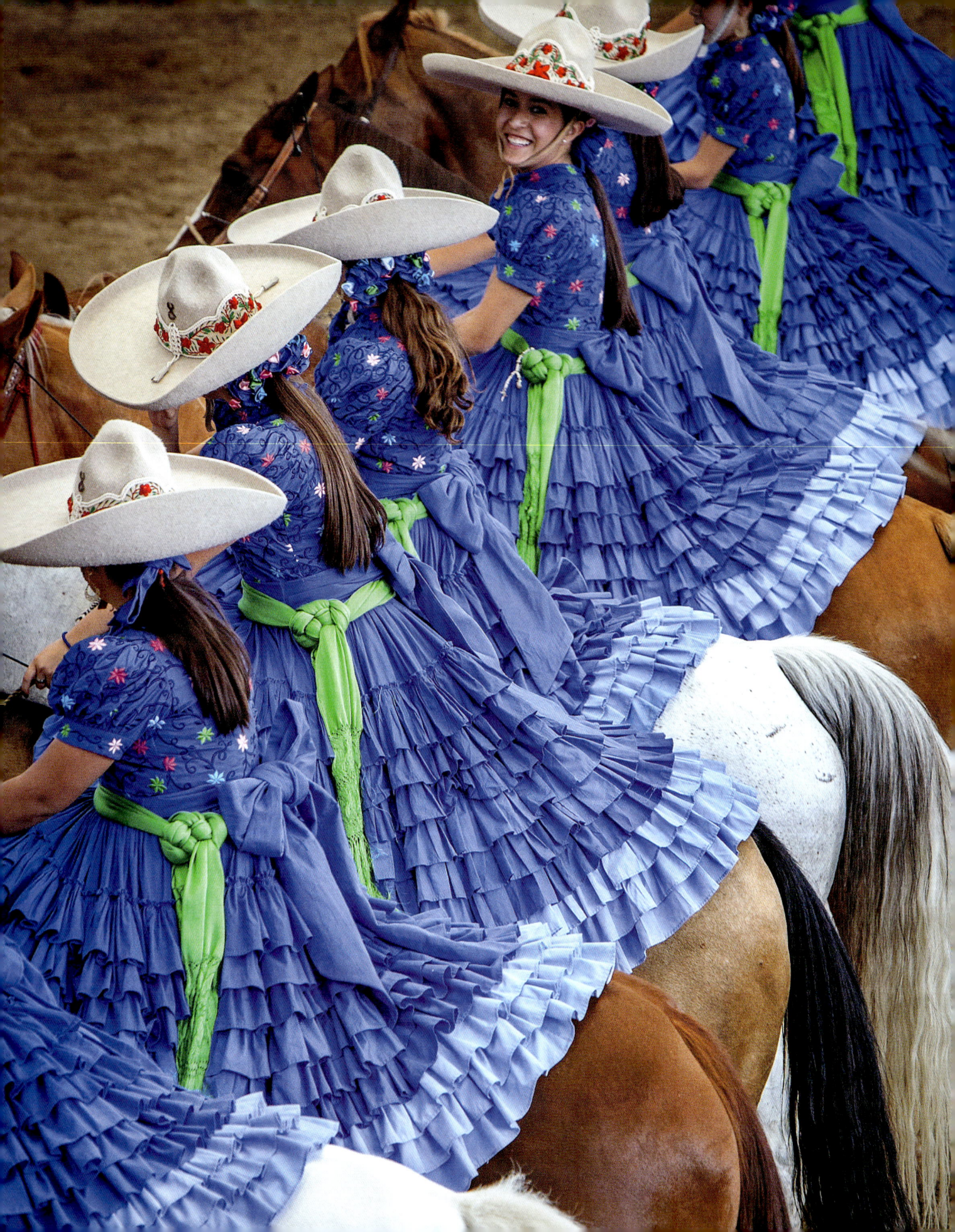

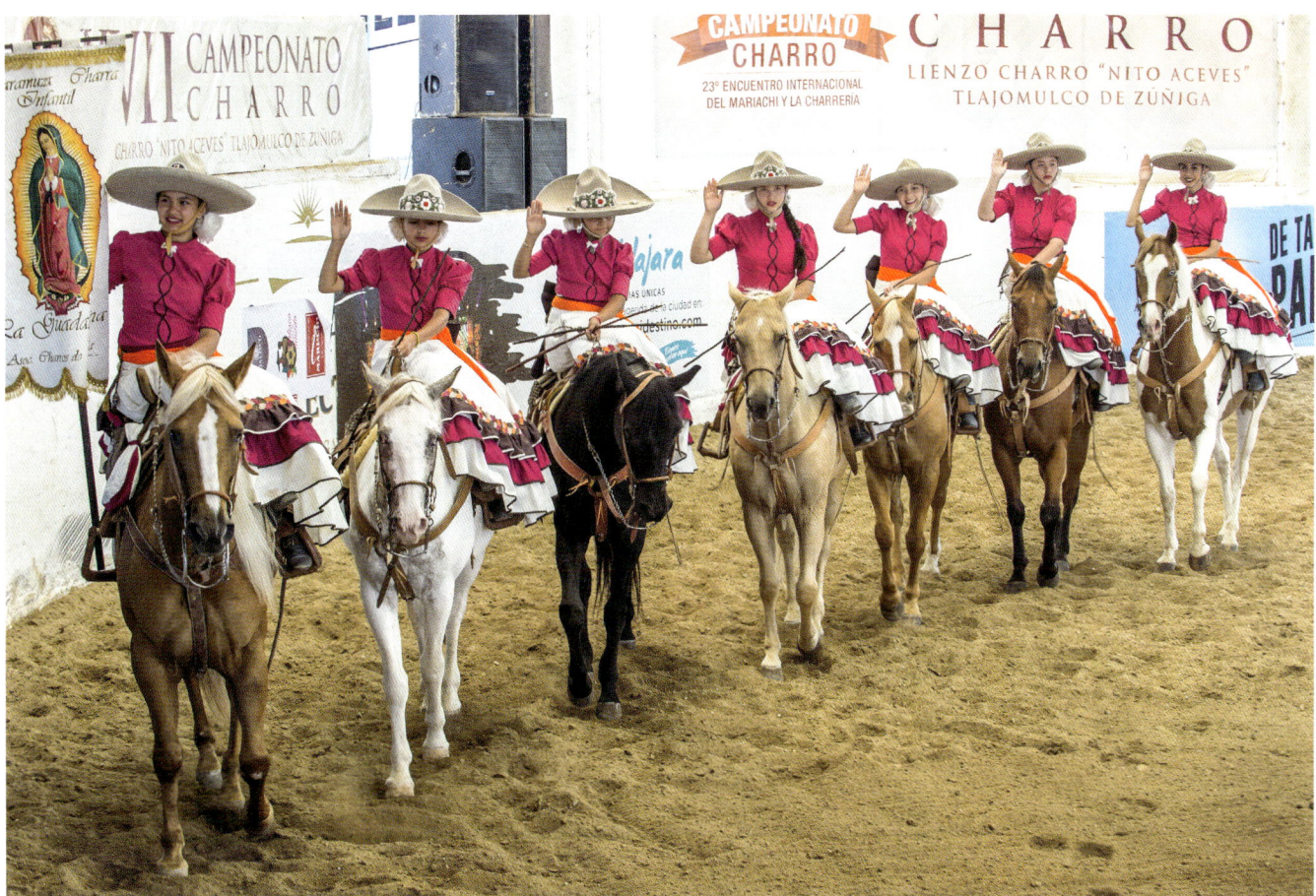

Charras perform at the 2016 International Mariachi & Charrería Festival in Guadalajara, Mexico.

A troupe of escaramuza riders at a charreada rodeo in Guadalajara, Mexico.

horseback. They sport traditional outfits inspired by Adelitas, a popular term for the women who fought in the Mexican revolution.

Both charrería and escaramuza are rooted in tradition and pay homage to the core of Mexican charro culture. Two notable escaramuza teams that play a vital role in preserving charrería traditions include: Escaramuza las Margaritas and Escaramuza Charra Villa de Guadalupe.

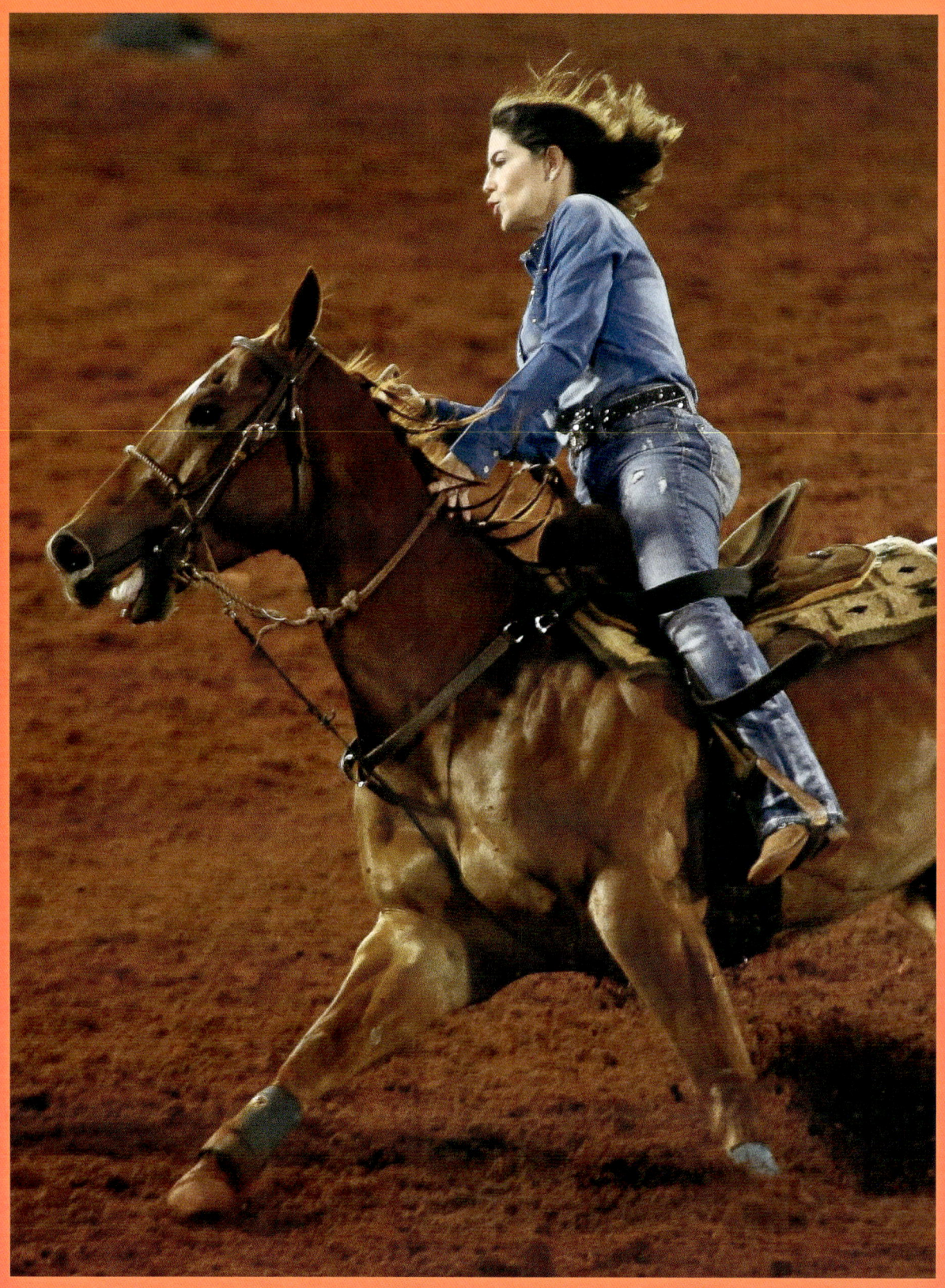

Cowboys and Cowgirls Across Continents

A cowgirl rides at the 2022 Festa do Peão de Barretos in Brazil.

Even farther south is the Festa do Peão de Barretos, a rodeo in Barretos, Brazil. It is widely considered the world's largest rodeo, with more than one million visitors each year. American rodeo has a huge influence on the sport in Brazil, which began more than fifty years ago in the South American country. The Western sport that is the most popular in Brazil is bull riding. They also have a traditional Brazilian long rope competition known as Laço Comprido, where riders use a long rope to lasso a steer while galloping on horseback, to showcase precision and skill.

Some of the best professional bull riders who dominate the bull riding industry hail from Brazil. Some notable riders include Adriano Morães, Silvano Alves, Renato Nunes, and Kaique Pacheco. Brazilian bulls tend to be larger and feistier than their American counterparts, which is believed to give the Brazilians a leg up when they come to the United States for bull riding.

Brazil is also home to some incredible cowgirls, including Renata Simonetto, a fierce competitor in the long rope category, and Lettícia Pessin, a champion barrel racer who earned the title at the International Rodeo at just fourteen years old. Other champion Brazilian barrel racers include Fatiana Ferreira and Thais Munique.

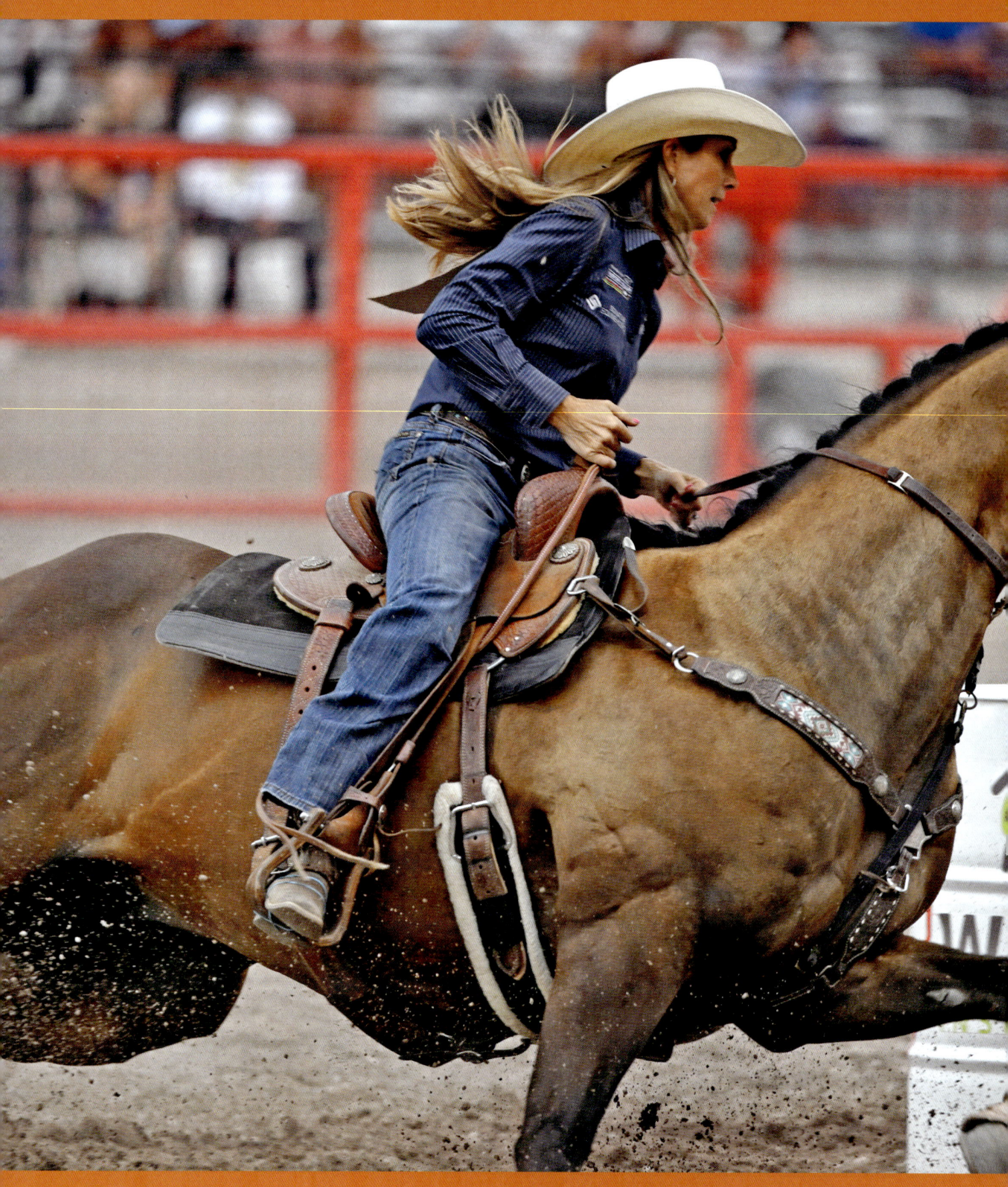

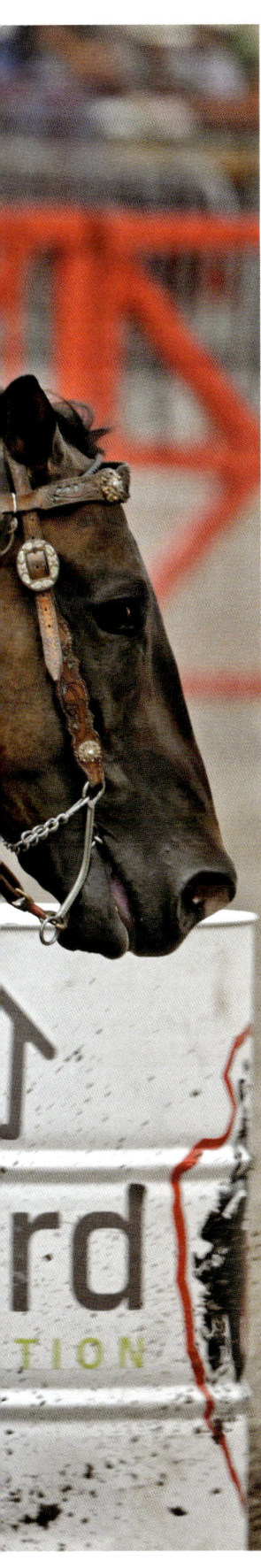

← Kassie Mowry competes in Barrel Racing at the 2023 Cheyenne Frontier Days Rodeo in Wyoming.

Across the pond, equestrian roots run as far back as recorded history can go. And though Europe has always had a history of using horses for activities like fox hunting, racing, hunter jumping, and cross country, Western culture hasn't been as widely adopted. However, there are still many major Western influences in events that take place in Europe.

For instance, Germany hosts Europe's largest Western riding fair, the Americana, which happens biennially in Friedrichshafen. It's a popular event that hosts thousands of participants and includes many parts of Western culture, including reining, cutting competitions, ranch classes, saloon-style entertainment, and more.

One notable cowboy includes German reining rider and trainer, Grischa Ludwig, who became an NRHA (National Reining Horse Association) Million Dollar Rider in 2023. Some influential European cowgirls include Cira Baeck, a Belgian rider, who became the first European woman to join the NRHA Million Dollar Rider list; and Nina Lill, a talented German rider who became the youngest woman on the German team to win gold in the FEI European Reining Championship.

Italy also hosts the Pordenone rodeo, an Italian hoedown that celebrates the American West with cowboy hats, line dancing, a mechanical bull, and country music. One notable Italian cowgirl is Carmelina Colantuono, referred to in Italy as "the last cowgirl." She leads annual cattle drives along ancient herding trails, known as tratturi. While Italy has developed its own unique take on Western traditions, the broader European rodeo scene owes much of its growth to American military influence during and after World War II.

The United States military brought rodeo to Europe in a big way when Alan Jacob, a US Navy veteran who served for four years during World War II, had the idea to start up a touring rodeo in Europe. Similar to the Wild West shows from American history, this rodeo tour began in Italy and crisscrossed the continent. US Army Europe would later become involved, and Jacob's rodeo proceeds began to be funneled to the Army Morale Fund. Through this endeavor, the European Rodeo Cowboy Association (ERCA) was born. The group has flamed out over time, but the rodeos Jacob produced generated more than $1 million for service members stationed in Europe until his passing in 2003.

Jumping Down Under to Australia, Western culture is alive and thriving. The only thing comparable to the massive cattle drives happening across the

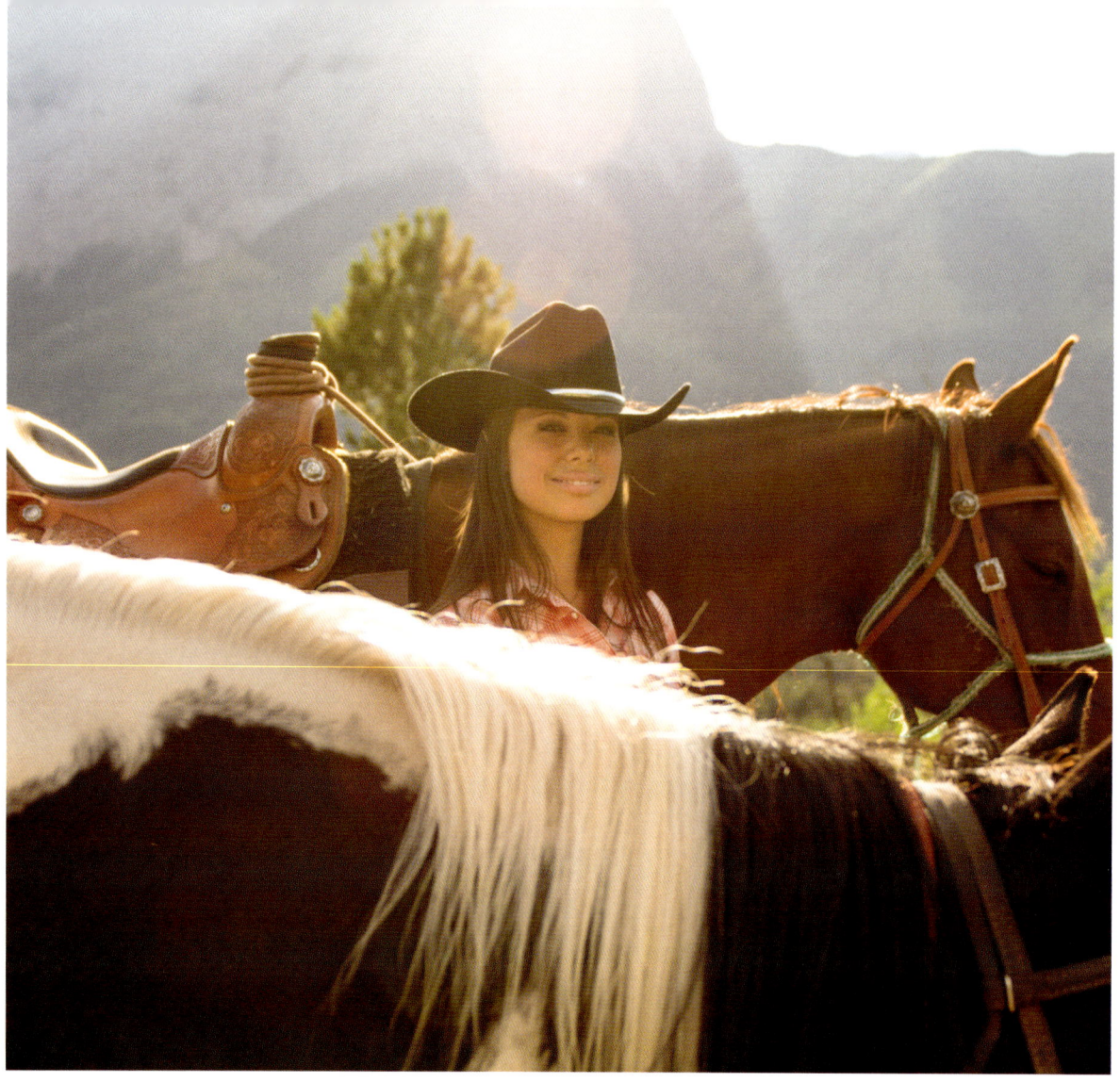

United States in the nineteenth century were those drives taking place in the twentieth century in Australia. Both Aboriginal women as well as white women were often hired as drovers in Australia's Northern Territory, and in Queensland. They faced similar dangers to those faced by American women who drove cattle, but overall, it was much more widely accepted to embrace the rural lifestyle as an Australian woman.

Like America, Australia has its own history of touring Wild West shows, which increased the popularity of the sport of roughriding—or rough stock riding as we know it in the States—including bareback, saddle bronc, and bull riding. Bushmen's Carnivals were the Australian equivalent of American rodeos, and they originated in the 1920s around Northern New South Wales. Over the next decade, American rodeo would have a huge influence on these shows with the additions of clowns, ropers, trick riders, and more. These events are still held today in the main towns

← A cowgirl in Canada soaks up the sunshine and the fresh mountain air in the best of company.

→ **NEXT PAGE** A woman out for a sunset horseback ride in Botswana.

of cattle country, across the eastern states of Australia and the state of South Australia.

In 1944, Sydney, Australia, became the home of the Ladies' Rodeo Club (LRC), and subsequently became a popular city for rodeo. Eventually, the National Rodeo Association (NRA) would form in the 1960s as the fastest growing rodeo association in Australia. They offer the same rodeo sports for women as we do in the States, with Barrel Racing and Breakaway Roping being primary events for the ladies to participate in. Additionally, like American rodeo culture, they take pride in their rodeo royalty, hosting queen and princess competitions at several rodeos throughout the season.

One woman in particular has been a standout when it comes to driving more patrons to the sport in Australia. In 2014, then-twenty-one-year-old Eileen Hettich became the first woman in Australia to compete in the steer wrestling. German-born Hettich was taking time away from her medical studies in Germany when she visited Australia on vacation. While there, she not only fell in love with the Northern Territory's rugged lifestyle, but also with a roughrider named Johno. The couple loaded up to the Mount Isa Mines Rotary Rodeo to compete in their respective events, and Hettich was determined to at least try the bulldogging, as it was an event she loved to watch. Hettich caught her steer but wasn't able to turn him over. Regardless, she is the first woman in the country to attempt a sport intended for the largest and strongest men in rodeo.

Another notable woman bringing clout to female rodeo competitors in Australia is Indigenous cowgirl Lani Jackson of the Ngāti Tūwharetoa tribe. Jackson holds an unprecedented record of Open Barrel Racing titles in Australia's barrel racing scene, and more notably just won the inaugural New Zealand Rodeo Cowboys Association Breakaway Roping championship.

While rodeo has been a little slower to take off in Australia, the performance horse world has moved at lightning speed. Just like in the United States, women are quickly finding their seat at that table. While many performance horse professionals come to the States to get full-time jobs and better opportunities, women are seeing more and more places to rise to success on their native continent. The rise of events like the Australian Cowgirl, the Australian iteration of Art of the Cowgirl, features Australia's Greatest Horsewoman competition, an event rapidly gaining in popularity even in its US version. Like its American counterpart, the Australian Cowgirl will feature horsewomen, artists, silversmiths, saddle makers, and more. These women gather annually to celebrate Australian cowgirls, their history, and the contributions they will continue to make to Australian Western culture.

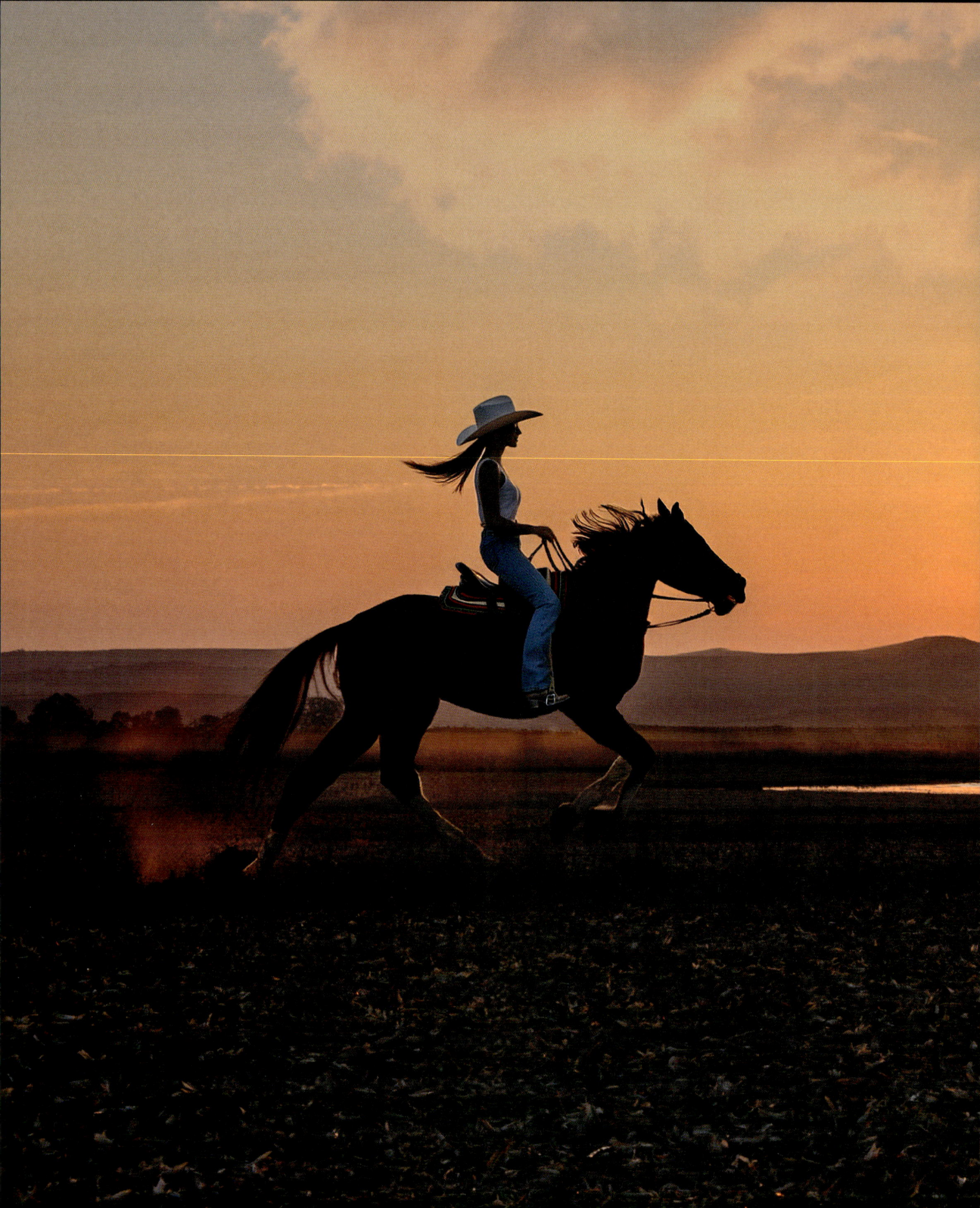

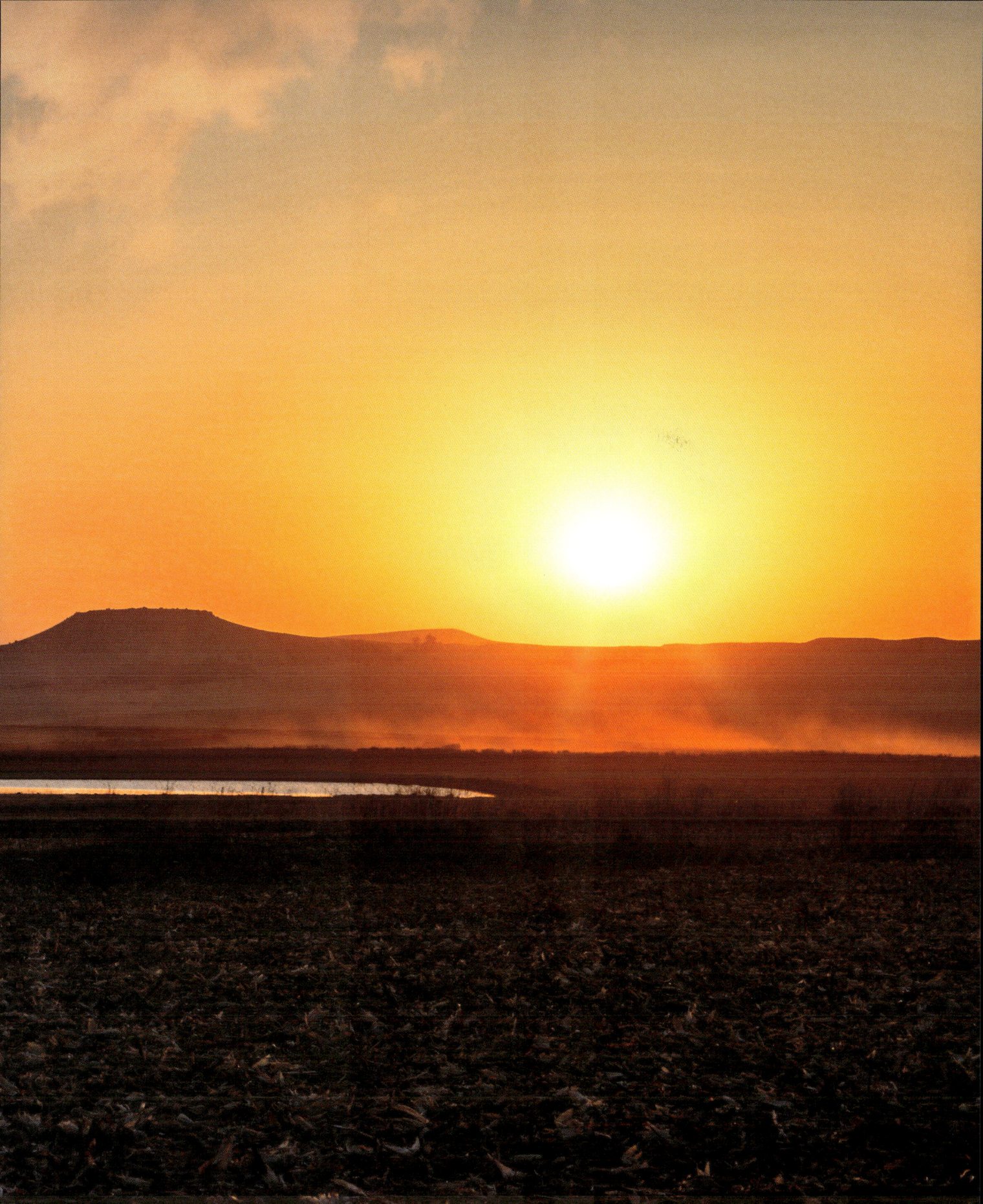

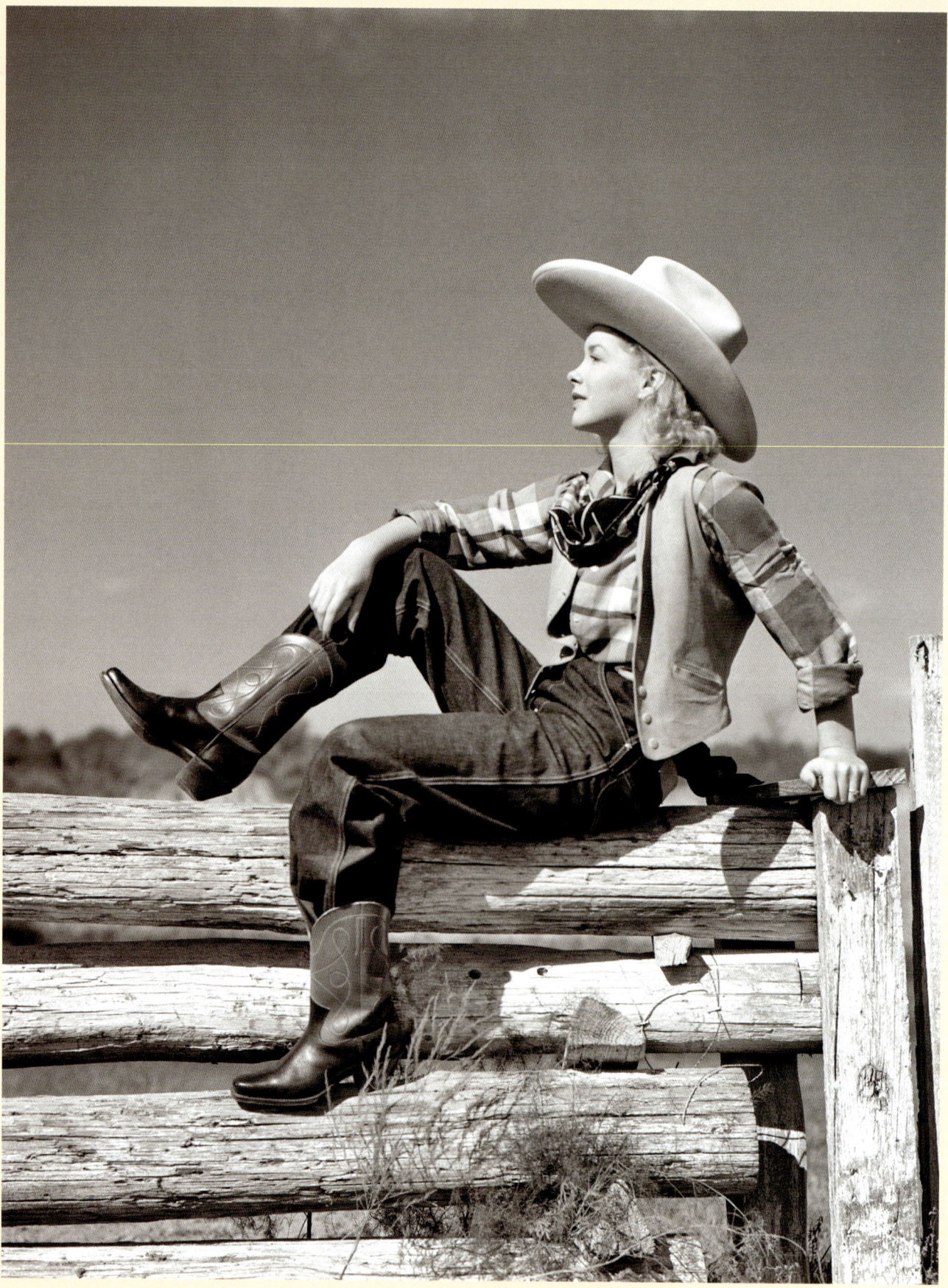

Quintessential Cowgirls

← Vintage cowgirl fashion from the 1940s.

The cowgirl spirit would be nothing if not for the fearless women who unabashedly pioneered the way for a girl in a modern man's world. These women saw what cowboys were doing and knew they could do it just as well as—or dare we say better than—the boys. They forged new paths of action, never afraid to step up when the opportunity presented itself. It's this kind of tenacious initiative that makes cowgirls who they are.

Their existence stands on the backbone of women who weren't afraid to stand up for themselves, stand up for others, and make a little noise. These women followed in the footsteps of the cowgirls before them, pulling them from Wild West shows and cattle drives, and transforming them into modern day ranching queens, proving they've got grit, bronc riding skills, and brains.

I hope you see the cowgirl spirit all around you in this life, but I also want you to have a clear idea of a working cowgirl, and be able to draw inspiration from her life and the things she had to overcome. There are women who make a living on cattle and ranching, and they deserve for you to know their names; they deserve to be celebrated.

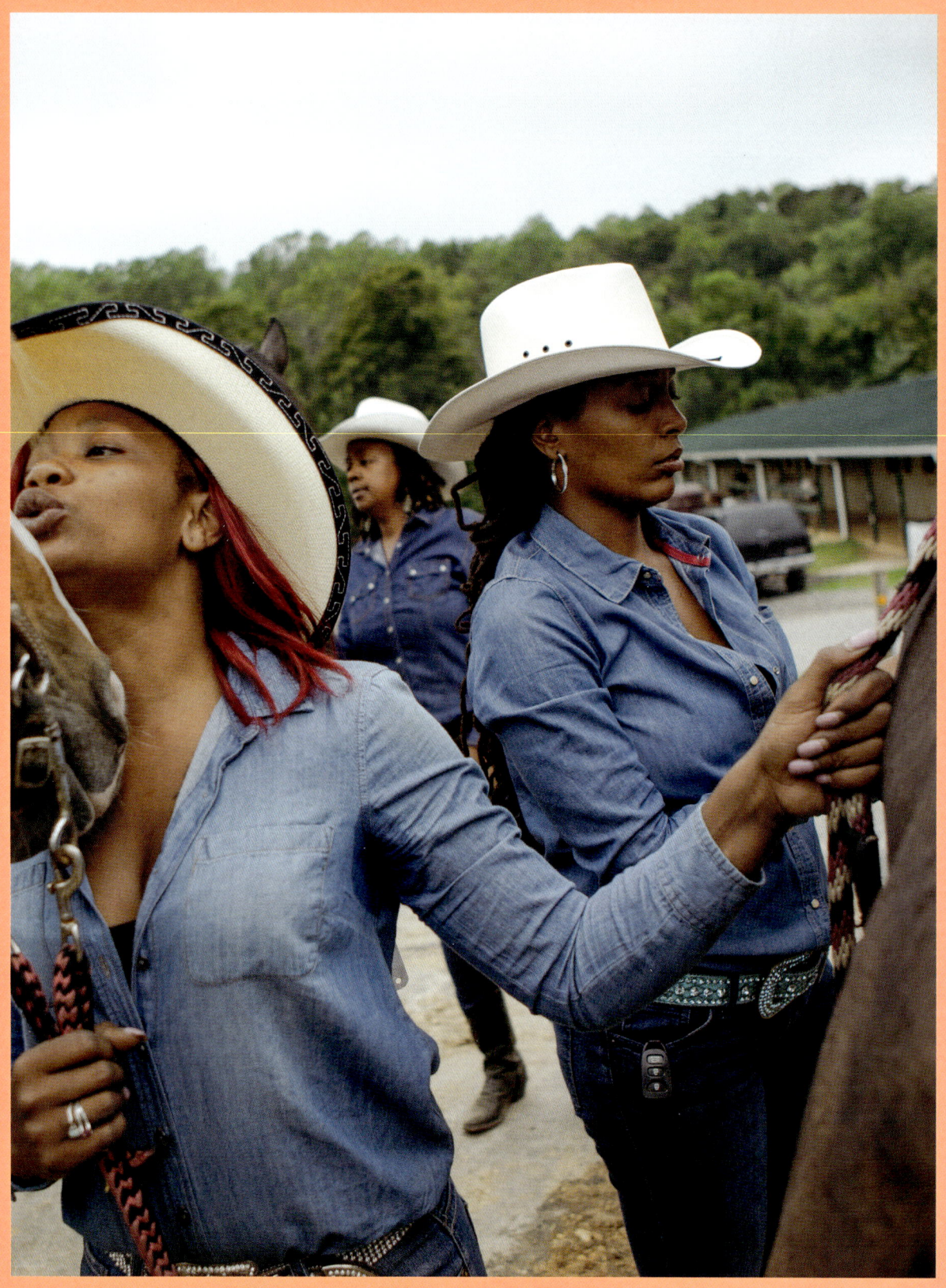

Kisha Bowles and Brittaney Logan
The Dynamic Duo

Nothing compares to the connection between human and horse. The members of Cowgirls of Color (including founder Kisha Bowles, seen here on the right) came later to the sport than many competitors, but they have become dedicated riders and spokeswomen for Black rodeo culture.

Brittaney Logan ("Britt Brat") and Kisha Bowles ("KB") are the incredible founders of Cowgirls of Color, an all-Black, all-female rodeo team, established in 2016. Originally from the Washington, DC area, their introduction into the world of rodeo began after meeting Dr. Ray Charles Lockamy, a seasoned horseman who guided them into horseback riding and competitive rodeo.

While Logan had started riding horses in her twenties, developing a love for rodeo life and accepting the challenges that came with it, Bowles discovered her passion for horse riding in her late thirties, finding comfort in the practice during a time of grief, after her mother passed away. She found respite in horseback riding, becoming attached to the sport.

Together, both women trained in the Maryland countryside under Lockamy's mentorship and eventually competed in events like Bill Pickett Invitational Rodeo. Their efforts have not only brought attention to the contributions of Black women in rodeo but have also inspired others to challenge stereotypes and embrace the Western lifestyle.

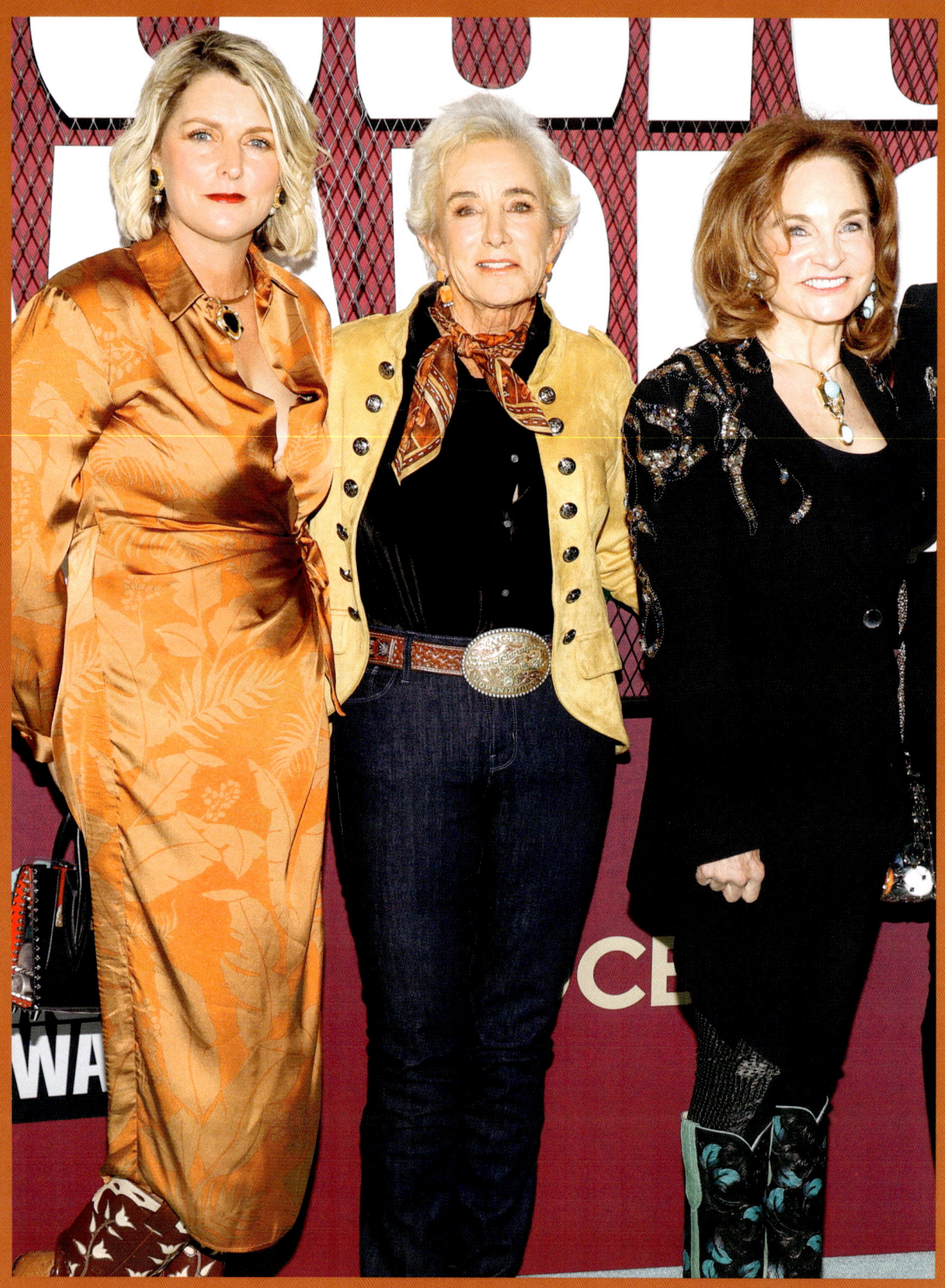

Lindy Burch
Cutting's Trailblazer

← Lindy Burch (center) with Jess Pounds (left) and Kit Moncrief (right) at the 2023 CMT Music Award.

Lindy Burch has been blazing trails in the cutting pen since she first swung her leg over a horse. Cutting—a sport derived from cattle drives in which the Cow Boss used a horse with "cow sense" to separate individual cattle away from the herd for medication, branding, or weaning—has been historically male-dominated. That is, until Burch came along. Burch never really worried about whether being a woman would limit her opportunities—she simply let her skill do the talking. Now a respected trainer and cutting horse champion, Burch's accomplishments in the arena bred opportunity and credibility for the women who would follow in her footsteps.

In 1979, Burch was the first woman to claim the NCHA Open Futurity Reserve Championship. The following year, in 1980, she became the first woman to win the NCHA Open Futurity, setting a record score of 225.5. The victory was unprecedented—the record score, set by a woman, from California of all places. The boys had no choice but to take this West Coast cowgirl seriously. To this day, Burch remains the only woman who has won the iconic event, but her streak wouldn't end there.

She shattered records again in 1995 when she became the first rider in history to win all four rounds of the NCHA Open World Finals, and again when she scored a historic 233 at the 1998 NCHA Open World Finals. In 2000, she became the first woman to win the NCHA Open World Championship. The same year, she was elected as the first (and still the only) female president of the NCHA. She was inducted into the National Cowgirl Hall of Fame in 2001.

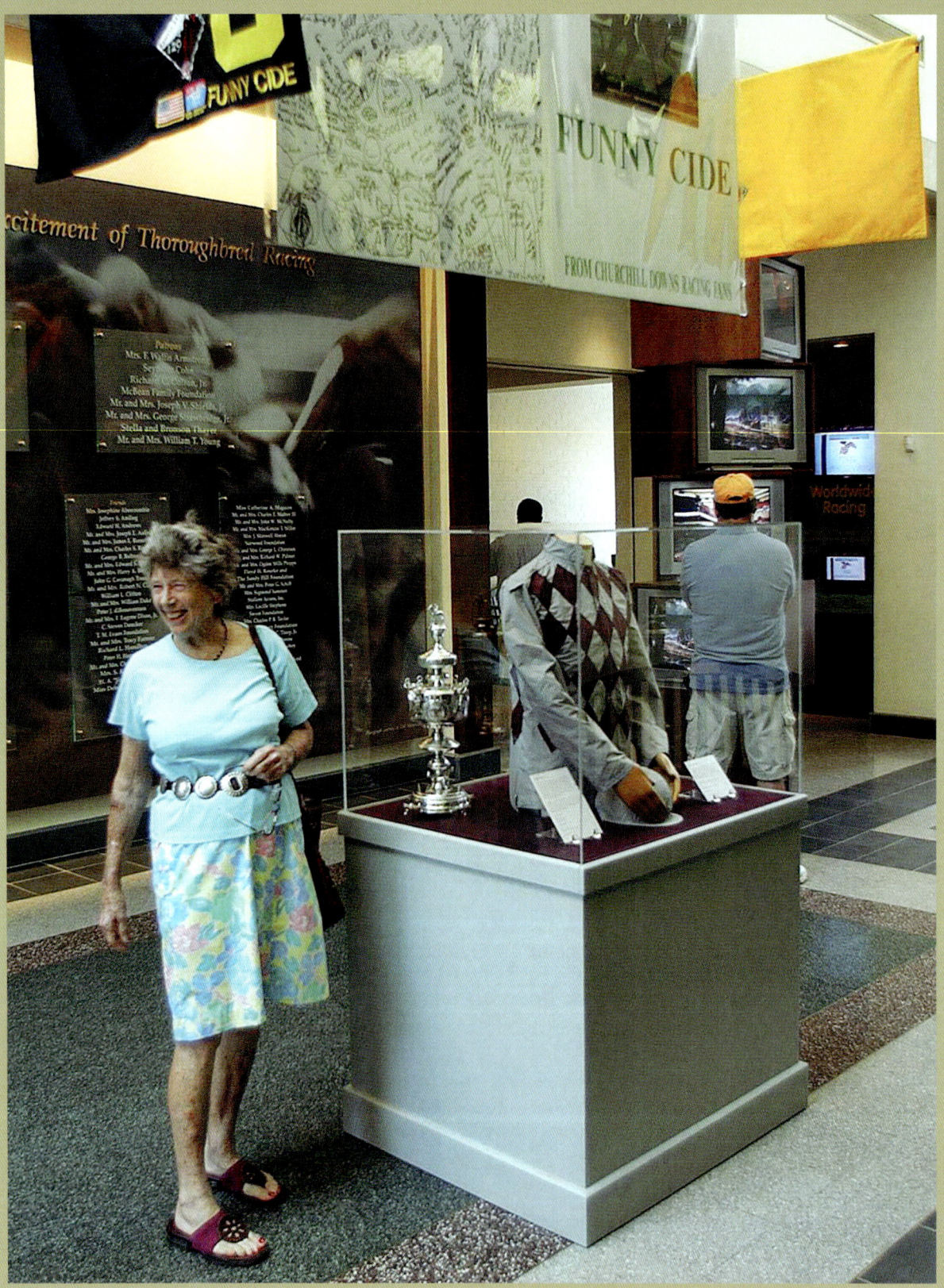

Helen Groves
Cutting's First Lady

Born in 1927 in San Antonio, Texas, Helen Groves hailed from a long line of prolific ranchers. Groves was the only daughter of Robert Justus Kleberg, Jr., a renowned rancher who managed the iconic King Ranch in south Texas and developed the Santa Gertrudis breed of cattle—the first distinct American breed.

Raised on the King Ranch, Groves was taught from a young age to protect livestock and take care of the land. As an adult, Groves oversaw the Buck & Doe Run Valley Farms in Chester County, Pennsylvania; Silverbrook Farms in Staunton, Virginia; and Silverbrook Ranches in Texas. She focused on breeding programs at the King Ranch, raising the best Santa Gertrudis cattle and American Quarter Horses in the country. As the King Ranch horses established their dominance in National Cutting Horse Association arenas and competitions, so did Groves. She became known as the "First Lady of Cutting," campaigning two of her horses in competitions all over the country.

Her equine interest expanded into the thoroughbred world, a new area for cowgirls. Groves made her mark when she led King Ranch's Assault, a thoroughbred horse, into the winner's circle after his 1946 Triple Crown victory—making him the only Texas-bred winner of the Triple Crown to this day.

Thanks to Groves's innovation, the King Ranch remains family-owned and -operated and still retains all the land it held. Groves died in May of 2022, leaving behind a massive void in the Western industry. Her spirit lives on in each and every cowgirl who dares to step out of her comfort zone.

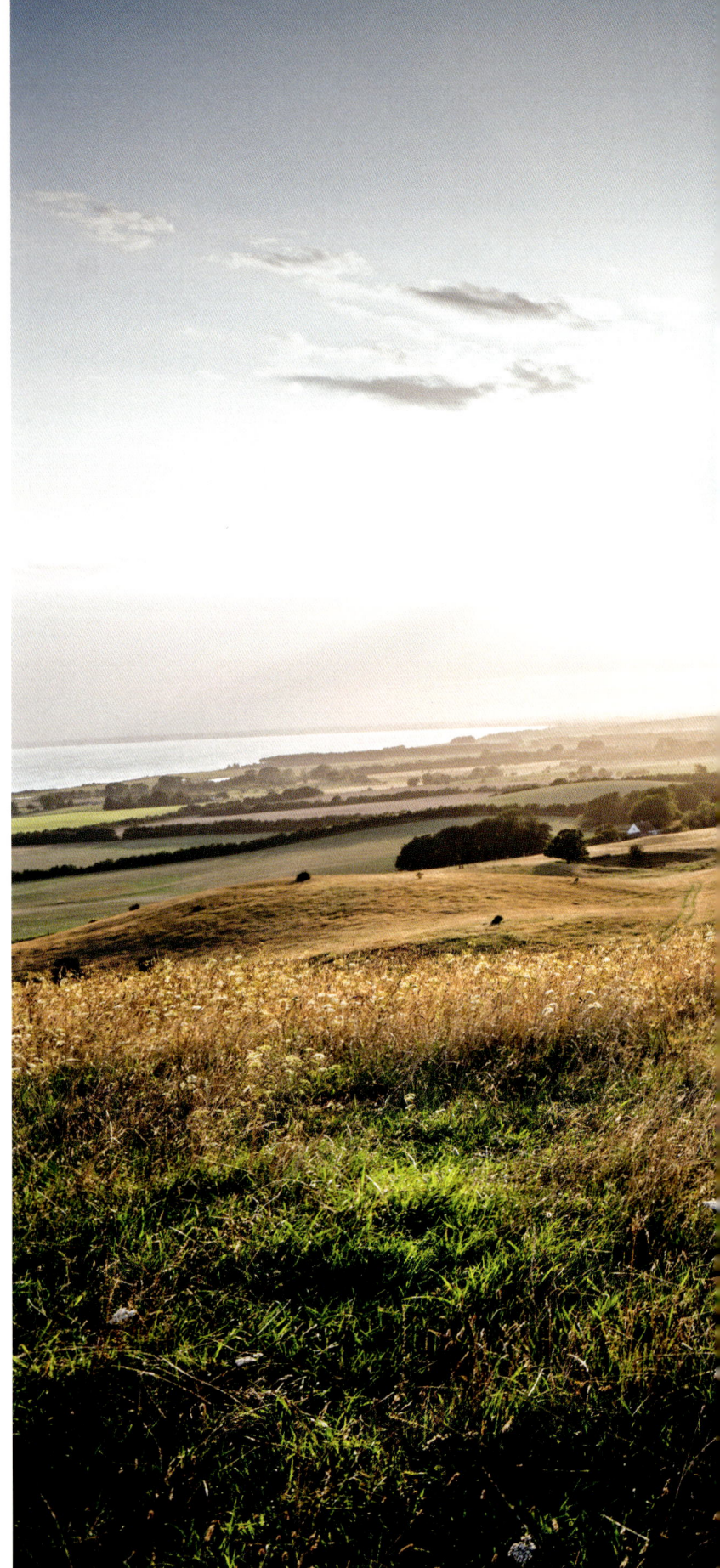

→ Grazing at golden hour.

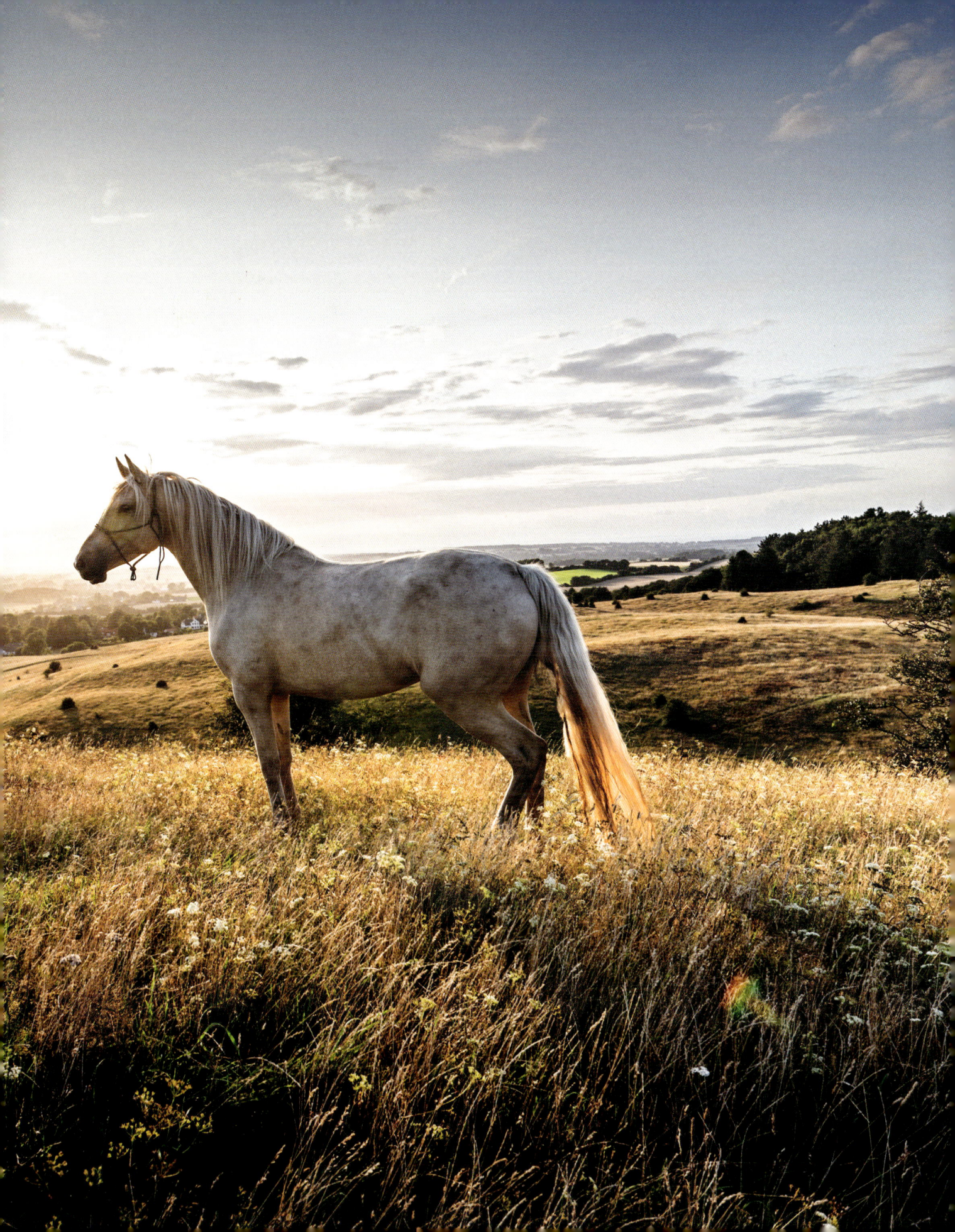

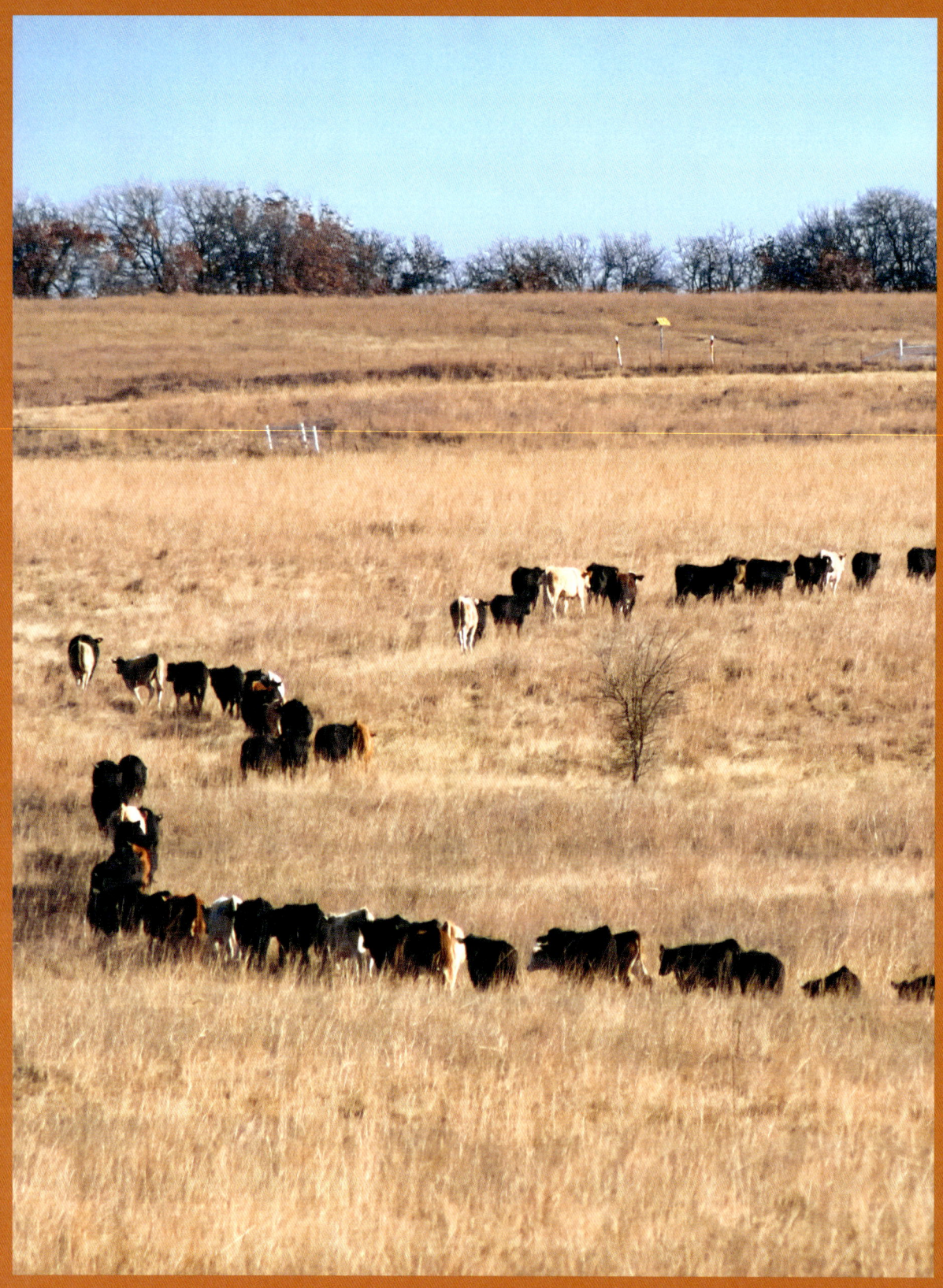

Whitney Hall
The Young Gun

Whitney Hall is young—but she has the oldest Western soul I have ever known. I write about her often—almost every time I write about cowgirls. Her dad, Shannon Hall, is one of the greatest horse trainers of his generation—maybe even of all time. Great horsemanship is in Whitney's blood, to say the least.

Hall is an accomplished horsewoman, winning nearly $300,000 in the cutting horse pen alone, not including her accolades in the ranch rodeo space. She is a member of "Team Espuela," which has won multiple Art of the Cowgirl All-Girls Ranch Rodeo championships. And in 2022, Hall won the title of World's Greatest Horsewoman.

What really makes Whitney special, though, is her heart. When the Smokehouse Creek wildfire ripped through west Texas, claiming countless livestock and burning more than one million acres (four hundred thousand hectares) of land, Hall encountered an older gentleman who couldn't save his calves, and she jumped into action to help. She contacted friends, who showed up with trucks and trailers to house about half the calves. The other half went home with her.

Whitney and her mother shared photos of the injured calves on social media. They received an outpouring of support and donations from friends and got to work trying to save the calves' lives. They covered their eyes, which were damaged from smoke. They salved and wrapped their burned hooves and legs. They bottle fed them and kept them warm. They didn't lose a single calf. I can't think of anything more tangible—more central to Western culture—than Whitney's display of cowgirl spirit.

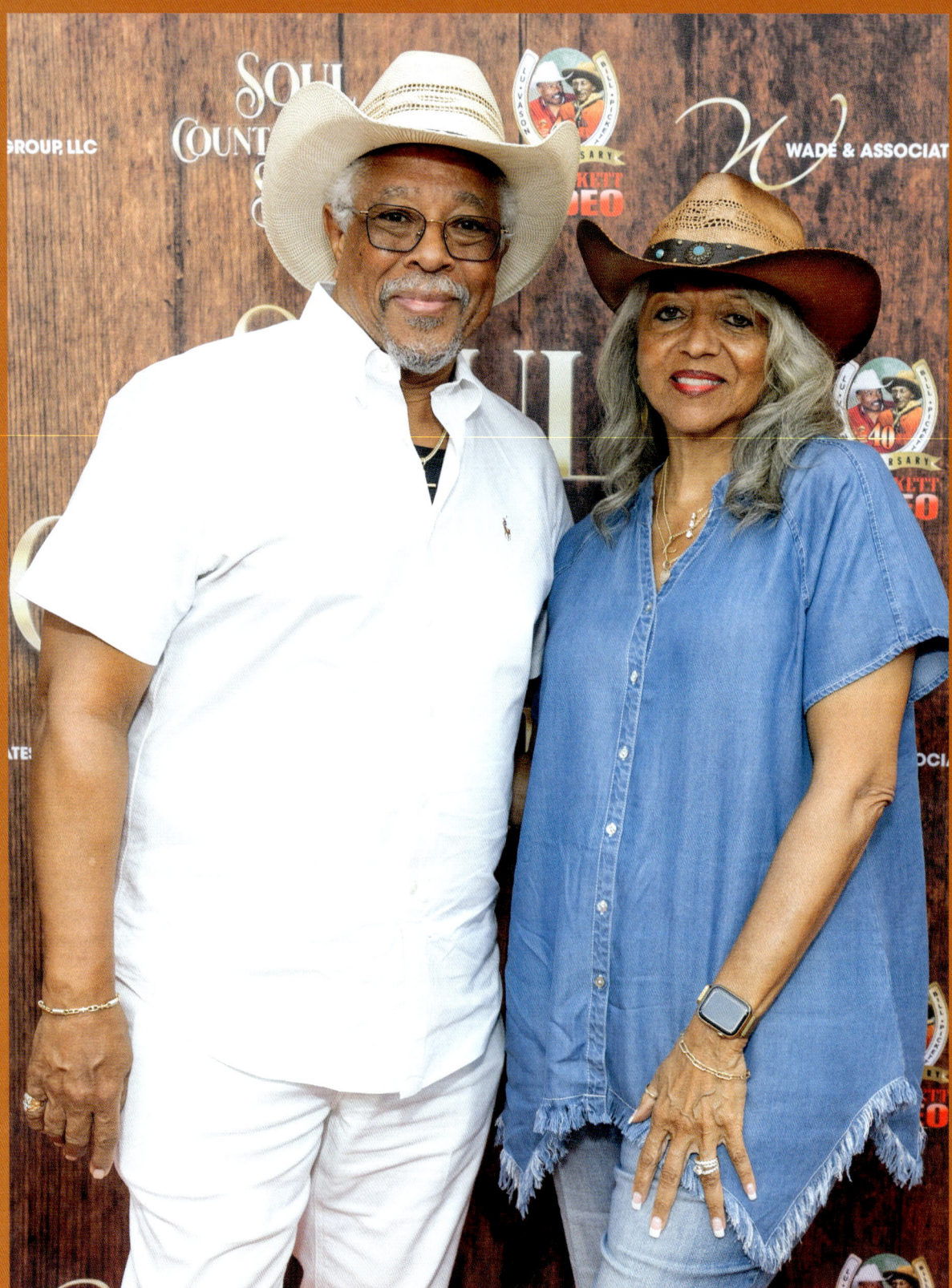

Valeria Howard-Cunningham
The Rodeo Entrepreneur

← Valeria Howard-Cunningham (right) at the 2025 Soul Country Music Star Regional Finals at the Autry Museum of the Ameican West in Los Angeles, California.

Valeria Howard-Cunningham is the President and Producer of the Bill Pickett Invitational Rodeo (BPIR), the longest-running Black touring rodeo in the United States. She took the reins of the BPIR from her husband, rodeo founder Lu Vason, when he passed away in 2015. Vason started the Bill Pickett rodeo in 1984 to celebrate and preserve Black cowboy culture. He wanted to create a space where passionate performers, vendors, and fans could come together to learn about the history of Black cowboys and cowgirls and carry that legacy forward into the future. Howard-Cunningham has been an exceptional steward of Vason's vision—in her decade-plus at the helm of the organization, she has produced sold-out rodeos in more than twenty cities throughout the country, partnered with the Professional Bull Riders (PBR) to make BPIR the first all-Black rodeo to be aired on national television, and launched a series of grants and workshops to help BPIR participants grow their rodeo careers.

While she's never competed in the rodeo herself, Howard-Cunningham has empowered countless young men and women to pursue their Western dreams. Her commitment to holding the door open for others is an example of cowgirl generosity in action.

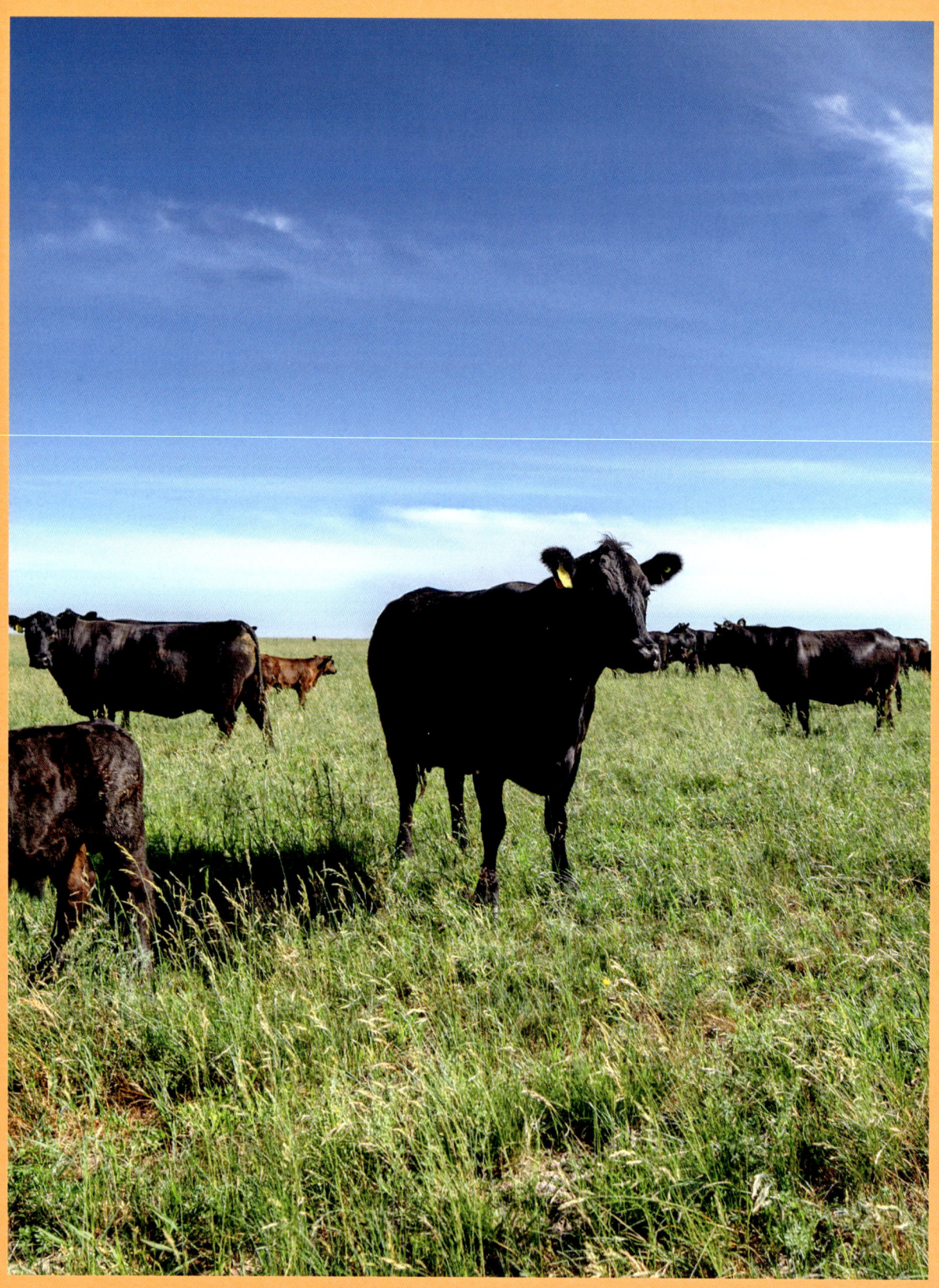

"Little Anne" Marion

The Daughter of Ranching

In addition to their performance horses, Four Sixes Ranch is known for their Black Angus cattle.

Anne Marion, "Little Anne," was born an American heiress and in line to inherit one of the largest ranches in the country. She could have easily rested on her birth-given laurels but instead chose to dive head first into the family business and learn everything there was to know about owning and running a ranching and equine business. Anne was born in Fort Worth, Texas, in 1938, to a stockbroker, and a horsewoman who was the granddaughter of Four Sixes Ranch founder Samuel Burk Burnett. While Anne was raised in Fort Worth, Texas, she spent her summers in Guthrie, Texas, on the ranch.

Little Anne inherited the Four Sixes Ranch and took over as the president of Burnett Ranches. She then purchased three award-winning racehorses and kept 160 broodmares, or mares that were bred for their outstanding bloodlines and performance record, on the ranch. She is known for her outstanding innovation on the Four Sixes, diversifying their business from cattle alone to include performance horses, racehorses, and a legendary breeding operation.

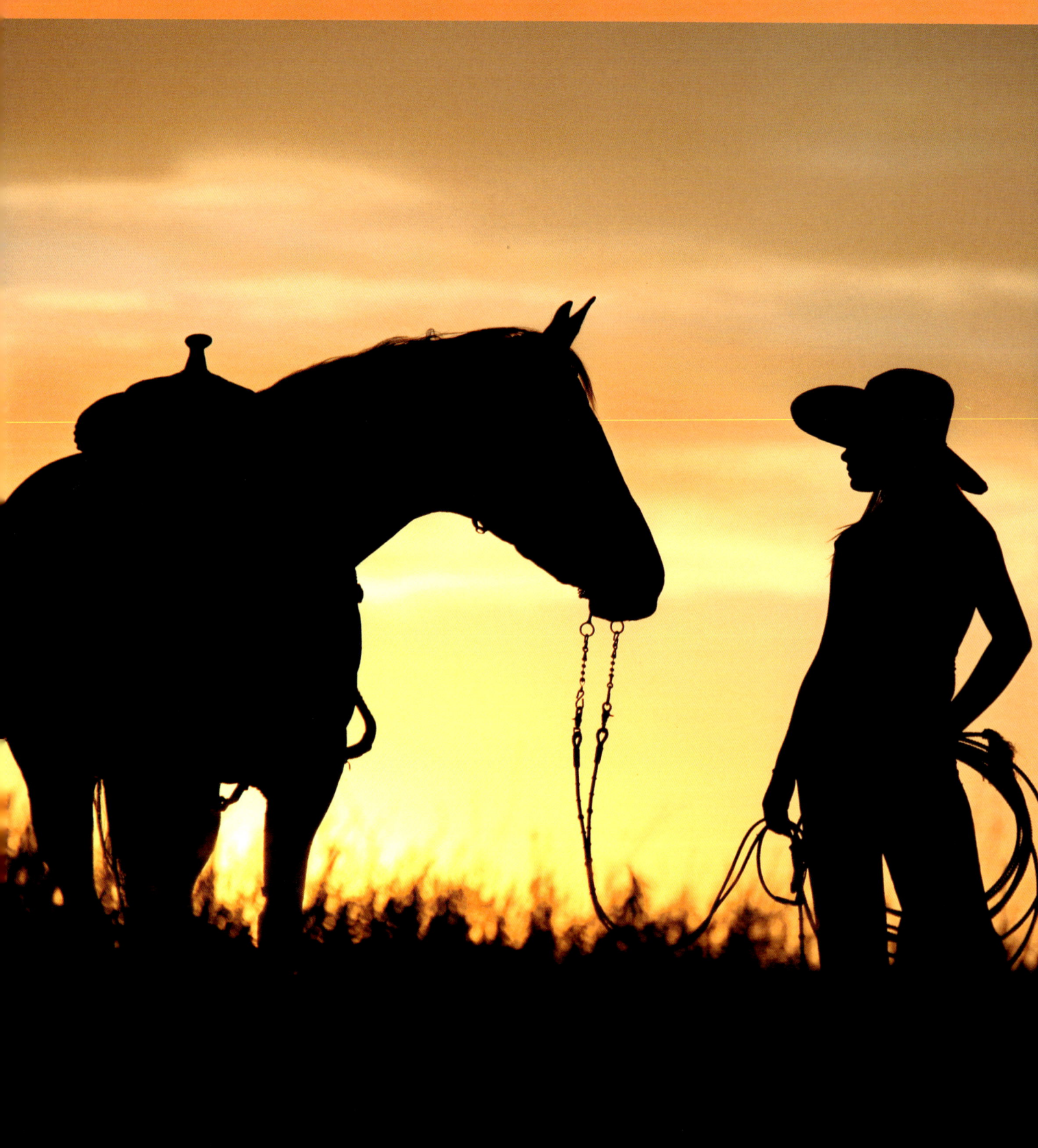

Little Anne received the National Golden Spur Award from the National Ranching Heritage Center in 2001 and was inducted into the National Cowgirl Hall of Fame in 2005, the American Quarter Horse Hall of Fame in 2007 and the Hall of Great Westerners at the National Cowboy & Western Heritage Museum in 2009. She died in February of 2020, but her legacy will live on in the hearts of cowgirls and changemakers forever.

← Cowgirl culture is about hard work and dedication, but it's also about freedom, joy, and celebrating life's small beautiful moments.

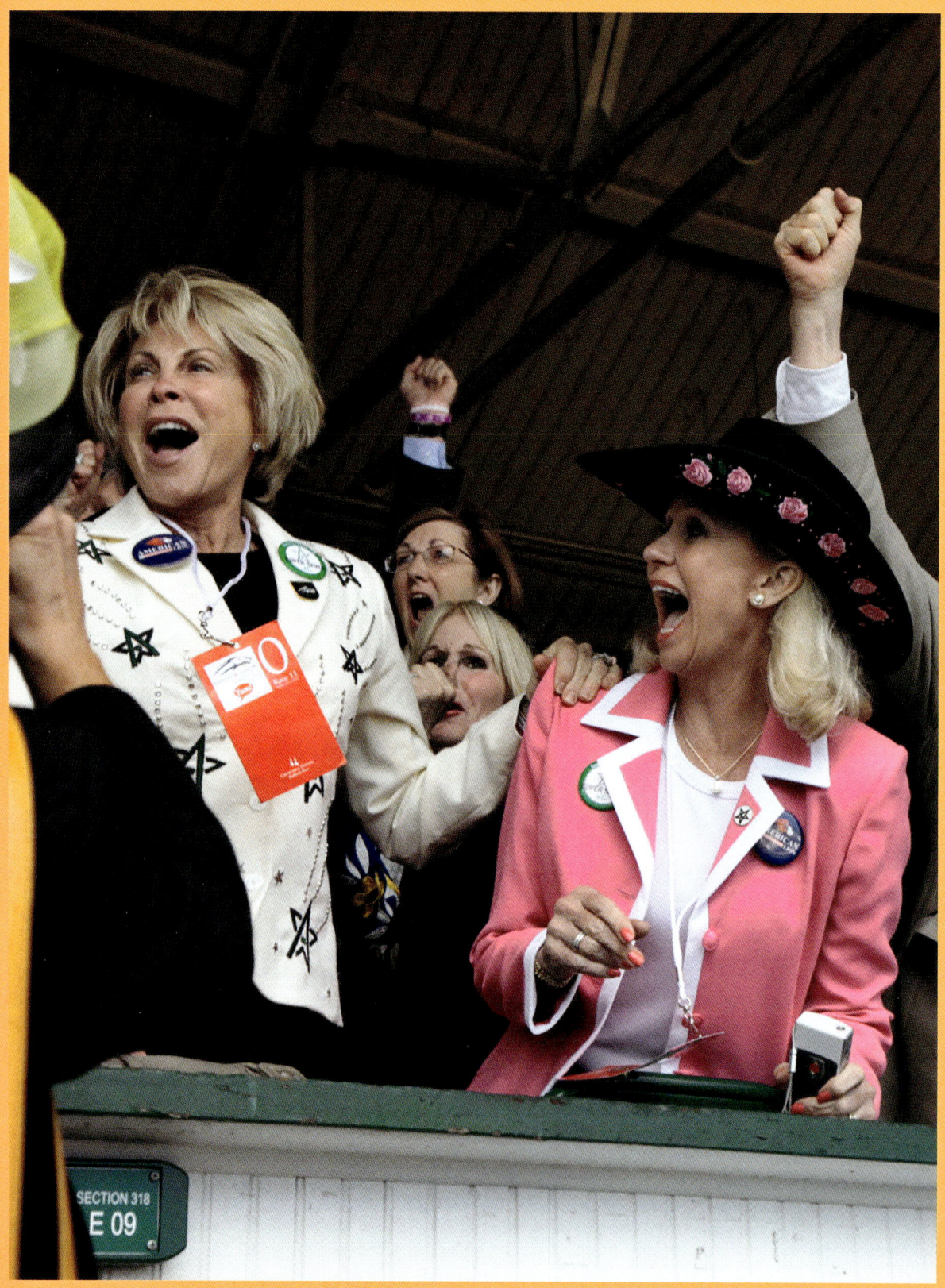

Pam Minick
The Rodeo Queen

Pam Minick (right) celebrates with Susan Casner (left) as Casner's horse Super Saver wins 2010 Kentucky Derby.

Pam Minick was raised in Las Vegas, Nevada, with her sister. The girls didn't own horses, but after they learned to ride at the local 4-H there was no turning back.

Minick went on to have an illustrious rodeo career. She won Miss Rodeo America in 1973. She was the WPRA Champion Breakaway Roper in 1982. She qualified for the Women's National Finals Rodeo eleven times. Pam also served as the WPRA president and her role in television and movies only increased the popularity of the sport. But Minick's biggest contribution to the sport of rodeo has been raising awareness through her commanding media presence.

She has hosted or commentated on more than one thousand rodeos, events, and country music programs. Her name in the rodeo community is known by all—she is the ultimate ambassador for the sport. Her accolades include the 1992 Coca-Cola Woman of the Year Award, the 1994 Lane Frost Award, the 1998 Tad Lucas Award for the National Cowboy & Western Heritage Museum, the 2006 Great Woman of Texas Award, and the 2016 *Western Horseman* Women of the West Award. She has also been inducted into the National Cowgirl Hall of Fame, the Texas Cowboy Hall of Fame, the Texas Trail of Fame, the Texas Rodeo Cowboy Hall of Fame, and the National Multicultural Western Heritage Museum and Hall of Fame.

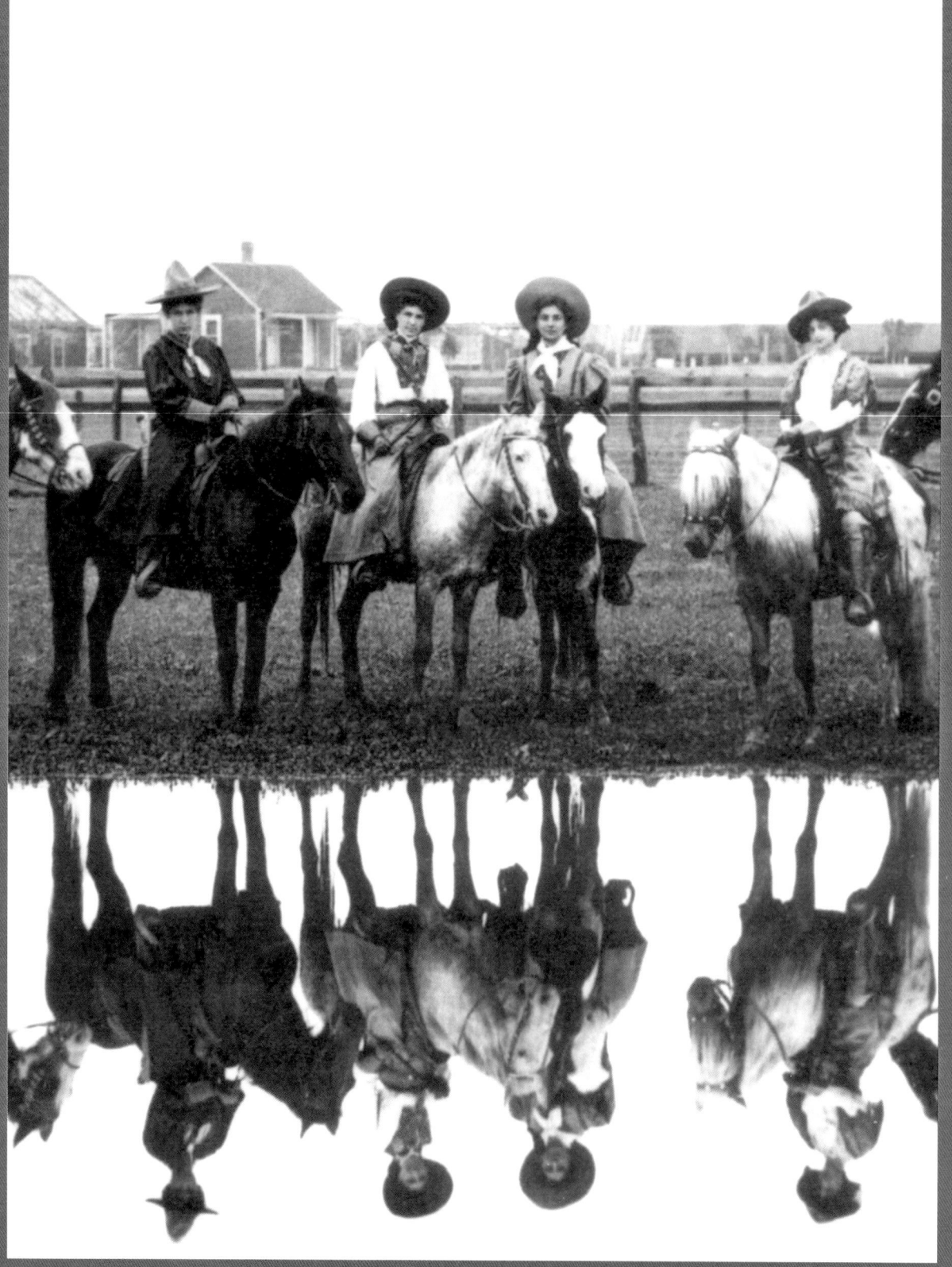

Jimmie Munroe
The Equal Pay Activist

← A line-up of cowgirls at the Miller Brothers' 101 Ranch, circa 1900.

Jimmie Munroe was born with a love of rodeo pulsing through her veins. Her grandfather, one of the Miller Brothers who established the iconic 101 Ranch Wild West Show, passed his talent for roping and riding on to Jimmie.

Munroe won the 1975 National Intercollegiate Rodeo Association All-Around, as well as the Women's Professional Rodeo Association All-Around, the Tie-Down Roping, and the Barrel Racing championships that same year. She dedicated her life to the sport of rodeo, serving as the WPRA president for fourteen years. During her tenure, she campaigned fiercely to increase the prize money for women's rodeo competitions to equal the men's prize payouts.

In 1992, Munroe was inducted into the National Cowgirl Hall of Fame for her contributions to women's rodeo, and in 1996, was awarded the Tad Lucas Award from the National Cowboy & Western Heritage Museum—an award reserved for women who have exhibited extraordinary characteristics while promoting and upholding the Western industry. She was also inducted into the Texas Rodeo Cowboy Hall of Fame in 1997, Texas Cowboy Hall of Fame in 2003, and the ProRodeo Hall of Fame in 2019.

Munroe's legacy will carry on in the sport of women's rodeo and in her daughter, Tassie, who brings Munroe's tenacity to everything she does.

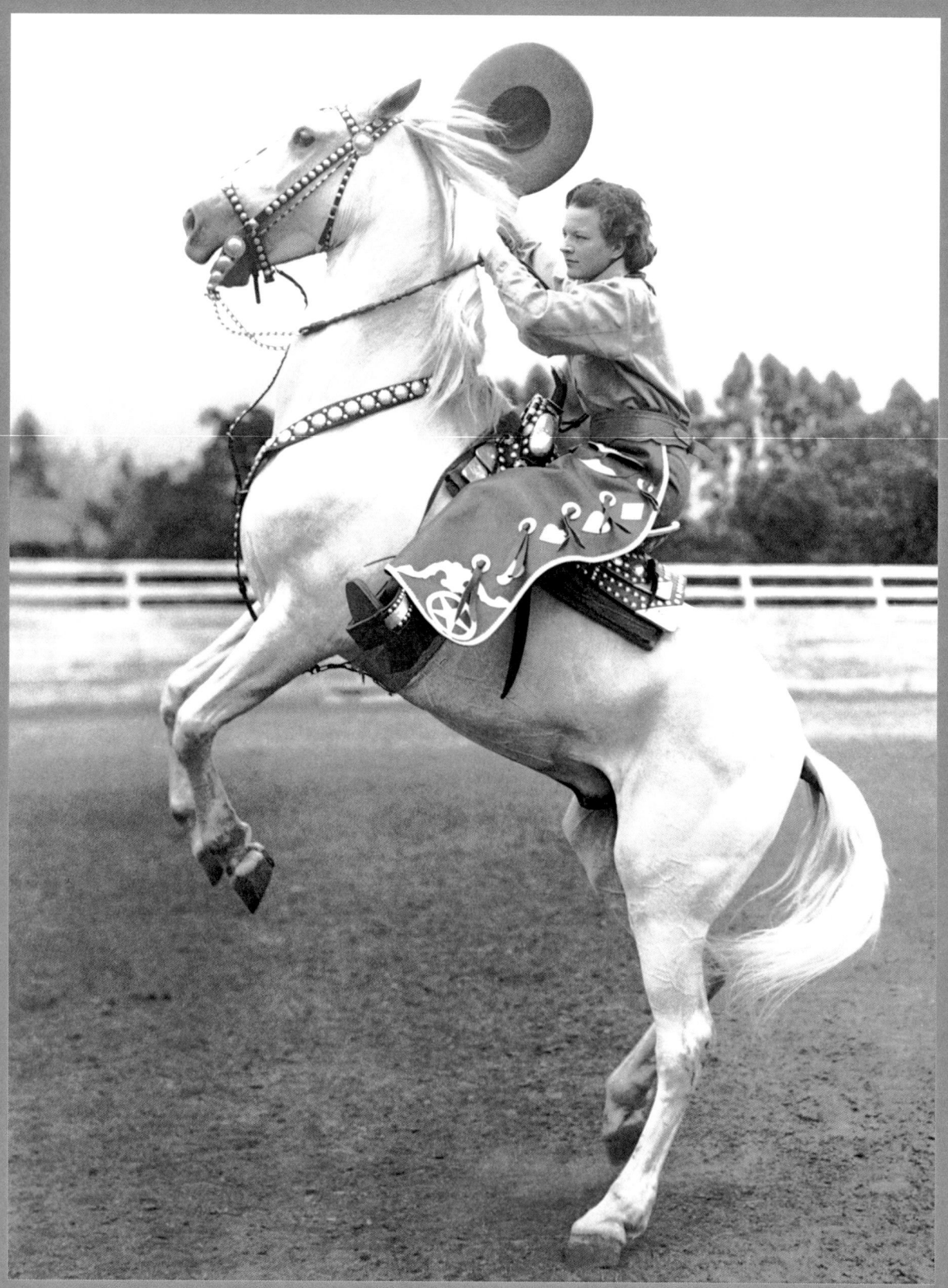

Everybody Wants to Be a Cowgirl

A cowgirl from Santa Barbara practices for the California Rodeo in Salinas in 1934.

The women I've covered thus far are just a glimpse into the kind of person it takes to be called "cowgirl," but so many others are worthy of the title—whether their impact is industry-wide or just on their own family and friends. These women make it easy to celebrate cowgirl culture.

We talk a lot about the Western way of life, or the way of the cowgirl, being an aspirational way to live. In reality, though, the lifestyle is not glamorous. It's relentless hours, unforgiving conditions, and countless setbacks. The work is hard, unpredictable, and physical. Vacations are mostly non-existent, because livestock and land never sleep. But the freedom that comes with this life—the freedom of passion, of dreaming, of trailblazing—is immeasurable.

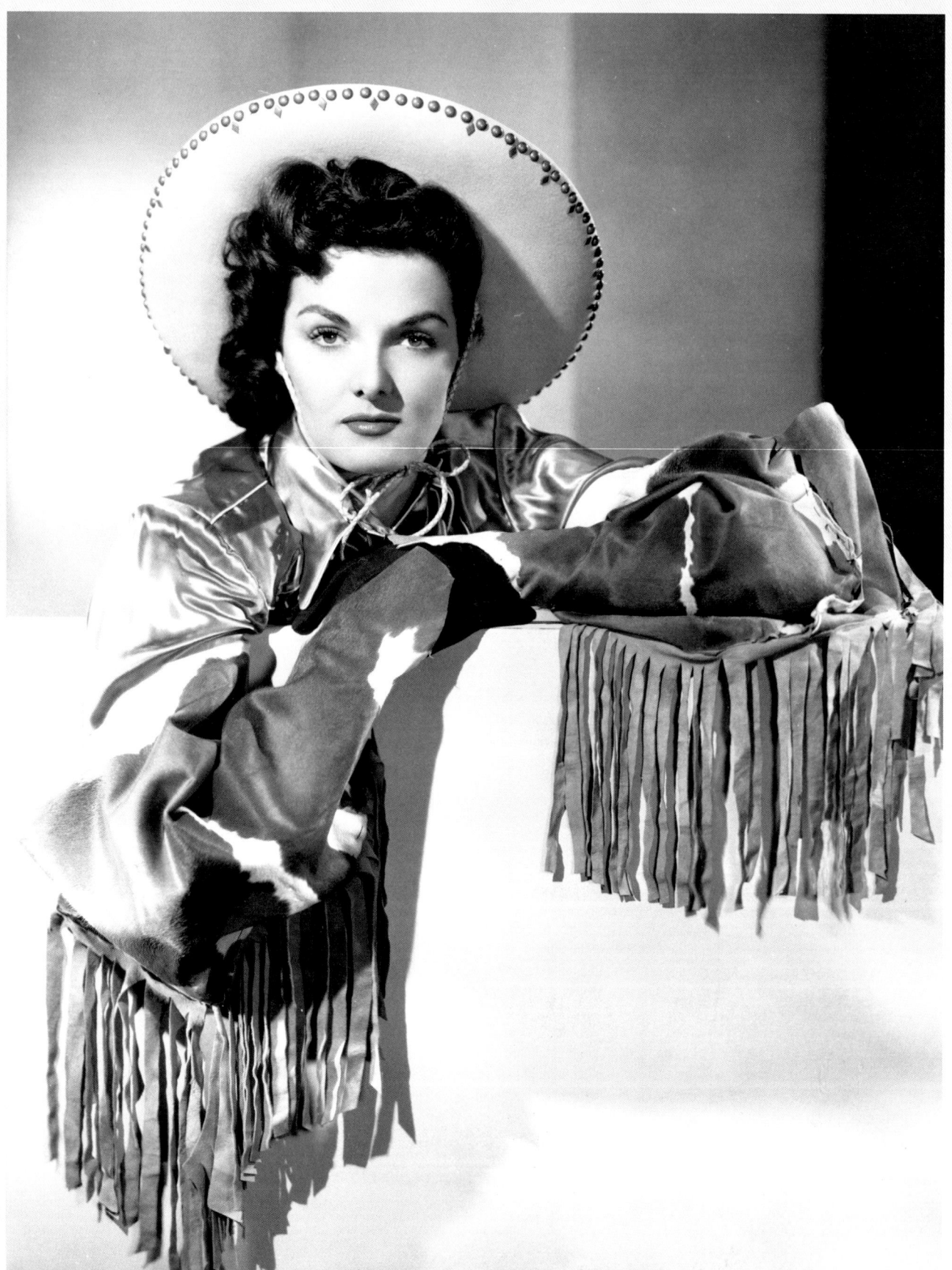

From Homestead to Household Name

There is controversy and tension in Western culture over the mainstream use of "cowboy" and "cowgirl." Some think the terms should be reserved for those embedded in the Western industry, while others believe that anyone can embody the cowgirl (or cowboy) spirit.

Despite the different ways of thinking, these groups share one common thread: If you're going to dress like us, talk like us, and call yourself a cowgirl, you had better be a good steward of the brand. There are a few mainstream cowgirls who have been just that, and thanks to them, cowgirl culture is as hot as ever. These iconic Western women aren't famous for their accomplishments on the ranch, but they represent cowgirl values in popular culture—in music, television, and film. And while these women may be "all hat, no cattle," their tenacious spirit and love of Western culture makes them worthy of the cowgirl title.

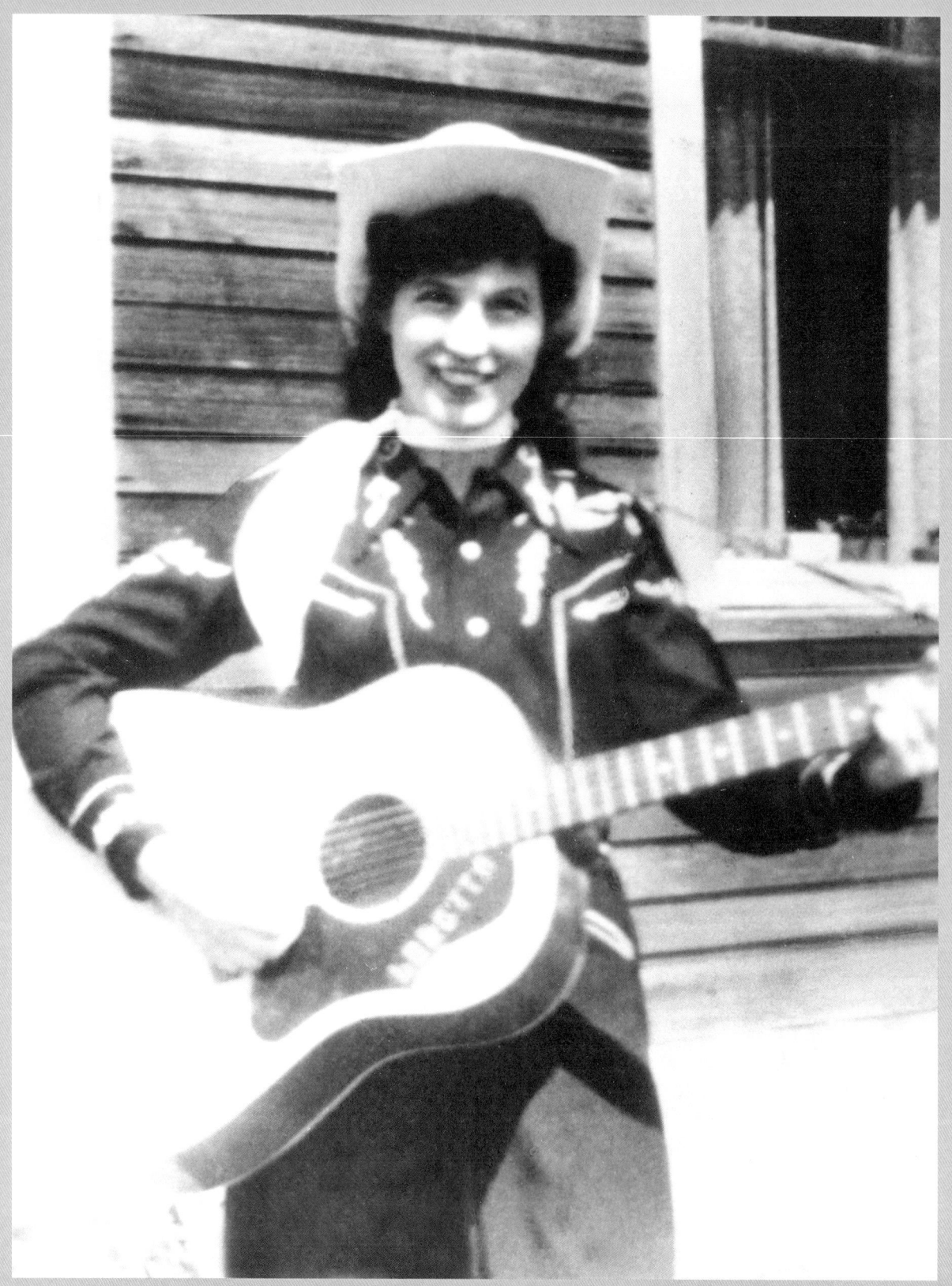

Country Goes Cowgirl

Loretta Lynn
with her acoustic
guitar, circa 1960.

There are a few women in country music who stand above the pack when it comes to their accomplishments and ability to push through the noise and trends, and stay true to themselves. Their passion and drive helped them to set records and turn heads doing it, and forced an entire industry to start taking women seriously—that's the recurring theme for the cowgirl.

It started with Loretta Lynn.

Loretta Lynn

Lynn married a rodeo cowboy and the pair hosted rodeos at their ranch in Tennessee. Lynn's music career was long and illustrious—she was known as the first "queen of country music." She was the first woman to be named Entertainer of the Year by the Country Music Association, besting the likes of Merle Haggard, Charley Pride, and other huge names in the industry. Her win cleared a trail for more passionate and talented women in country music to come after her and accomplish big things.

Lynn released her last album in 2021. For her entire career, she notably sported old-fashioned dresses adorned with lace or an old-school stitch pattern. Her prairie style and soothing vocals are reminiscent of a ranch woman—headstrong and hardworking, but soft and feminine by nature. While her contributions to country music blazed trails for young women coming behind her, many of them would choose to take their own, bold approach to the business.

Dolly Parton

Dolly Parton is one of the most beloved household names of all time. While her big blonde hair and bold style draw you in, you stay for her kind nature and incredible sense of humor—and her incredible songwriting. Parton leans into her image and uses it to her advantage. She never backs down from the things she wants to accomplish, but she faces every obstacle with such class and grace.

She began as a songwriter and found success in that part of the industry, but when she was ready to take to the stage herself, she did so in a bold way, with glittering outfits and a level of sex appeal that the country music industry had never really experienced before. She was hard to ignore, and that was the point. Parton went on to win numerous awards, including Entertainer of the Year for both the Country Music Association (CMA) and the Academy of Country Music (ACM) Awards.

Her personality was too big to be confined to radio, and she went on to be featured in movies, like the comedic film *9 to 5*, *The Best Little Whorehouse in Texas*, *Steel Magnolias*, and countless guest roles or surprise appearances in other television shows and movies. She also opened her own production company, which produces films, television shows, and musicals. She is a country music icon and carries the tenacious spirit of the cowgirl—bold and confident in all she does, but humble and kind beyond compare.

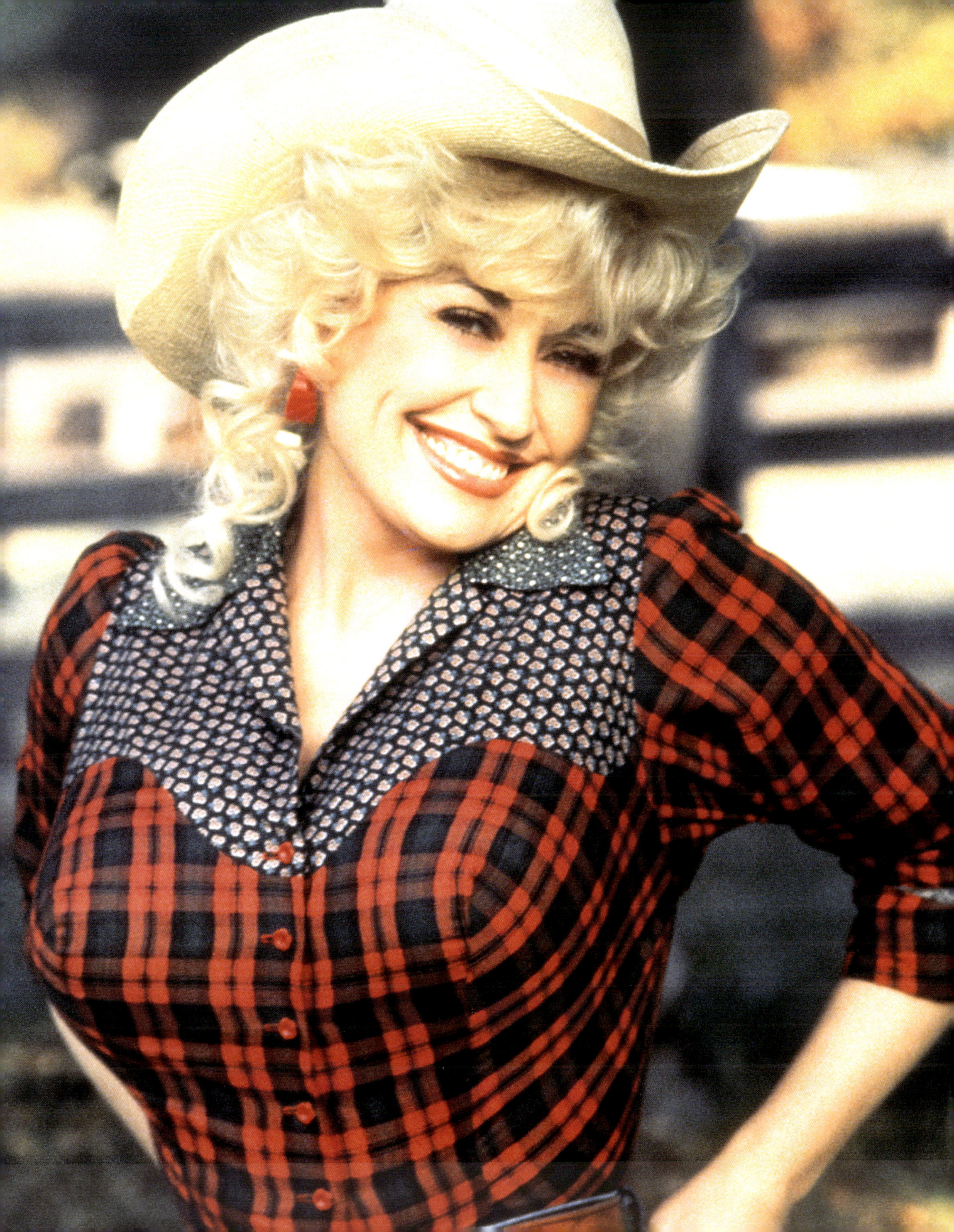

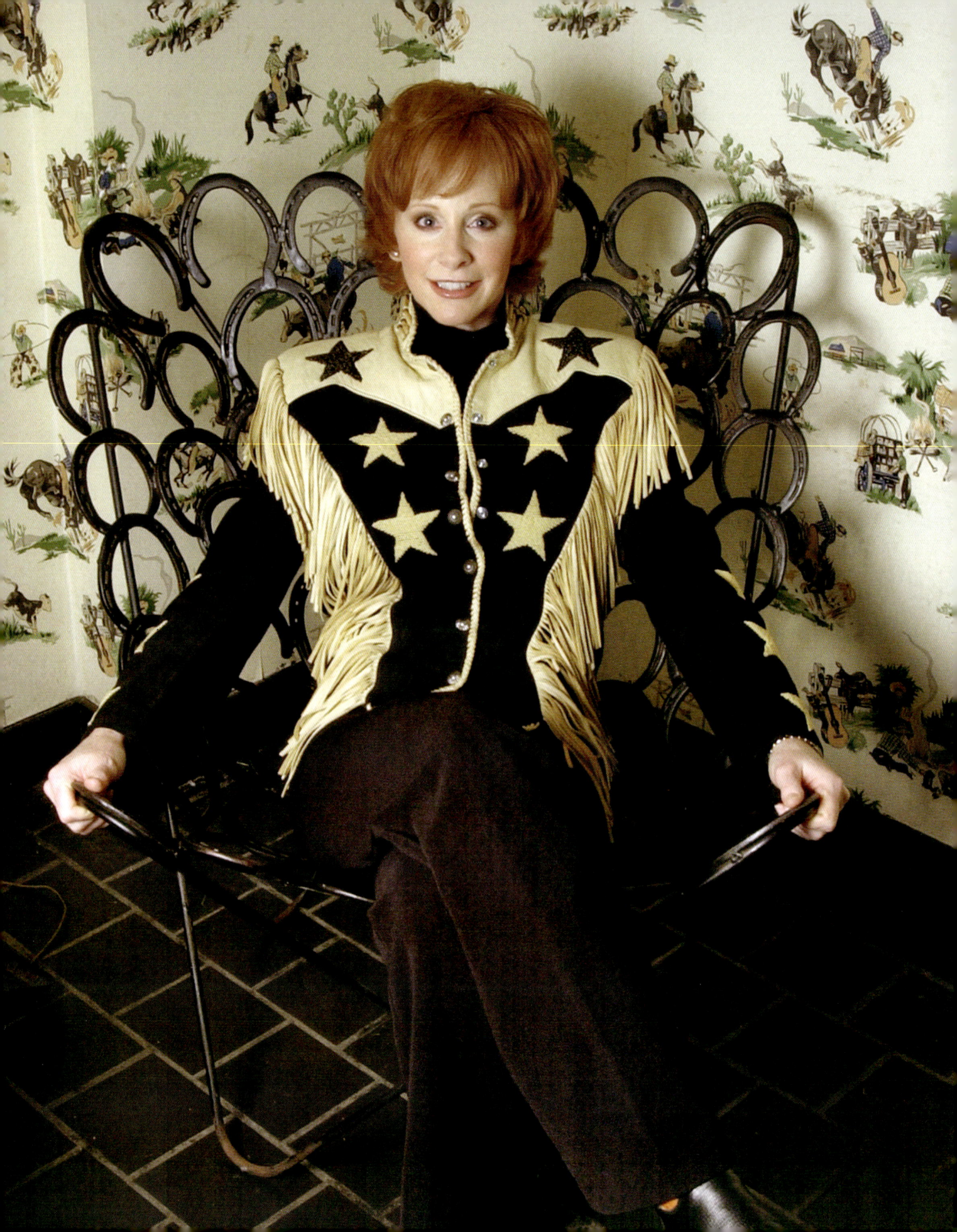

Reba McEntire

Singer-songwriter-actresses were having a moment in the '90s, especially when Reba McEntire came onto the scene. The country music icon—dubbed the new "queen of country,"—saw success like few women in country music had ever seen. McEntire was born to a world champion steer roper, and her family owned a cattle ranch. Every family member took turns helping with the cattle, but her passion for music developed at an early age. Her career, though illustrious and full of incredible achievement, often felt like it was out of her control. She spent decades at the mercy of record labels, until she fired her manager and formed her own entertainment company in the late 1980s. From that decision alone, McEntire was able to work on her own ventures and has seen immense success in the country music and television industries since then.

In 1991, eight members of McEntire's touring band were killed in an airplane crash in San Diego, California. Dolly Parton was among a small group of other country music artists who helped Reba rebuild her band so she could continue on her tour that year, seeing it through while nursing the devastating loss of her close friends and colleagues. She released the album, *For My Broken Heart*, and dedicated it to those deceased members of her band. It's her best-selling album to date. Her career continued to see incredible success and proved that when hard work backs talent, you can reach unfathomable milestones. In her fifties, McEntire became the oldest woman to ever have a No. 1 hit on country music charts.

She is often regarded as one of country music's most influential female singers and commended for staying true to her vocal style for more than four decades of work. Not to mention, she is known for being one of the most kind, humble, and likeable women in the entertainment industry. She has always had a little cowgirl in her from a young age, but even if she hadn't been someone who rode horses and worked a cattle ranch, her faith, tenacity, and drive to take her life into her own hands and be her own agent of change is cowgirl enough for me.

← Reba McEntire poses at the Cowgirl Hall of Fame, circa 2000.

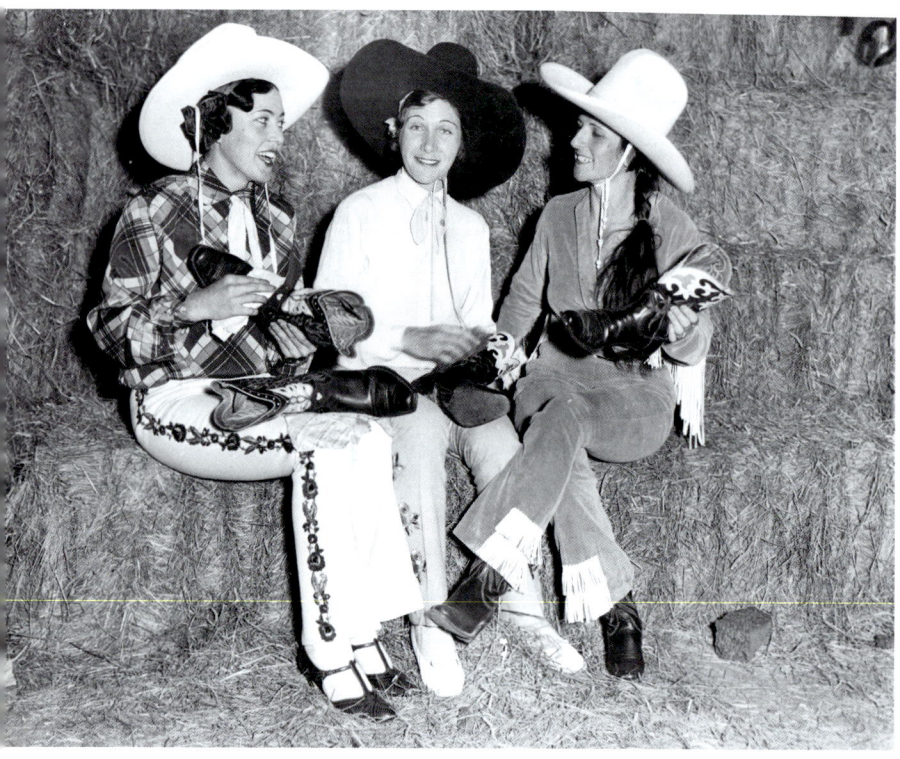

← American cowgirls Lucyle Roberts (1909-1995), Alice Greenough (1902-1995), and Reine Shelton (1902-1979) polishing their boots before a 1933 charity rodeo at Madison Square Garden in New York City.

→ A portrait of Linda Martell, circa 1969, in Nashville, Tennessee.

Linda Martell

Another influential country singer who has made her fair share of impact on future generations is Linda Martell. Born as Thelma Bynem in 1941, she became a pioneering woman in country music, becoming the first Black woman to perform in Grand Ole Opry. Her most iconic moment includes breaking the racial barriers in an industry typically dominated by white artists.

Although she began her music journey performing as Linda Martell and the Anglos in the gospel and R&B arenas, she transitioned to country music after being discovered singing at an Air Force base and her career has been mostly in the country industry. Her 1969 hit single, "Color Him Father," reached the Top 25 on *Billboard* country charts.

Even though she had an amazing talent, Martell faced many challenges, including racism and industry conflicts, which eventually led to her retiring from music in 1974. However, her contributions have continued to inspire generations of artists. She was honored with the CMT Equal Play Award in 2021. She broke many barriers in the country industry, embodying the bravery and determination of the cowgirl ethos.

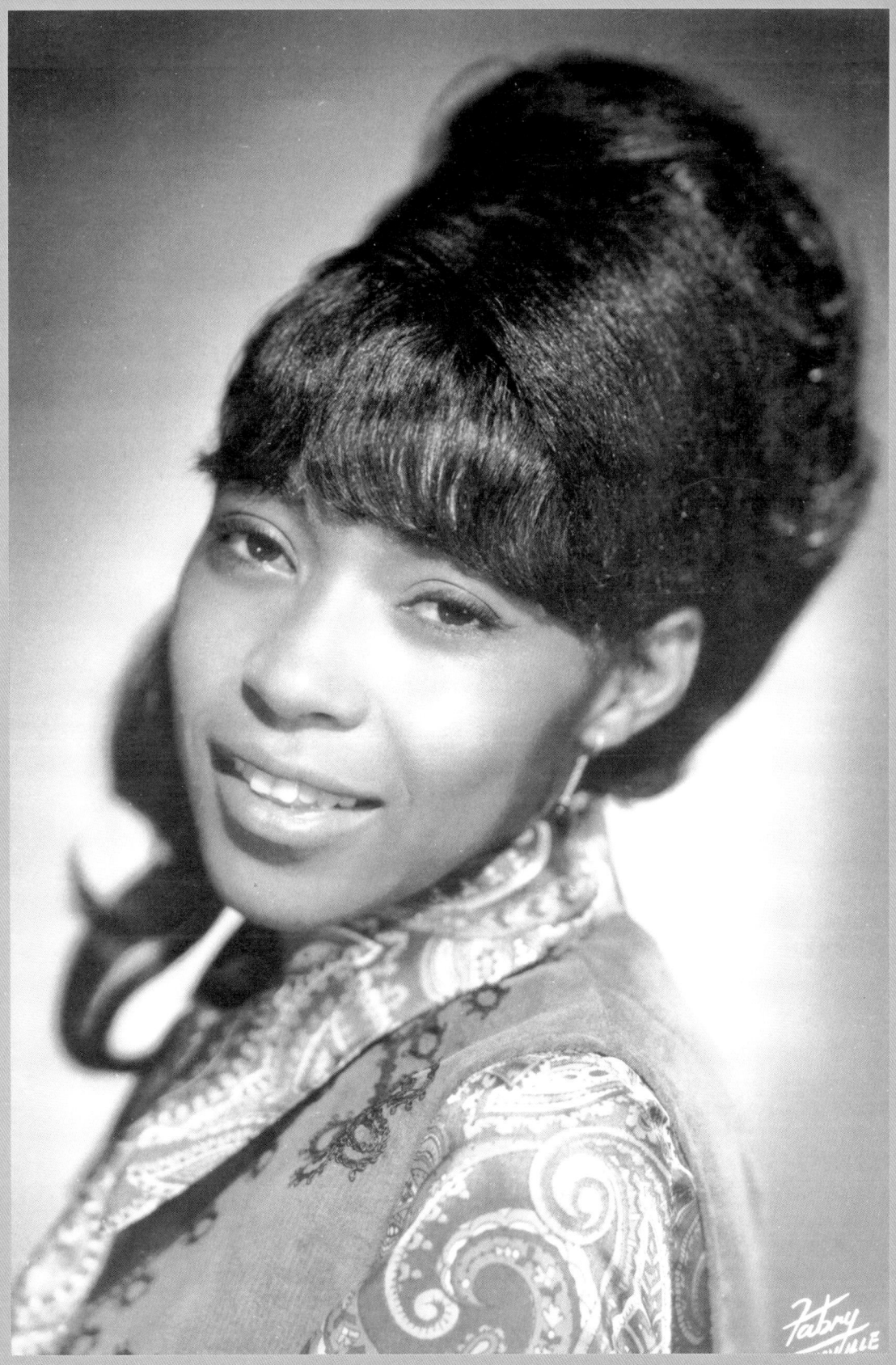

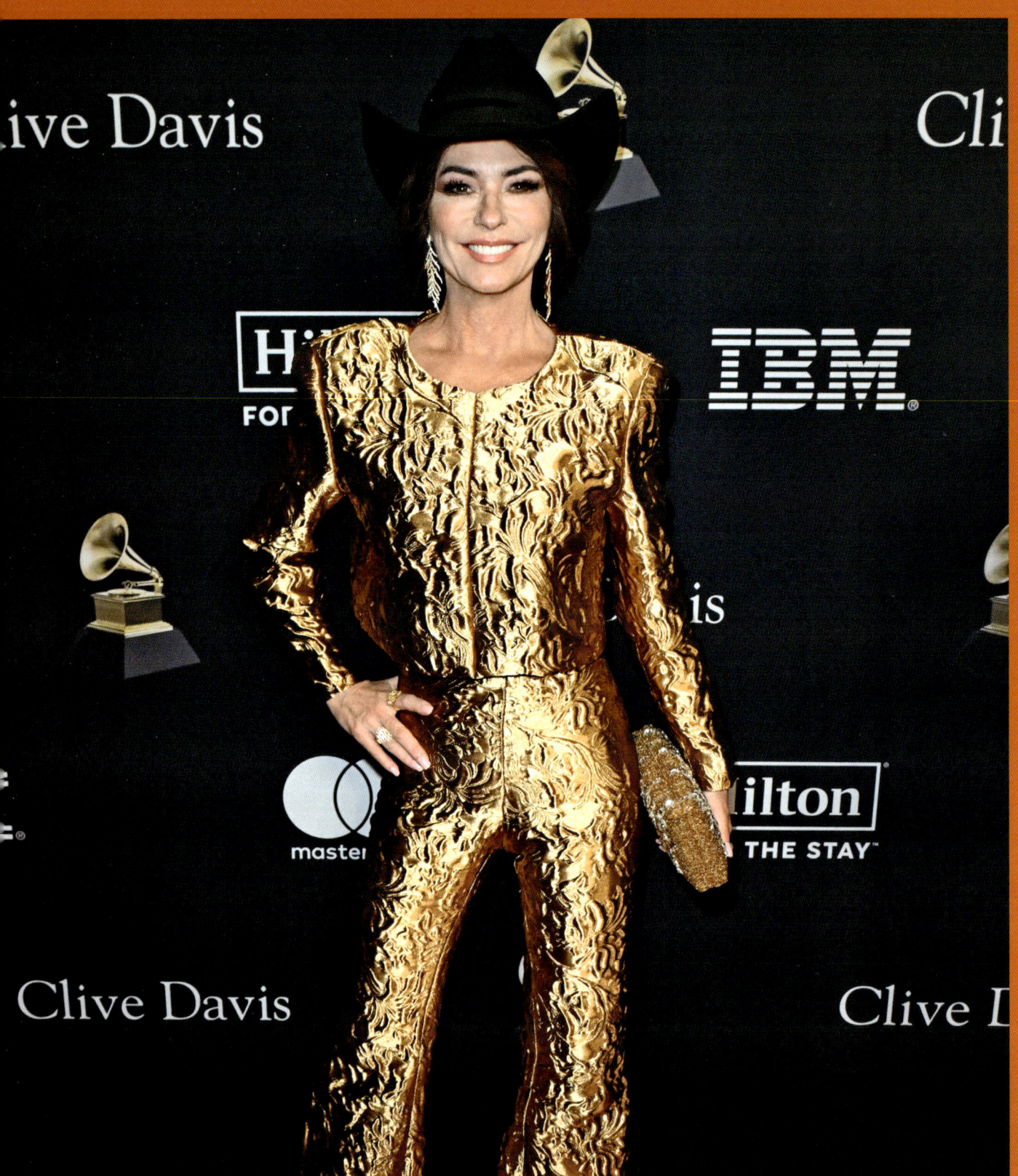

142

Shania Twain

Speaking of iconic artists who have overcome adversity, it'd be remiss not to mention fashion and country music icon, Shania Twain. She is the best-selling female country music artist in history, and she overcame enormous hurdles to get there. As a child, Twain was subjected to divorced parents and a volatile and often abusive relationship between her mother and stepfather. Additionally, her family experienced severe poverty, and she began singing in bars at the age of eight just to help put food on the table.

Twain persevered through her turbulent childhood and grew into an impressive young singer-songwriter. Through a series of events, she ended up in the presence of Mutt Lange, who had produced some of the biggest rock albums of all time. The pair began working together and fell in love. The album Mutt produced catapulted her to the top of music charts everywhere, both in pop and country.

If you were a '90s country music fan, you'd be hard-pressed to forget Twain's "That Don't Impress Me Much" music video, where she strutted in full cheetah print in the desert. She commanded the room in her "Man! I Feel Like A Woman!" video in a menswear-inspired top hat and black tuxedo coat, and sported classic Western in a denim-on-denim ensemble (also known as a Canadian tuxedo) for the "Any Man Of Mine" video.

In 2003, the artist contracted Lyme disease, which caused nerve damage to her vocal cords. Five years later, Twain very publicly separated from her husband after his affair with her best friend. She was out of the spotlight for nearly ten years, returning to the stage in 2012. She released her sixth studio album in 2023 and has had a resurgence of iconic and whimsical fashion moments over recent years, reestablishing herself as the pop country diva of this generation.

It's not Twain's tie to horses and cattle that makes her an ambassador for the term "cowgirl," or even her tie to country music. It's the manner in which she overcame the obstacles she faced, and she became stronger for having faced them. She could have easily retired when she fell ill, having already accomplished something so special, but she worked to continue to pursue her dreams. All the while, she made bold choices that felt right to her rather than conforming to the status quo. That's the spirit of the cowgirl.

← Shania Twain at the Recording Academy and Clive Davis's Salute to Industry Icons Gala before the 2024 Grammy Awards in Beverly Hills, California.

Beyoncé Knowles Carter

In 2022, Beyoncé was photographed for the cover of *British Vogue* on the back of a horse. The following year, the singer set out on her Renaissance World Tour, where she closed the concert by riding onto the stage atop a disco horse, aptly named "Reneigh," to sing her hit "Summer Renaissance."

But this was not Bey's first flirtation with country Western music and aesthetics. The song "Daddy Lessons," from 2016's *Lemonade*, opens with a bluesy horns section and a spirited "yee-haw." Beyoncé later released a version of the song that features the beloved country music trio The Chicks.

In March 2024, Beyoncé went from disco cowgirl to full-on Western when she announced the release of her new album, *Cowboy Carter*, and its first single, "Texas Hold 'Em." The album went on to win Album of the Year and Best Country Album at the 2025 Grammy Awards, making Beyoncé the first Black woman to ever win in the Best Country Album category—and the first Black woman to win Album of the Year since Lauryn Hill in 1999. Her tour for the album was the highest grossing country music tour of all time.

As an artist, Beyoncé is innovative and authentic at the same time. Like any good cowgirl, she pushes the envelope while always remaining true to herself.

Mickey Guyton

I cannot finish this section without talking about Mickey Guyton. Born in 1983 in Arlington, Texas, she was the second oldest of four children. Her family was consistently moving within Texas due to her father's engineering career. While it exposed her to many diverse environments in the area, it also exposed her to some experiences with racial discrimination. She is most famously known for her powerhouse of a voice and deep lyrics. She began her career by moving to Nashville in 2011 and signing with Capitol Records Nashville.

Her introduction to the country industry began with her critically acclaimed debut single, "Better Than You Left Me," which released in 2015. Her heartfelt song reached the Top 40 on the *Billboard* Country Airplay chart. However, that doesn't compare to the success of her 2020 single "Black Like Me," which addressed racial inequality and marked a pivotal moment in her career.

The single earned her a Grammy nomination. She also became the first Black woman to cohost the Academy of Country Music Awards and continues to be a staple in the country arena. Her music reflects the resilience and independence of the cowgirl spirit.

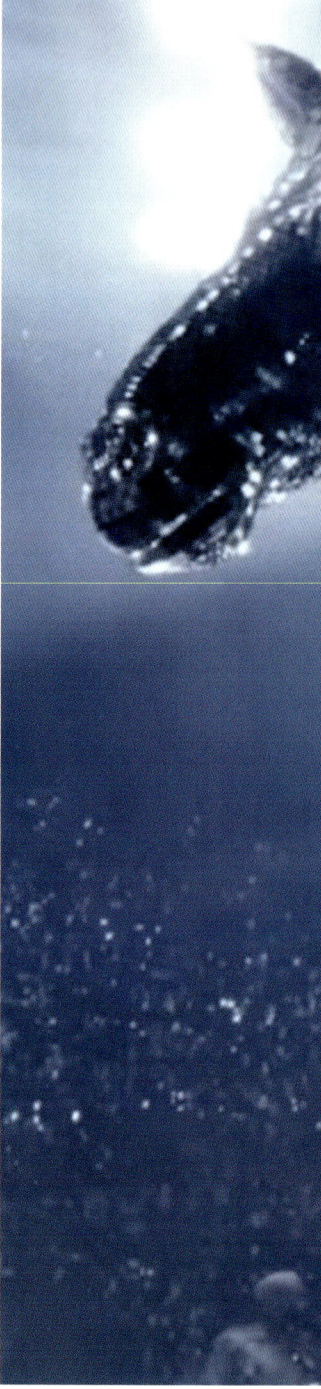

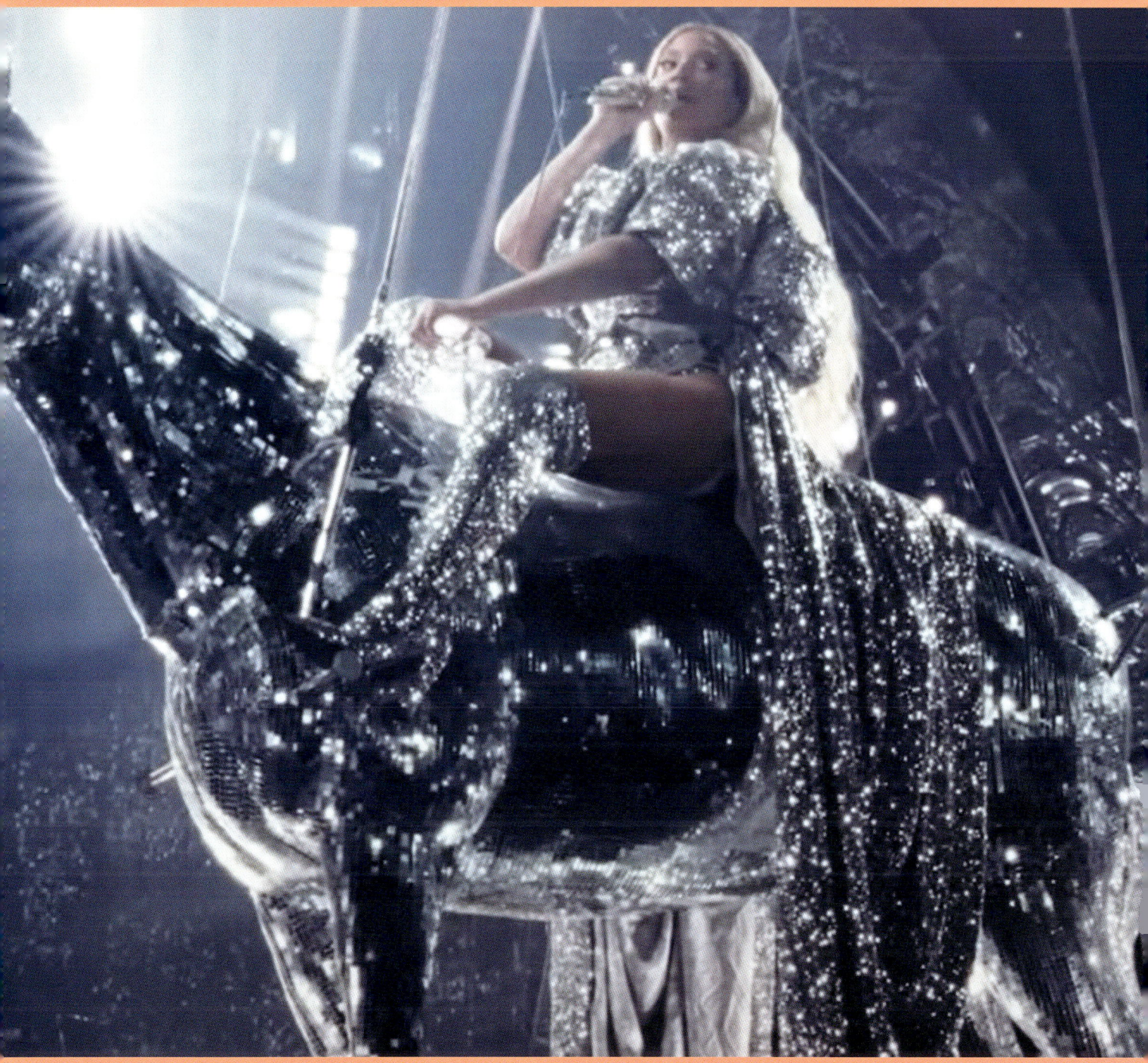

↑ Beyoncé on stage astride Reneigh in
Renaissance: A Film by Beyoncé.

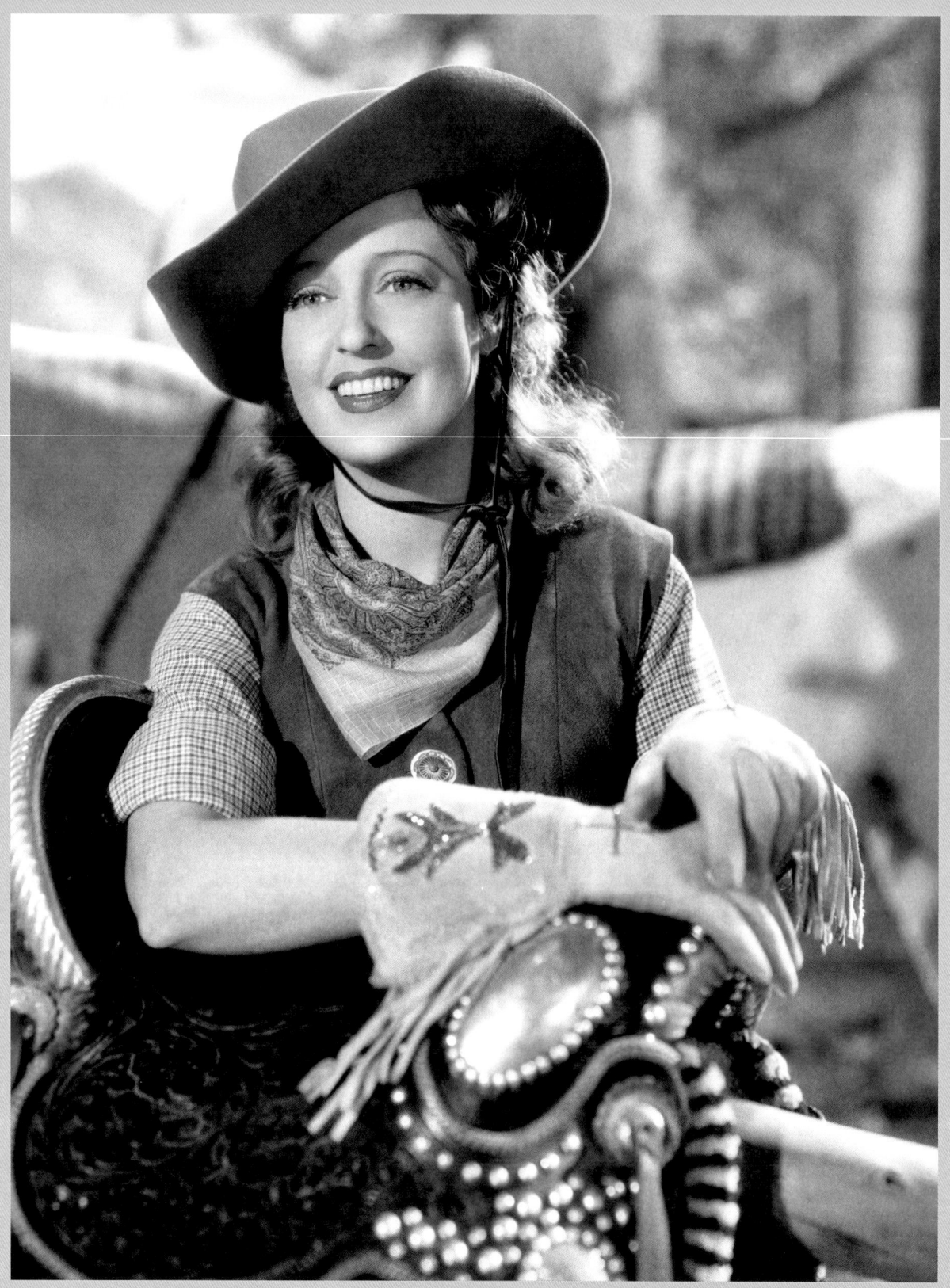

It's Cool to Be Cowgirl

Jeanette MacDonald (1903-1965) in a publicity portrait for the 1938 film *The Girl of the Golden West*.

The country music industry is not the only place cowgirls made their mark on pop culture. Portrayals of cowgirls on television and movie screens have allowed the young girls at home to find the same inspiration as the boys did with John Wayne, Roy Rogers, and Val Kilmer. (If you don't know where Val Kilmer ties into all of this, your movie library is lacking an important cultural gem!) Hailee Steinfeld played Mattie Ross in the remake of the Western classic *True Grit*; Kerry Washington played Broomhilda, an enslaved woman who showed incredible bravery and resilience in the modern Western *Django Unchained*; and Cate Blanchett played Maggie Gilkeson in *The Missing*; and those are just a few of the major actresses who have brought the spirit of the cowgirl to life on the silver screen.

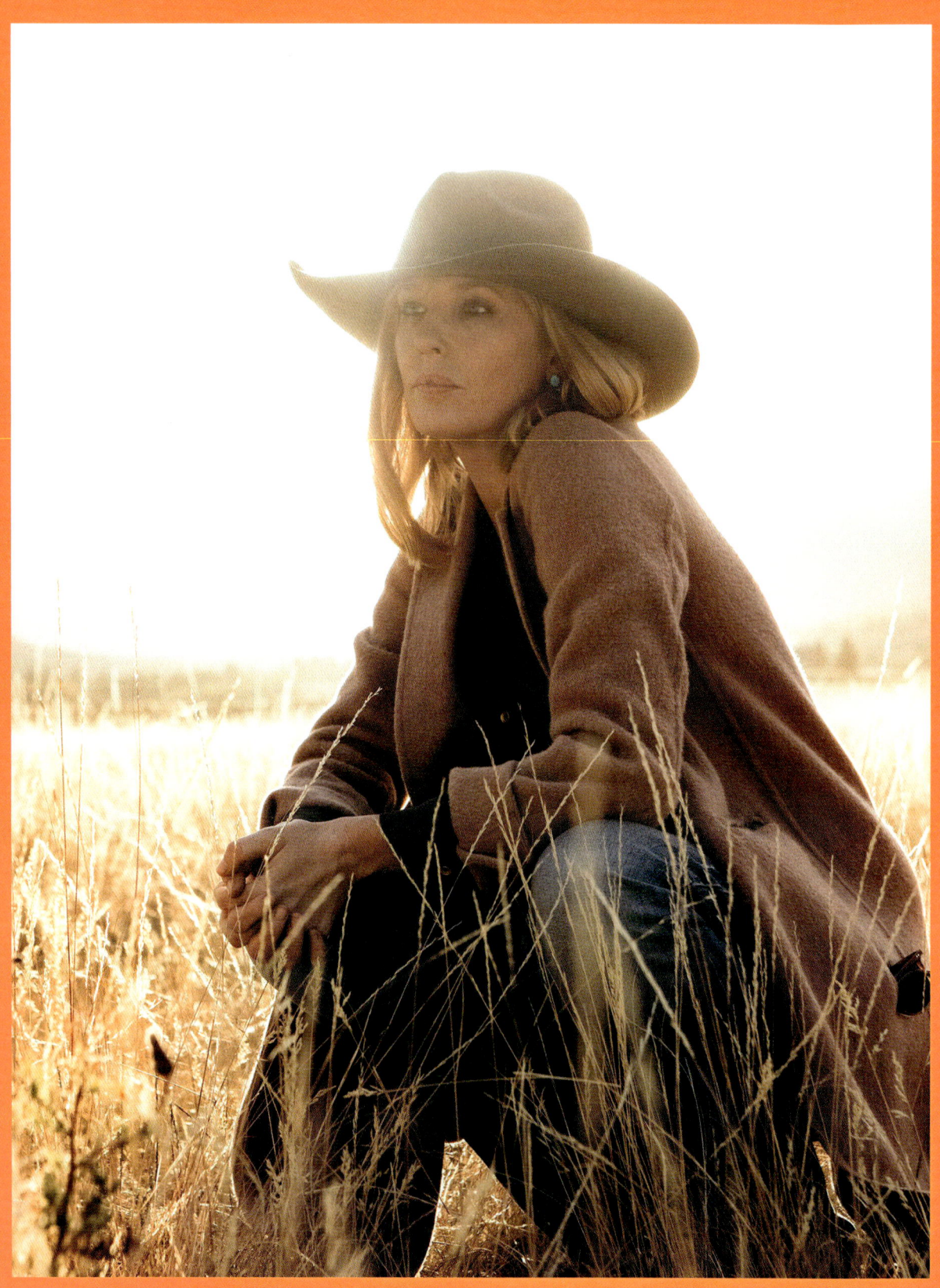

The Yellowstone Effect

Taylor Sheridan's *Yellowstone* is one of the most widely adopted and fawned-over pieces of Western media in existence. The creator has effectively immersed himself and his actors in the culture, allowing them to depict Western life in an accurate way.

Characters like Beth Dutton and Rip Wheeler captivate audiences with their compelling story arcs and strong personalities. And in real life, many of the cast, guest stars, and crew of the popular series—such as Jake Ream, Kory Pounds, and Ethan Lee—actually make a full-time living on ranches or doing some sort of Western work. This component of authenticity is part of why viewers all over the world are so infatuated with the series and its subsequent spinoffs, *1883* and *1923*. Many scenes were shot on real working ranches, like the Four Sixes Ranch in Guthrie, Texas, and Bosque Ranch, (formerly Silverado on the Brazos,) in Weatherford, Texas, both of which Sheridan now partially owns. Other scenes were shot at Will Rogers Coliseum, and in the historic Fort Worth Stockyards in Fort Worth, Texas, also known as "Cowtown" for its historic roots as a pinnacle cattle market. These Western settings, away from the stages of Hollywood, have made a difference in the impact the show has had on viewers.

While the series itself has come to a messy end with its lead actor making a very public exit, the craze it created is going strong and shows no signs of slowing down. The show is changing Western culture as we know it.

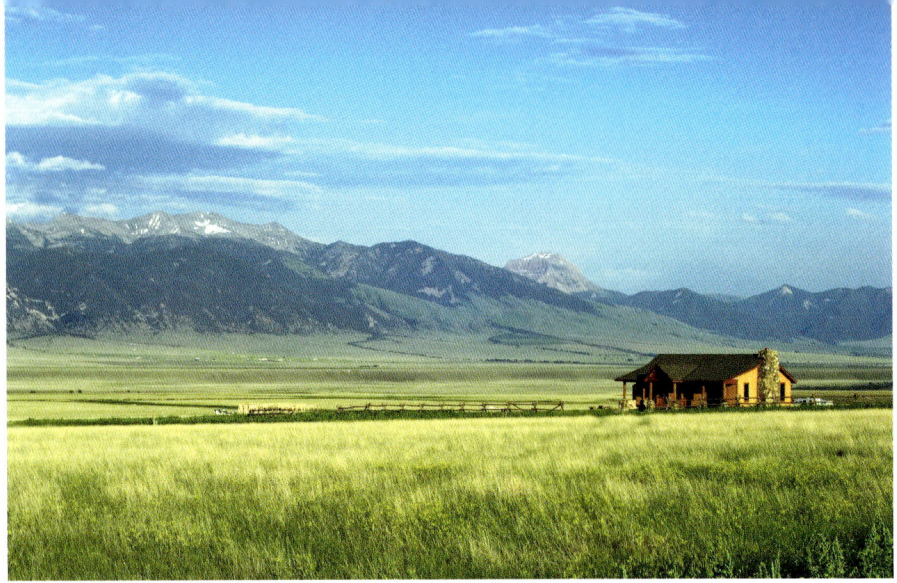

↑   A ranch house in scenic Montana.

→   A herd of wild horses stands majestically in a meadow.

We're seeing an influx of interest and money that feels unprecedented. The Montana tourism industry surged after the first season aired, stirring admiration for the rugged landscape and the rural American way of life, and hiking up land prices in the process. While some locals might rue the new traffic, the spike in tourism has undeniably increased revenue for the state of Montana and created numerous new job opportunities. The show's soundtrack has featured country music from many artists from indie or "Texas Country" circles who are now being streamed worldwide and selling concert tickets globally because of the show's notoriety. Not to mention, we're seeing shops who sell non-traditional luxe Western wear start carrying heritage brands like Kemo Sabe, City Boots, and many more.

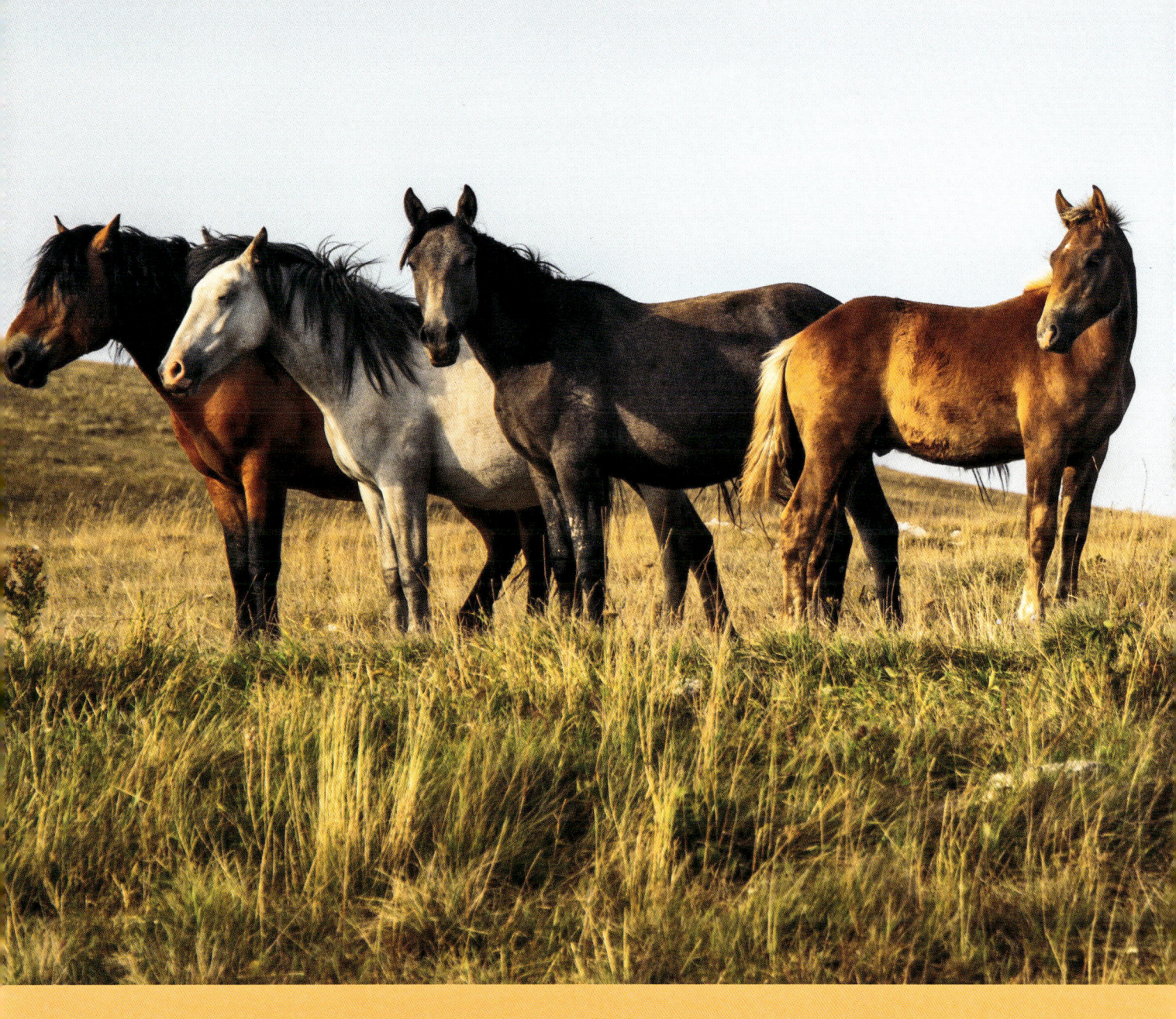

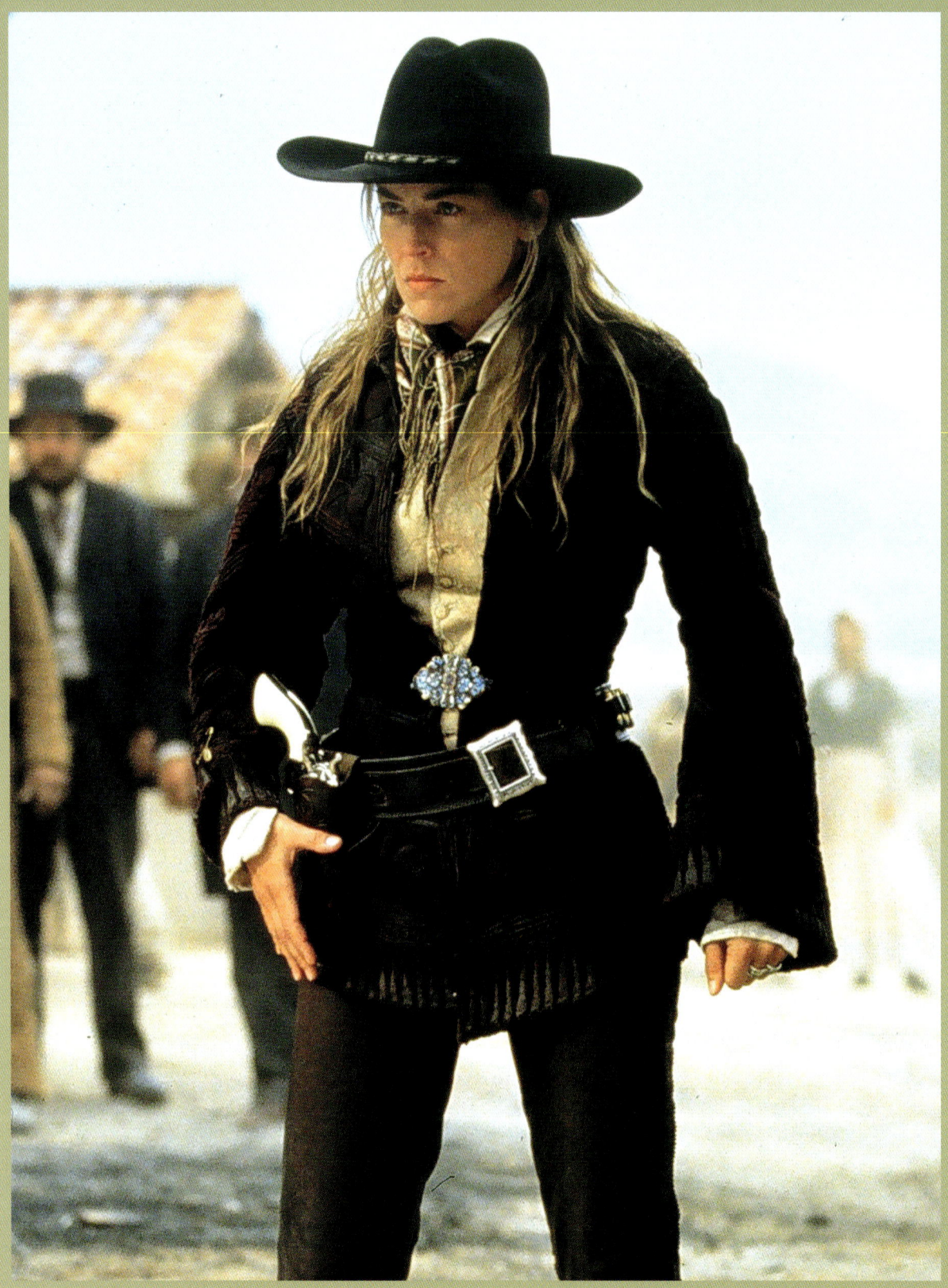

Hollywood's Gone Country

← Sharon Stone in the 1995 film *The Quick and the Dead*.

Beth Dutton isn't the only cowgirl character in Hollywood making waves with her aesthetic and fierce personality.

Barbie's release in 2023 had a standout Western moment when Barbie and Ken find themselves exploring new territory in the streets of California in their cowboy and cowgirl getups. Kendall Jenner has long been an equestrian but has also been spotted recently shopping at Kemo Sabe in Aspen, on the hunt for the perfect cowboy hat. And of course, super model Bella Hadid has taken the West by storm since she began dating cutting-horse trainer Adan Banuelos and competing in the sport of cutting. Hadid took to the streets of Times Square to host a cutting-horse exhibition alongside her new beau, before finishing out the year as the National Cutting Horse Association's Limited Aged Event Rookie of the Year—a huge accomplishment in the Western community. Shortly after, Hadid took to the silver screen in a guest role, playing the girlfriend of *Yellowstone*'s Travis Wheatley, played by the show's writer and producer, Taylor Sheridan.

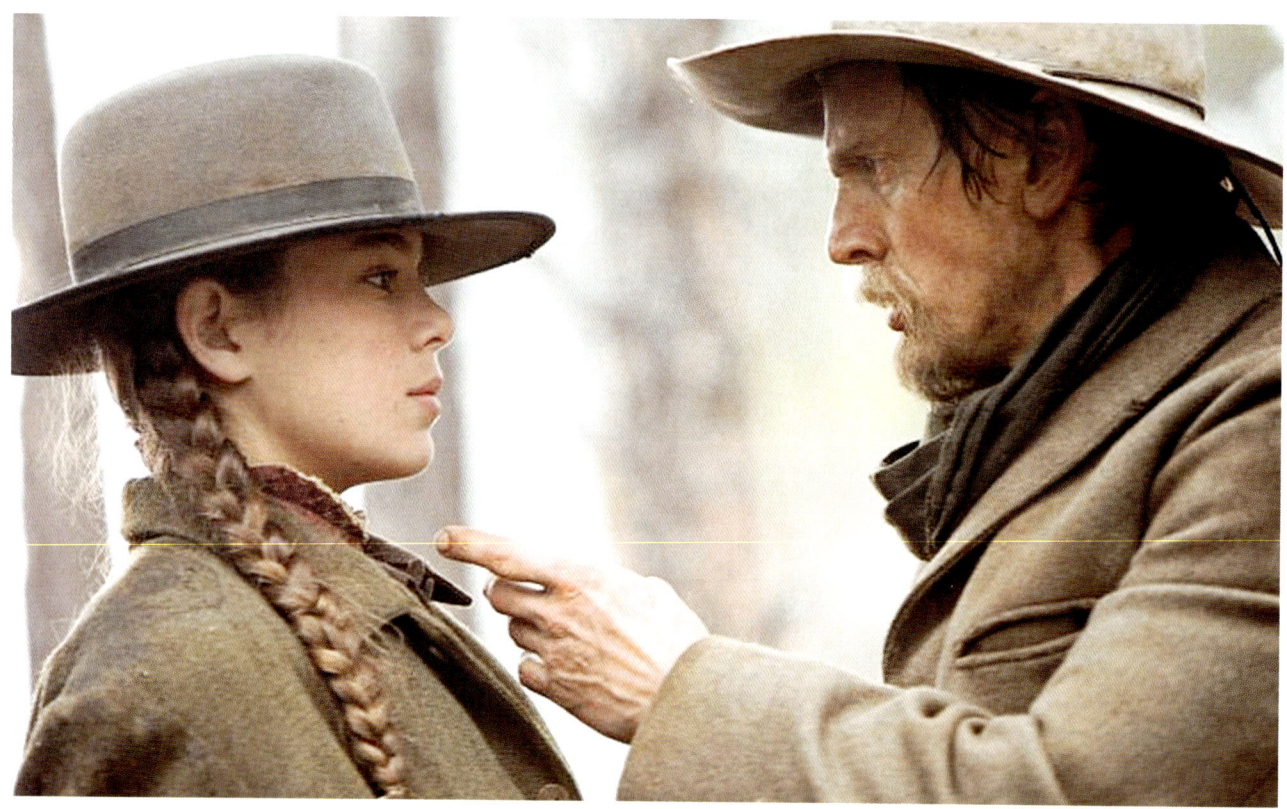

↑ Hailee Steinfeld and Barry Pepper in 2010's *True Grit*.

→ CLOCKWISE Michelle Dockery in the 2017 Netflix miniseries *Godless*. Nicole Kidman in the 2008 film *Australia*. Natalie Portman in the 2015 film *Jane Got a Gun*.

In addition to *Yellowstone* and its many spin-off series, many high-profile Western films were made from 2010 to 2019, including movies such as:

* *The Revenant (2015)*

* *Django Unchained (2012)*

* *The Hateful Eight (2015)*

* *The Magnificent Seven (2016)*

* *True Grit (2010)*

* *Hostiles (2017)*

* *Hell or High Water (2016)*

* *Wind River (2017)*

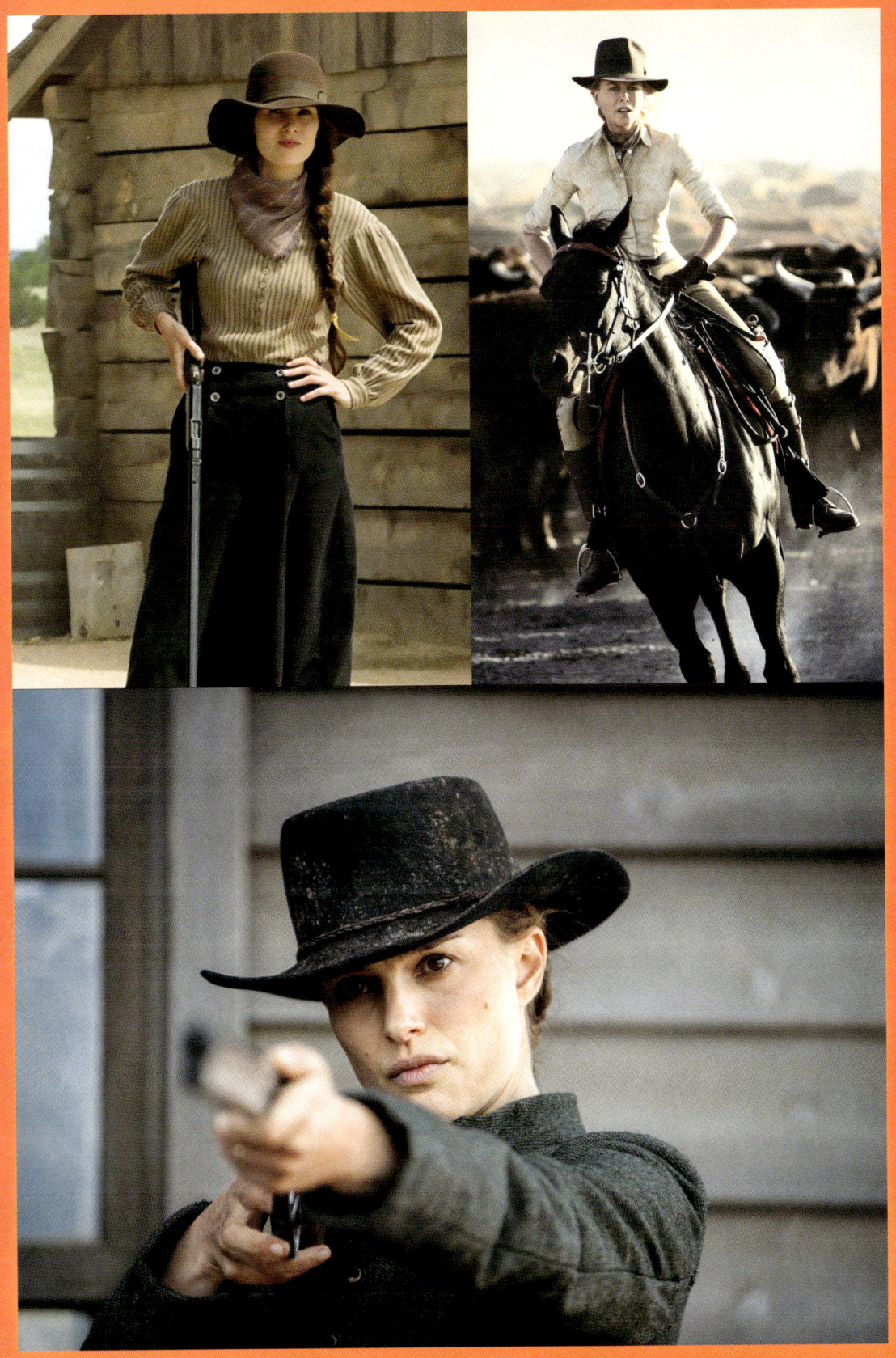

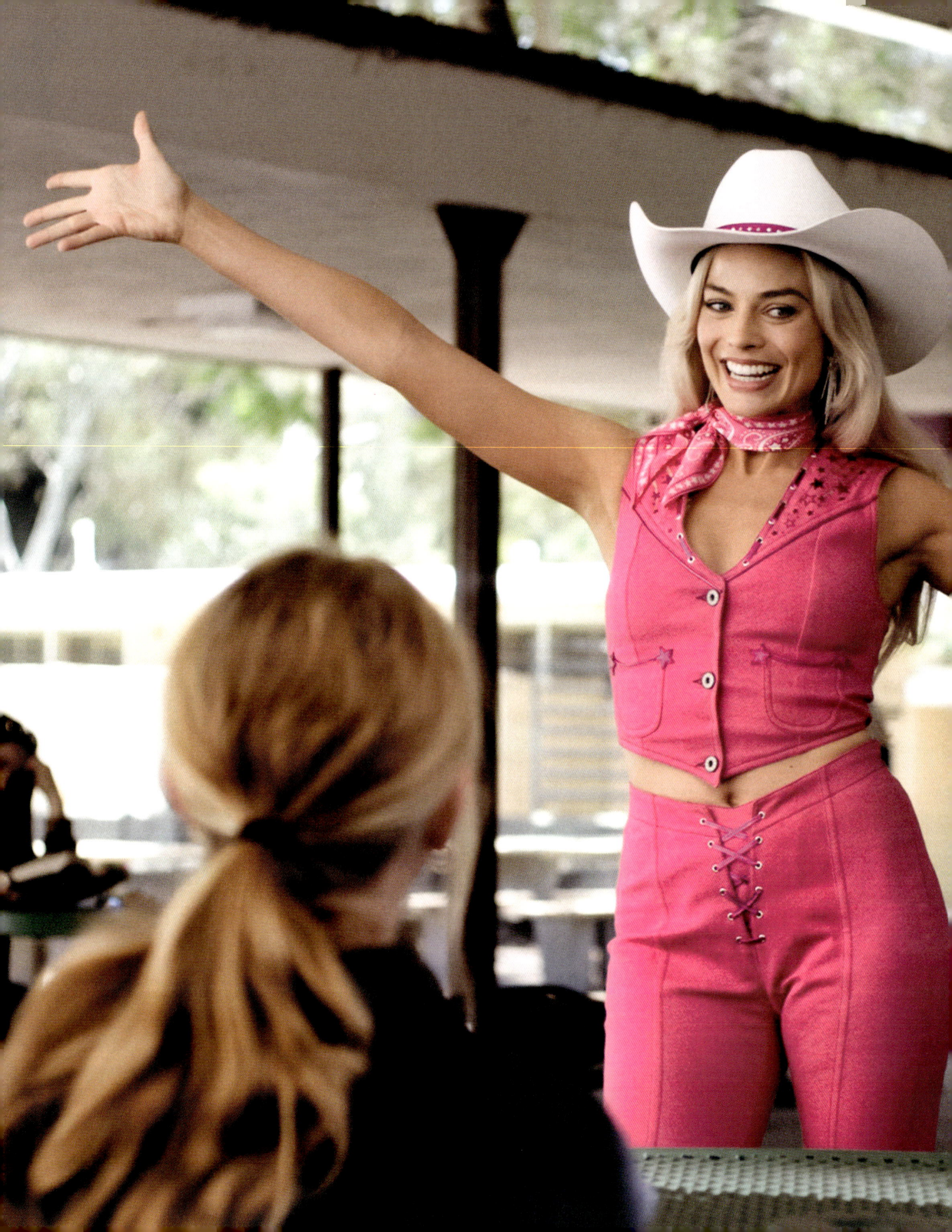

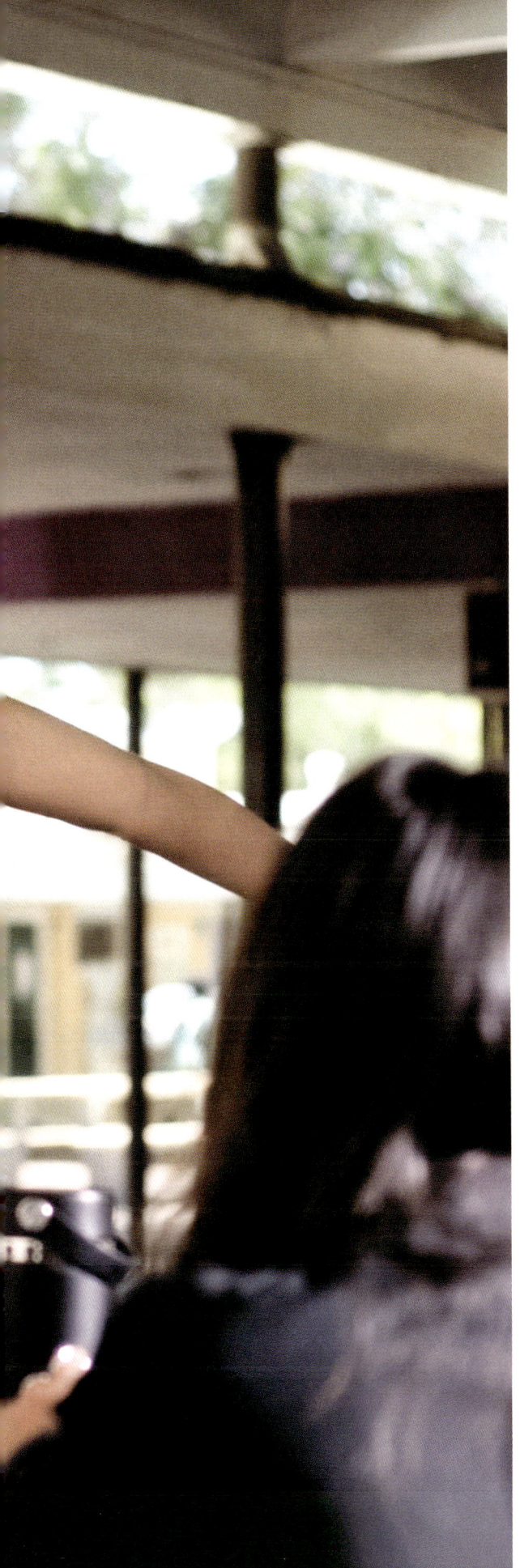

← Margot Robbie as Barbie in Greta Gerwig's 2023 film.

There is something aspirational and rugged about the cowgirl and the Western life that our country longs for. Now that country is back, I don't foresee it going anywhere, anytime soon. Whether you are someone who is riding the fence lines daily and branding calves in the spring, someone who took a dude ranch vacation and fell in love with the lifestyle, or someone who loves to hit the Las Vegas strip in December in a killer pair of cowboy boots for the National Finals Rodeo, there is a space for any and all Western enthusiasts to celebrate the spirit of the cowgirl.

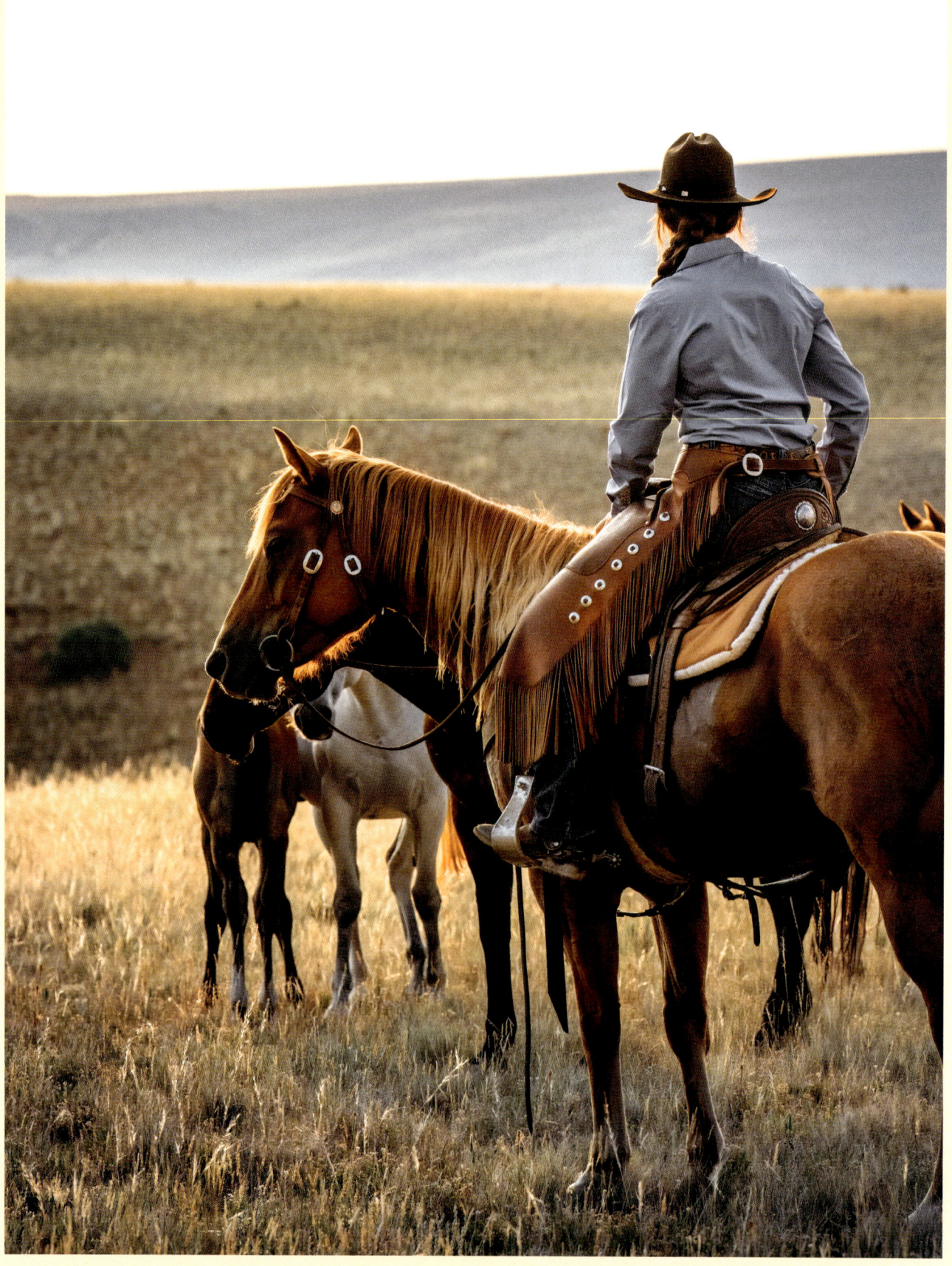

In Our Cowgirl Era

Cowgirl fashion has taken its own eras tour. In the late 1800s, cowgirl "fashion" was entirely based in practicality. Western women wore bonnets, or hats, and boots, and picked up many fashion concepts from the Indigenous peoples they encountered. They adopted fringes—a Native American design that keeps water from soaking into the leather—wore gemstones, and used hides for warmth and protection. Skirts became split skirts. Split skirts became frontier pants. Frontier pants were traded in for denim pants, which offered unmatched durability and protection from the elements.

The uniform of the modern working ranch cowgirl hasn't changed much from those days, though the quality and technology are always evolving and improving. Most ranch women wear cowboy hats, button-down shirts or T-shirts, jeans, a great pair of worn-in boots, and leather gloves, when necessary. The evolution has halted outside of fabric durability and performance. Cowboy fashion is largely the same.

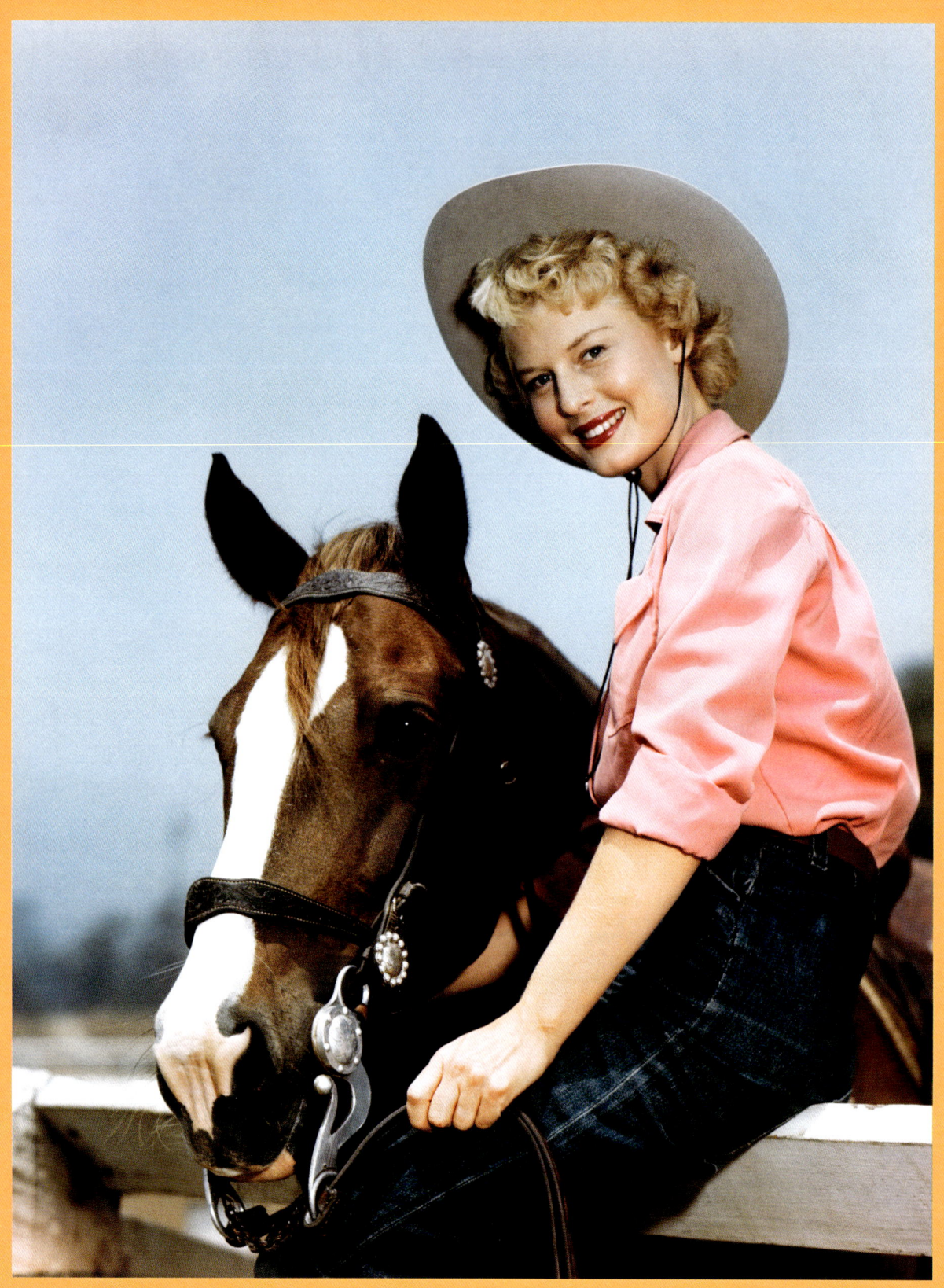

Trends Through the Modern Years

← An example of modest cowgirl fashion from the 1940s and '50s.

↱ NEXT PAGE
A cowgirl-themed chorus line, circa 1935.

Cowgirl street fashion has seen some incredible eras over the years. Rodeo queens got the ball rolling with what I consider to be business casual—if business casual was full leather: blazers, dresses, blouses, pencil skirts, and pants all made from thick leather in tons of beautiful colors and adorned with crystals, yoking, piping, fringes, and embroidery. The outfits look as though they weigh around forty pounds and the style hasn't changed much through the years—though the shoulder pads have slightly decreased in size and the cowgirls' hair is a more manageable height. The original rodeo queen was crowned at the Pendleton Round-Up in 1910. Even then, the garb was a full leather pant suit and a classic western hat. Rodeo queens were the original fashionistas, and they haven't strayed far from their roots.

Early 1900s

Fashion was limited in the early 1900s. Women were largely confined to hoop skirts and long sleeved blouses that buttoned up the front. They wore bloomers beneath the skirt, especially those women who were often horseback. A wild rag or silk scarf was often applied to ensure protection from wind and dust, and leather boots were the only appropriate shoes for a rural woman.

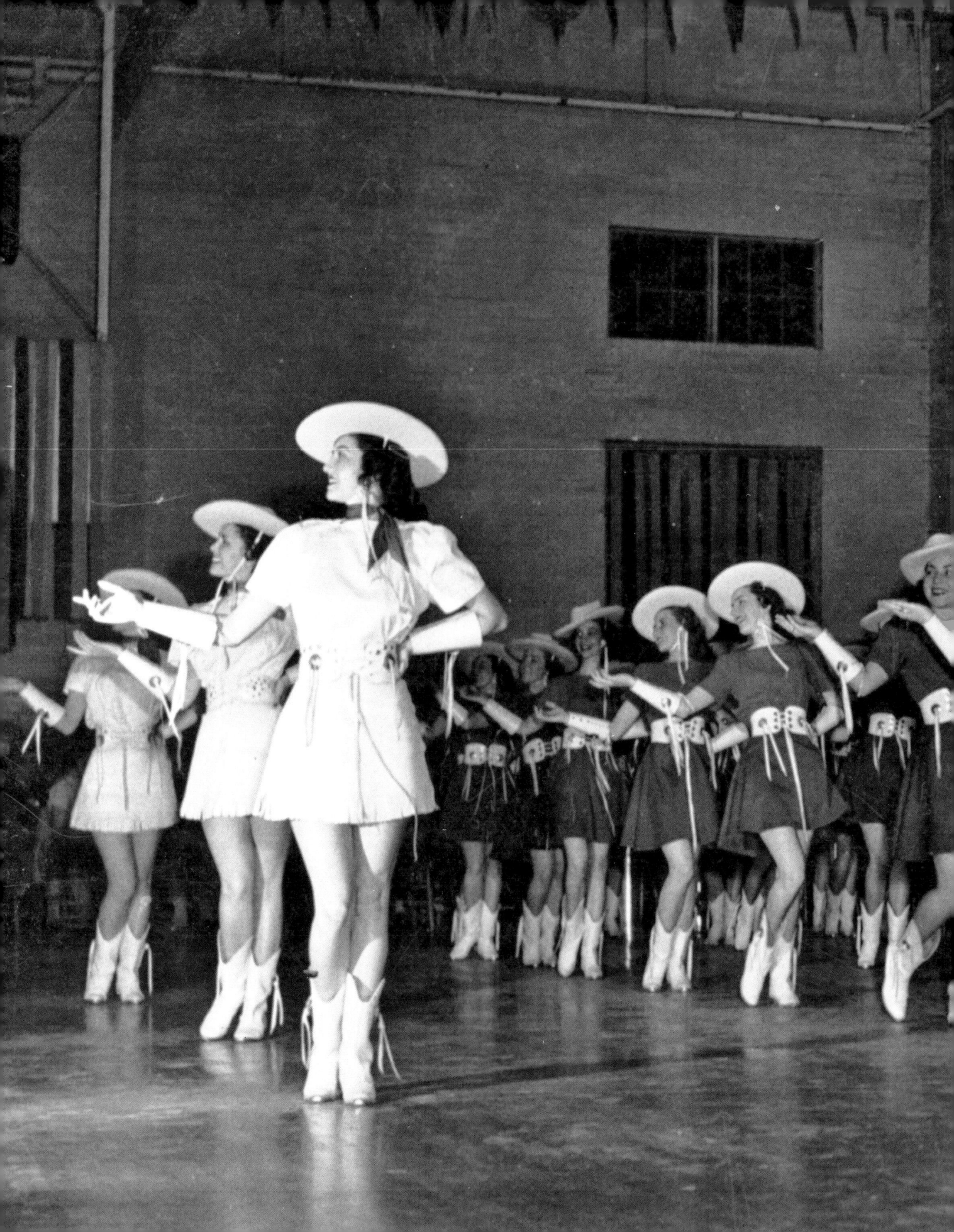

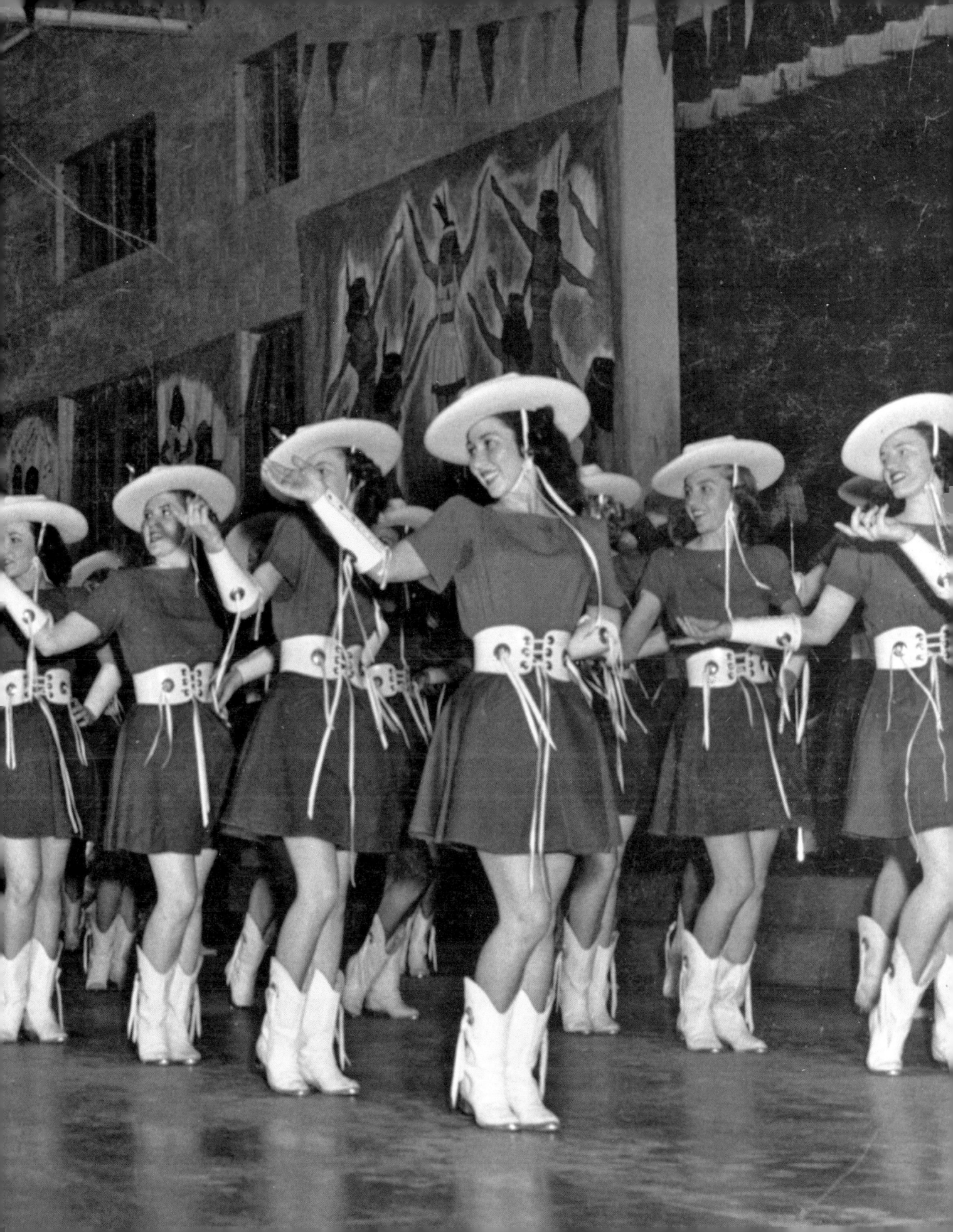

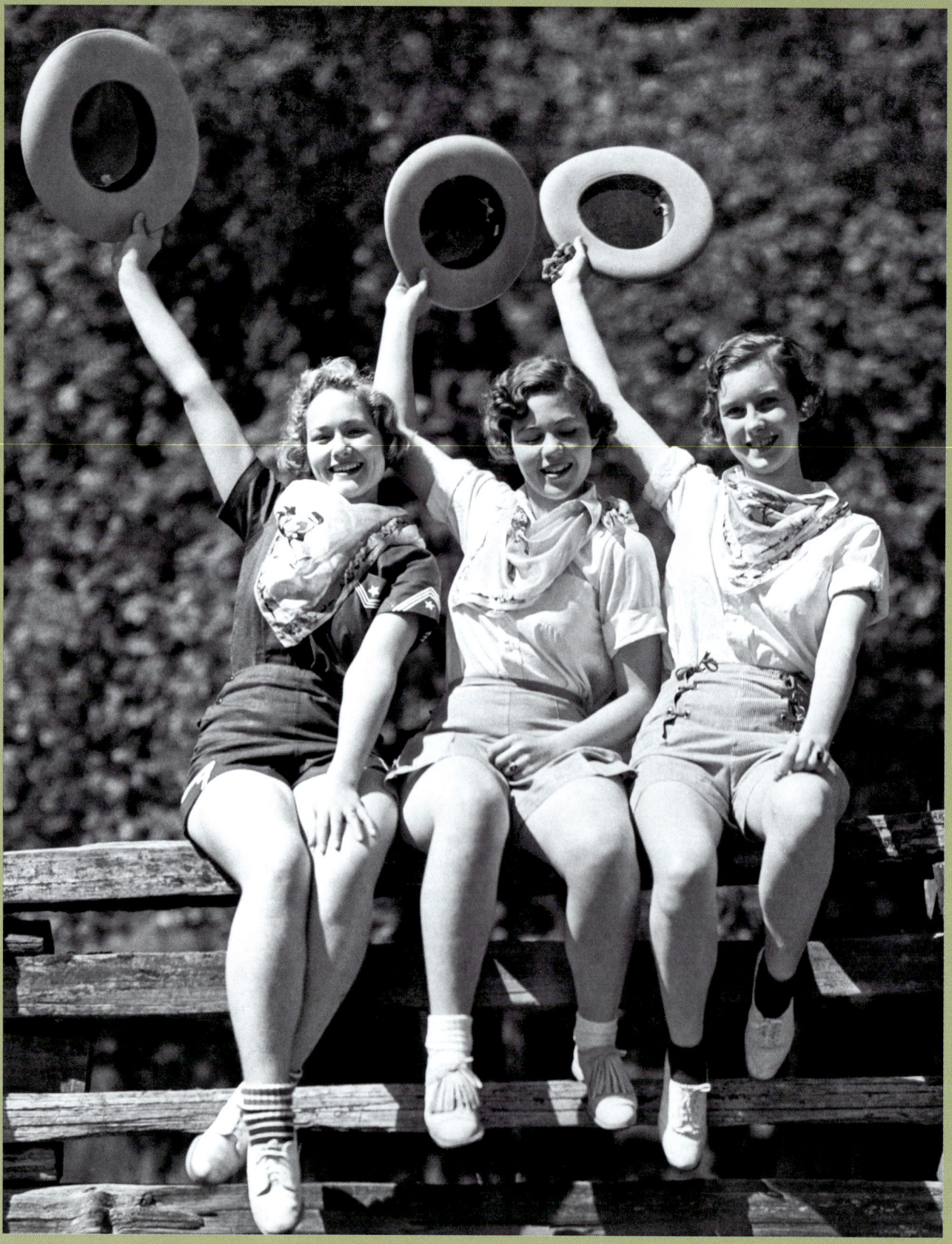

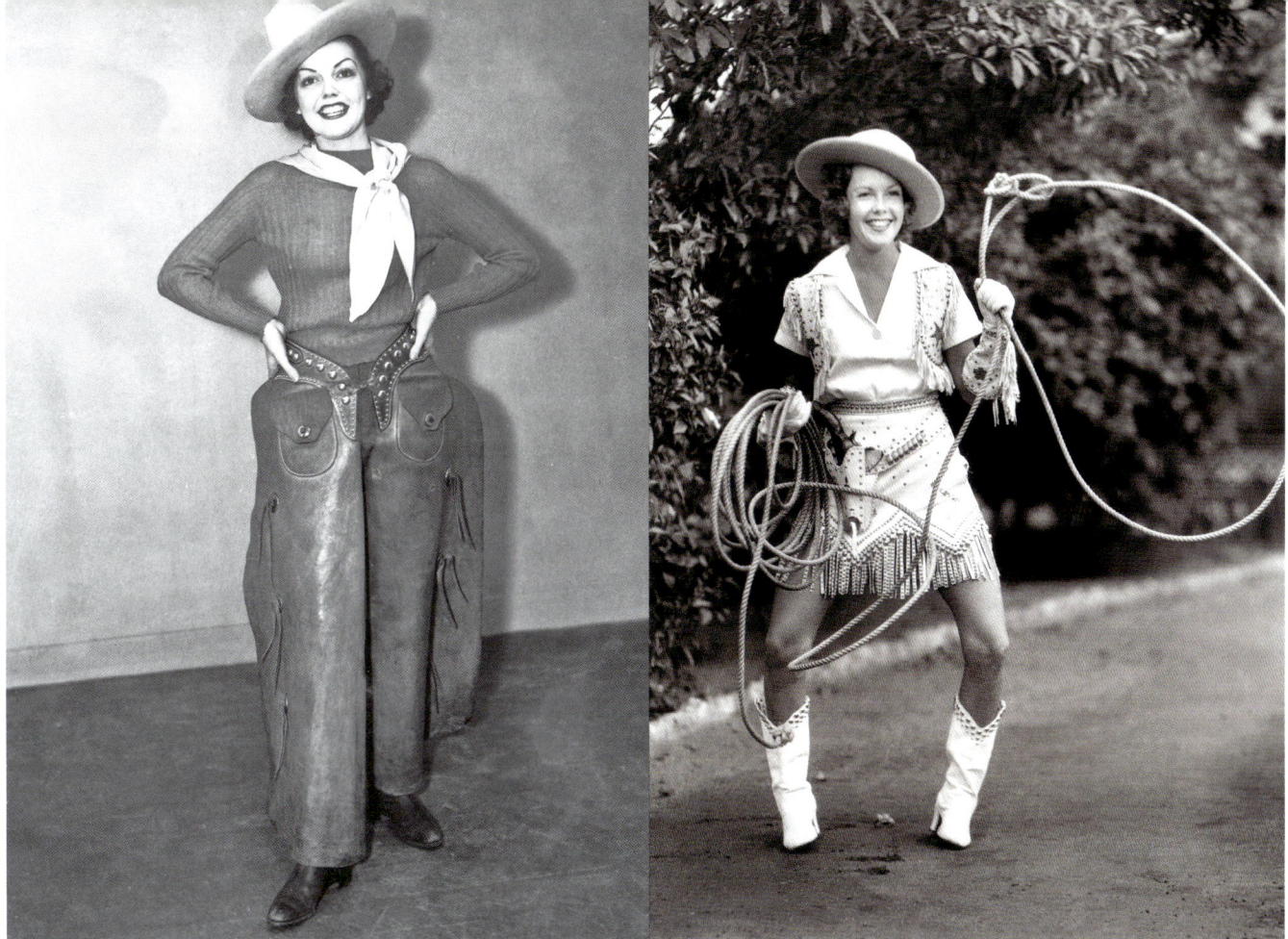

↑ A woman sporting a cowboy hat and chaps, circa 1940.

⇢ American comedy actress Dorothy Lee (1911–1999) in a Western-inspired promotional shoot. Lee was a star of stage and screen in the 1930s.

⇠ Three young women in Western wear at the 1936 Frontier Days celebration in Willits, California.

1930s

Pants finally become accessible and adopted by Western women in the 1930s with the rise of culottes. The wide-leg pants fit perfectly inside of a boot shaft at the shin and allowed women to ride comfortably without worrying about skirt placement. This decade also brought about a slight decrease in hat brim size to a more modern and manageable width.

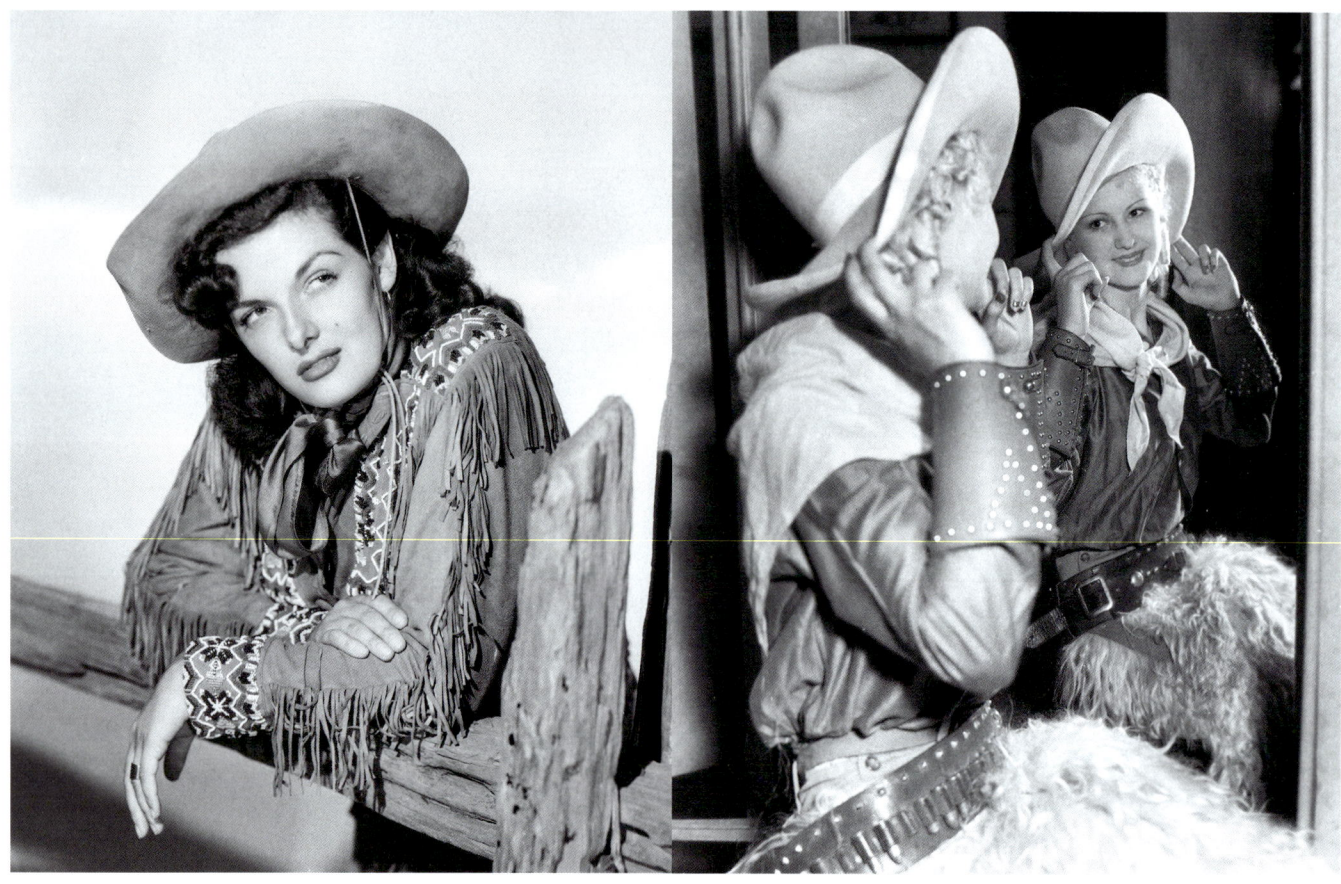

← American actress Jane Russell in a promotional photograph for the 1948 film *The Paleface*.

↑ A promotional shoot for a Southern California rodeo, circa 1950.

→ Elizabeth Taylor in the 1956 film *Giant*.

1940s to 1950s

In the 1940s, we begin to see some individualized and feminine fashion in the Western world. Pants became tailored for women with a tighter, more form-hugging fit, and a boot cut. Blouses also became more fitted, makeup use was on the rise, and the stampede string, or the string that fastens under your chin to help keep your hat from flying away, was widely being adopted by women. Cowgirl fashion of the 1940s is completely iconic and so different from any era the industry had seen prior.

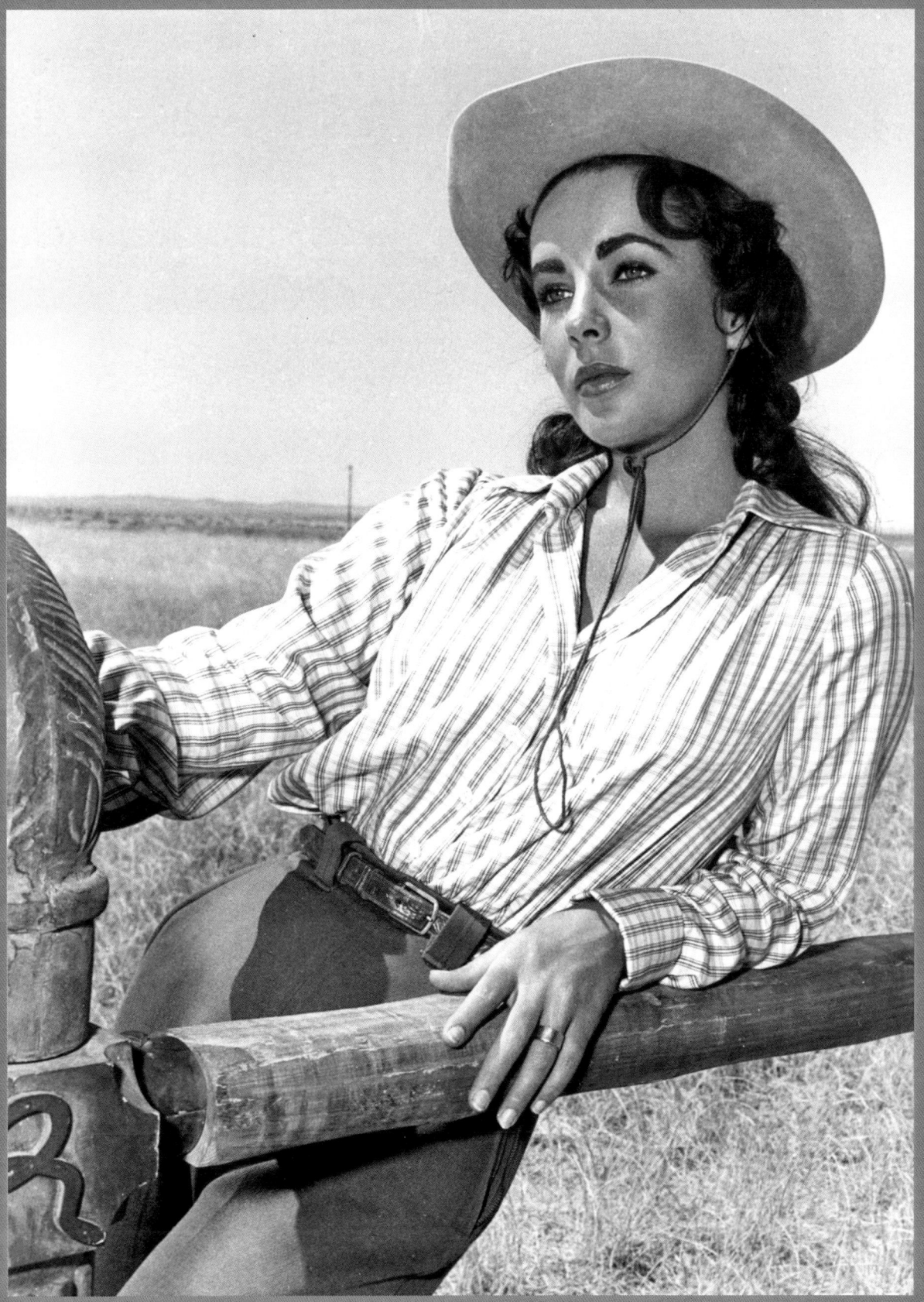

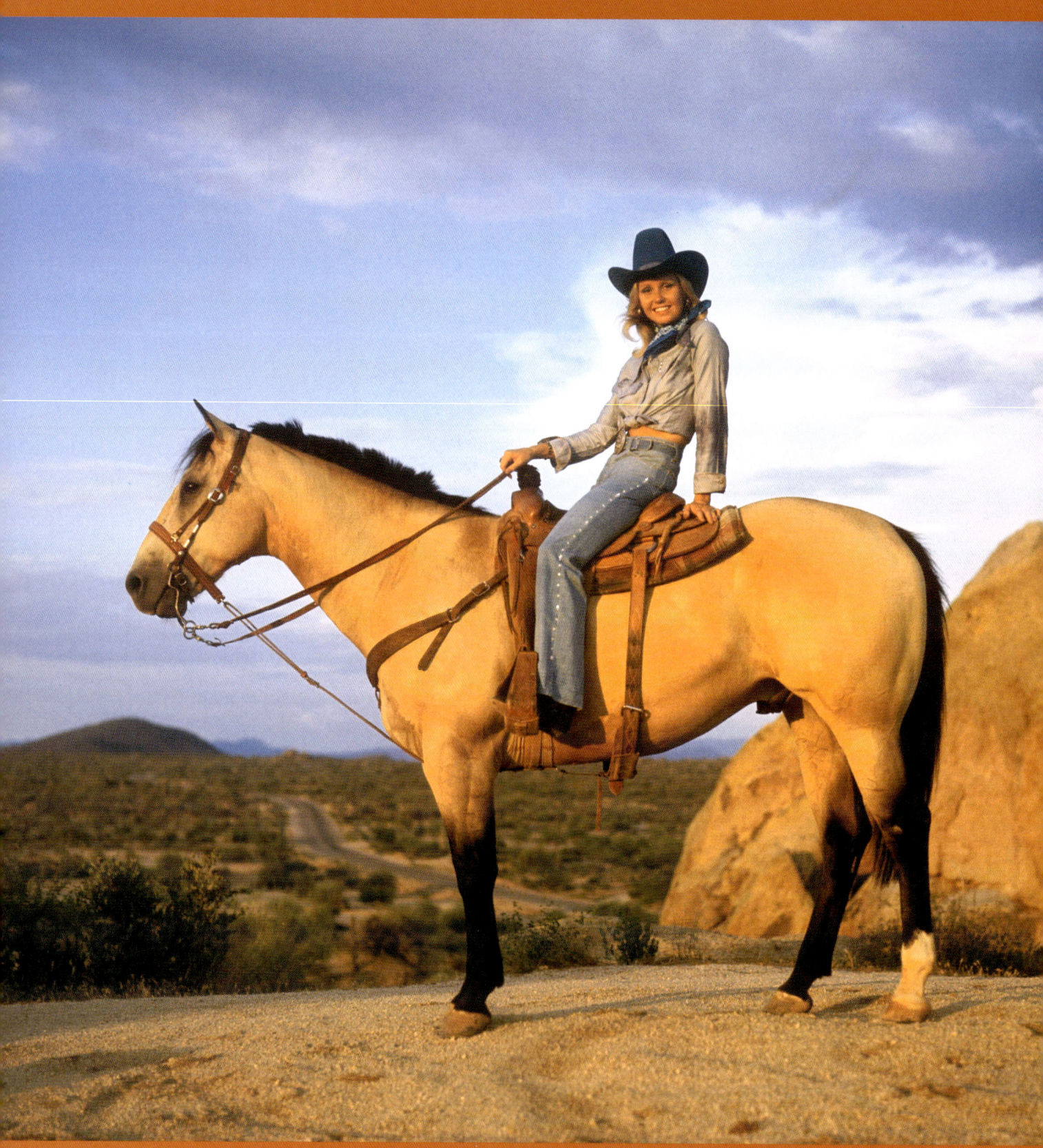

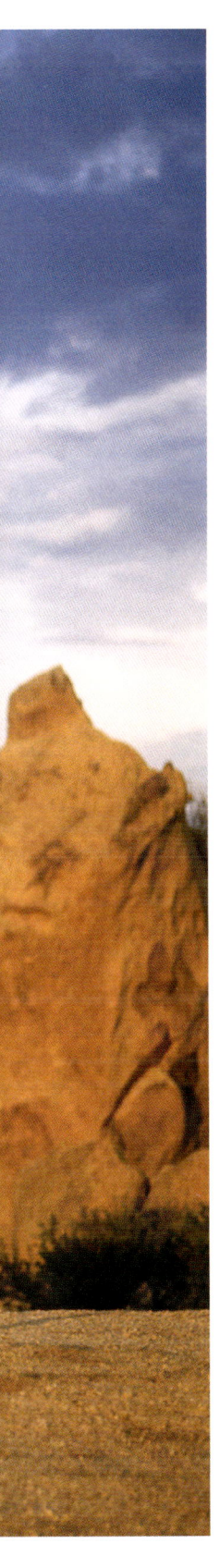

→ Man's best friend? A dog can be a cowgirl's best friend too. (Second to her horse, of course.)

← A model shows off 1970s cowgirl fashions.

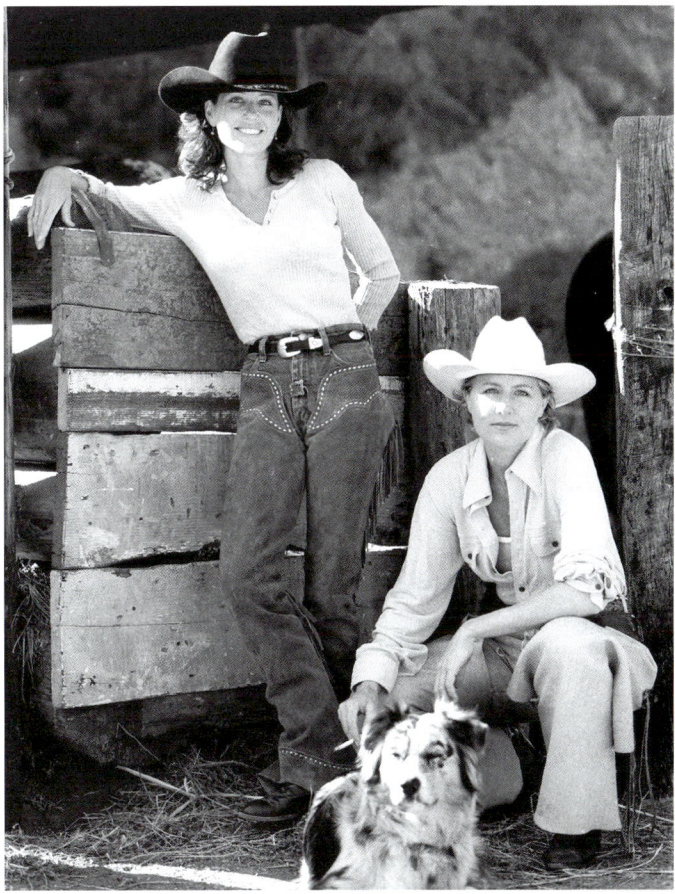

1960s to 1970s

While cowgirl fashion was still widely individualized during this time period, we did see a huge trend change in the brim of hats. During the 1960s, the classic "cattleman's crease" shape—a sharp creased brim that was no more than three-and-a-half or four inches (8.9 or 10 cm) wide—surged in popularity, paired with a tall, classically shaped crown. Unsurprisingly, while hats were getting tighter, pants were getting wider. The wide leg, parachute-style pants this era was known for applied just as much to the Western industry as it did anywhere.

1980s

The 80s was our first real glimpse of modern Western wear. Rockies denim emerged on the scene, jeans had a more classical fit, and men's and women's fashion began to overlap in many areas. The hat creases relaxed a bit, though the cattleman's crown was still king. This era of Western fashion is very classically cool.

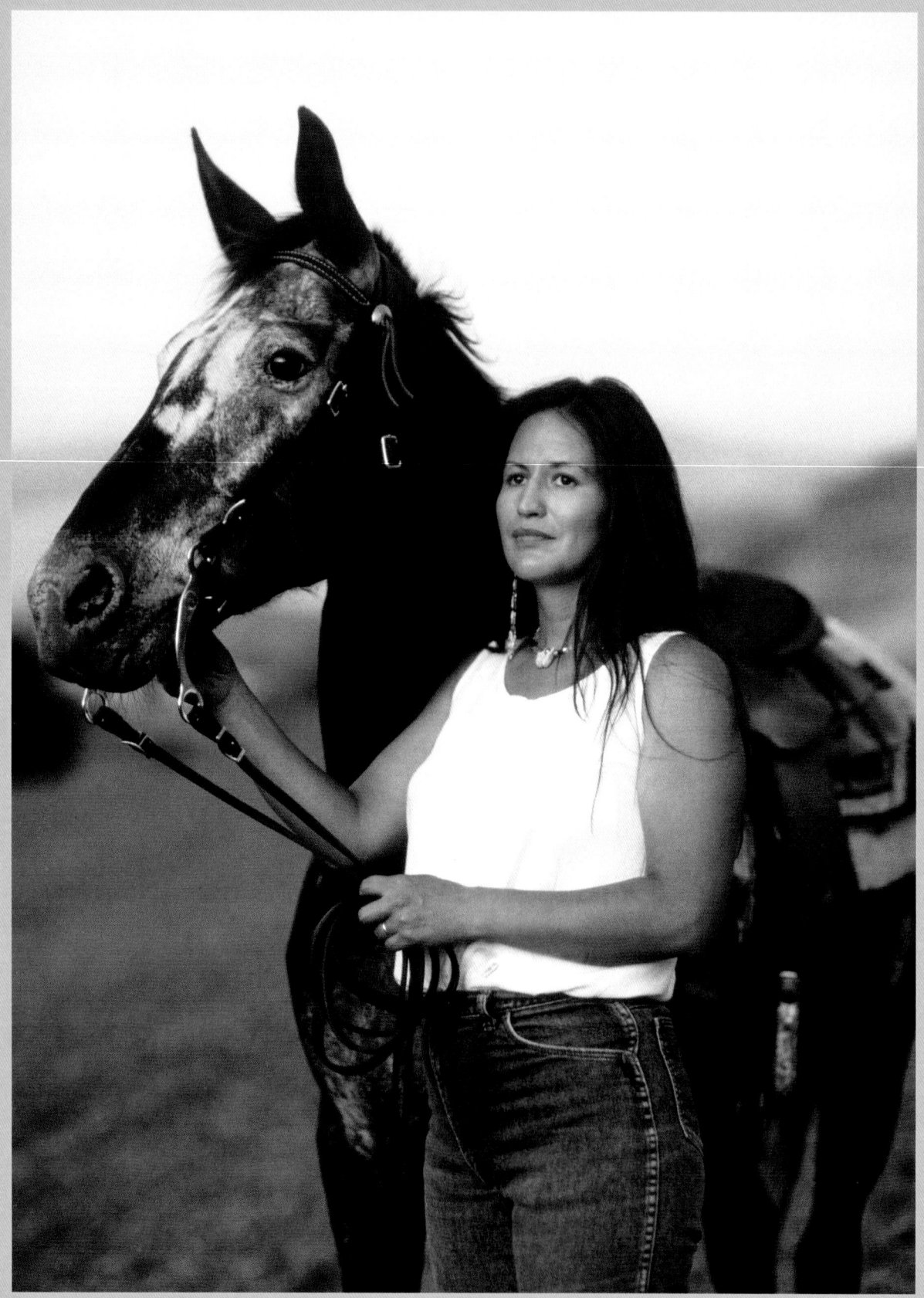

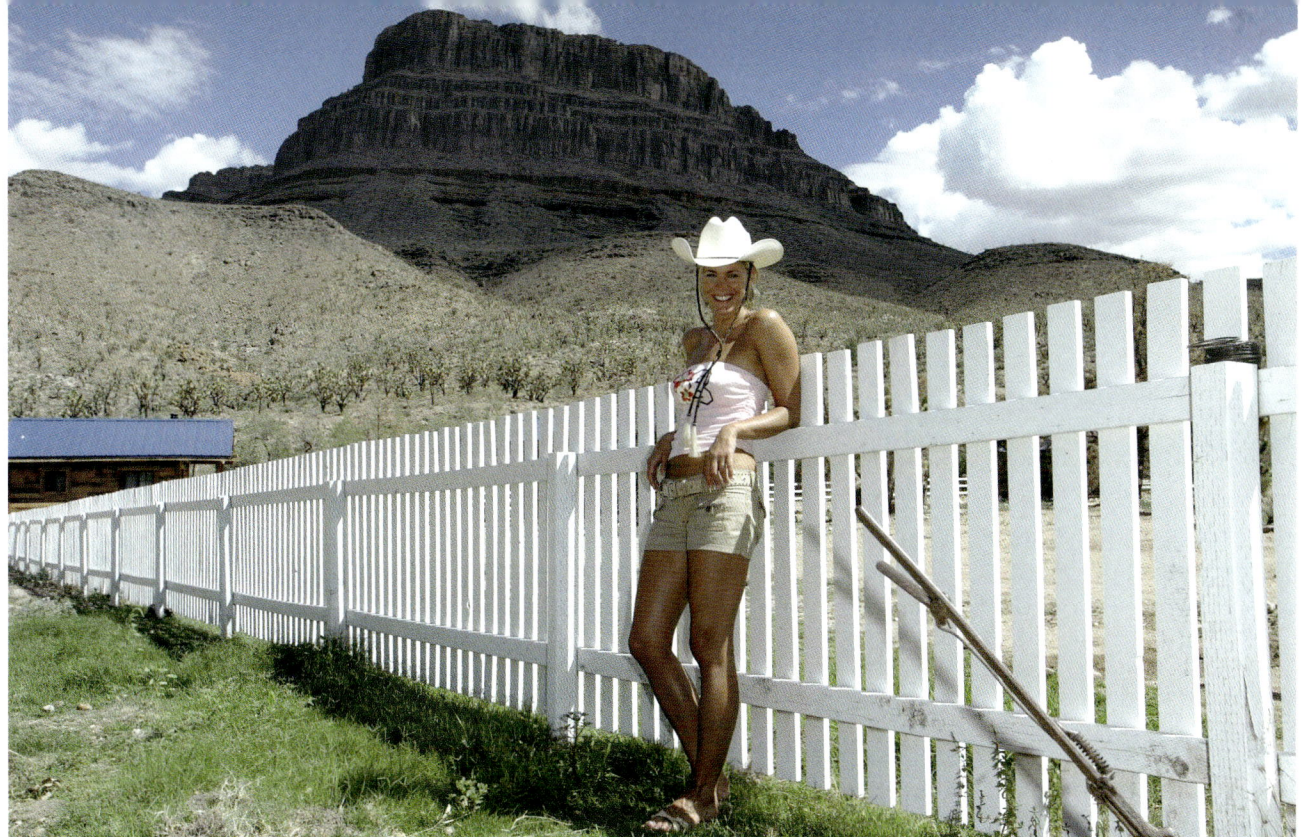

↑ Scottish TV presenter Jenni Falconer goes Western in 2003 for an episode of the British morning news program *Entertainment Today*, filmed in the American Southwest.

← Former Nez Perce Tribal Executive Committee member Carla HighEagle, seen here with her horse in the early 1990s.

1990s

We saw colored Rockies denim jeans take over the Western fashion scene for most of the '90s. The jeans were sky-high waisted, had a straight or slim leg, and the denim came dyed in every color and print under the rainbow. There were no back pockets, which was thought to accentuate a women's— ahem—assets, and the jeans were often paired with a loud, printed, long-sleeved shirt. Lace-up boots were all the rage at that time too.

Early 2000s

The early 2000s saw the rise of the denim miniskirt, which was paired with boots, two or three Hollister tank tops layered on top of one another, and a curled-up straw cowboy hat. This look took the concert world by storm and even made its way onto a few red carpets.

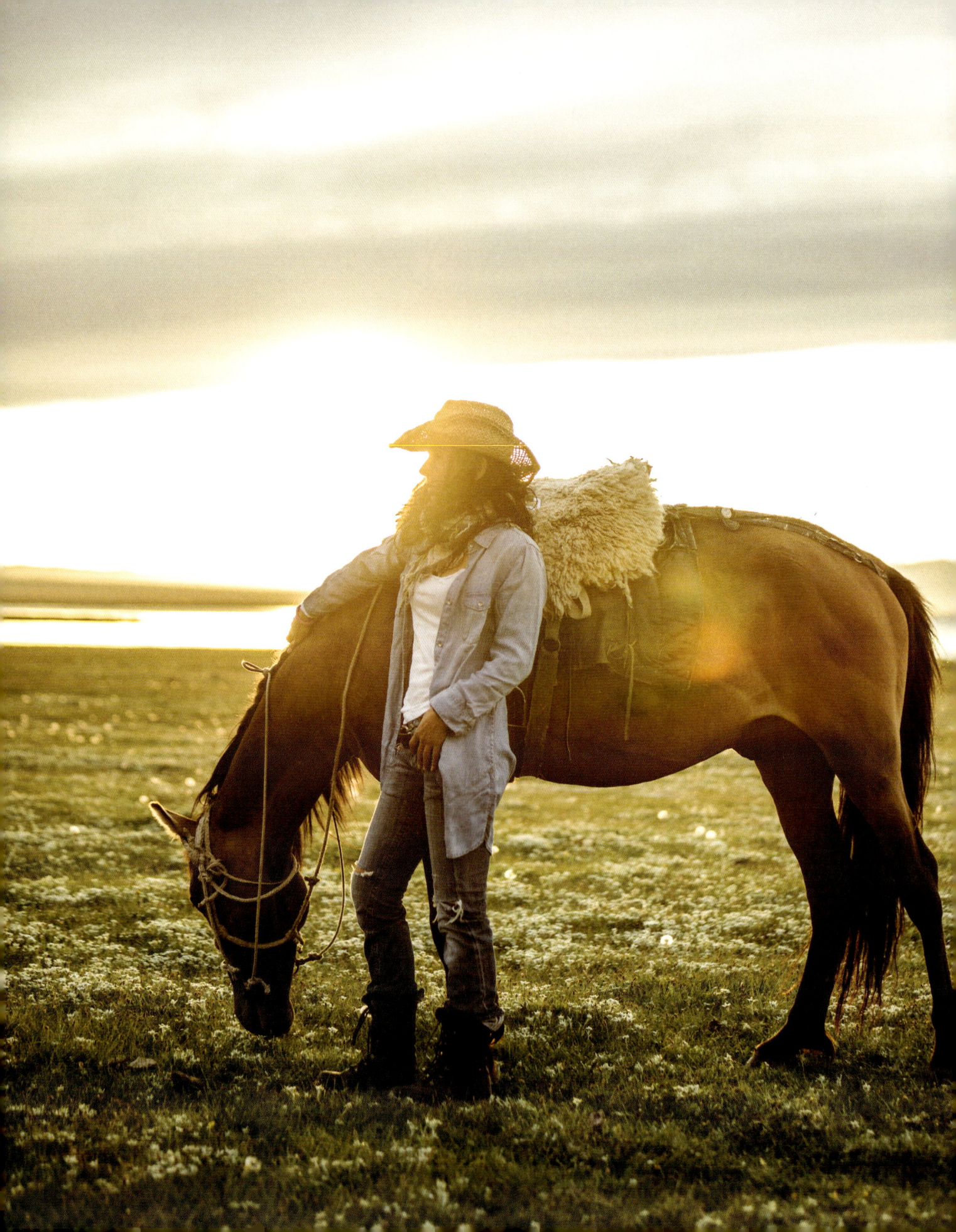

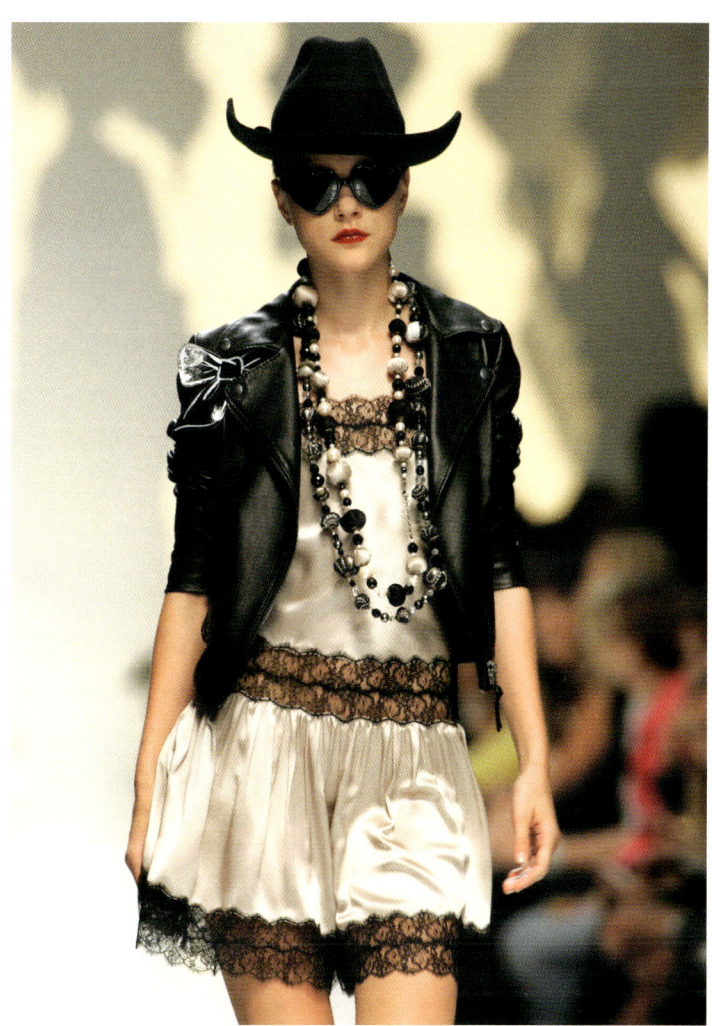

→ A model walking a runway in Milan, showing off Moschino's ready to wear, Western-inspired fashions from their 2006 spring/summer collection.

← A cowgirl in distressed denim, lined lace-up boots, and a woven straw hat.

2010s

The 2010s brought us Miss Me jeans, and there is not one father in the world who drove a car with leather seats who doesn't know what I am talking about. (I was banned from wearing these to the barn because my dad realized I was scratching up the seats of our leather saddles. Yikes.) The low-rise Miss Me jeans, with completely stone-encrusted back pockets and a boot cut, were truly the most iconic look of this era.

The age of lace came next. Every girl at every rodeo or every Country Western concert owned a romper, dress, or jumpsuit that was entirely lace, save for the skin-colored paneling that was built in. This outfit, paired with the Taylor Swift tight curls (circa *Speak Now*) and an overly tooled pair of boots, was—as the kids say—chef's kiss. Shortly after lace, came the exact same stylings but with sequins or some combination of the two.

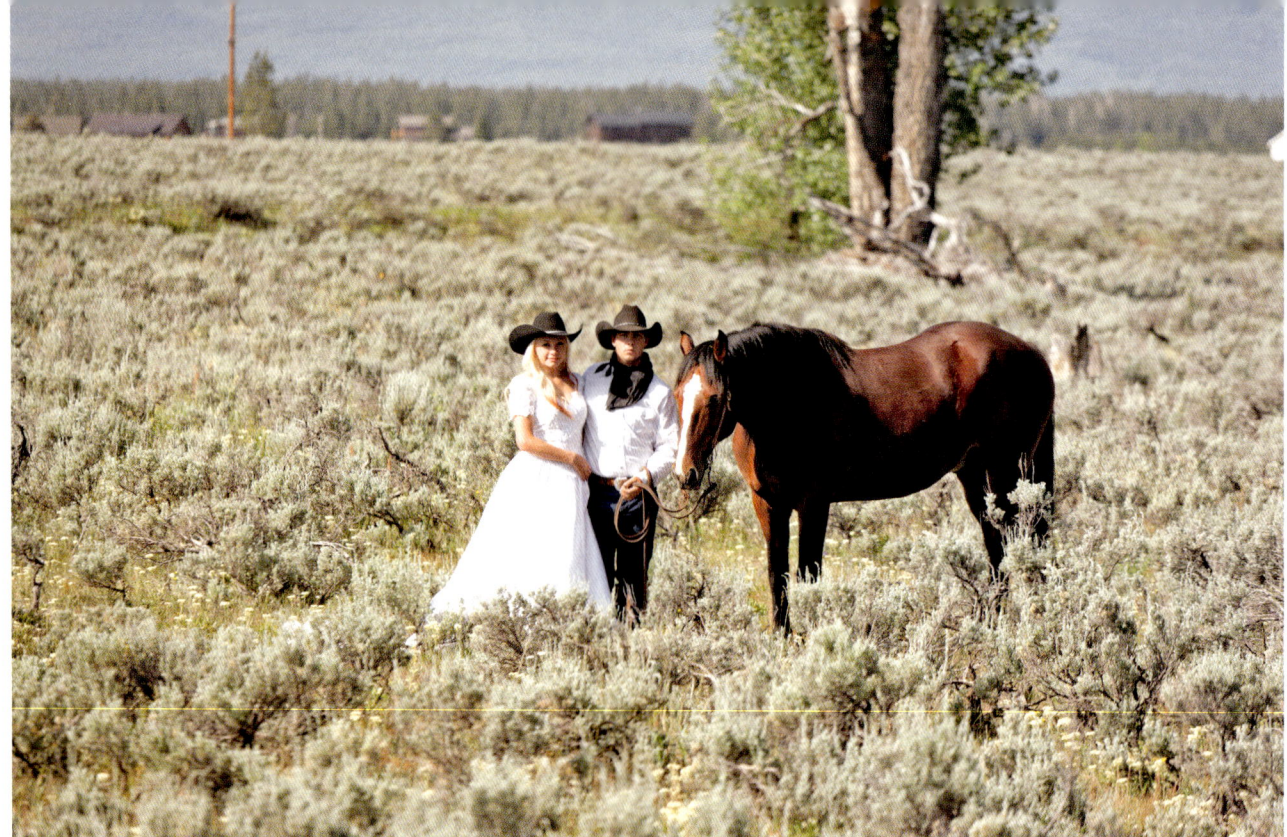

↑ A Stetson-sporting couple pose for their wedding photo with a horse on Parade Rest Guest Ranch in West Yellowstone.

→ Watch out for those embroidered pockets!

Present Day

The last ten years or so have been so good for Western fashion. Maybe it's the Western effect on media or maybe we all just grew up and got smart, but we are finally in a Western fashion era that is exactly what it was always meant to be—unique to each and every person.

The entire spirit of the cowgirl was built on women who weren't afraid to be themselves and go against the grain, and Western fashion finally adopted the same mentality. The diverse and beautiful stylings of today's Western fashion are far more elevated and sophisticated than anything the industry has seen before, and that is spilling over into mainstream media and pop culture.

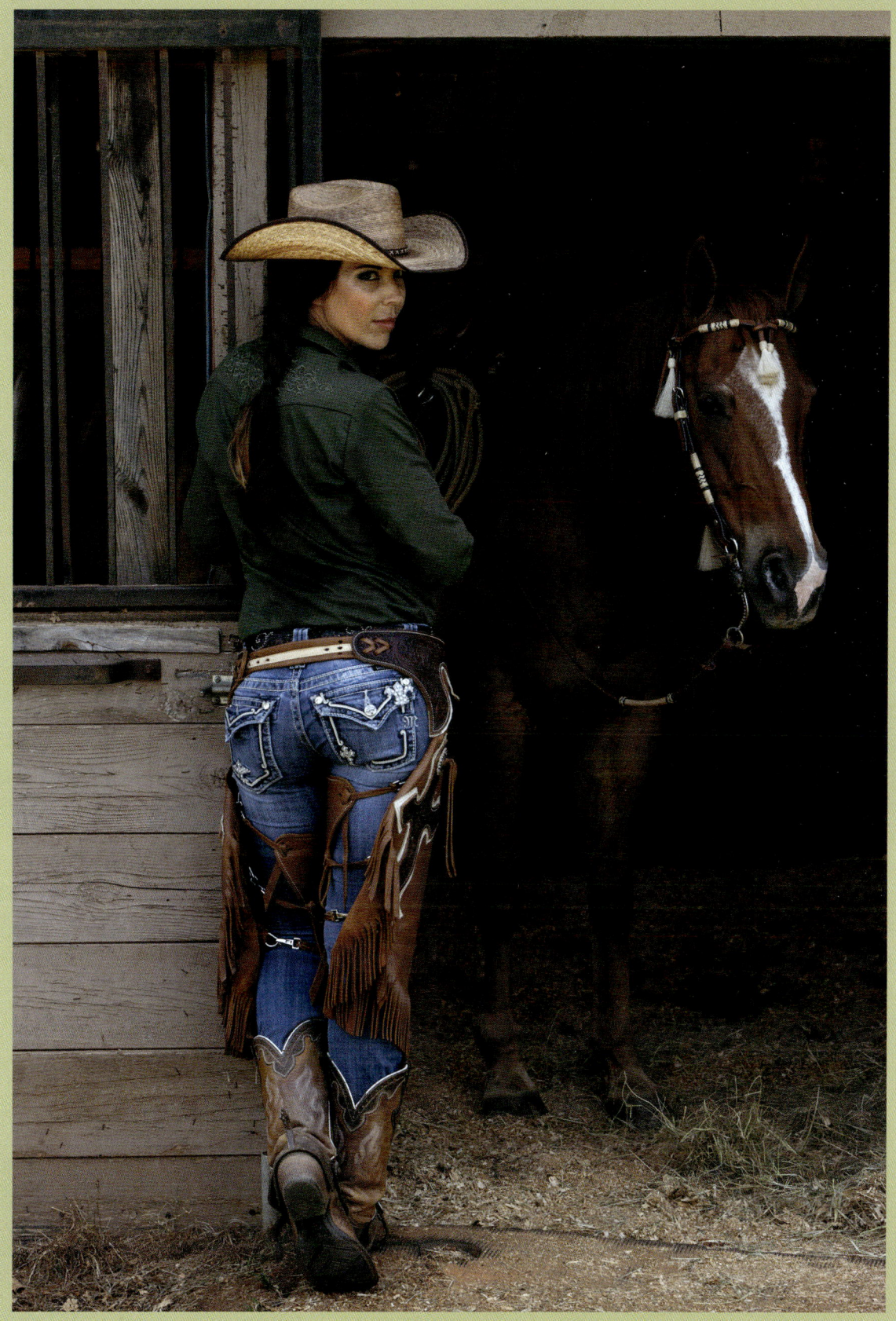

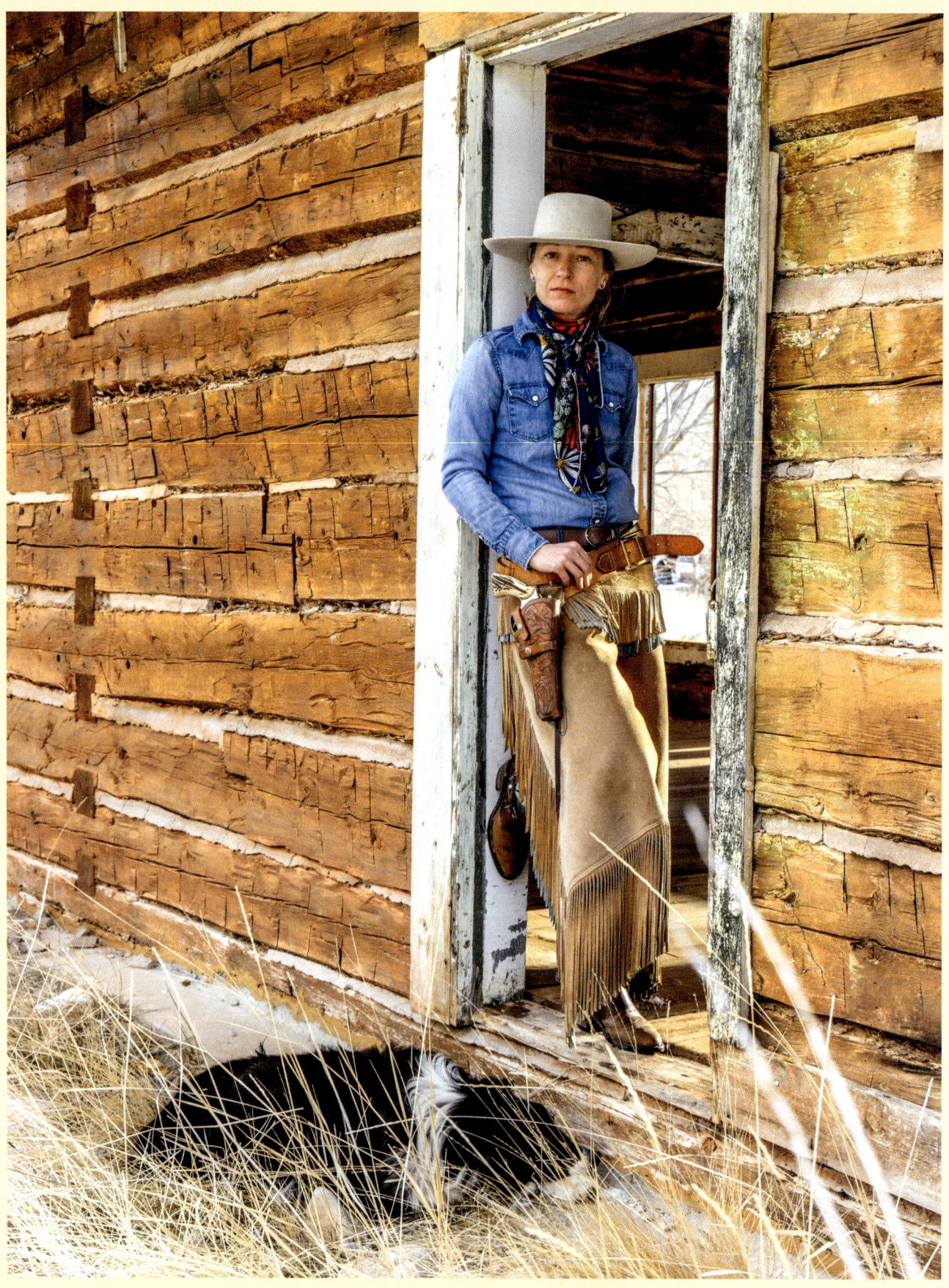

Cowgirl Essentials

← A portrait of a female wrangler
   at Hideout Horse Ranch
   in Wyoming.

Western fashion didn't start with the Country Music Association Awards. In fact, its origins can be traced back to the nineteenth century—maybe even further—when Western settlers began interacting with Indigenous peoples. Much of what is at the forefront of modern cowgirl fashion today has a direct tie to the Old West.

The look of a cowgirl can take many forms—what she wears on the ranch, to the rodeo, to a movie premiere, or to a professional event all varies greatly. Every cowgirl has her own look, and individuality is one of the most celebrated pieces of the culture. Cowgirl style consists mostly of bold colors and patterns that are heavily influenced by Southwestern culture, as well as rodeo and rock and roll.

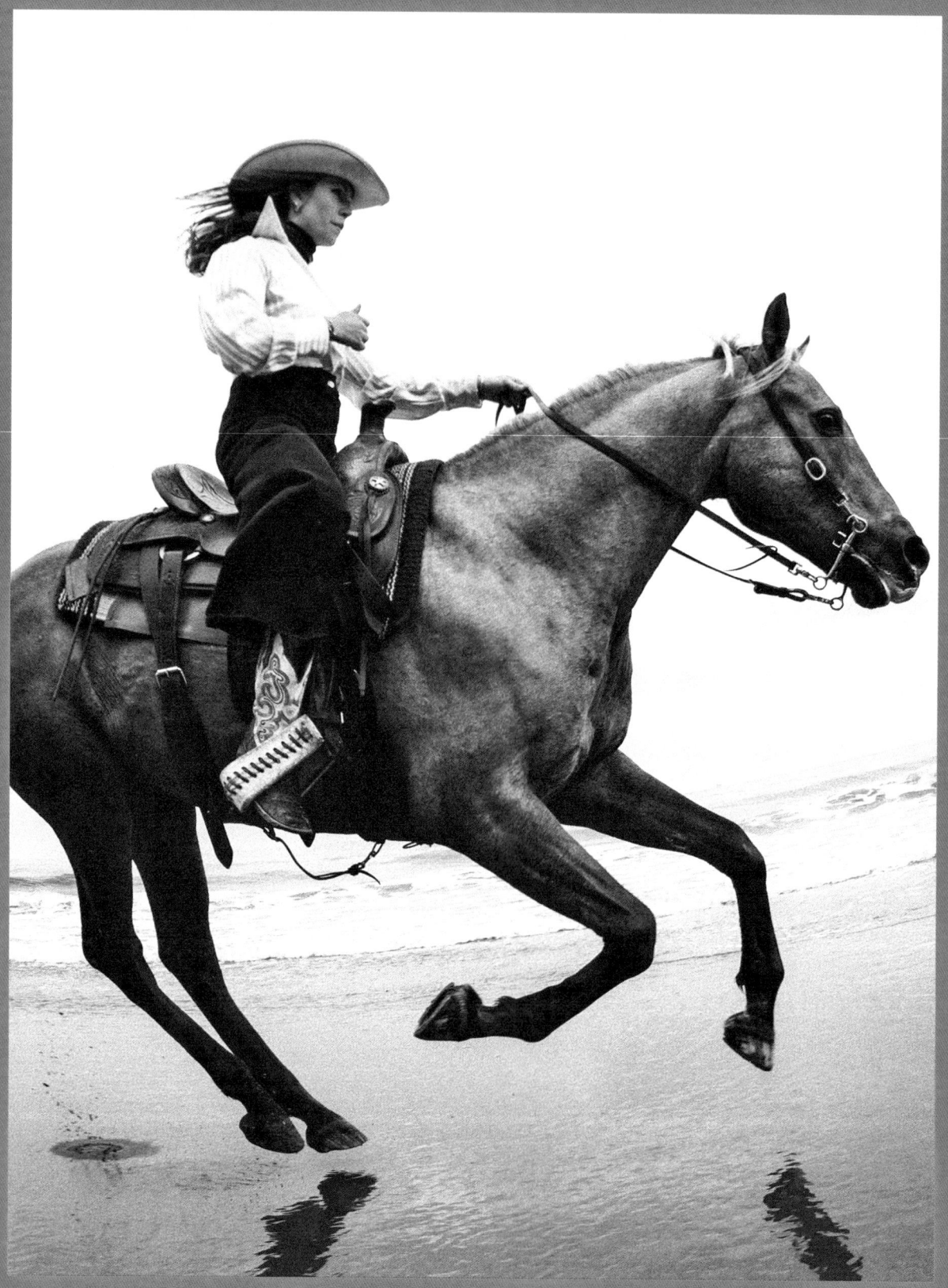

The Cowboy Hat

Perhaps the most recognizable piece of the cowgirl's—or anyone's—Western wardrobe is the cowboy hat. It's notably the most recognizable symbol of the West in general, and it's an important accessory in every cowgirl's wardrobe.

Hats come in all different shapes, sizes, and tiers of quality. The end-use should drive the choice. Traditionally, the brims were wide. The origin of the cowboy hat hailed from early settlers wearing wide-brimmed palm or straw hats to help guard their faces and necks from the hot sun on long rides. It's widely accepted that this influence came from the Mexican sombrero. In the 1860s, John Stetson designed the Boss of the Plains hat, which was a fur felt hat made to be more durable, waterproof, and lightweight. The natural curving of the brim and pinching of the crown came over time, as the felt wore away from being constantly moved and squeezed. Eventually, this style became what we know as the modern cowboy hat.

Women's hats then were more modest than the traditional cowboy hat. They had shorter brims, dainty crowns, and a more refined crease. As women got more involved in the sport of rodeo and on cattle drives, they favored the men's version for more practical use. And now, as the hat has moved to the forefront of Western accessories, it's taken on an iconic and playful vibe.

In addition to the hat choices the wearer already has to make, such as brim size, crown shape, and fur quality, a massive variety of colors are now in play. Many cowgirls go for a charcoal or navy blue, which still gives the same classic vibe as the traditional black felt hat, but with slight variation. Others go for a bolder look and choose green, red, and even pink.

The hats are adorned with hat bands and band accessories like pins, feathers, jewels, or otherwise. While a classic shape with a creased brim between four and five inches (10-12.7 cm) is most widely chosen for Western fashion, the "open-road" style with a short brim (usually under three inches, or 7.6 centimeters), as well as the wide, flat brim hat, and the pencil brim hat are becoming increasingly popular, paying homage to the traditional cowboy hats of yesteryear. Additionally, short brims are in, with rough stock riders—generally known to be the fashionistas of the rodeo world—beginning to go back to an old-school three-and-a-half inch (8.8 cm) brim with a tall crown.

Beyoncé sported her classic Stetson at the 2024 Grammy Awards, and there are plenty of other impressive hat makers out there (my personal favorites are Greeley Hat Works, American Hat Company, Serratelli Hat Company and JW Brooks Custom Hat Co.). For the truly trendy, tourists are flocking to their nearest Kemo Sabe for hats at a competitive price that reflect a vibe more reminiscent of the southwest than the true cowboy style. Kemo Sabe has been worn by the likes of Jennifer Lopez, Kevin Costner, Kyle Richards, Rihanna, Shania Twain, Kendall Jenner, Cher, and more. The Kemo Sabe shops can be found in both Aspen and Vail, Colorado; Park City, Utah; Jackson, Wyoming; Whitefish, Montana; and, as of 2025, in the Fort Worth Stockyards.

→ Beyoncé performs songs from her album *Cowboy Carter* at the NFL 2024 Christmas Day Halftime Show.

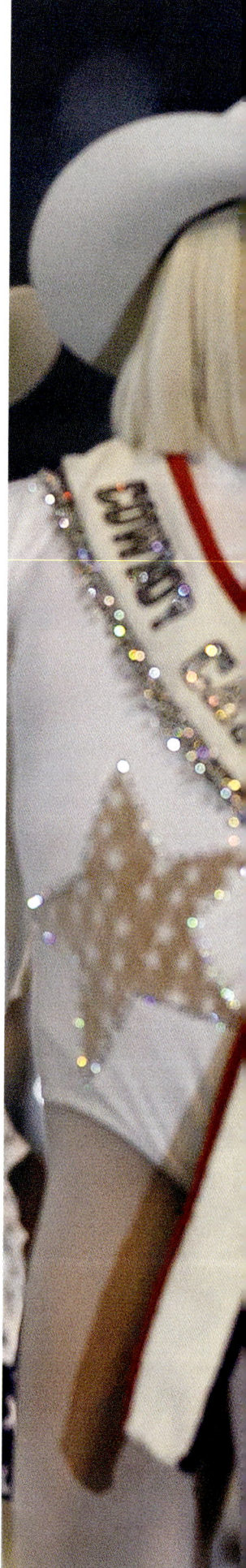

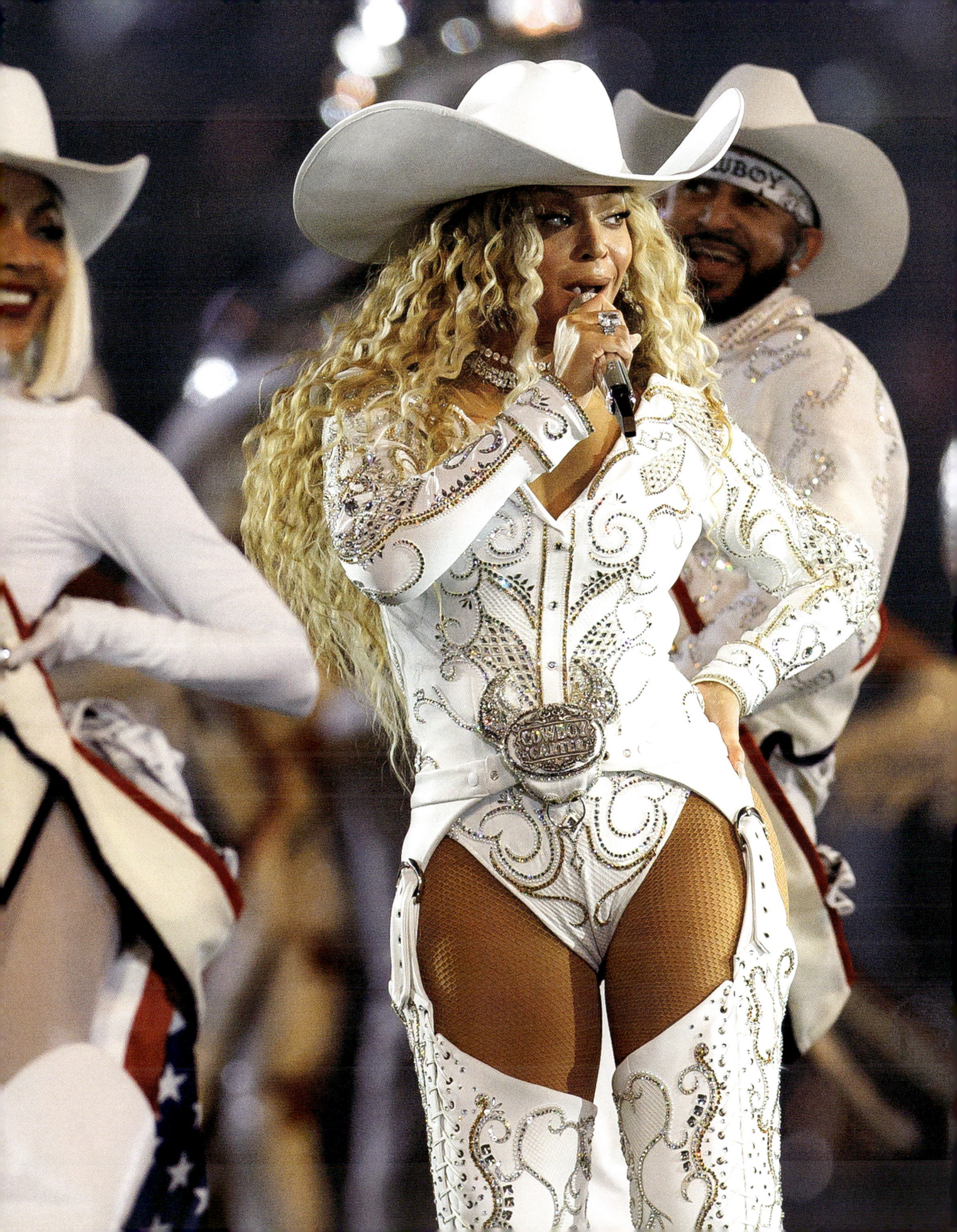

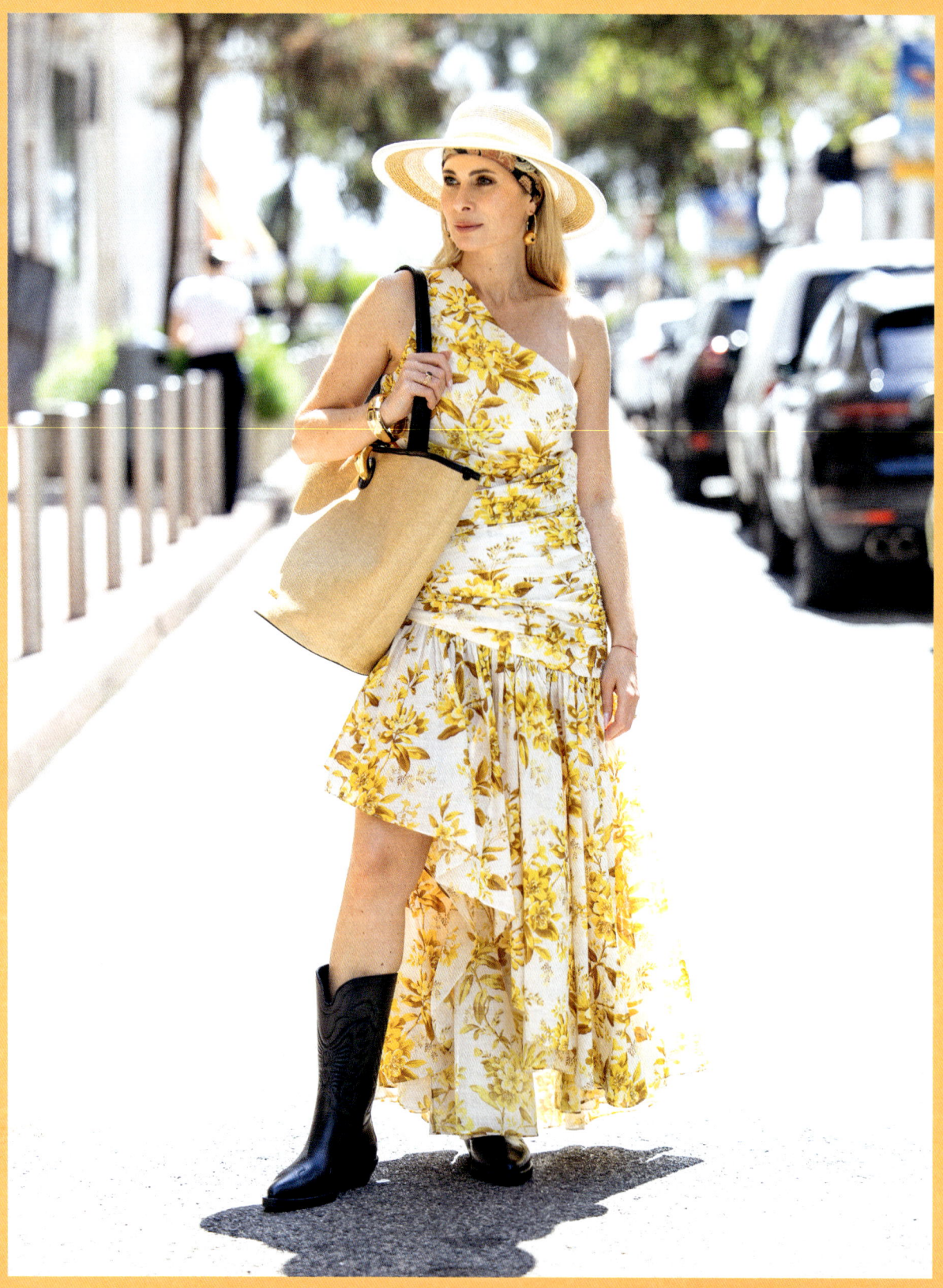

Boots

Fashion influencer Iryna Thater shows off her Dior cowboy boots at the 2025 Cannes Film Festival.

Boots are a lot like hats—they are a very personal accessory and vary widely based on use. I have a set of Justin work boots, and I have about six pairs of fashion boots from various brands like Old Gringo, Ariat, Black Star, and more. I would say such is the case for most cowgirls.

The biggest differentiators between pairs of cowboy boots are color, material, toe style, and shaft height, or the part of the boot that goes around the calf. The more exotic the boot leather, the more expensive the boot gets. They range from leather and ostrich to alligator and tons of other exotic hides like hippo, stingray, and shark. The leather for the boot top, or the part that goes over the foot, can range from simple, smooth leather to finely and ornately tooled or stitched leather, in neutrals or fun colors.

The first iteration of fashion boots featured a shorter shaft height, a round, lifted "walking heel," instead of a "riding heel," which is flatter, and jewel tone colors. Shaft heights were often only ankle or mid-calf height, versus the standard thirteen-inch (33 cm) shaft. Now, we are seeing far more boots with a tall shaft used in Western fashion—usually around eighteen inches (46 cm)—which hits just above the knee. This look elongates the leg and looks great with a Western skirt or dress.

Most fashion boots also feature a narrower toe style, contrary to a classic round- or square-toed Western riding boot. They are often completely pointed or have a very narrow square: no more than an inch or two. Finally, trends are moving away from ornate leather tool or stitch work, and toward more vintage-style patterns and icons. The muted colors are elevating looks, making them feel classic and expensive.

Boots are sadly one of the things falling victim to the fast-fashion market, with low-quality knockoffs popping up all over fast-fashion sites. For the highest quality leather and craftsmanship, cowgirls shop the real thing, at stores such as CITY Boots, Petite Paloma, Lane, Old Gringo, Miron Crosby, Lucchese, Serna, Anderson Bean, and others like them.

183

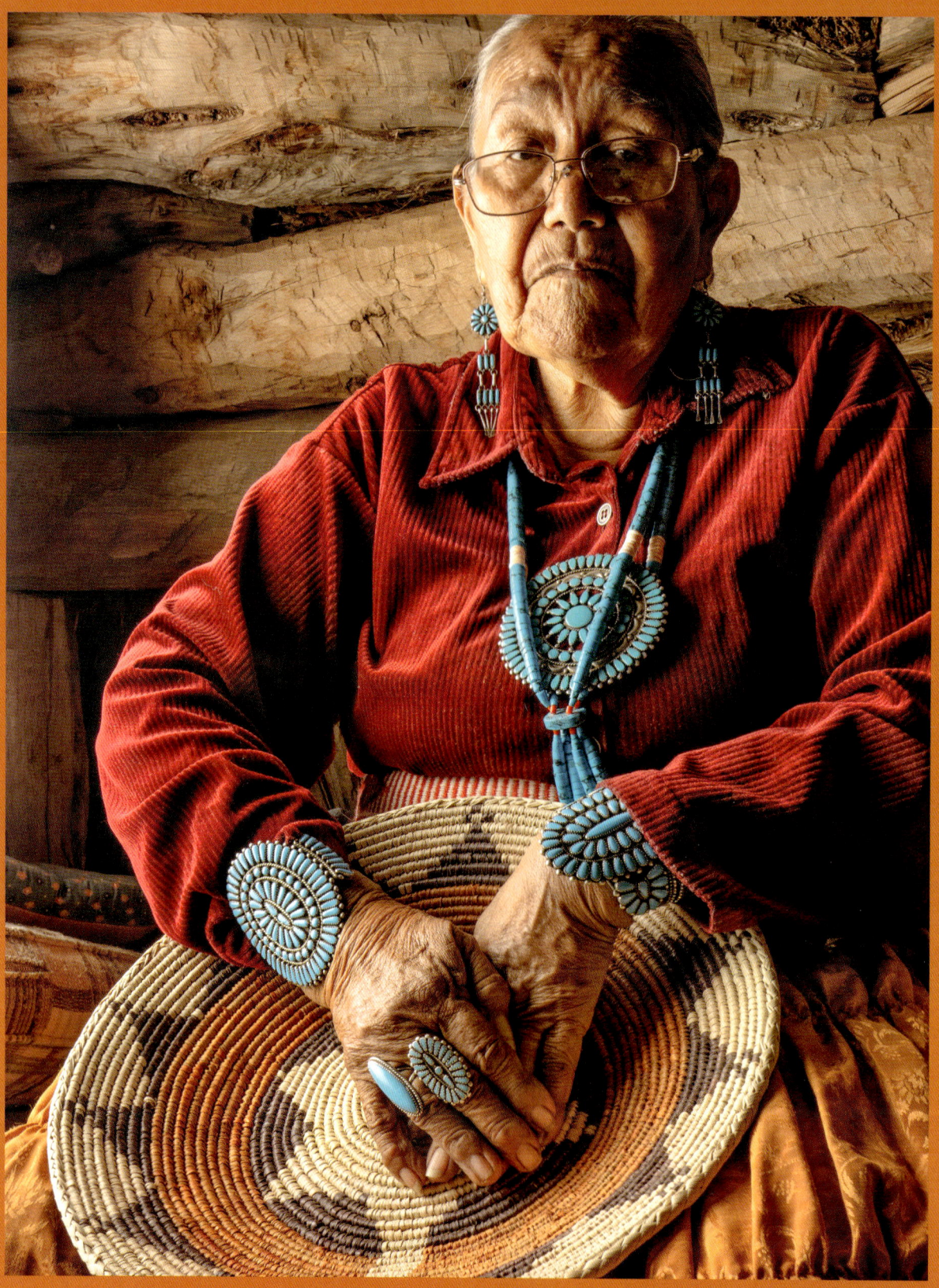

Turquoise

← A Navajo woman in her eighties wearing beautiful turquoise jewelry.

Most cowgirl jewelry is silver and turquoise. American turquoise has been mined all over the southwest, from Colorado and New Mexico all the way to California and Nevada. In fact, evidence suggests that Indigenous tribes were mining turquoise roughly 1,200 years before the Spanish arrived on the continent. American turquoise is considered the most valuable variety of the stone by collectors, because it comes in all grades and colors.

Many of the turquoise jewelry styles worn by cowgirls (and cowboys) were developed and popularized by Native American makers and designers. The Zuni word for turquoise translates to "sky stone" in English, and in several Indigenous cultures, such as the Zuni, Apache, Navajo, and Hopi tribes, the stone is associated with both water and sky.

The stone was used frequently in the aforementioned Indigenous communities in the southwest as a symbol of protection, strength, and good fortune. When cowboys came across Indigenous communities on their journeys west, they began to interact with elements of their culture, including clothing. Cowboys and their families subsequently began incorporating turquoise jewelry into their own lifestyles.

Turquoise is the top fashion stone of the Western community by far. It's a symbol of culture, and of status. Depending on their budget, you'll see cowgirls (and sometimes men too) wear the gem on rings, bracelets, necklaces, earrings, hat bands, belts, and more. Its value changes based on its hardness, matrix pattern, color, and the mine from which it originated. Each turquoise mine in the country assigns different values to its stones based on the supply and demand of that particular mine. It's the only gemstone in the world where two stones of the same quality from two different mines will often be priced differently.

The most expensive American variety of turquoise is the spider web matrix pattern. There are also rare and unique color varieties, such as lime green, fossil, pale white, yellow, and even brown. The price can vary anywhere from one dollar per carat to $300 per carat. The most popular American mines include the Royston, Blue Moon, Kingman, Morenci, Bisbee, Sleeping Beauty, and others. Most of the mines are located in Arizona and Nevada and are known for their unique colors and matrix patterns.

While all turquoise jewelry is derived from and inspired by Indigenous culture, not all stones are Indigenous turquoise. Shoppers must be diligent in finding jewelers who responsibly source their turquoise for the most authentic product. Faux turquoise is not only misleading to consumers, it also tarnishes the significance of the stone for Indigenous communities, who still use it in jewelry making and in important ceremonies. Real turquoise will have a slightly rougher finish than fake, and it won't be scratched as easily. It should also be slightly heavier than a faux counterpart. A quick online search should easily help buyers find reputable jewelry makers who sell authentic turquoise, but if you're looking for a quick recommendation, I would start with Mud Lowery and Montana Silversmiths for the best quality turquoise and silver. Always ask your seller for a certificate of authenticity if you're unsure. You can also buy directly from Native American-owned businesses, or dealers who work closely with Indigenous makers and designers.

Trendsetters and cowgirls are using turquoise in so many new and fun ways, such as in ear crawlers and hat bands, to elevate and dress up any Western look.

Ever the belle of the turquoise ball, though, is the coveted squash blossom. Usually made of turquoise and sterling silver, the squash blossom necklace is the most recognizable and traditional piece of turquoise jewelry on the market. The necklace, said to have originated in the Navajo and Plains Indigenous communities, has two major design components: the naja pendant, a crescent-shaped pendant at the center of the necklace, and beads that look like flowers beginning to bloom. Usually, in between the squash blossom beads are plain or ornate silver beads. They began as somewhat simple pieces of jewelry, but over time have become status symbols, often using large, expensive stones and high-quality silver. The necklaces range from dainty and understated to bold, statement pieces. They've been seen on superstars like Cher, Beyoncé, Jason Momoa, Drew Barrymore, and more.

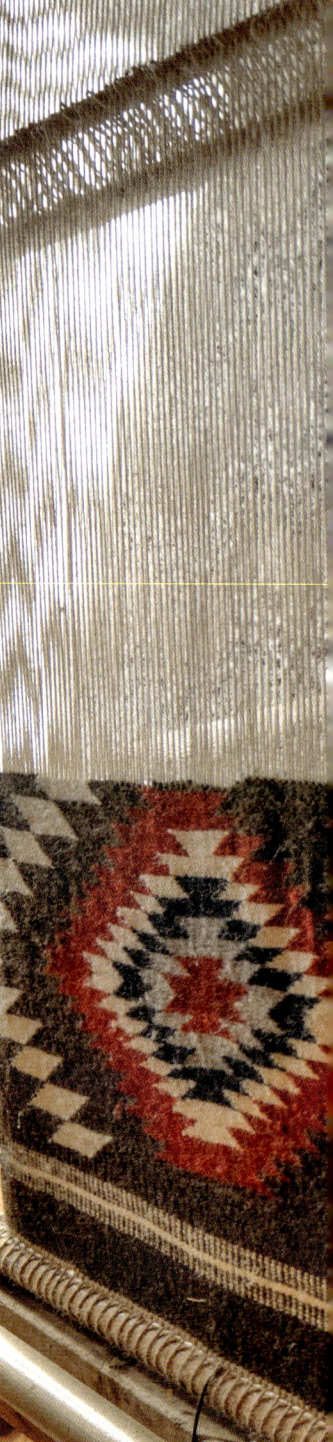

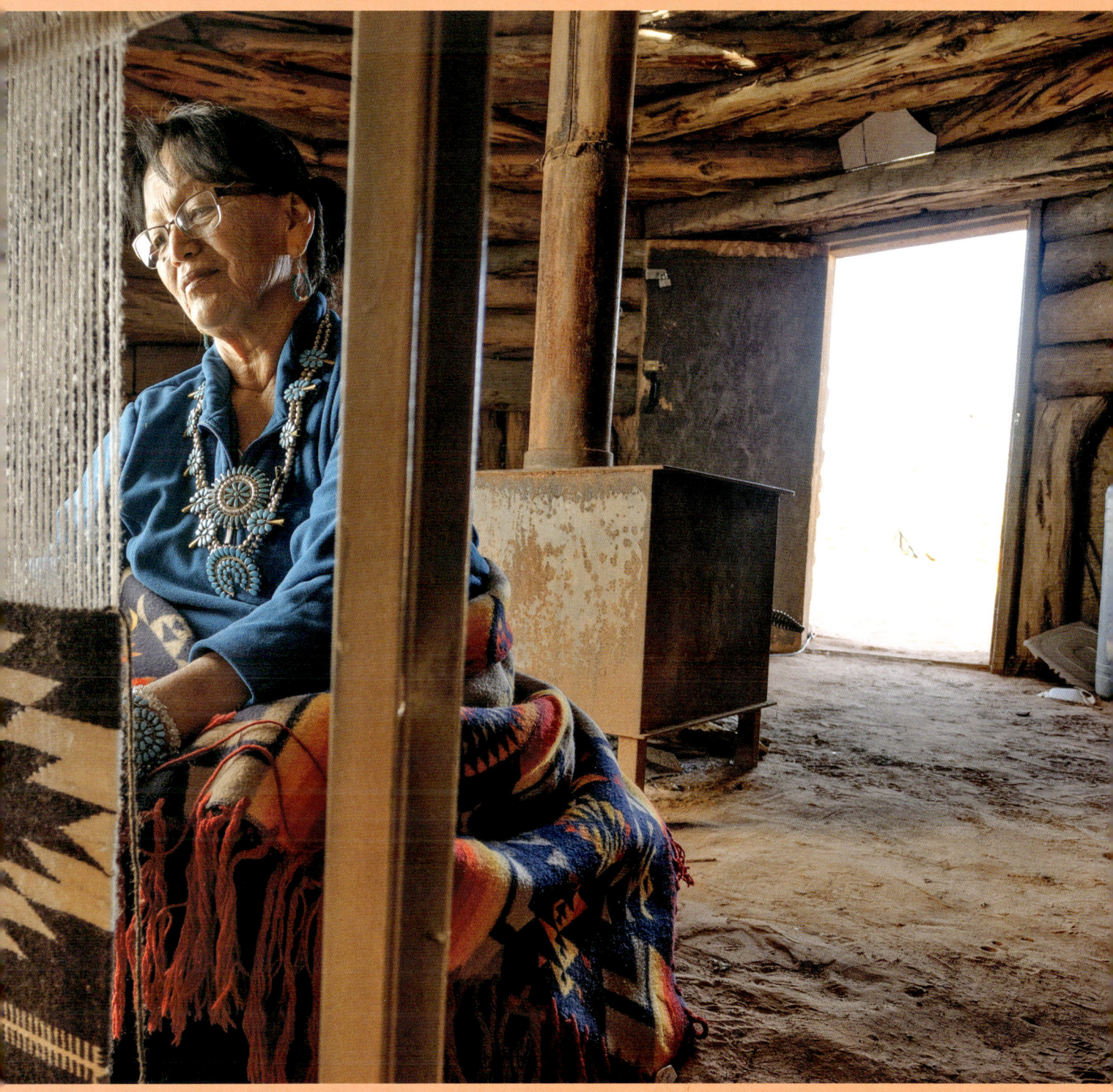

The iconic textile and jewelry designs of Navajo artisans have become synonymous with the American Southwest.

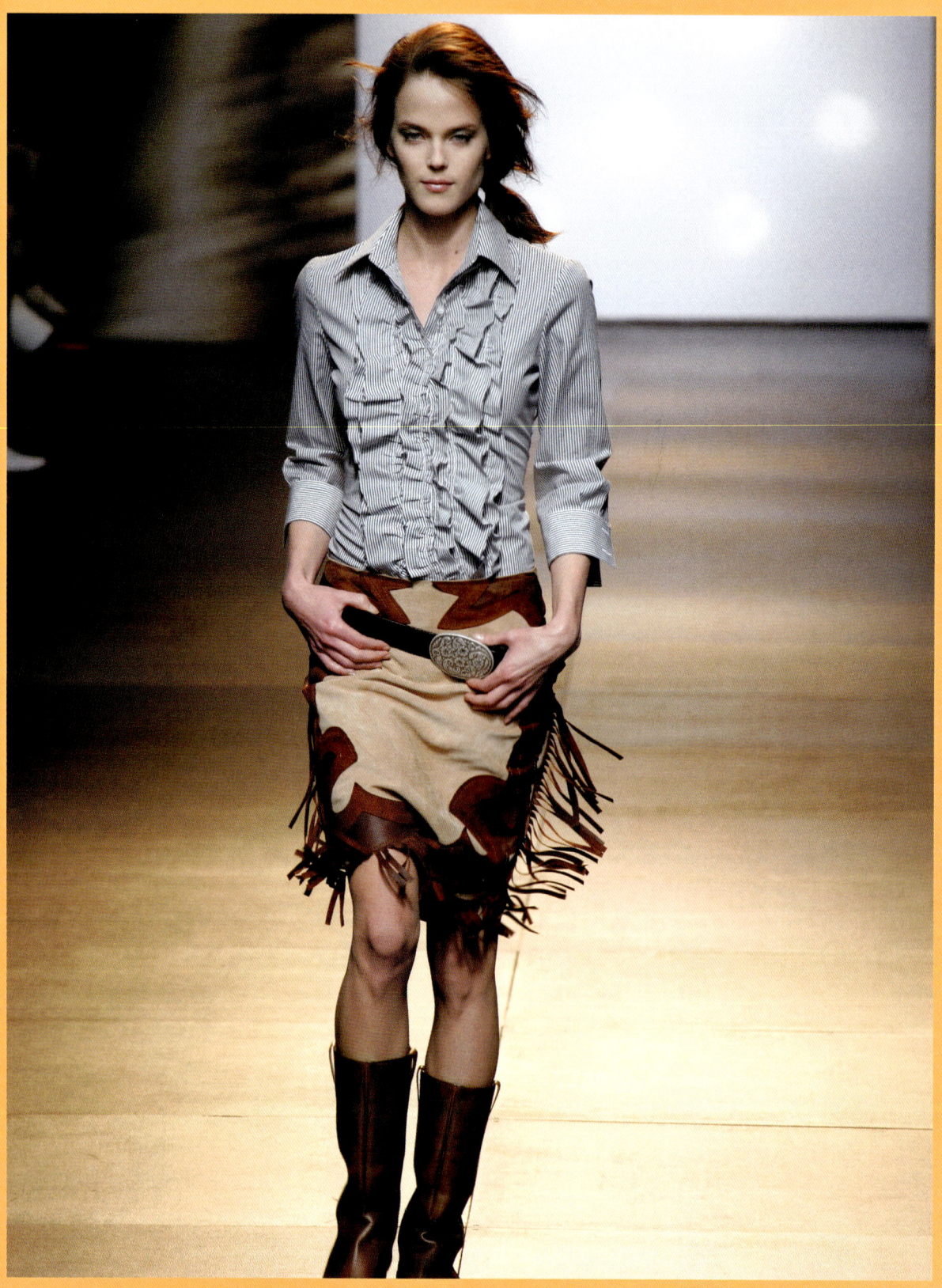

Leather

← A Milan runway look from fashion brand Philosophy's autumn/winter 2005/6 ready-to-wear collection.

Western fashion is also known for its use of leather. Indigenous peoples on the American continent used leathers and hides as protective clothing. Leather has been used in Western and Southwestern fashion for more than seven thousand years, but Western trends are exploring the use of leather in new ways.

Beyond the cowboy boot, belt, and leather jacket, leather is being incorporated into accessories like jewelry, bags, and more. Trending right now is the incorporation of leather patches onto the legs or hips of jeans and skirts. It's a creative way to break up an everyday simple style, and it pays homage to the Western tradition of wearing leather chaps while working cattle. Jackets are adorned with leather fringes to add a more dimensional texture to any style.

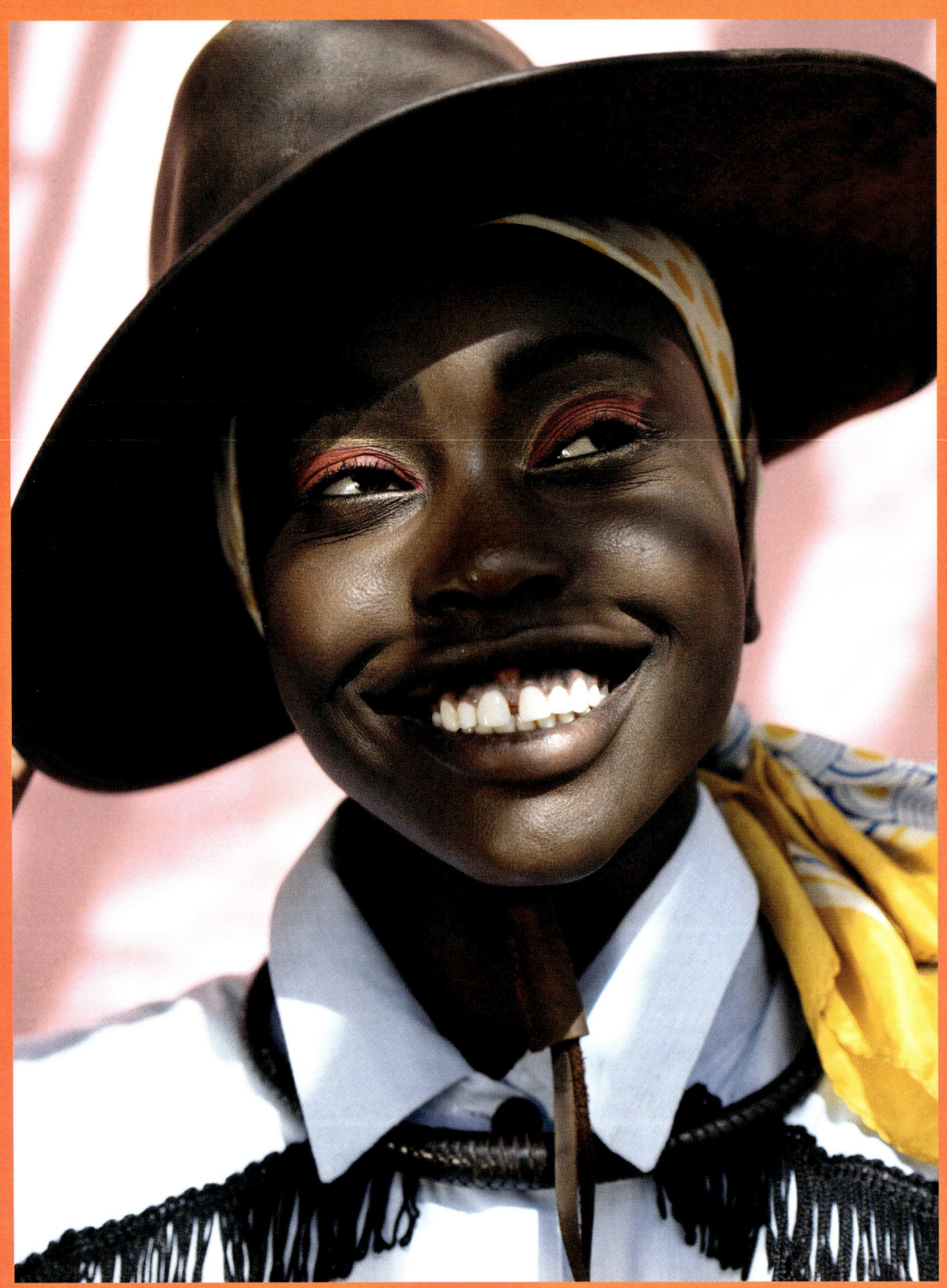

Creative Adaptations

← A cowgirl's best accessory: confidence.

One thing about cowgirls is, if the perfect accessory doesn't exist, they'll just DIY it. One of my favorite trends is the personalization of Louis Vuitton bags, where the designer takes a Louis Vuitton classic leather bag, deconstructs it, and then puts it back together with a Western twist, using thick leather stitching and trim, silver and turquoise stones, tons of leather fringes and braids, silver buckles and clasps, and an endless list of other customizations. Of course, all of this is done in partnership with the French fashion house and is completely legal. The fashion brand Leatherandvodka (pronounced leather and vodka) have really perfected this art.

Speaking of a good do-it-yourself project, my favorite fashion trend in the Western community is taking real, tangible, and everyday Western items and turning them into accessories. At the 2024 National Finals Rodeo, Shaley Ham (or as she is better known on social media, "West Desperado") used a snaffle bit—a common piece of tack for horse owners—and attached it to a leather strap to create the ultimate cowgirl belt. The bit itself was the focal piece in the front where the buckle would normally be. This trend screams horse girl in the best way.

I have also seen spur rowels used as necklace pendants or earrings, horseshoes strung together to make a concho-style belt, rodeo contestant back numbers sewn onto denim jackets as patches, and many other creative customizations, from hat to boots.

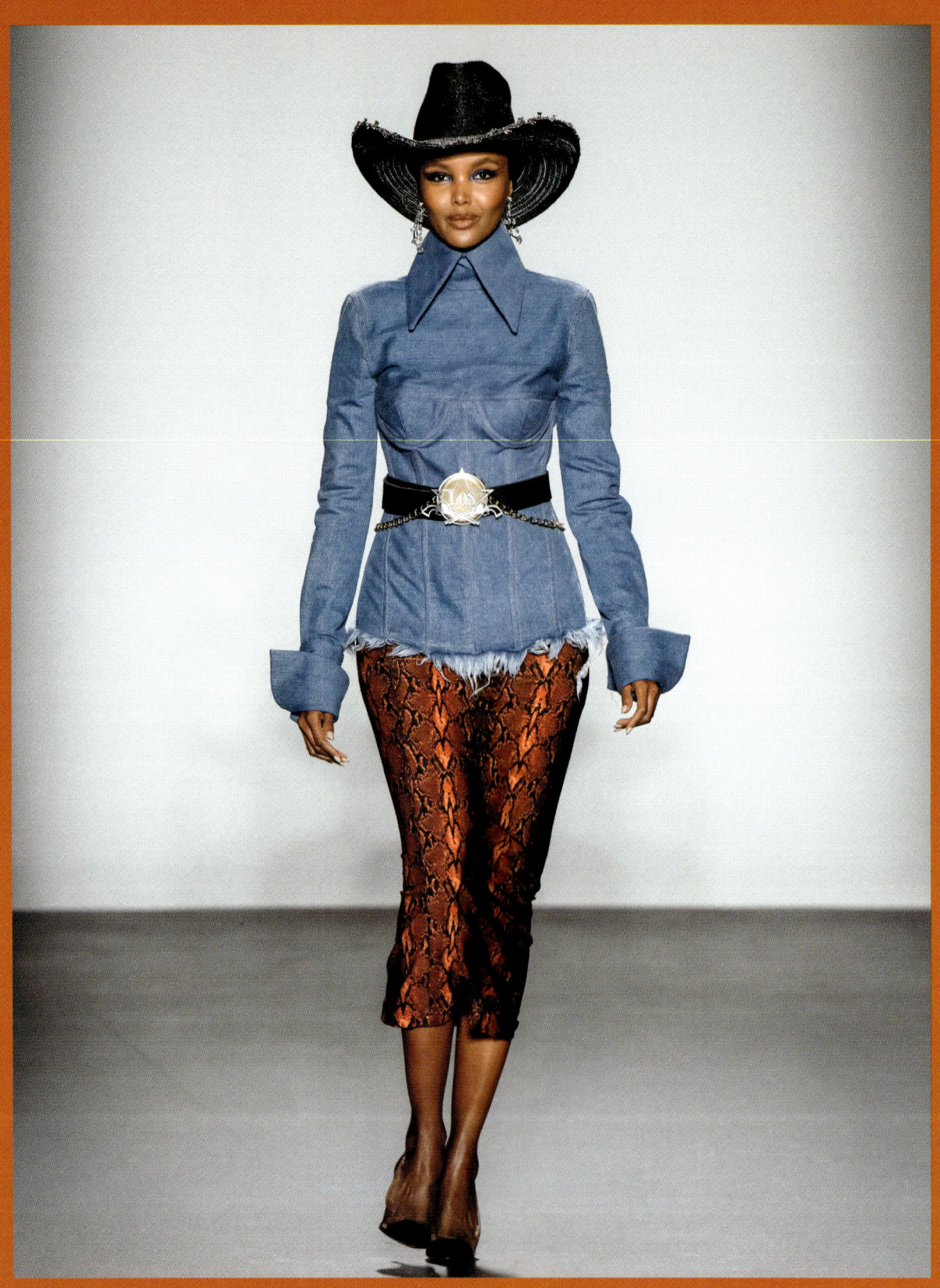

Haus of Cowgirl

Cowgirl fashion has had its moment on the runway too. While Ralph Lauren has always been a brand on the fringe of the Western space, recently, other major fashion houses adopted the Western aesthetic.

The Louis Vuitton fall 2024 men's fashion show featured old-school Western-style embroidered blazers, leather, denim, fringes, cowboy hats, belt buckles, turquoise jewelry (including turquoise grills), and more. In this show, the creative director, Pharrell Williams, wanted to illuminate the roots of the American Western wardrobe. It was epic.

Prada's spring/summer 2025 preview also featured Western-inspired clothing, with the women's line being described as a journey through Western women's fashion clichés. The fashion house has also launched Western-inspired leather boots.

Celine Homme's fall/winter 2024 collection by Hedi Slimane has been described as "cowboycore," and incorporated wide-brimmed hats, heeled cowboy boots, and Western desert scenery, giving it a 1970s vibe with a modern take on tailoring and cuts.

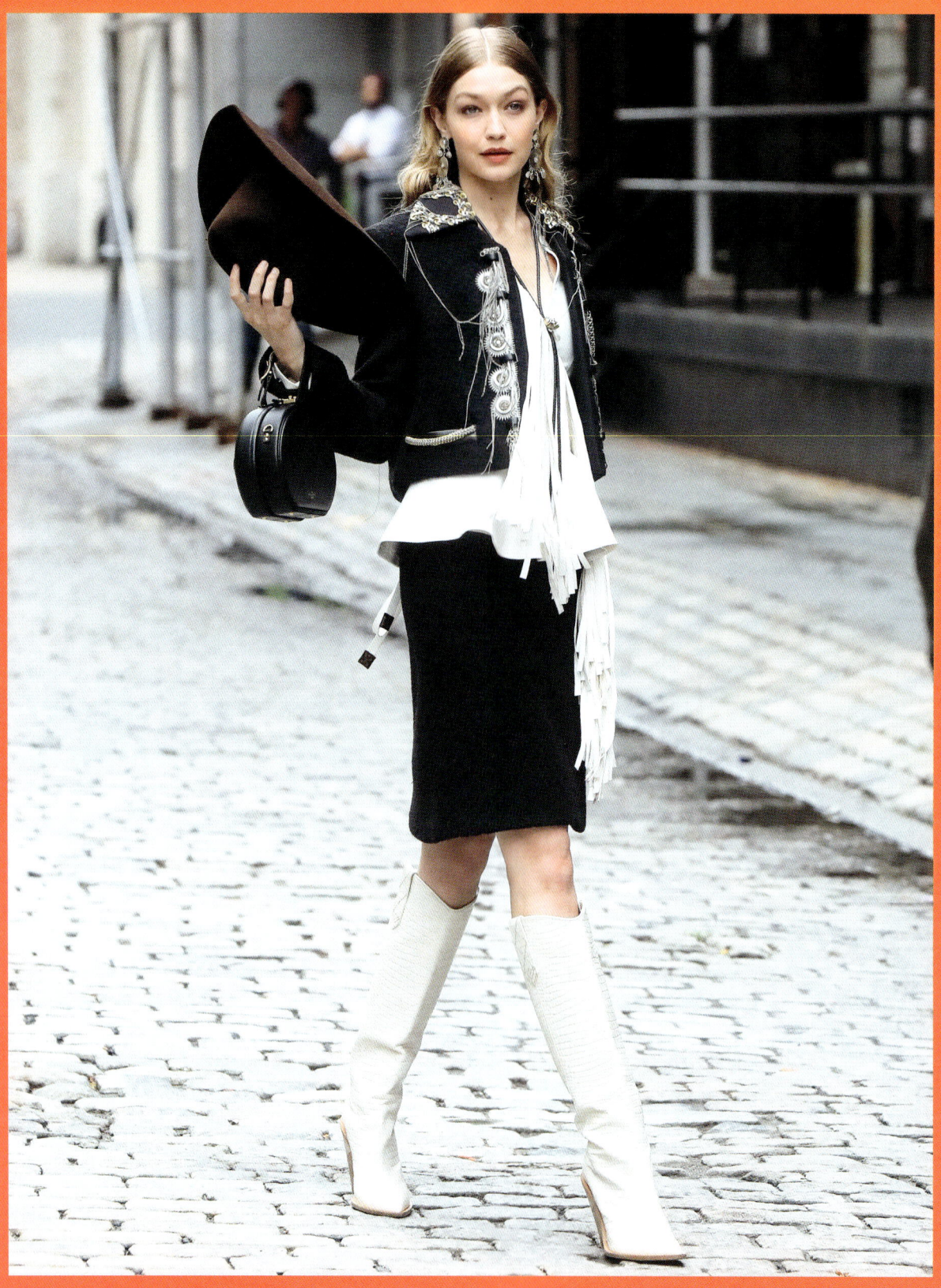

When Western Went Viral

Across the internet, the cowgirl has been going viral. From coastal cowgirl fashion to cowgirl copper hair, the idea of being able to tap into a more wild and carefree version of ourselves has everyone eager to adopt the cowgirl lifestyle in some way, shape, or form.

One of the most used songs on social media reels in 2024 was Dasha's "Austin." The country-feeling ballad had girls and guys across the apps leaning into their line-dancing skills and kicking up their boots. That song was followed closely by Ella Langley's "You Look Like You Love Me."

Cowgirl Copper, another viral internet video trend, featured women requesting a very specific shade of red-toned hair that is reminiscent of Annie Oakley, or Jessie from Toy Story. The color is said to be reminiscent of the American West with its rich, warm, golden and copper tones.

Space Cowgirl became one of the most popular bachelorette party themes of the last couple of years, with women sporting a fun combination of pinks, purples, sequins, and fringes. This was also done in various iterations like Disco Cowgirl, Last Rodeo, Cosmic Cowgirl, and so on. The theme originated after Kacey Musgraves's Grammy-winning album *Golden Hour* was released, which took the world by storm with its flowy, vibey, soothing music.

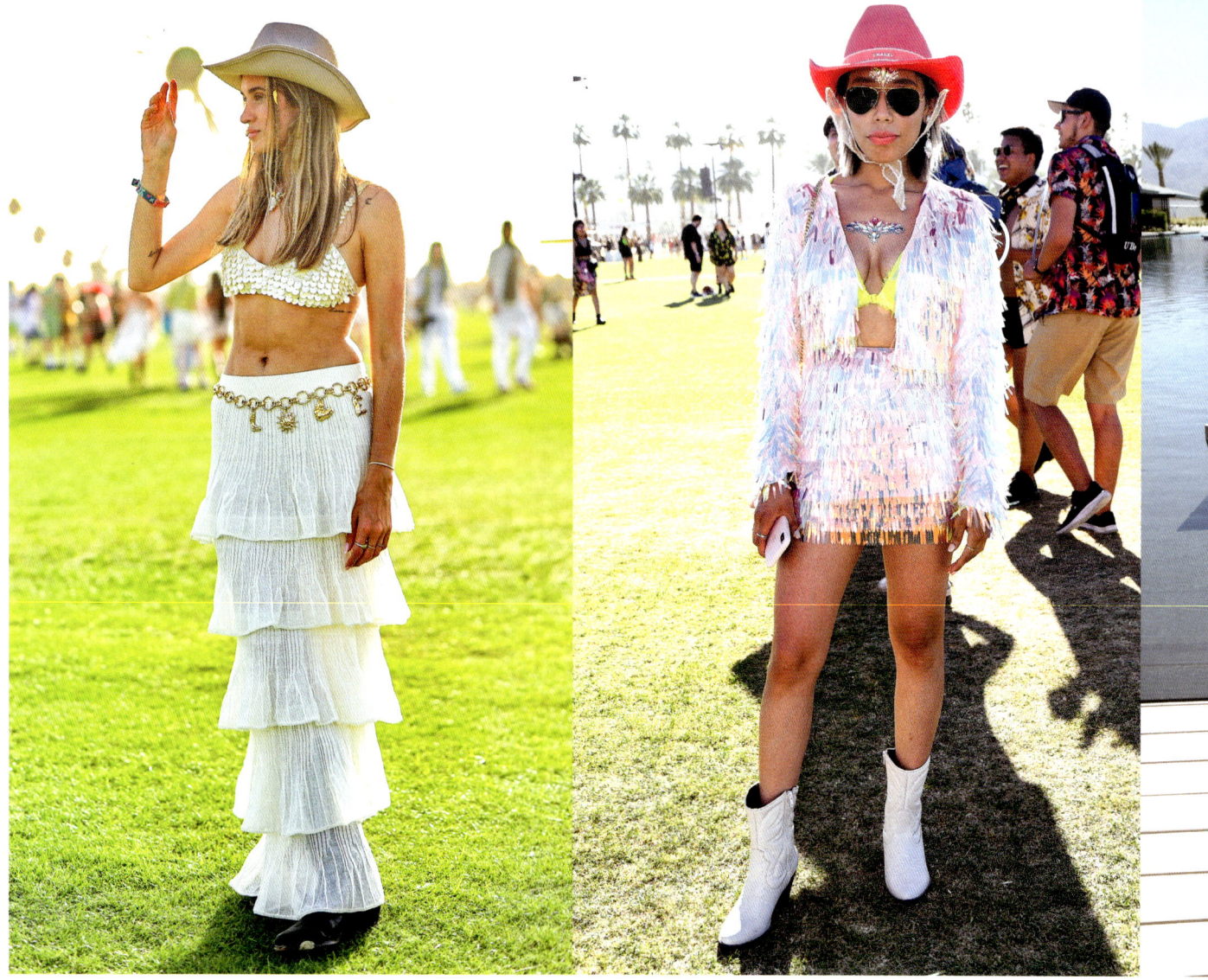

Perhaps the viral internet trend that really took mainstream fashion by storm, though, is the #coastalcowgirl look. Coastal cowgirl is a look that is carefree, light, airy, summery, and relaxed. It isn't too fussy—it looks thrown together and effortless. It's elevated with breathable fabrics and textures. The hair is loose and beachy, the skin is sun-kissed, and the vibes are immaculate. The coastal cowgirl is fun, easygoing, and the girl who many aspire to be. She is the perfect combination of the cowgirl spirit and the coastal pace of life, where things just move slower—kind of like the West.

There are a few standout Western fashion icons who are an instant inspiration for the ultimate cowgirl style. These cowgirls exude confidence, from the ranch pasture to the rodeo arena.

Shaley Ham is one of rodeo's most iconic fashion influencers. She puts her unique style and brand on every outfit, often creating something

← A whimsical Western-inspired festival look, this one spotted at Coachella in 2024.

↑ Coachella festival-goer sporting a pink cowboy hat and white cowboy boots in 2019.

→ Model and actress Olivia Culpo at a 2018 party thrown by Dream Hotels and Republic Records in California.

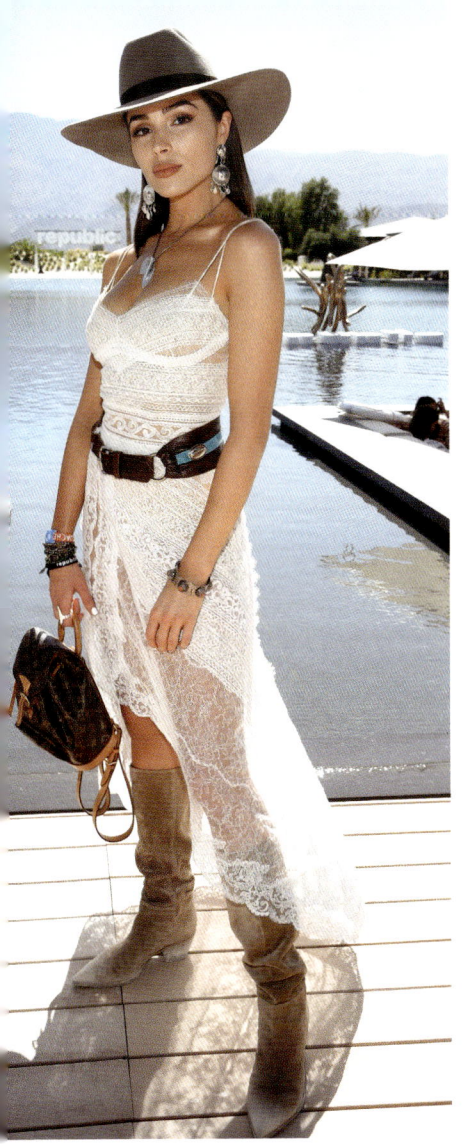

herself to bring the whole vision together. She left her full-time corporate job to pursue her passion for Western fashion and has been an all-out success. Ham is all about lace and fringes, and she has an epic collection of accessories and boots.

Shelby Mayfield is the sister of Shad Mayfield, the world champion tie-down roper. The former can go from old-money glam to cowgirl queen in seconds. Her look is always elevated but somehow seems more attainable for the average person because the pieces she uses are timeless staples. My favorite thing about this influencer is that she often opts to pair her Western outfits with stilettos instead of boots, which feels true to who she is, and I love the way she incorporates that into her everyday fashion.

Danielle Reinhart is a cowgirl by trade and married to a tie-down roper. Dani sports a more conservative, classic cowgirl style and puts her own flair on each and every one of her outfits. She self-describes her style as "corporate cowgirl," which is perfect, because her looks are completely appropriate for both the boardroom and the rodeo stands. Reinhart has found a way to be effortlessly and beautifully Western without sacrificing modesty, which you can tell is more her comfort zone.

Marijka Hunsaker is another cowgirl influencer with a style all her own, but an important pillar of her brand is dressing modestly. Marijka seeks out tea-length skirts and shoulder-covering blouses and sweaters for her dressier outfits, but can just as often be found in jeans, ball caps, and T-shirts. I love Hunsaker's style for its ultimate accessibility and for the way it's completely true to her brand and the space in which she feels most comfortable.

On the other hand, Siobhan Hilliard rocks an edgy, bold Western style I adore. What I find most unique about Hilliard's style is that her pieces are generally not Western by nature, but she creates her signature Western brand by accessorizing with pieces that tie the outfit back to cowgirl culture. Whether it's a turquoise accessory, a fun rodeo ball cap, a concho belt, or a fringe jacket, her style doesn't scream Western and yet you know it is. I love the way these outfits are always bold and yet somehow not overwhelmingly Western. This style is timeless and sexy.

With these examples in mind, cowgirl fashion is not one-size-fits-all. There is something for everyone in the space—the working ranch cowgirl, the fashionistas, the conservative cowgirls, and the eclectic. What makes the styles fun is when a cowgirl stays true to herself and lets her personal brand shine through. When her personality shows up, so does her confidence.

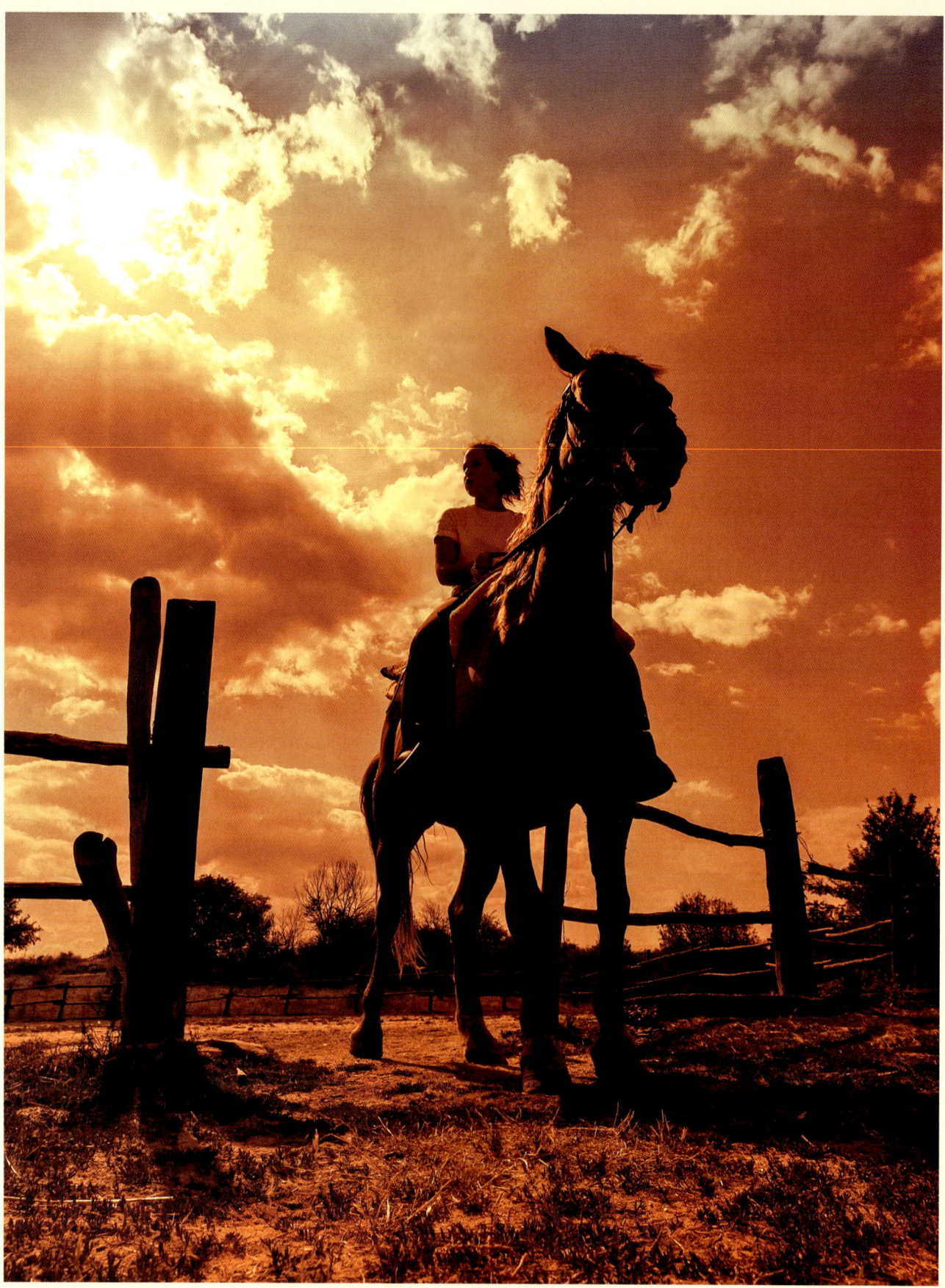

The Cowgirl Spirit

← The world looks wider from the saddle.

What makes or breaks a cowgirl is what lies underneath—what's in your heart, your mind, and your soul. Being a cowgirl isn't about titles or riding with the boys—it's about embracing cowgirl spirit in everything you do. Tenacity, fearlessness, passion, and kindness are values we can all carry with us, embodying the essence of a cowgirl, wherever life takes us.

You can be a rodeo queen and sport full sequins and crystals and embody the cowgirl spirit. You can work from home in sweatpants and a T-shirt and never step foot in a competitive arena and also have the spirit of the cowgirl within you. All of this to say, if you have the fire and passion for Western life—if you are bold, brave, and confident—you are already embodying the cowgirl ethos.

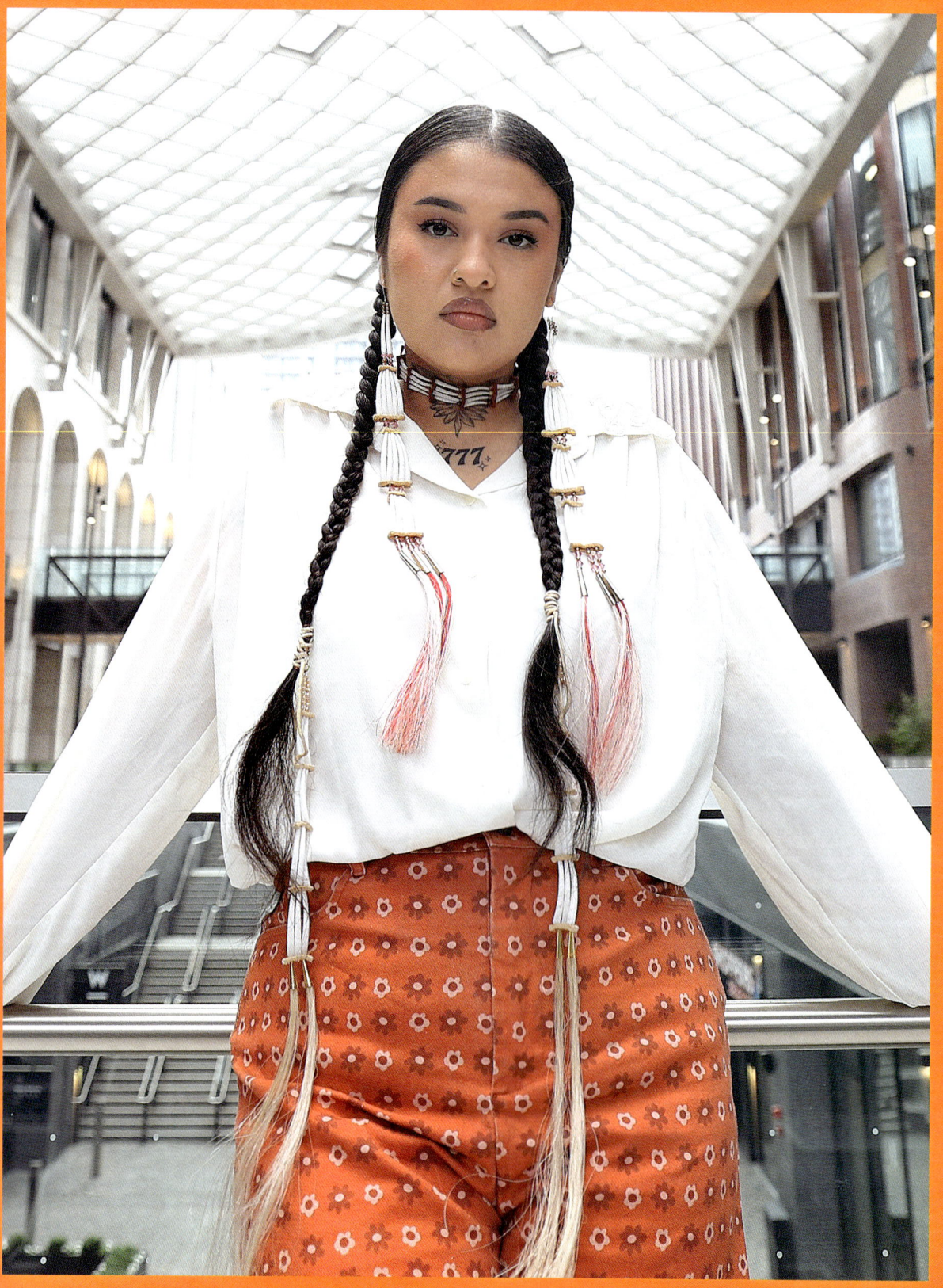

Living the Dream

← Musician and
activist Tia Wood.

We've gone through some true cowgirls and Western fashion icons, but this section is about the women whom I consider to be beacons of cowgirl culture, regardless of how often they are actually on horseback.

Dream chaser Lexi Hoagland is the founder of a group called Cowgirls & Cocktails. She started this group with the goal of building more community among Western women—to build a longer table instead of a taller fence. Originally from Denver, Colorado, she moved to Fort Worth for work. A triplet with two brothers, she was raised with Western culture and values. Within a year, Hoagland grew Cowgirls & Cocktails into a business development group with more than six hundred industry professionals and three areas of operation. The group hosts monthly events for women to gather, network, learn, and engage.

Courtenay DeHoff is also doing similar work with Fancy Lady Cowgirl, an event that is a blend of fancy and ranchy. This gathering celebrates the unique journeys of women as they harness the cowgirl strength within, with a focus on six core cowgirl principles: courage, originality, worthiness, grit, integrity, and resiliency.

Tia Wood is an Indigenous Plains Cree and Salish singer and content creator. She educates people on Indigenous culture while also incorporating Western fashion into her looks and videos. Combining her Indigenous roots with pop influences makes her voice a popular standout. She debuted her music to the world with her EP, *Pretty Red Bird*, in 2024.

And it's not just her voice and music that stand out, but her commitment to advocating for her community and shining a spotlight on missing and murdered Indigenous women.

Alli Addison is the creator of Milton Menasco, an apparel brand marrying old-school equestrian class with a bold, Western flare. She has used her platform to connect two worlds that have long been divided by their opposite cultures. Her designs are timeless yet edgy. She has worked within the Western community to elevate women and give them the confidence to step outside the traditional Western box. Addison is outspoken, fun, creative, and a cowgirl at heart.

Adrian Brannan is a singer and songwriter who hails from a ranching family. With her collection of vintage boots, long blonde curls, and million-dollar smile, you'd never guess by looking at her that Adrian is in law school at Georgetown University in Washington, DC You'd also never guess she is a retired ranch bronc rider, or a survivor of domestic abuse. Adrian wrote *Dear Cowgirl: Letters to Women* in 2018, while she was growing her own cattle herd and attending college. The book is a collection of letters and reflections aimed at giving advice to other domestic abuse survivors. Dear Cowgirl became an entire social media movement and her second book, *Dear Cowgirl: 100 Poems of Hope*, was published in 2022. She is continuing to work on more music. Adrian's steadfast nature and unbreakable spirit is the epitome of the cowgirl ethos.

These women are special, but they are not unlike many women around the world who possess these same characteristics. You don't have to seek them out—the cowgirl spirit is recognizable from the minute you meet it. You just have to know what you are looking for.

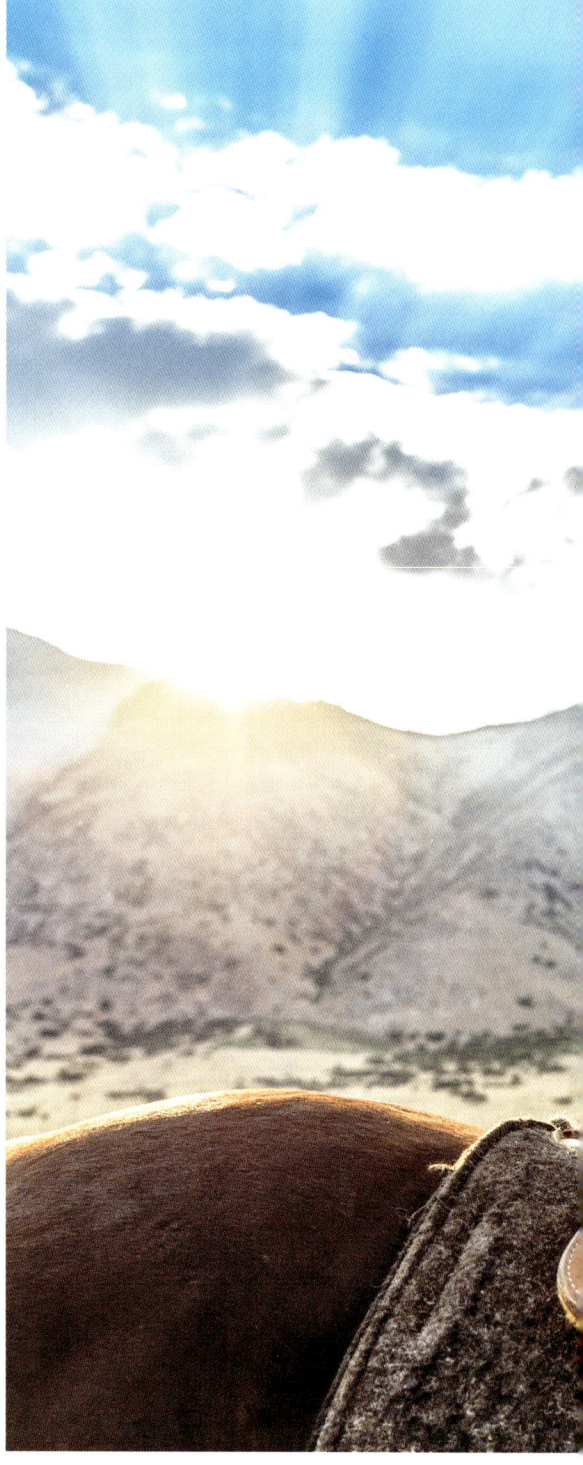

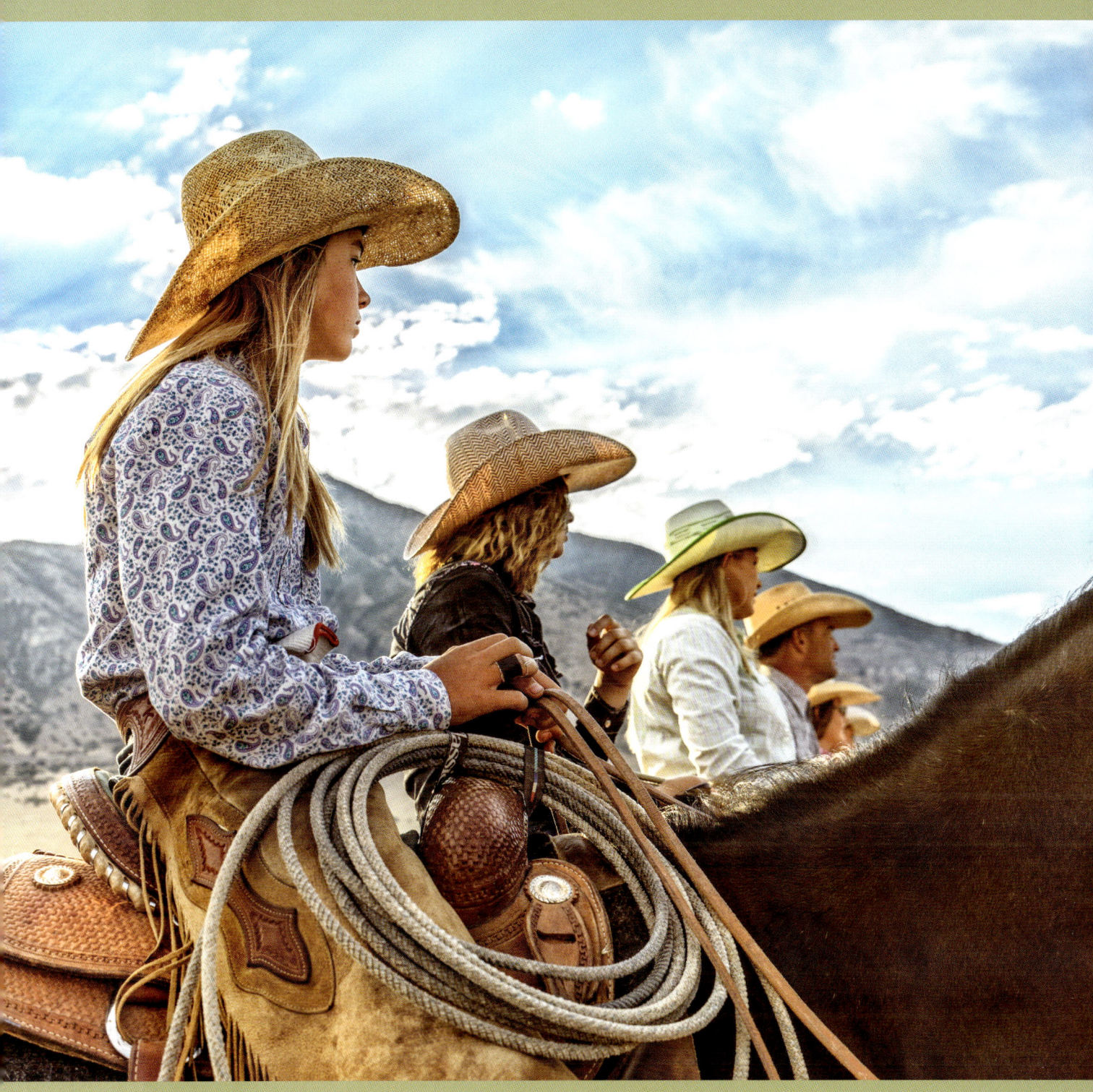

↑   A morning ride.

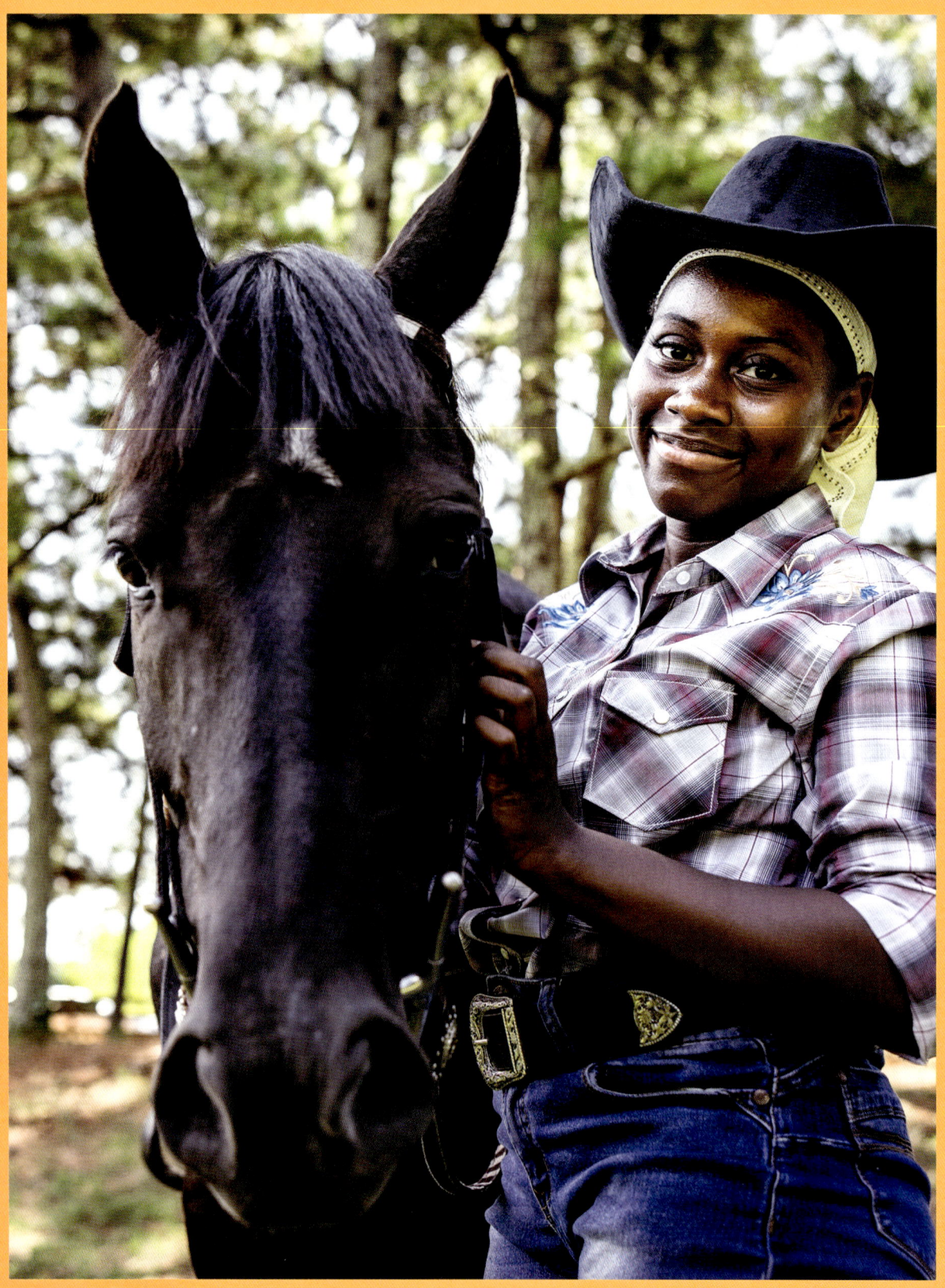

The Cowgirl Next Door

← Happy horse, happy heart.

When you think about the women you know who live like cowgirls—women who are kind by nature, who are fair and just, who work hard for the things they love, and who care deeply about their inner circle—who do you think of? If we want cowgirl culture to survive and be passed on to the next generation, we can't be afraid to encourage young women to saddle up and go for the things they want.

Living like a cowgirl doesn't have to mean branding calves and throwing a rope. It can be women who seek their purpose and pursue their goals. It can be women paving new roads for the ones who will come after them—women who are unafraid to make waves and break stigmas. It can be a single mom working two jobs. It can be a teacher who goes out of her way to help her students succeed. We all know someone who lives like a cowgirl—but are we celebrating her cowgirl spirit?

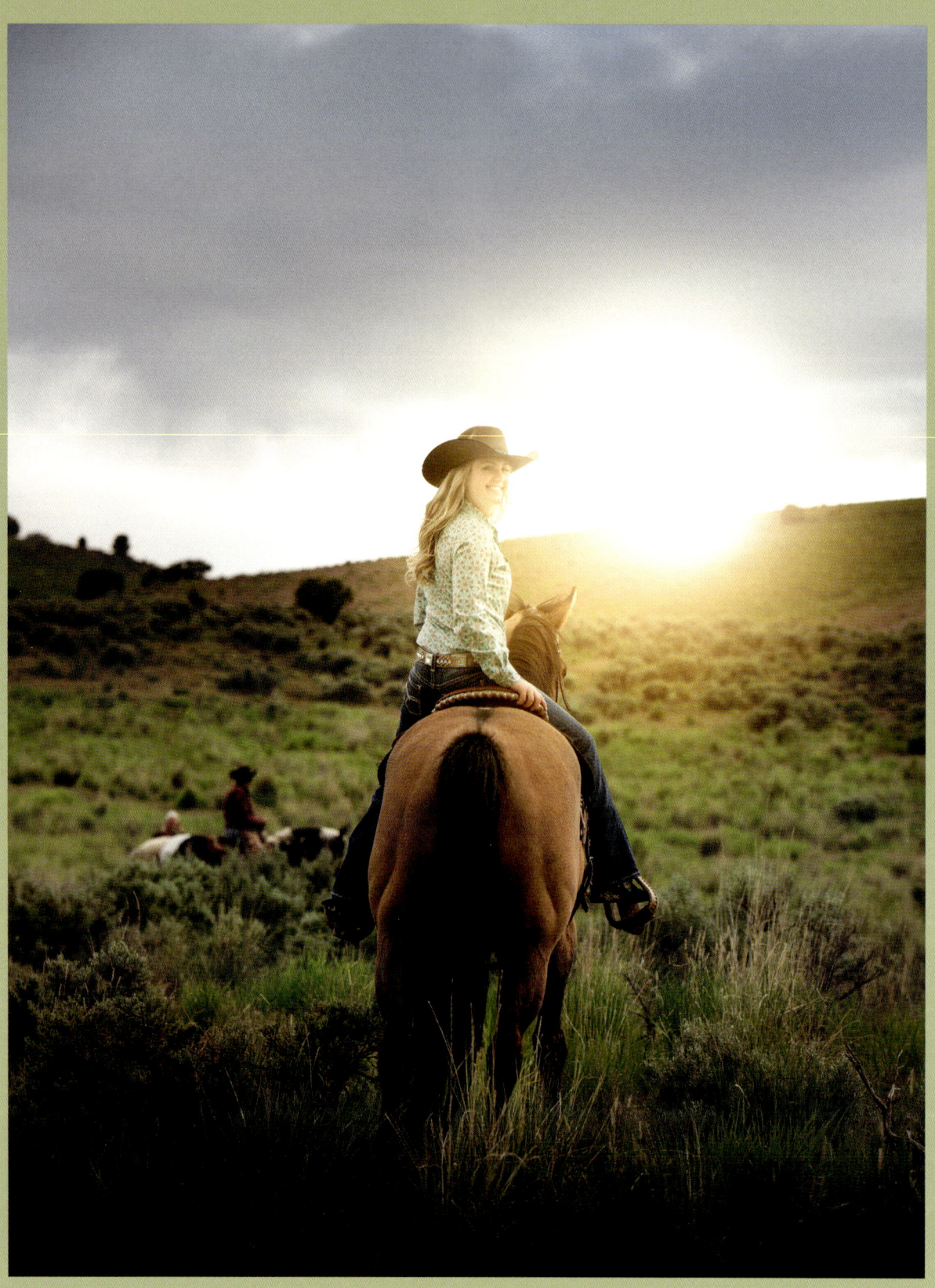

Conclusion
The Cowgirl Legacy

← Keep chasing that horizon.

The problem remains: How do we grow the cowgirl brand without diluting the integrity of the word? Cowgirl culture is already in the mainstream; that train left the station years ago. So how do we ensure the name "cowgirl" is stewarded in a way that brings pride and honor to the Western industry and to the incredible women before us who have worked so hard to ensure cowgirls had a place in this world?

How do we get real-life cowgirls and mainstream cowgirl enthusiasts to sit at the same table? Do they need to? I think the answer is no. All we really need is for every cowgirl, in spirit or profession, to understand our history. If we understand the women who started this whole thing—the ones who pretended to be men to keep themselves safe on cattle drives; the ones who risked their lives in Wild West shows so women could break into rodeo; the ones who demanded equal pay or faced racial discrimination; and the ones who have gone toe to toe with cowboys every day since—we will have a better respect for the term "cowgirl."

We don't diminish the integrity of the cowgirl by using her name to describe someone who doesn't truly uphold cowgirl values. We don't throw the term around based on someone's appearance alone. We reserve the esteemed title of "cowgirl" for those women advancing Western culture, upholding our strict code of ethics, showing courage and determination and kindness in all they do. We hold the cowgirl to a higher standard, and we encourage everyone to embody her spirit, regardless of their

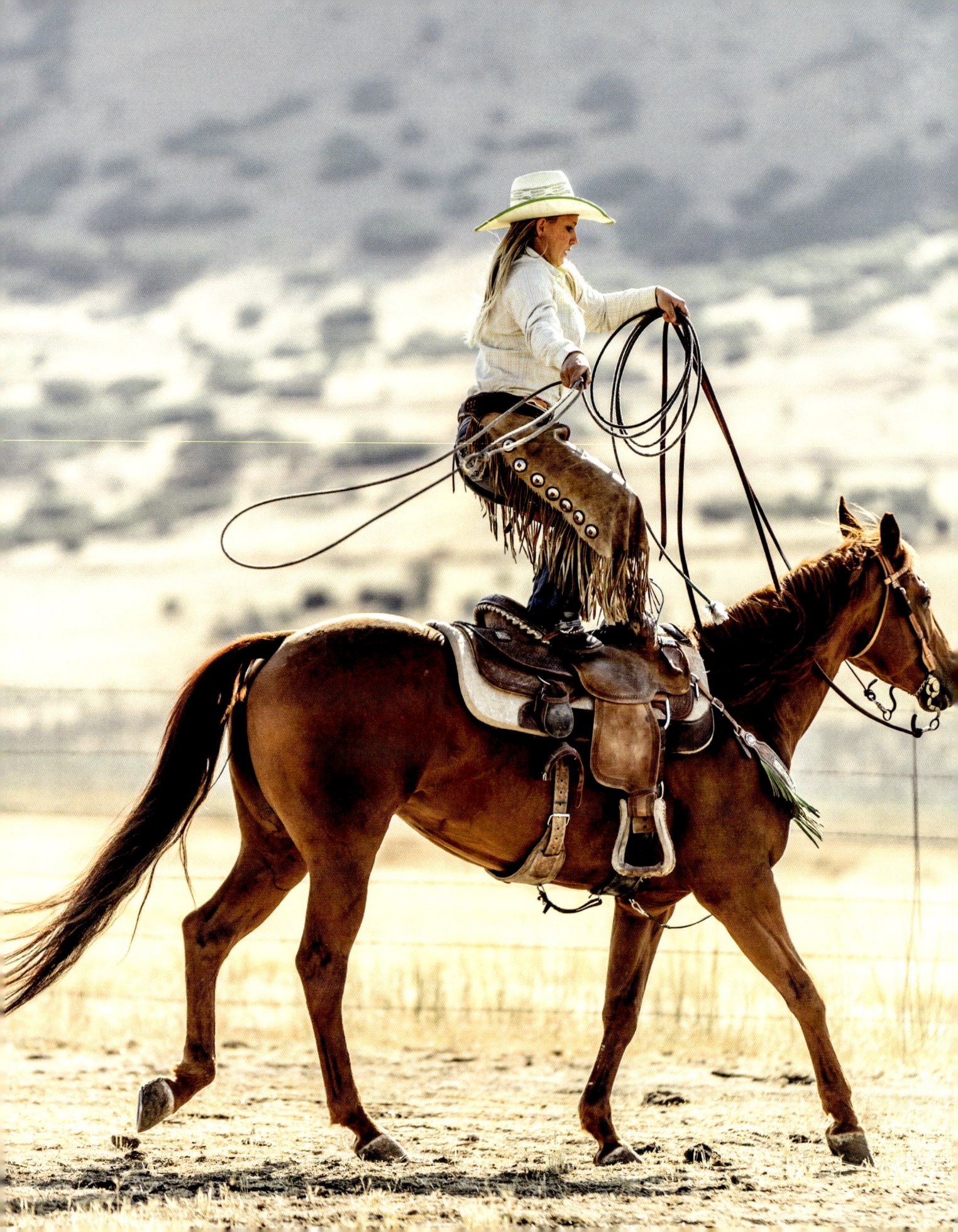

background or environment. We make cowgirl a term any woman would be proud to carry.

The history behind cowgirl culture is important because it helps us understand where cowgirls started and gives us hope for the future. But if we are going to progress, respect has to be mutual. Working cowgirls have to appreciate the extent to which our culture is beloved and celebrated across the world. Cowgirl enthusiasts have to respect the origin of the cowgirl, and ride for that brand. Both cultures have to celebrate the individuality and complexity of the other. When we embrace women who are unafraid to blaze their own trail, make a name for themselves, and take charge of their own lives, regardless of whether they are doing it from the back of a saddle or the front of a stage, we all win.

As long as women keep pushing the envelope, the cowgirl legacy lives. It will live on through inspiration and innovation in the workplace, it lives in the ever-evolving but always classic fashion that is inherently American, it lives in every little girl who sees a horse for the first time and feels something open up deep inside her. It lives in the legacy of the cowgirls in the history books and it will live in the cowgirls who continue to break ceilings and make strides in their own right.

Don't sleep on your dreams. Take the first step. Lift up the people around you as you make your way to the top. Never lose sight of life's most precious gifts. Buy the boots. Wear the hat. Bring individuality to all you do. Take pride in your work. Ride off into the sunset of the life you built for yourself—that's the cowgirl way.

← A cowgirl practicing her trick riding skills.

Cowgirl History
Timeline

1830

GODEY'S LADY'S BOOK FIRST STARTS CIRCULATING

Godey's Lady's Book was a popular magazine for women that circulated from 1830 to 1898 and was instrumental in reinforcing how people thought women should behave and what would later become known as the Cult of Domesticity. Notably, Black women and other Women of Color were excluded from the Cult of Domesticity due to slavery, sharecropping, displacement and other acts of colonial violence that prevented them from existing in domestic spaces. Even as *Godey's Lady's Book* popularized ideas of what "true womanhood" meant, women began challenging the limited roles the Cult of Domesticity laid out for them.

1848

WOMEN'S RIGHTS AND HEADING WEST

1848 was a busy year for cowgirls as it marked the beginning of the California Gold Rush that inspired American men and women to start heading west as well as the first women's rights convention held in Seneca Falls, New York.

1862

THE HOMESTEAD ACT OF 1862

With the rise of ranches in the West, women took a pivotal role in managing the land and animals, especially whilst the men were away on cattle drives. In 1862, unmarried women over the age of twenty-one were granted the ability to claim up to 160 acres (65 hectares) of land to manage their own ranches in the west, though Black women and other Women of Color were excluded until 1866.

1883

BUFFALO BILL'S WILD WEST SHOW

Buffalo Bill's Wild West Show opens in Omaha, Nebraska. Wild West shows like Buffalo Bill's showcased the horsemanship and ranching skills of talented men and women, though these displays could often be dangerous. Buffalo Bill's Wild West Show ran until 1915.

1885

THE BIRTH OF THE "COWGIRL"

The term "cowgirl" is first used in print, referencing the popular Wild West shows, though many women during this time participated in cattle drives, often disguising themselves as men to do so.

1891

BERTIE BROWN

Bertie Brown was one of the first Black women to successfully manage a homestead on her own in the state of Montana. She is known for defying the odds in time when opportunities for Black women were scarce. She's also well-known for creating her own moonshine in the time of prohibition.

1929

DEATH OF BONNIE MCCARROLL, THE RODEO ASSOCIATION OF AMERICA, AND THE BAN OF WOMEN FROM RODEO

In 1929, rough stock rider Bonnie McCarroll died during a Wild West show from an injury she sustained during the bronc riding event. Her death led to the formation of the Rodeo Association of America to help govern and standardize the sport of rodeo. Unfortunately, this also included banning women from participating in rodeo competitions.

1936

THE RODEO COWBOYS ASSOCIATION

Rodeo contestants, fed up with the restrictions placed on them by the Rodeo Association of America, which was made up entirely of event organizers and producers, formed the Rodeo Cowboys Association (RCA), the first contestant-led rodeo organization. The RCA advocated for contestant rights and safety as well as fair compensation. The RCA still excluded women and cowboys of color at this time, however. The RCA was renamed to the Professional Rodeo Cowboys Association (PRCA) in 1945.

1948

THE GIRLS RODEO ASSOCIATION AND THE WOMEN'S PROFESSIONAL RODEO ASSOCIATION (WPRA)

As women were still banned from joining the RCA, thirty women joined together to form the Girls Rodeo Association (GRA), the first organized rodeo association for women and the first professional sports organization in the US created by and for women. The GRA created the rodeo event of barrel racing, which has become one of the most popular and exciting events in rodeo and is still mostly competed in by women. The GRA eventually led to the creation of the Women's Professional Rodeo Association.

1955

THE RODEO COWBOYS ASSOCIATION AND BARREL RACING

In 1955, the Rodeo Cowboys Association, formerly the RAA, signed an agreement with the GRA that the RCA would encourage rodeos to include barrel racing at their events.

1967

BARREL RACING AT THE NATIONAL FINALS RODEO

The Professional Rodeo Cowboy Association introduced barrel racing into the National Finals Rodeo, though the prize money awarded to the women's event was far less than the men's payout.

1969

LINDA MARTELL PERFORMS IN THE GRAND OLE OPRY

Country singer Linda Martell made history as the first Black woman to perform in the Grand Ole Opry, breaking racial barriers in a field dominated by white performers.

1972

LORETTA LYNN WINS ENTERTAINER OF THE YEAR

In 1972, Loretta Lynn, otherwise known as the first "queen of country music," was the first woman to be named the Entertainer of the Year by the Country Music Association, beating out a number of male entertainers and paving the way for other talented women to come.

1980

PRIZE MONEY EQUALITY

In 1980, the GRA refused to participate in any PRCA rodeo that refused to offer a prize payout to women at least equal to the lowest paying men's event. That year, 98 percent of PRCA rodeos met this requirement, encouraging women to develop their skills and compete in the PRCA rodeos, including the National Finals Rodeo.

1987

CHARMAYNE JAMES TAKES NUMBER 1 FOR THE NATIONAL FINALS RODEO

Charmayne James was the first woman to earn the number 1 spot at the National Finals Rodeo, less than a decade after the increase in pay for women competitors. Sherry Cervi in 1995 and Mary Burger in 2016 are the only two other women to achieve this coveted title.

1998

EQUAL PAY FOR BARREL RACING

In 1998, the PRCA began awarding the same amount of money to women as men in the barrel racing competition at the National Finals Rodeo.

2000

LINDY BURCH WINS NCHA OPEN WORLD CHAMPIONSHIP

Lindy Burch was the first woman to win the NCHA Open World Championship in 2000, and that same year was elected as the NCHA's first and only female president. Burch had a career of record and glass-ceiling breaking before her victory in 2000: in 1979, she was the first woman to win the NCHA Open Futurity Reserve Championship; in 1980, she was the first woman to win the NCHA Open Futurity (and setting an impressive record while she was at it); in 1995, she was the first rider, man or woman, to win all four rounds of the NCHA Open World Finals; and in 1998, she set a record that lasted thirteen years at the NCHA Open World Finals.

2016

BRITTANEY LOGAN AND KISHA BOWLES FOUND COWGIRLS OF COLOR

Brittaney Logan and Kisha Bowles founded Cowgirls of Color, an all-female, all-Black rodeo team, bringing attention to the contributions of Black women in rodeo.

2025

BEYONCÉ WINS GRAMMY FOR BEST COUNTRY ALBUM OF 2025

Beyoncé made history with her 2024 album, *Cowboy Carter*, when it won the Best Country Album of 2025, making her the first Black woman to win the Best Country Album Grammy Award.

2026

PROFESSIONAL BULL RIDERS (PBR) LAUNCHES THE PREMIERE WOMEN'S RODEO

This year, a new, wholly-owned brand built to become the preeminent platform for women's rodeo athletes worldwide will launch, opening the door even wider for future cowgirls.

Resources

The Professional Rodeo Cowboys Association (PRCA): Based in Colorado Springs, it is the world's oldest and largest rodeo-sanctioning body. It champions the traditions of the West, organizes premier rodeo events, supports youth programs, and collaborates with organizations like Tough Enough to Wear Pink and the ProRodeo Hall of Fame. Learn more at prorodeo.com.

The WPRA (Women's Professional Rodeo Association): Based in Colorado Springs, it works alongside the PRCA to create opportunities for women to compete in rodeo and earn equal payouts. Learn more at wpra.com.

The Cowgirls of Color: Based in Maryland, this is an all-Black women's organization that aims to break racial barriers in the sport of rodeo. Learn more at: cowgirlsofcolor.wixsite.com/cowgirlsofcolor

The American Quarter Horse Association (AQHA): Based in Amarillo, Texas, it is the world's largest breed registry and membership organization. It promotes humane treatment and supports members competing nationwide. Learn more at AQHA.com.

The National Cowboy & Western Heritage Museum: Located in Oklahoma City, it is the leading institution for Western art and culture. Formerly the National Cowboy Hall of Fame, it preserves and showcases artifacts to celebrate the American West's legacy. Learn more at nationalcowboymuseum.org.

The ProRodeo Hall of Fame and Museum of the American Cowboy: Based in Colorado Springs, it preserves rodeo history and its impact on Western American culture. It honors notable competitors and works alongside the WPRA and PRCA to inspire future rodeo stars. Learn more at prorodeohalloffame.com.

The National Cowgirl Museum and Hall of Fame: Located in Fort Worth, this museum celebrates women whose courage, resilience, and independence helped shape the West. It features interactive exhibits, a research library, and over 4,000 artifacts honoring more than 750 remarkable women. Learn more at cowgirl.net.

The Texas Cowboy Hall of Fame: Located in the Fort Worth Stockyards, it honors 160 Texans who have excelled in rodeo, ranching, and Western culture. Learn more at tchof.com.

The Art of the Cowgirl: This annual event celebrates women's contributions to ranching and the Western lifestyle through trade shows, craft showcases, and competitions. It raises funds for traditional cowgirl trades and features events like the Kimes Ranch World's Greatest Cowgirl and the Wrangler All Women's Ranch Rodeo. Learn more at artofthecowgirl.com.

The Australian Cowgirl: Held in Tatura, Victoria, this spinoff of Art of the Cowgirl celebrates Australian cowgirls and supports horsewomen and artists through mentorship. Events include Colt Starting, Reining, Cutting, and Australia's Greatest Horsewoman. Learn more at theaustraliancowgirl.com.au.

National Finals Rodeo: Hosted annually in Las Vegas, this event showcases the top 15 riders competing for world championships over ten nights. Highlights include Cowboy Christmas, trade show events, and rodeo-adjacent competitions like Barrel Racing and Breakaway Roping. Details at nfrexperience.com.

Fancy Lady Cowgirl: Courtenay DeHoff's event unites women from all walks of life to embrace the cowgirl spirit through motivational talks, networking, and immersive experiences. Find out more at courtenaydehoff.com.

Cowgirls and Cocktails: Lexi Hoagland's community connects over 600 women in the Western industry around Dallas/Fort Worth. Monthly meetups foster mentorship, friendships, and collaboration. Follow on Instagram at @cowgirlsandcocktails_.

COWGIRL: This bi-monthly publication celebrates modern cowgirls with content on lifestyle, style, and music, as well as the annual *COWGIRL* 30 Under 30.

Western Horseman: Since 1936, this monthly magazine has covered Western culture, competitions, and lifestyle. Explore more at westernhorseman.com.

Of the West: A resource connecting job seekers with Western industry employers, from ranch roles to corporate positions. Discover opportunities at ofthewest.co.

References

CHAPTER 1: THE WEST GOES COWGIRL

Frontier Institute. "Black History Month in Montana." Accessed April 15, 2025. https://frontierinstitute.org/black-history-month-in-montana/.

National Park Service. "African American Homesteaders in the Great Plains." Accessed April 15, 2025. https://www.nps.gov/articles/african-american-homesteaders-in-the-great-plains.htm.

ScholarWorks, University of Montana. "Conference Abstracts." Accessed April 15, 2025. https://scholarworks.umt.edu/umcur/2022/330/2/.

University of Missouri System. "Women and the Cult of Domesticity." Accessed April 15, 2025. https://umsystem.pressbooks.pub/alpt1865/chapter/women-and-the-cult-of-domesticity/.

CHAPTER 2: NOT HER FIRST RODEO

Cowboys & Indians. "Nat Love: The Legendary Cowboy of the American West." Accessed April 15, 2025. https://www.cowboysindians.com/2025/02/nat-love-the-legendary-cowboy-of-the-american-west/.

COWGIRL. "The African American Women of the Wild West." Accessed April 15, 2025. https://www.cowgirlmagazine.com/the-african-american-women-of-the-wild-west/.

Essence. "It's Not Our First Rodeo: Black Women in the Wild, Wild West." Accessed April 15, 2025. https://www.essence.com/news/not-our-first-rodeo-black-women-wild-wild-west/.

Nat Love. Life and Adventures of Nat Love, Better Known in the Cattle Country as "Deadwood Dick," by Himself. Accessed April 15, 2025. https://uncpress.org/book/9781469633220/life-and-adventures-of-nat-love-better-known-in-the-cattle-country-as-deadwood-dick-by-himself/.

National Cowboy Museum. "Breaking Trail: The Life of Bill Pickett." Accessed April 15, 2025. https://nationalcowboymuseum.org/blog/breaking-trail-the-life-of-bill-pickett/.

Professional Rodeo Cowboys Association. "Rodeo Association of America, Rodeo Cowboys Association, Girls Rodeo Association, The Original Horsemen." Accessed April 15, 2025. https://www.prorodeo.com.

CHAPTER 3: WESTERN LIFE AROUND THE WORLD

Afar. "Meet Mexico's Youngest Generation of Rodeo Riders." Accessed April 15, 2025. https://www.afar.com/magazine/the-new-generation-of-women-competing-at-mexican-rodeos.

Americana. "Official Event Page." Accessed April 15, 2025. https://www.americana.de/en/.

ExpoBeds. "Americana Event Overview." Accessed April 15, 2025. https://www.expobeds.com/event/americana.

EQ Fest. "Miguel Vega Profile." Accessed April 15, 2025. https://www.eqfest.com.mx/miguel-vega.

FEI. "FEI European Reining Championships for Seniors, Juniors, and Young Riders." Accessed April 15, 2025. https://inside.fei.org/media-updates/fei-european-reining-championships-seniors-juniors-and-young-riders.

Mazatlán Post. "Escaramuzas: The Female Rodeo Queens of Mexico." Accessed April 15, 2025. https://themazatlanpost.com/2019/01/01/escaramuzas-the-female-rodeo-queens-of-mexico/.

Paniolo Preservation Society. "Hall of Fame Inductees." Accessed April 15, 2025. https://paniolopreservation.org/nine-new-hall-of-famers/.

Quarter Horse News. "Cira Baeck Joins NRHA's Million Dollar Rider List." Accessed April 15, 2025. https://www.quarterhorsenews.com/2018/12/cira-baeck-joins-nrhas-million-dollar-rider-list/.

RodeoWest. "Competidoras e Rainhas – As Mulheres No Mundo Country." Accessed April 15, 2025. https://blog.rodeowest.com.br/mundo-country/competidoras-rainhas-mulheres-mundo-country/.

Smithsonian. "Cowboys in the Tropics: A History of the Hawaiian Paniolo." Accessed April 15, 2025. https://www.smithsonianmag.com/blogs/smithsonian-center-folklife-cultural-heritage/2021/05/12/cowboys-tropics-history-hawaiian-paniolo/.

Western Horseman "Jineteadas: Festivals & Folklore." Accessed March 2025.

Western Horseman. Pimienta, Paola. "Escaramuza: Women of the West." Accessed April 2025.

Montana Tourism Department. "Assessing the Impact of the Yellowstone TV Series on Montana's Tourism Economy." https://www.bber.umt.edu/pubs/econ/FilmIndustryImpact2022.pdf

CHAPTER 4: QUINTESSENTIAL COWGIRLS

Essence. "Meet The Co-Founders of 'Cowgirls of Color' — A Rodeo Group Aiming To Change The Face Of Riding" Accessed April 15, 2025. https://www.essence.com/news/money-career/cowgirls-of-color-rodeo-group/.

National Cowboy & Western Heritage Museum. "Anne Marion, Helen Groves." Accessed April 15, 2025. https://www.nationalcowboymuseum.org.

National Cowgirl Museum and Hall of Fame. "Classic Cowgirls: Anne Marion, Helen Groves, Jimmie Munroe." Accessed April 15, 2025. https://www.cowgirl.net.

National Cutting Horse Association. Accessed April 15, 2025. https://www.nchacutting.com.

Oxbow Ranch. "Lindy Burch." Accessed April 15, 2025. https://www.lindyburch.com.

Performance Horse Central. "Lindy Burch." Accessed April 15, 2025. https://www.performancehorsecentral.com.

Vintage Vandalizm. "Badass Black Cowgirls of History." Accessed April 15, 2025. https://vintagevandalizm.com/blogs/news/famous-black-cowgirls-of-history.

Women's Professional Rodeo Association. "Girls Rodeo Association, Women's Professional Rodeo Association, Jimmie Munroe, Lindy Burch, Pam Minnick." Accessed April 15, 2025. https://wpra.com/.

CHAPTER 5: FROM HOMESTEAD TO HOUSEHOLD NAME

BlackPast. "Mickey Guyton Biography." Accessed April 15, 2025. https://www.blackpast.org/african-american-history/mickey-guyton-1983/.

Britannica. "Linda Martell Biography." Accessed April 15, 2025. https://www.britannica.com/biography/Linda-Martell.

Rolling Stone. "Linda Martell: Country's Lost Pioneer." Accessed April 15, 2025. https://www.rollingstone.com/music/music-features/linda-martell-black-country-grand-ole-opry-pioneer-1050432/.

CHAPTER 6: IN OUR COWGIRL ERA

Rare Historical Photos. "The Cowgirls of the West in Rare Photographs, 1860-1930." Accessed April 15, 2025. https://rarehistoricalphotos.com/cowgirls-west-photographs/.

Vintage Dancer. "Vintage Western Wear for Women 1930s, 1940s, 1950s." Accessed April 15, 2025. https://vintagedancer.com/vintage/1930-1950s-western-wear-for-women-and-men/.

CHAPTER 7: COWGIRL ESSENTIALS

National Cowboy & Western Heritage Museum. "History of the Cowboy Hat." Accessed April 15, 2025. https://nationalcowboymuseum.org/explore/history-of-the-cowboy-hat/.

Museum of Indian Arts & Culture. "Turquoise, Water, Sky: The Stone and Its Meaning." Accessed April 15, 2025. https://www.indianartsandculture.org/whatsnew/&releaseID=292.

CHAPTER 8: THE COWGIRL SPIRIT

Cowboys & Indians. "21 Western Influencers To Follow in 2021." Accessed April 15, 2025. https://www.cowboysindians.com/2021/05/21-western-influencers-to-follow-in-2021/.

ELLE Canada. "Tia Wood Is a Cree and Salish TikTok Creator Sharing the Beauty of Her Culture Online." Accessed April 15, 2025. https://www.ellecanada.com/culture/society/tia-wood-is-a-cree-and-salish-tiktok-creator-sharing-the-beauty-of-her-culture-online.

NUVO magazine. "Tia Wood Paves the Way for Indigenous Artists." Accessed April 15, 2025. https://nuvomagazine.com/daily-edit/tia-wood-paves-the-way-for-indigenous-artists.

Image Credits

Index

Acknowledgments

First and foremost, thank you to my husband, Nathan Devan. Despite our already very full plates, you never hesitated to support me and cheer me on through this endeavor. You told all of your friends I was writing a book before I even knew for sure if I was writing a book. You have picked up and continue to pick up so much of my slack at home and with our children so that I never have to sacrifice the projects I want to pursue, and you will never know how much that means to me.

To my mom, who kept my sons on multiple days so I could go hole up somewhere and write. Thank you for always stepping in when we need you. There are so many things over the past four years I would never have been able to pursue if it hadn't been for your willingness to be so involved in our children's lives.

To my dad, the original cowboy in my life, thank you for always being the ultimate supporter in everything I do and having a genuine interest in what I am working on. I wouldn't know anything about this life if it weren't for you. Thank you for making me do things I was afraid to do when I was young so that I could grow up to be someone who isn't afraid to try. I am so grateful for how I was raised by both you and mom and for the lessons I learned from our life.

To my grandmother, Dixie, thank you for being the greatest cowgirl I know. Your passion for life and unending love for your family is something that should be written about in history books, and you'll likely never get the recognition you deserve. I know you don't care about that, but I wish everyone in the world could know you.

To my boys, Jameson and Boston, you have changed my life in infinite ways and pushed me to make huge life changes that allowed me to be the best mom I know how to be. If it weren't for the two of you, I never would have had the push I needed to make those changes and be in the incredible position I am in now with so many incredible opportunities. Everything I do is to make you proud. I hope you think I'm a cool mom when you find this book in our attic someday.

Finally, to the cowgirl trailblazers in the Western industry, thank you for showing all of us that we do not have to be victims of circumstance, we can all do important things, and we never have to sacrifice kindness and grace to create real change. You are the source of all my inspiration, and I am so grateful to honor just a few of you in this book. In the words of the great Judy Wagner, "nice job, cowgirls."

About the Author

Amanda Devan grew up around Fort Worth, Texas in a family of cowboys, cowgirls, and horsemen, with multiple family members who trained cutting horses and ran cattle full-time. After graduating from Texas A&M University with a degree in Agricultural Communications and Journalism, she began her career at RIDE TV (now GAC Family), where she served as the Director of Marketing and oversaw a variety of operations and projects for seven years.

After getting married during a global pandemic and giving birth to her first child in 2021, she took over as the editor of the *Cutting Horse Chatter, the official publication of the National Cutting Horse Association. Shortly thereafter, she became the editor for the historic Western Horseman*, a magazine truly made for the cowboy and cowgirl spirit.

Outside of work and motherhood, her passions and simple pleasures are Aggie football, slow days with family on the ranch, a chelada or margarita on a patio, and chips that don't break in the queso.

First published in 2026 by Epic Ink, an imprint of The Quarto Group,
135 West 36th Street, 13th Floor, New York, NY 10018, USA
(212) 779-4972 www.Quarto.com

EEA Representation, WTS Tax d.o.o.,
Žanova ulica 3, 4000 Kranj, Slovenia.
www.wts-tax.si

Epic Ink titles are also available at discount for retail, wholesale, promotional,
and bulk purchase. For details, contact the Special Sales Manager by email at
specialsales@quarto.com or by mail at The Quarto Group, Attn: Special Sales
Manager, 100 Cummings Center Suite 265D, Beverly, MA 01915 USA.

10 9 8 7 6 5 4 3 2 1

ISBN: 978-0-7603-9863-0

Digital edition published in 2026
eISBN: 978-0-7603-9864-7

Library of Congress Control Number: 2025938773

Group Publisher: Rage Kindelsperger
Creative Director: Laura Drew
Senior Acquiring Editor: Nicole James
Managing Editor: Cara Donaldson
Editors: Keyla Pizarro-Hernández and Natalie Butterfield
Cover Photograph: Phyllis Burchett
Back Cover Photograph: Christy Berry / Arcangel Images
Interior Design: Annie Marino

Printed in Huizhou City, Guangdong, China TT012026

↑ TITLE PAGE A woman in a cowboy hat silhouetted against the sunset.